Libraries in Post-Industrial Society

Libraries in Post-Industrial Society

Edited by Leigh Estabrook

A Neal-Schuman Professional Book

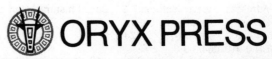 ORYX PRESS

Operation Oryx, started more than 10 years ago at the Phoenix Zoo to save the rare white antelope—believed to have inspired the unicorn of mythology—has apparently succeeded.

An original herd of nine, put together through Operation Oryx by five world organizations, now numbers 34 in Phoenix with another 22 farmed out to the San Diego Wild Game Farm.

The operation was launched in 1962 when it became evident that the animals were facing extinction in their native habitat of the Arabian peninsula.

Copyright © 1977 by Leigh Estabrook
Published by The Oryx Press
3930 E. Camelback Road
Phoenix, AZ 85018

Printed and Bound in the United States of America

Library of Congress Cataloging in Publication Data
Main entry under title:

Libraries in post-industrial society.

(A Neal-Schuman professional book)
Bibliography: p.
Includes index.
CONTENTS: Bell, D. Welcome to the post-industrial society.—Stearns, P. Is there a post-industrial society?—Harrington, M. Post-industrial society and the welfare state. [etc.]
1. Libraries and society—Addresses, essays, lectures. 2. Libraries—United States —Adresses, essays, lectures. 3. Social history—20th century—Addresses, essays, lectures. I. Estabrook, Leigh.
Z674.L46   021'.00973   77-8928
ISBN 0-912700-00-9

To Carl

Contents

Foreword

John Donne's "Send not to hear for whom the bell tolls, it tolls for thee" is the message that Leigh Estabrook spells out and amplifies for librarians. Hers is a vital contribution to every librarian who will heed the message not as a death knell but as a call of alarm, and who will respond to that call not by barricading the book stacks but by climbing to the library roof to survey and to grasp the vast changes sweeping over the world of information resources.

The dimensions of change are many. Most significant are changes in clientele. Information haves and have-nots remain, but their locales and their needs are no longer precisely as they were when the Library of Congress or the Carnegie system of libraries were created. Much has been written, both fanciful and realistic, about changes in the tools of information handling and the new opportunities they afford for serving diverse clienteles. There the message sums up as "Send not to hear for whom Ma Bell tolls, she tolls for thee." Not least are the institutional changes that encompass the emergence of new organizations, public and private, tax-supported and fee-supported, that compete with traditional libraries and library services in serving many publics and that afford great new opportunities for librarians.

This volume emphasizes the personal dimension, the professional future of librarians themselves. Disdaining both the humble hand-wringing and the arrogant solipsism that disgrace the profession's reflex response to change in the world around it, Professor Estabrook has boldly stepped out into that world. She has brought back the gifts of community with other professions, or opportunities to learn from wider experience, of sustenance to be gained from understanding and sharing that experience, and of the challenges of translating that experience into vigorous public service.

These essays will be valued by every colleague who wants not merely to survive but rather to grow in professional competence, stature and capacity for public service.

Anthony G. Oettinger

Preface

Post-industrial society is a term coined by sociologist Daniel Bell to describe his view of the changes society is presently undergoing. According to Bell, passage from an industrial into a post-industrial phase of society is signalled by "the accumulation and distribution of theoretical knowledge . . . as a directive force of innovation and change"—an "information society." The implications of this definition, whether one agrees or disagrees, is worth the attention of the library profession. The articles selected for inclusion in this book represent an attempt to bring together a wide variety of viewpoints on current social, economic, political, and technological changes in society that are relevant to librarianship, with specific reference to changes in work, organizations, and services. While there has been no attempt to cover all issues related to library and information services today, material has been drawn from a range of scientific and social scientific journals and books, both scholarly and popular; and one previously unpublished work is included. Only two of the authors are librarians, although several others are vitally concerned with the problems of library and information science.

The intent of this collection is to present ideas which are not generally discussed in the library press: to provoke and to inform the reader. Many authors express views which conflict with commonly held positions on libraries and librarianship; but each one, in discussing developments in non-library organization and occupations, draws attention to the similarities between groups and libraries. Specific reference to developments in librarianship which pertain to the problems being discussed in the selected articles is made in the introduction. The bibliography which follows the last section of readings provides citations to related library literature.

Acknowledgements

This book would never have been compiled had it not been for Professor Estelle Jussim's original conceptualization and proposal of the topic and Patricia Glass Schuman's encouragement. Caroline Couglin offered insight into how to organize the material. Three research assistants—Judy McCormack Gleason, Eric Johnson, and Eleanor Strang—were creative and thorough in working on the tedious details of gathering permissions and bibliographic items and indexing the book. June McGough and Mary Duggan provided special support.

My thanks to each of these individuals, to the Emily Hollowell Fund for Research which provided partial financial assistance, and to the publishers and authors who generously allowed their material to be included.

Introduction

Librarians today are increasingly finding themselves in the position of their clients: they need information that is at once highly specialized and inter-disciplinary. All sorts of libraries are now considered "special libraries," and separate professional functions within these organizations require greater technical skill and specialization from those who perform them. At the same time, there is a constant interaction between libraries and the society within which they exist.

If one looks at education for library and information service, it is apparent that in curriculum design, continuing education programs and recruitment more and more attention is being paid to training individuals for technical and specialized work. There is also a growing emphasis on research that can provide a theoretical base for such work; and, while there is much still to be learned, librarians seem to have a sense of what needs to be done and what information must be acquired in order to develop greater professional expertise.

Less clearly controlled are the vast areas of research outside library and information science that seem to have immediate relevance for library services. Librarians draw on findings from communication theory, organizational behavior, psychology, sociology, and other sciences and social sciences. But, the citations in library literature are predominantly to other library literature. Librarianship certainly shows nothing unique in this phenomenon: communication theorists cite other communication theorists; sociologists, other sociologists. This can be seen as one indication of the problem every field has in incorporating into its scholarship the materials from other disciplines.

The problem is more than academic. It bears directly on the performance of professionals within their field: on their interpretations of their role in society; on their perceptions of their relationships to those with whom they work, both inside and outside of their specialty; and on their understanding of what goals they should pursue. Within librarianship this problem is illustrated by the way in which librarians have sought to understand their role in society. In professional meetings, published articles, and general conversation, librarians are concerned with the social, technological, and economic changes we see affecting their profession. One attempt to understand the general impact of these changes, which has attracted much interest from those concerned with library and information services, is found in the work of the sociologist Daniel Bell and the vision of post-industrial society which he has created. (Bell was a keynote speaker at the 1975 American Society for Information Science meeting in Boston, and he was sought after to address the American Library Association convention in Detroit in 1977.) Bell's work is attractive because his description of the major transitions currently occuring in Western capitalist cultures seems to imply that society is moving in directions that will result in the increased importance of library and information science to society.

Bell's central thesis is that the managerial elite which currently dominates society is gradually being replaced by a "knowledge elite." Indications of this process include: (1) the transition from a goods-producing to a service-producing economy; (2) the growing influence on society of professional and technical workers; (3) the increased importance of theoretical knowledge to those involved in policy formulation; (4) increased concern with technological growth; and (5) the management of large-scale systems through the complex manipulation of information.

In his key words, "knowledge," "professional," "service," "technological," and "information," we read a future in which there will be a dramatic boost of libraries importance to society. At the same time, we survey the current developments in our profession—the financial crises, lack of user response, our inability to achieve a central position in society—and sense failure. To read Bell is thus both a promise and a rebuke.

One way of explaining current difficulties in librarianship is to blame the victim—to argue that in fact librarians are responsible for their failures to assume a dominant role in society. A second interpretation might begin by blaming Bell, or at least by suggesting his visions of society may be incorrect, for Bell is only one of many social theorists writing of social change. Bell's term "post-industrial" has been used by liberals, Marxists, and conservatives. Any attempt to consider libraries in society must take into account the various interpretations of social change by sociologists, economists, historians and others. To date discussions among librarians about the nature of our profession in the context of the social changes described by Bell rest upon limited assumptions. The articles that follow offer a spectrum of views on this issue.

THE NATURE OF POST-INDUSTRIAL SOCIETY

The first section of this book considers the nature of the post-industrial society. The decisions librarians make daily—both minor and major—are affected by the assumptions they make about society: what we believe it is and how we wish it to be. For example, a decision to extend outreach services to home-bound individuals is based on demographic data about the number of people who might require such service and also on the priorities of the library in allocating scarce resources. The report of the National Commission on Library and Information Science makes certain basic assumptions about social and technological change. In projecting plans for library development it clearly reflects the values of its authors on priorities for library service. Similarly, the forthcoming White House Conference on Library and Information Services will probably reflect, in the concerns it addresses, the assessment of its planners and participants of the nature of post-industrial society and the role libraries should fulfill.

The five articles in this section all consider explicitly the fundamental issue of determining the nature of society. In an article from *Physics Today,* Daniel Bell presents his view of post-industrial society, with an emphasis on his position on the role of theoretical knowledge in such a society. Peter N. Stearns, in a general response to Bell, attacks the entire notion of post-industrial society on the basis of historical evidence and suggests that the distinction drawn by Bell between industrial and post-industrial society may not be valid. A further response to Bell is given in Michael Harrington's article, in which he too disputes the validity of the transitions postulated by Bell, particularly those which relate to the distribution of wealth and power in society.

Each of the last two articles in this section treats a central question raised in the reading of the first three: how accurate can social forecasting be? Heilbroner, in a comment on his book, *An Inquiry Into the Human Prospect,* evaluates the reliability of short-term and long-range forecasting. He argues that it is possible to anticipate *general* trends and future developments of society—and offers the fatalistic view that many devastating changes are bound to occur. He is less sanguine about anyone's ability to predict smaller changes—to flesh out the details of how and when the larger changes will come about. But Amitai Etzioni disagrees with Heilbroner; arguing that near-term forecasting is much more reliable than long-range. He also raises the important problem of the relationship between policy making and social forecasting.

While each of these articles is concerned explicitly with what the author believes to be the nature of post-industrial society, each also contains implicit assumptions about what the author wishes it to be.

PROFESSIONALS IN POST-INDUSTRIAL SOCIETY

The articles in this section are concerned with various aspects of professionalization—a subject of immediate concern to librarians who often find themselves categorized as semi-professionals by sociologists. Statements by Bell and others that ours is a professionalizing society, as well as trends within librarianship itself, lend credence to the beliefs that the status of the profession is increasing. At the same time we find ourselves in an ever tightening job market in which the absolute number of librarians being hired is decreasing. Library technical assistants are being hired for formerly professional positions. Union membership is increasing in all types of libraries, with the resultant schism between library workers and library management. These trends can be interpreted as a sign of decreasing professionalization.

There are a number of possible ways of trying to understand this conflicting evidence. John McKinlay considers professionalization *per se* to be a false issue in his article on "The Professional Regulation of Change." Instead, he looks at the ways in which certain dominant occupational groups assert power in society and attempt to ensure that social change is in their best interests. His concern is with the relative social power of professional groups.

Marie Haug also views professionalization in terms of power relationships, but her argument differs from McKinlay's. In "The Deprofessionalization of Everyone?," she takes issue with those social theorists who think that society will become dominated by professional groups. She presents evidence that, as clients gain increased information about their own needs and the type of service which they should expect from professionals, the professional loses some of his or her authority and autonomy. The traditional distinction between client and professional becomes less meaningful.

Chamot's article about professionals in unions is markedly different in approach. He examines the changing work situation of professionals and the growth of white collar union membership. The place of the professional worker in unions provides special problems, argues Chamot, because of the professionals' expectations that they will have greater autonomy in their relationship with clients and in determining conditions under which they work. Unionization becomes both a symptom and a cause of conflict over decision making.

In Ivar Berg's "The Licensing of Paraprofessionals," a problem is discussed which relates to the use of technical assistants in libraries, an issue relevant to discussions concerning certification of librarians and accreditation of library schools. Berg believes that in measuring the competency of an individual, it may be valuable to establish criteria which evaluate a variety of dimensions of an individual's performance. He also believes that current trends in the educational system will support extension of the criteria used to measure professional performance.

Hooyman and Kaplan discuss a most immediate problem for 85 percent of librarians—the role of professional women in "New Roles for Professional Women." They investigate the ways in which the influence of women in human service professions is minimized and offer an outline of a training program for overcoming—or at least modifying—some of the barriers to effective participation by women. References in this article also draw attention to some of the more significant current scholarship in this area.

ORGANIZATIONS IN POST-INDUSTRIAL SOCIETY

A number of the articles in the section on professionals underline the importance of the organizational context within which professionals work. Librarians' traditional views of their function within information organizations are undergoing a rapid transition as we increasingly find our role defined as library manager. We are asked to deal with the worker/manager conflict in different roles—sometimes as professionals, sometimes as managers—and are confronted with rapidly changing styles of management and an increasing demand both from workers and from clients for a greater role in defining organizational goals and in decision making. (The arguments for community control were not just arguments of the 1960's.) At the same time pressure is felt from above: from state and federal governments and related organizations.

Kenneth Alexander's "On Work and Authority" considers the general question of worker participation and managerial authority and a number of the more specific historical and contemporary developments that inhibit movements toward increased shared authority. Some of the areas he identifies are the spread of employee unionism and the mutual fear and distrust by labor and management.

The first of these areas is also of concern to Chapman and Cleaveland in their article on public service. Pressures for centralization and de-centralization, increased citizen involvement, and the impact of technological change are considered as major factors which affect the administration of public service organizations. From these they see three major tendencies which will affect public administration in the 1980's: a move toward increasing flexibility; an opposing move toward increasing rigidity; and an indication that the administrative process is becoming more complex.

Mott also writes about public service, but his immediate concern is the relationship of public bureaucracies to attempts by communities to organize themselves. Specifically, he argues that the relationships which public bureaucracies establish between themselves and governmental and private agencies are antithetical to responsiveness to community needs. He bases this conclusion on the difficulties which exist in mobilizing numerous bureaucracies to work together to resolve community problems—problems that are multi-dimensional and cannot be treated by only one agency. The solution, he argues, lies in legislation and policy formation that leads toward agencies working together.

While Mott looks first toward the federal government, Elazar, in his article, looks toward state governments. Elazar is less concerned with legislation which leads to bureaucratic cooperation than with legislation which can legitimize community control. Describing a number of the problems which arise from community control and are as yet unresolved, he nonetheless feels that the fight for community control has accomplished some important goals.

Rosengren's article on "The Careers of Clients and Organizations" looks at bureaucratic organizations not in community terms, but in terms of the way in which they relate to individual clients. He believes that organizations should be looked at in the terms of the ways in which they change over time, and not in static terms. Viewed historically, organizations can be seen to vary in the way in which they relate to their clients and the extent to which they intervene in the life of their clients. While Rosengren's theory is presented in sociological terms and slips sometimes into technical terminology, his insightful ideas are extremely interesting for librarians and well worth considering.

Nicholas Henry's work on copyright is familiar to librarians. In "Knowledge Management," he addresses the broad issue of the new roles of scientific and social scientific information in the public policy-making process, suggesting that this process may be dramatically altered by new information technologies. Henry also discusses some of the current ways in which public policy-makers are dealing with the sudden influx of information.

SERVICES IN POST-INDUSTRIAL SOCIETY

Of all the topics considered in this book, "Services" is the most difficult. It involves consideration of technological change as well as change in clientele. Services expand and change as a result of new technology. Technological developments allow better coordinated services as well as the establishment of more specialized services. New client demands (e.g., for non-English materials), changing educational patterns (the burgeoning of adult- and continuing-education programs), and demographic trends (such as the decline in undergraduate enrollment) demand responsive services.

Weizenbaum's "On the Impact of the Computer on Society" jousts with commonly held opinions that the computer has had a major societal impact. What are important, he argues, are the side-effects which have resulted from new computer technology. Weizenbaum insists that human questions must be asked—and answered—by human beings, not by machines.

In a substantially different analysis, Parker and Dunn examine information technology in terms of its mechanical potential. Cable television, satellite communication, and other forms of communication technology are discussed with reference to their economic, social, and educational potential and government planning for their implementation and use.

Hechinger's brief article discusses major educational changes which are directly affecting library and information services: adult and continuing education. He is sensitive to the special needs of older students as well as the social importance of expanding opportunites for higher education.

"The Underlying Assumptions of Advocacy Planning" deals with two issues of importance to information professionals today: (1) the role of advocate, and (2) the assumptions of political pluralism. Since librarians face varied demands for service from a multiplicity of special client groups, we must try to reconcile conflicting requests. If we act as advocates, we find ourselves in the position of trying to respond to these special groups while not losing support from more politically influential people. Mazzioti's article provides a thorough foundation for investigating these problems.

Raymond Williams debates an area which is of paramount concern to public librarians: the relationship between high culture and popular culture. In discussing popular culture he makes a crucial distinction between cultures developed *by* a people and that developed *for* a people. He then looks at the revitalizing, creative impact that popular culture can have on high culture.

LIBRARIES IN POST-INDUSTRIAL SOCIETY

Each of the sections in this book implicitly concern, libraries in the post-industrial society. The four articles in this section explicitly discuss librarianship and information services as they are developing or might be expected to develop in the near-future.

Robert Taylor, Dean of Syracuse University's School of Information Studies has stated that in a metaphorical sense we are moving from a

Ptolemaic world with the library at the center to a Copernican one with information at the center and the library as one of its planets. Each of these articles speaks to that point of view.

Owens, writing on "The Information Function," seeks to establish "A Theoretical Basis for the Development of Information Networks and Centers" and proposes that information systems be developed that allow users to become "information literates." Several major analyses of information needs and information use are drawn on to develop his model.

Swartz is also concerned with current studies of information needs and use, but he uses the material as a basis for a critical analysis of library cooperation. He finds that in terms of fulfilling user information needs, cooperative systems will not be successful unless there is interaction between client and professional in determining the way in which cooperative systems should develop.

Salton's article entitled "Proposals for a Dynamic Library" develops a model for a specific type of mechanized library environment. Also concerned with user needs, he sees the relationship between the user and the library as a dynamic one. This is an extremely technical paper, but even to those who become discouraged by charts, tables, and formulae, Salton's ideas should provide an imaginative framework for library service.

The final paper was written by Kas Kalba, and while it relates most specifically to the problems of public libraries, it deals more generally with the relationship of libraries to other information sources. Kalba looks at three possible roles libraries can assume and evaluates the potential and problems of their functioning in these roles.

As varied and diverse as these articles are, they are only a small portion of the scientific and social-scientific literature which has been written on topics of concern to librarians. As the profession begins to include more members from outside disciplines in its research and teaching, it is hoped that such materials will become more accessible to all concerned with library and information services and that interdisciplinary findings will become an important part of the critical thinking and concerns of librarianship. Many have read a promise of significant societal change into Bell's theory of a professionalizing society and the growth of a knowledge elite in which librarians will play an important role. Yet, theorists like Haug, Harrington, Kalba and others present evidence against this. Current research indicates that all professional groups are *losing* power and authority in society. There is also evidence that although the information sector of the economy may continue to grow rapidly, that government agencies and corporations—not libraries or other human services—will be the major organizations involved in the information business. Tomorrow's "knowledge elite" may look very much like today's "managerial elite." But Bell's writings should be neither a promise or a rebuke to the library profession. He provides one way of viewing the social order of which we are a part. Understanding Bell, and others, offer us a chance to better understand our role and the social forces that shape it. The lesson to be learned from those writing in other disciplines is that if we are committed to providing access to information as a *human* service, then we must actively work for social changes which will enable us to do so. Often, this may entail working against the prevailing trends. To do this, we must not only comprehend these trends, but incorporate this knowledge into the philosophy and practice of librarianship.

Leigh Estabrook

Contributors

Kenneth O. Alexander, "On Work and Authority," reprinted with permission from *American Journal of Economics and Sociology* (January, 1975) pp. 43–54. He is a member of the faculty of the department of business at Michigan Technological University.

Daniel Bell, "Welcome to the Post-Industrial Society," reprinted with permission from *Physics Today* (February, 1976) pp. 46–49, copyright © American Institute of Physics. Bell is professor of sociology at Harvard University. His most recent book is *The Cultural Contradictions of Capitalism*, published in 1976.

Ivar Berg, "The Licensing of Paraprofessionals," reprinted from *Education and Urban Society*, vol 8, no 1 (November, 1975) pp. 104–119 by permission of the author and publisher, Sage Publishers, Inc. Berg is in the department of sociology and anthropology at Vanderbilt University. He is the author of *Education and Jobs: The Great Training Robbery* (1970).

Dennis Chamot, "Professional Employees Turn to Unions," reprinted with permission from the *Harvard Business Review* (May–June, 1976), copyright © 1976 by the President and Fellows of Harvard College, all rights reserved. He is assistant to the executive secretary of the Council of AFL-CIO Unions for Professional Employees.

Richard Chapman and Frederick N. Cleaveland, "The Changing Character of the Public Service and the Administrators of the 1980's," reprinted with permission from *Public Administration Review* (July/August, 1973) pp. 358–365, published by the American Society for Public Administration. Chapman is a senior research associate at the National Academy of Public Administration in Washington, D.C. Frederic N. Cleaveland is provost of Duke University. In 1974 he was elected chairman of the National Academy of Public Administration.

Daniel J. Elazar, "School Decentralization in the Context of Community Control," reprinted with permission from *Phylon*, vol 36 (December, 1975) pp. 385–394, copyright © Atlanta University. Elazar is on the faculty of Temple University in the department of political science. His most recent book, published in 1976, is *Community and Polity: The Organizational Dynamics of American Jewry*.

Amitai Etzioni, "Futures Analysis," reprinted with permission from *Vital Speeches of the Day*, vol 10 (March 1, 1976) pp. 307–309, published by City News Publishing Company. Etzioni is in the department of sociology at Columbia University. He has written extensively on social change and occupational development.

Michael Harrington, "Post-Industrial Society and the Welfare State," reprinted with permission from *Dissent*, vol 23 (Summer, 1976) pp. 244–252. Harrington is a member of the editorial board of the journal *Dissent*. Two of his most recent books are *Socialism* (1972) and *Twilights of Capitalism* (1976).

Marie R. Haug, "The Deprofessionalization of Everyone?" reprinted from *Sociological Focus*, vol 8 (August, 1975) pp. 197–213, with the permission of the author and the North Central Sociological Association. Haug is a professor in the department of sociology at Case Western Reserve University. She has written many articles on the sociology of occupations.

Fred M. Hechinger, "Education's New Majority," reprinted from *Saturday Review* (September 20, 1975) pp. 14–16ff, with the permission of the author. Hechinger has been a member of the editorial board of *The New York Times* since 1969. He has contributed articles on education to *Harper's*, *The Reporter*, *Saturday Review of Literature*, and *McCall's*.

Robert Heilbroner, "Second Thoughts on the Human Prospect," reprinted with permission from *Futures*, vol 7 (February, 1975) pp. 31–40. Heilbroner is on the graduate faculty of the department of economics at the New School for Social Research in New York City. He has written numerous books, including *An Inquiry into the Human Prospect* (1974), and *The Future of Business Civilization* (1976).

Nicholas L. Henry, "Knowledge Management," reprinted with permission from *Public Administration Review* (May/June, 1974) pp. 189–195, published by the American Society for Public Administration. Henry is the director of the center for public affairs at Arizona State University. He has recently written *Copyright-Information Technology-Public Policy: Public Policies-Information Technology* (1976).

N. R. Hooyman and J. S. Kaplan, "New Roles for Professional Women," reprinted with permission from *Public Administration Review* (July/August, 1976) pp. 374–378, published by the American Society for Public Administration. Nancy R. Hooyman is an associate professor in the school of social development at the University of Minnesota; Judith S. Kaplan is assistant dean at the school of social development at the University of Minnesota.

Kas Kalba, "The Information Marketplace," originally presented as a speech to the Harvard Ukranian Research Institute, December 14, 1976, printed by permission of the author, copyright © Kas Kalba. Kalba is president of Kalba-Bowen Associates, Inc. of Cambridge, Massachusetts and a visiting lecturer in the department of political science at M.I.T. He is also a Research Fellow of Harvard University's Program on Information Resources Policy.

Donald Mazzioti, "The Underlying Assumptions of Advocacy Planning," reprinted by permission of the *Journal of the American Institute of Planners*, vol 40 (January, 1974) pp. 38, 40–47. Mazziotti is the chief planner at the program and policy analysis section of the Bureau of Planning of the city of Portland, Oregon.

John B. McKinlay, "The Professional Regulation of Change," reprinted from *Sociological Review Monograph* 20, pp. 61–84 with permission of Sociological Review. McKinlay is a professor in the department of sociology at Boston University. He has recently edited *Processing People: Cases in Organizational Behaviour,* published in 1975.

Paul E. Mott, "Bureaucracies and Community Planning," reprinted with permission from *Sociological Inquiry,* vol 43, no 3–4 (1973) pp. 311–323. Mott is a professor in the department of sociology, Wharton School of Finance and Commerce, at the University of Pennsylvania. He edited, with Michael Aiken of the University of Wisconsin, *The Structure of Community Power* (1970).

Anthony G. Oettinger is Gordon McKay Professor of Applied Mathematics, Professor of Information Resources Policy, and Chairman of the Program on Information Resources Policy at Harvard University. He has written *Elements of Information Resources Policy: Library and Other Information Sources* (1975) for the National Commission on Library Information Science.

Major R. Owens, "The Information Function: A Theoretical Basis for the Development of Information Networks and Centers," reprinted with permission from *Drexel Library Quarterly* 12 (Janurary–April, 1976) pp. 7–26. Owens is a New York State Senator from Brooklyn. He is a frequent contributor to the library press.

Edwin B. Parker and Donald A. Dunn, "Information Technology: Its Social Potential," reprinted with permission from *Science,* vol 176 (June 30, 1972) pp. 1392–1399, copyright © 1972 by the American Association for the Advancement of Science. Parker is a member of the department of communications of Stanford University; Donald A. Dunn is a member of the department of engineering and economic systems at Stanford University.

William R. Rosengren, "The Careers of Clients and Organizations," reprinted with permission of the publisher from *Organizations and Clients* edited by William R. Rosengren and Mark Lefton (Columbus, Ohio: Charles E. Merrill Publishing Company, 1970) pp. 117–135. William R. Rosengren is in the department of sociology and anthropology, University of Rhode Island.

Gerald S. Salton, "Proposals for a Dynamic Library," reprinted with permission from *Information-Part 2,* vol 2, no 3 (1973) pp. 5–27, copyright © 1973 by Science Associates. Salton is in the department of computer science at Cornell University. His most recent book is *Dynamic Information and Library Processing,* published in 1975.

Peter N. Stearns, "Is There a Post-Industrial Society," published by permission of Transaction, Inc., from *Society,* vol 11, no 4, copyright © 1974 by Transaction, Inc. Stearns is a member of the faculty in the department of history at Rutgers University. Since 1967, he has also been the managing editor ot the *Journal of Social History.* Two of his most recent books are *Western Civilization: An Overview* (1975) and *Industrial Societies* (1975).

Roderick G. Swartz, "The Need for Cooperation Among Libraries in the U.S." reprinted with permission from *Library Trends,* vol 24, no 2 (1975) pp. 215–227. Swartz is librarian at the Washington State Library, Olympia, Washington.

Joseph Weizenbaum, "On the Impact of the Computer on Society," reprinted with permission from *Science,* vol 176 (May 12, 1972) pp. 609–614, copyright © 1972 by the American Association for the Advancement of Science. Weizenbaum is a professor of computer science at the Massachusetts Institute of Technology. He is the author of *Computer Power and Human Reason: From Judgement to Calculation,* published in 1976.

Raymond Williams, "On High and Popular Culture," reprinted from *The New Republic* (November 23, 1974) pp. 13–16 by permission of The New Republic, copyright © 1974. Williams is professor of drama at Jesus College, Cambridge, England. His latest work is *Marxism and Literature.*

Libraries in Post-Industrial Society

PART

I

THE NATURE
OF POST-INDUSTRIAL
SOCIETY

Welcome To the
Post-Industrial Society

by Daniel Bell

A number of countries in the West, the United States among them, are now passing from an industrial into a post-industrial phase of society. The change primarily affects the socio-technical dimensions of society and is generally independent of the nature of political change or political structure. The main difference between an industrial and a post-industrial society is that the sources of innovation in a post-industrial society are derived increasingly from the codification of theoretical knowledge, rather than from "random" inventions. Every society in human history has been dependent upon knowledge, but it is only in recent years that the accumulation and distribution of theoretical knowledge has come to the fore as a directive force of innovation and change.

INFORMATION SOCIETY

A post-industrial society is basically an information society. Exchange of information in terms of various kinds of data processing, record keeping, market research and so forth is the foundation for most economic exchanges. Data-transmission systems are the transforming resource of the society, just as in an industrial society, created energy—electricity, oil, nuclear power—is the transmuting element, and natural power—wind, water, brute force—is the transforming resource of the pre-industrial society. The strategic resource of the post-industrial society becomes theoretical knowledge, just as the strategic resource of an industrial society is money capital, and the strategic resource of a pre-industrial society is raw materials. Thus, just as capital and labor frame the problems of an industrial society, so information and knowledge frame the problems of a post-industrial society. Instead of a society based on a labor theory of value, the central idea of which comes from Adam Smith or Karl Marx, the post-industrial society rests on a knowledge theory of value—that is to say, value is fundamentally increased, not by labor, but by knowledge.

TALENTED TINKERERS VERSUS SCIENTISTS

The industries that have come forth as representative of the last third of the twentieth century are science-based industries, which derive fundamentally from the application of the findings of theoretical knowledge. These twentieth-century industries differ radically from nineteenth-century industries, which are still the major industries in Western society—steel, automobiles, electricity, telephone and aviation. These can all be regarded as nineteenth-century industries, even though steel began in the eighteenth century with Abraham Darby and the coking process, and aviation was invented in the twentieth century with Wilbur and Orville Wright at Kitty Hawk, because they were founded or created by talented tinkerers, men who worked independently of the scientific establishment and were ignorant of many of the theories of basic science. Sir Henry Bessemer, who created the open-hearth process, knew little of the work of Henry Sorby on metallurgical properties. Thomas Edison, who was a great genius in creating the electric light, the motion picture and the gramophone, was literally mathematically illiterate. Alexander Graham Bell was an elocutionist who invented the telephone largely to amplify sound so that deaf people could hear, and he knew nothing of the work of James Maxwell on electromagnetism. In a similar way Guglielmo Marconi invented the radio with little theoretical knowledge of the fundamental physical principles he employed.

These nineteenth-century industries contrast strongly with twentieth-century industries, which derive directly from the investigations of scientists into the basic phenomena of nature and the application of this research to technological problems. The basic research of I. I. Rabi and Charles H. Townes into the possibility of sending a molecular beam through an optical field led to the creation of a maser and then a laser, and this in turn led to Dennis Gabor's development of the hologram. William B. Shockley's research on transistors is responsible for a huge transformation in modern electronics, and the work of Felix Bloch on solid-state physics is the basis of much of computer technology. Theoretical knowledge in the twentieth century is organized and used in a radically different way than in the nineteenth century. Advances in twentieth-century technology are dependent upon the progress of basic research and the codification of theoretical knowledge, as well as upon science's sense of direction and sense of search. For this reason the first truly modern industry is the chemical industry, because a base of theoretical knowledge is necessary in order to manipulate macromolecular structures and develop new products and new techniques.

Just as twentieth-century industries have not replaced the basic nineteenth-century industries, however, the post-industrial society does not replace or displace an industrial society. Rather, the whole structure is a system of superimposed layers, like a palimpsest. An industrial society does not displace an agrarian society, except in numbers. Agriculture in the United States today is important in that it furnishes food for our society and a large part of the rest of the world, but only 4% of the U.S. labor force is involved in food production. But just as an agricultural base still exists, an industrial base still exists.

DESIGN OF THE SOCIETY

One other aspect is crucial to an understanding of the way in which the sense of one's world is colored by socio-technical changes. This is the so-called "design of the society." A pre-industrial society is a game against nature, a game in which one is subject to the vicissitudes of wind and water, the depletion of the soil and the never-ending turn of the seasons. The rhythms of life are played out against a conflict with the elements. An industrial society is a game against fabricated nature, in which Man has used energy to make large machines that add to his power to transform his world. But a post-industrial society is a game between persons, between teacher and student, doctor and patient, research team members, and so forth. It means that in the experience of most of our lives, Nature is excluded, except as recreation, and things are excluded, except as hobbies. The basic experience of each person's life is his relationship between himself and others. This state is rather unique in Man's existence. Most of the coding of Man's behavior has been predicted by his role as a member of a hunting society or an agrarian society, in which he was forced to use his ingenuity against Nature. The Man–machine relationship is a fairly recent phenomenon in terms of Man's history and Man's experience. But the Man–Man relationship has never been the central issue in terms of his history or his attempts at survival.

The problem with the exclusion of Nature and things, with inter-personal relationships as the focus of each man's thoughts and actions, is the fact that people do not know how to live easily with one another. We often need an external artifact, such as Nature or machines, in order to weld us together or to discharge our aggressions. This point is important because the one other element that is crucial to a sociological understanding of the modern world, particularly the post-industrial society, is the increasing multiplication of interactions between persons. If there is any single char-acteristic that is true of our time, it is not so much the increase in the pace of technology, but the increase in the number of personal transactions we experience. A person born in 1830 would have experienced a steam engine and a steamship, just as a person born in 1930 would have experienced television, space satellites and commercial jet transportation. The great difference does not seem to be the acceleration of change, but the en-largement of an individual's world that accompanies the advance of technol-ogy. There is a tremendous change of scale in the number of persons one knows or knows of. Developments in transportation and communication have extended each person's pool of potential interaction from a village to a city to a nation and beyond.

THE LIMITS OF THE SCALE

This change of scale is a central issue as we approach the twenty-first century. John von Neumann pointed out about twenty years ago that the rapid development of modern technology increased speed not so much by shortening the time requirement as by increasing the areas affected by its development. The reason is clear. Since most time scales are fixed by human reaction time, by physiological processes, the increase in speed of technolog-ical processes enlarged the size of political, economic and cultural units that are affected by technological operations. That is, instead of performing the same operations as before in less time, now large-scale operations can be performed in the same time. This important evolution has a natural limit—the earth's actual size. This limit will soon be approached.

In one sense the first limit was reached in the geopolitical sphere. As von Neumann pointed out, World War II was in many ways the last war of mass human civilization because it was the last war in which there was sufficient land area for a large army to retreat, as the Russian army could still retreat from the Germans. But there is no retreat from intercontinental ballistic missiles. We have reached an absolute limit in that respect.

In other senses, too, we are reaching the limits of our physical world. We are now in a situation of "real time" in almost every part of the world. The revolution in telecommunications, which is in many respects the last major revolution in the twentieth century, allows for immediate exchange of information, financial transfers throughout the world, the shipping of news and so forth, all almost immediately to every part of the globe. There is a very real question of what happens when the whole world becomes part of a world-interactive network and the increase in interaction is brought to its outer limits.

It was once suggested that 5,040 persons was the optimum size for the city-state, based on the fact that it took at least half a day per year for each person to have at least some intercourse with another individual. Athens, the largest of the Greek city-states, had at its peak 40,000 male citizens, with the quorum in the assembly fixed at 6,000. The number of adult citizens in New Zealand is about 30 times that of Athens, in the Netherlands 100 times, in France 500 times, in the U.S. 2,500 times, and in India about 6,000 times that of Athens. In the face of this, what does participation mean? What is the character of human contact? What are the limits of human comprehension?

PROBLEMS FOR INSTITUTIONS

The increase of scale creates two effects that pose problems for the institutions that govern the post-industrial society. One is that the increase of scale in communications and transportation extends the range of control from a center of power, particularly when there is a command-and-control system. (A wit once remarked that Stalin was Genghis Khan with a telephone in one hand.)

A second problem is that the linear extension does not simply make an initial institution large, but creates a threshold that transforms it. A university that has 50,000 students is not the same university as one with 5,000 students, even though the name may be the same. The Harvard University of 1869 under Charles Eliot is not the Harvard of today. Its entire structure is vastly different.

This refers to something familiar to all physicists—the notion set down by Galileo called the "square–cube law." If something doubles in size, it will triple in volume, but its shape will also change. The biologist D'arcy Wentworth Thompson once pointed out that Galileo said that if someone tried to build ships, palaces or temples of enormous size, the beams and bolts would cease to hold together. Nor can Nature grow a tree or construct an animal beyond a certain size and still retain the proportions and materials that sufficed for the smaller structure. The monster will fall to pieces under its own weight unless either the relative proportions are changed or a harder and stronger material is used. So it appears clear that a change in scale becomes necessarily a change in institution. The problem appears to be that institutions that double in size do not always take the appropriate shape.

POLITICAL PROBLEMS

The key political problems in a post-industrial society are essentially elements of science policy. Theoretical knowledge, the strategic resource of the post-industrial society, must be produced and distributed. This implies the care and nurturing of science and a research and development effort, and the identification of human capital becomes important in the development of the strategic resource. We know very little about identifying human capital, about spotting good people early and nurturing them, enriching their education, making them creative and innovating and developing opportunities for them. Even though we may have a surplus of educated labor at the moment, human capital is still a scarce resource in the society.

In the end a major political problem will be the post-industrial society's information policy. Whether a computer utility is established or a completely free market in computer systems is developed, various other dimensions of the politics of information handling will arise from the nature of information itself.

Is There a
Post-Industrial Society

by Peter Stearns

The Industrial Revolution constituted a vast change in human society, comparable to the transition from a hunting to an agricultural order. Not only where and how men worked but ultimately how they thought were profoundly altered. But the pace of change steadily advanced, so that less than two hundred years after industrialization began, yet another form of society is taking its place. New social relations, new forms of protest and a new mass culture mark the advent of a post-industrial society. The latter is as different from the industrial order as the industrial was from the agricultural.

Sound all right so far? The notion of a "post-industrial" or even a "post-modern" society is becoming increasingly current. It serves a variety of interests. All sorts of social scientists find validity in the concept. Sociologists have led the way, some delighting in an idea that frees them from much serious attention to history, but psychologists and even historians have joined the parade. Roger Lane, an historian, attributing the decline of crime in nineteenth-century England and, possibly, the United States to industrialization, dismisses the twentieth-century increase in crime as post-industrial. In other words, nineteenth-century specialists can defend the purity of their era against the contamination that has followed, while twentieth-century fans can trumpet the novelty of their own period. Advocates of youth culture have advanced their claims to a post-industrial society that will be dominated by the values of the young. Supporters of the aged could make an equal case, as the number and influence of older people will clearly grow in the foreseeable future. Apostles of economic affluence have made post-industrial society their own; Herman Kahn, particularly, has based his futurology on the notion that scarcity will have vanished by the year 2000. Not to be outdone, advocates of scarcity see post-industrial society as a return to nature—a "personal subsistence economy," according to Paul Goodman. Perhaps most telling is the fact that booksellers now see the post-industrial label as a way to sell books. A recently published study of aging, which itself makes no reference to a post-industrial concept and indeed sensibly discusses problems that began with advanced industrial society over a century ago, is touted in the dust jacket as addressing "a major dilemma of post-industrial society."

The concept also serves virtually any political tendency. Inspired by the anti-hierarchical implications of the May 1968 revolt in France, the sociologist Alain Touraine wrote an eloquent description of the new forces that must inevitably burst forth against the post-industrial technocratic system. For him and for other neo-Marxist scholars, the post-industrial idea not only denotes great change but provides hope for the future. Given the failure of classic industrial protest groups to deflect the course of industrial society, it is tempting to forget about them and to turn to new champions by asserting that the whole social situation has radically changed. Moderates, too, can hail post-industrial society, with only a few qualms, as the apotheosis of a new Establishment dominated by research scholars and other professionals, a modern version of a Platonic meritocracy. And an implicitly conservative, even reactionary, strand runs through many of the post-industrial visions, which seeks a reversal of the dominant organizational trends of industrialization itself. The variety of conceptualizations involved, in terms of scholarly as well as political orientation, is itself difficult to interpret. One might claim that such diverse support adds credibility to the idea of a post-industrial society. After all, conservatives and radicals came to agree that industrial society existed. But here the diverse, contradictory conceptualizations probably indicate the shakiness of the idea itself. Where there is scant basis in social reality, each claimant is free to insert his own judgment of selected contemporary trends and, above all, his own hopes and fears.

Admittedly, twentieth-century society, particularly that which took shape after World War II, is different from earlier industrial society. So why quarrel about a post-industrial concept? There is the obvious problem of choosing which post-industrial society we are heading into. The term itself is inelegant. Daniel Bell, one of its staunchest advocates, explains that it is meant to denote a transitional period in which the shape of the future cannot be clearly defined; he goes on, of course, to define the shape of the future. In fact, the term indicates the vagueness of most of the definitions: they are unable to capture the essential dynamic of a new age for the good reason that the dynamic they project is not new at all, but an elaboration of trends within industrial society itself. Above all, there is an inherent improbability in the idea of a second massive change—as opposed to a new stage within the industrialization process—occurring so soon after the first upheaval.

The notion of post-industrial society is an historical problem, involving major claims about the periodization of recent history. While industrialization began in the late eighteenth-century, its social impact spread to the bulk of society, even in England, only during the second half of the nineteenth-century. We need a clear notion of the long transition required to create the industrial order. Even when an industrial economy is well advanced, as has often been noted for late nineteenth-century Germany, the society may remain largely traditional. Hence in talking about "post-industrialization" one is often talking about a second upheaval within the span of a single century. It seems more economical, at the least, to consider contemporary society in terms of a new stage in a broader process rather than a really new order of the same magnitude as industrialization itself. And this question of magnitude is crucial: the post-industrial concept has never been subjected to a rigorous comparative scrutiny to see if it involves forces as powerful in their capacity to change human life as, it is generally agreed, the Industrial Revolution did.

Of course, advocates can return to the familiar cry of the increasing pace of change. Even historians too often uncritically accept the idea that the historical processes have massively speeded up. It is at least worth asking whether an artisan, born in the countryside and moving to an increasingly commercialized Paris around the middle of the nineteenth-century, was not more afflicted by the sense of overwhelming novelty than the New York office worker 12 decades later. For one of the features of industrialization was a gradual, often painful, conversion to a belief in change. Subsequent innovations, of course, cause new concern and new resistance, but do they alter the framework of existence as industrialization did in the first place? For example, do these innovations challenge basic understanding of what time is, as industrialization did—forcing people to move from a seasonal sense of time to an hourly schedule? Do they change the framework of human consciousness? This is the level at which the notion of a post-industrial order must be examined. Usually, however, a real comparison of magnitudes of change is neglected in favor of a terminology that capitalizes on the sense of change that industrialization itself created.

The need for a critical assessment of the post-industrial concept is underscored by the publication of Daniel Bell's *The Coming of Post-Industrial Society: A Venture in Social Forecasting.* The book has several levels, one or two of which barely touch upon the concept of a post-industrial society. There is considerable discussion of current events, projected for a decade or so. Hence we are told about the crisis in university financing, problems in the American balance of trade and a number of issues of government manage-ment. There are a few errors in presentation here, particularly about Ameri-can agriculture's role in world trade, but in general the discussion is sensible and unsurprising. At a related level, Bell returns to his concern about the counterculture, which may now worry him unnecessarily. He is at pains to deal with contemporary culture critics such as Ivan Illich. Here again, in Bell's mind, this canvassing of the contemporary American scene is related to his definition of post-industrial society; but the connection is extremely tenuous. The book does make serious claims about the nature of the post-industrial order, and Bell proudly notes his role in spreading the currency of the term since the early 1960's. It is on this level that the book requires serious evaluation.

Without question, Bell's defense of the post-industrial concept is more intelligent than most. He sees some of the key issues. He examines other definitions carefully and correctly dismisses most of them as frivolous or ill-founded. Hence he rejects the youth-oriented vision, the affluence vision, the return-to-nature vision. He does slight the neo-Marxists, which is un-fortunate because their conceptualization is quite close to his up to a point. Bell also rightly points out the deficiency in much sociological theory, in its applicability to contemporary society. Much of his book can be read as a thoughtful reassessment of some of the concepts of social structure that still rely too heavily on theories that were elaborated in the very early stage of industrialization. Implicity, Bell also reflects the distortions of contemporary social history, which has overstressed the very early industrial period and left the last hundred years badly underanalyzed. But, while Bell points out these deficiencies he does not offer an alternative. Despite his erudition, he does not use much of the historical and sociological work that is available; he neglects modernization theory, for example, leaving one to wonder whether post-industrial society involves a reshaping of modern values or whether the value system remains within a common framework. Above all, his repeated emphasis on the post-industrial concept distracts from an intelligent understanding of where we stand in relation to our recent past. In this, for all that his precise definition of post-industrial society differs from other theories, he shares the weakness of the whole post-industrial school.

Several conceptual problems must be emphasized. First, Bell is extremely hazy as to our present relationship with post-industrial society. At some points he stresses the transitional character of the present, but he also offers both text and charts—his book is full of charts and statistics, as if the future's map were spread before us—indicating that one post-industrial society does exist, and that is in the United States. A major claim, and perhaps a plausible one. But there is no comparative evidence adduced, save on two points. Bell compares government allocations on research and development, showing the American percentage lead. Yet this is not adjusted for different levels of military spending, though Bell mentions the problem in his text, or for the much higher social expenditures of other industrial governments. Bell also offers college enrollment figures, stressing America's lead in developing technically trained professionals. But he does not note that the basic difference in the concept of higher education long predates the contemporary period; he does not discuss the meaning of American college training compared to high-level secondary school training in Japan or Europe; and, although based at Harvard, he does not deal with the vast differentials within the American higher education system, which make generalization on the basis of official enrollments almost meaningless. Beyond these two pieces of evidence, we are asked to accept on faith the assertion that America has already entered a new era in contrast to other advanced industrial nations. Yet if Bell believes his own charts, he has a golden opportunity to prove how the new age differs from the old, simply by comparing the United States with, say, Western Europe.

More important, Bell has no real historical sense. He knows he must prove the existence of post-industrial society by historical reference, but he simply can't do it. First, he is with rare exceptions unaware of the magnitude of his claims about periodization. He shows some recognition that the Industrial Revolution brought about sweeping changes in the economic activities of most people, but he does not deal with the alterations in mentality involved. Therefore, his assessment of post-industrial society largely avoids the question of consciousness in favor of narrow occupational discussions. At some points he seems to be referring not to epochal change such as industrialization-modernization but to more modest periodization. He talks about changes in the nature of society every 50 years or so, which is nonsense if one refers to basic social change but more acceptable if alterations within a given framework are intended. Second, Bell's view of industrial society is that of early industrial England. He does not understand that by 1850 or even later the working class consisted of many service workers (or more properly partial service workers, as with many artisans) and certainly only a minority of actual factory labor. Hence his comparisons with what has occurred since then are at best oversimplified. Above all he does not know what to do with the century of industrial history after 1850 or 1870. Being an honest observer he often admits that trends he terms post-industrial are quite visible by 1870: the rise of white-collar workers, the speeding up of transportation processes and so on. But he offers no overall assessment of the society in which these developments took place. Should we call it pre-post-industrial? In fact, his references to the late nineteenth-century (and they could be multiplied more than he notes, as with the growing economic intervention of government) and to a maturing industrial society, are far more typical of the beast than the growing pains of the early nineteenth-century. Take one example Bell uses often: the changeover from industrial inventions devised by tinkerers, typical of early industrialization, to a con-juncture between science and technical research. The changeover began in the last half of the nineteenth-century, first in the chemical industry. This much Bell notes, but he simply doesn't follow through. If this association between science and industry is typical of post-industrial society, surely the decades between the rise of the chemical industry and the advent of the new society need assessment. Unfortunately, no assessment ensues.

Bell might answer that this problem is a rather pedestrian question of origins; what counts, as he often asserts, is the exponential increase in the speed of developments. "The idea of exponential curves—the acceleration of doubling rates of all kinds—has now become commonplace" (pp. 169-170). He applies this idea particularly to the increase of scientific knowledge, but also to the speed of transportation and the rapidity of commercial exploitation of technical advances. Accurate enough; but as a statement of historical periodization it simply won't wash. One epoch gives way to an-other, like agricultural society to industrial society, not because of a speed-up of existing processes but because of change in the framework in which change occurs. Knowledge is increasing, but is the framework in which knowledge is produced altered? A medieval Bell could have pointed to the exponential increase of theological knowledge in the thirteenth-century and claimed that the Middle Ages were over, with as much sense. Bell does not deal with the issue of framework and, in fact, he is talking about changes—important changes, to be sure—within industrial society.

And this relates to the final problem, which Bell shares with several other post-industrial theorists. With the advantage of hindsight, we know that the advent of industrial society involved not only new technology and business and government structures but also a new mental framework, as in the sense of time referred to earlier, that affected ultimately the whole population. Bell deals only with structures at the top. He talks about new knowledge, a new governing elite, but he does not address himself to the question of whether the basic value system of a whole society is being replaced. This problem, too, would have to be treated if the post-industrial concept were to be taken seriously.

This failure to deal with the underlying structure of society means that large areas of human behavior, which have changed in previous shifts from one kind of society to another, are given no attention. Family life is one example: within the industrial order some aspects of family life behave in cycles. Illegitimacy rates went up during the first phase of industrialization, then down after 1870 and more recently up again. Marriage age and rates of marriage fluctuate, but the cycles operate within a larger, common framework. Although illegitimacy rates vary, a tendency toward more frequent and expressive sexual intercourse seems basic to industrial society in the late nineteenth-century as in the present day. Putting it simply, industrial society has from its early stages made it biologically possible and emotionally desirable to make love more imaginatively and frequently than in traditional society. There is no indication that this pattern has been disrupted. Marriage rates vary but there are larger trends in family relations that still move in a direction predictable from nineteenth-century trends. The modern family involves an increasingly individual, affectionate relationship between husband and wife, which replaces economic production as the family's principal function (this is one reason, along with the fact that death more rarely dissolves a marriage, that divorce is an essential modern phenomenon as well when this new function is not being fulfilled).

Certainly contemporary society has not created a fundamentally new demographic pattern, which usually marks the birth of a really new stage in history. After the transitional phase in which population increased dramatically, industrial society settled down into a pattern of comparatively mild cycles based on substantial birth control. Family development shows a related continuum, particularly in the emotional attachment to children. The modern pattern of birth control, which, apart from the precise methods used, began by the middle of the nineteenth-century, developed in part because each individual child was cherished more affectionately and partly because the parents wanted fewer physical and economic burdens. Obviously the broader transformation of the family from a unit of production to a unit of affection and consumption continues. And overall it is difficult to perceive any major new transformation for the immediate future, granting that some aspects of family history operate in cycles rather than long-term trends. Again, one would expect such a transformation if society as a whole were undergoing basic structural change. The extended family may continue to weaken somewhat but this is not a new development and remains incomplete.

Citation of family, sex and demography may seem a bit unfair, for while they are a vital part of the broad process of industrialization as social historians are coming to understand it and therefore legitimately considered in assessing the post-industrial concept, they have not been invoked by the advocates of post-industrial society directly. This shows the limited criteria with which the post-industrialists are dealing. The criteria used are definitely important in any claim for a new historical epoch, but they prove inadequate by themselves. Three have been emphasized: social structure, which Bell deals with at length as do the neo-Marxists; social protest, to which Bell makes only passing reference but which is vital to the neo-Marxists; and technology.

Until Bell's study, technology, normally the most basic motor of social transformation, had not been elaborately assessed. It lurked in the background, and a mention of computers normally sufficed (as in Touraine's reference to a programmed society). Bell himself offers telling criticisms of the weakness of the technological factor in previous post-industrial argument, citing for example Amitai Etzioni's complete failure to substantiate his claim about a revolution in technology following World War II. We can grant a revolution in the area of information retrieval and a generally rapid pace of technological change, but it has not been proved that innovation is sufficient to alter the framework of life. Even in the information area, the notion of elaborate personal records and a steady speed-up in communication, was part of early industrialization; therefore, one wonders whether we have not simply elaborated on this base. Certainly it is questionable that contemporary technology implies a really new course, as opposed to a rapid evolution within an industrial framework; there is nothing clearly comparable to the application of fossil fuels to the production process. All this Bell largely grants. He reverts to the exponential rates of increase argument, but his basic statement is that there is no sign of a fundamental break in technology. Nor does he claim a basic watershed in levels of affluence. All this is cogently argued, and it would seem to put an end to some of the wilder claims about our futuristic future.

But Bell does not stop there. He knows he must have technological revolution if he is to have a new society, so he says that despite the lack of novel technology there is "something substantially new" about the whole process. This newness is that production technology is displaced, as the basis of social operations, by knowledge. Information replaces energy; the codification of theoretical knowledge replaces economic growth. And now that knowledge is becoming bureaucratized and specialized, and, of course, increasing exponentially, we have our equivalent of technological revolution. His discussion of changes in the organization of knowledge is in itself sensible enough, but of course these changes go back well into the Industrial Revolution itself. Problems in the bureaucratization and specialization of scientific knowledge were widely noted by 1900, so we can't go from this alone to the post-industrial society. What Bell must rely on is his reversion to exponential growth plus his statement that technology itself is unseated. While sympathizing with the logical necessity that moved Bell toward this position, I can only suggest that equally logical, and far more likely, alternative: that the claims to a distinctively new society can be abandoned.

Bell's conclusions about social structure follow fairly obviously from his analysis of technology, though they coincide with many other post-industrial arguments that did not have this peculiar base. Class structure is now derived mainly on differences in access to information or decision-making power, relating to educational level and position in a bureaucratic hierarchy. This, it is argued, contrasts with the industrial class structure, which, broadly speaking, separated property owners from nonowners. According to Bell the old upper-middle class gives way to scientists and other professions or (according to Dahrendorf) to a related managerial elite. For the neo-Marxists the working class becomes defined in terms not of poverty but of a lack of organizational control. Bell's emphasis is more in the steady diminution of the factory labor force and the rise of service workers and the white-collar sector.

This argument is substantially correct, but it involves two errors that detract from it as a proof of the existence of a new society. First, economic classes still exist and show every sign of enduring. Studies of the contemporary upper class, for example, reveal only a slight reduction in its property advantage over the rest of society. Bell's scientists and professionals work at best with the wealthy, and probably somewhat ambiguously under them, in shaping the course of society. Property ownership and decision-making remain intertwined. Moreover, the contemporary class structure is an evolution from earlier industrial class structure, not a fundamental departure from it. The pure property-owning criterion was a holdover from agricultural society, beginning to yield rapidly even by 1850 to a more bureaucratized class structure. Hence the emphasis on education by the middle class and the rapid modernization of the professions. Bell misses this entirely. He constantly talks of the rise of professions as if it were a brand new phenomenon. Yet while capitalists rose, both old and new professions defined themselves increasingly in terms of exclusiveness, advanced training and specialization—and this by the mid-nineteenth-century. Bell has nothing really to add to this, save to record the fact that the process has continued and that its relationship to capitalist property ownership remains ambiguous.

By the same token, at the other end of the scale, the nature of the industrial working class cannot be captured so easily as Bell imagines. It is true that the percentage of manufacturing workers crested in the later nineteenth-century and has usually declined since, in the advanced industrial countries. It is also true that some of the newer groups such as white-collar workers have not received enough study. But it is doubtful that the shift is as dramatic as claims of a move from a production economy to a service economy might indicate. Early industrial workers were preoccupied by problems of poverty, which had been exacerbated in the painful transition to industrial society, until about 1850. Relative poverty and, of course, lack of property continued to define the working class and many of its goals, but problems of society's organizational structure and workers' lack of decision-making power commanded attention quite early. At the same time, white-collar workers developed with some of the same attributes as workers —a lack of producing property and subjection to routinized work directed by large business or governmental organizations. They were not part of the same class and are not today, but their growing numerical importance does not create a really new set of social problems or values. There is, indeed, increasing evidence that white-collar workers will take over many of the organizational activities previously dominated by the blue-collar sector. In other words, the full implications of industrial class structure were not immediately worked out and are certainly not constant. What we see today is an evolution within this structure, not a break from it.

This can be illustrated by a brief outline of an unusually complicated social group: the lower-middle class. Shopkeepers were a relatively new element in the cities during the first phase of industrialization, before 1850 in Western Europe. Property owners, they formed the bulk of the lower-middle class, and they undeniably persisted into the twentieth-century as a major social category. But they were not an industrial class, for their motives and organizational sense were really traditional. Hence they stagnated economically even before 1850. They were, in other words, a large but essentially anachronistic product of a transitional period in which a traditional social and economic outlook could still survive even if transplanted to the growing cities. The modern lower-middle class of clerks and technicians, the white-collar class, was a product of the late nineteenth-century. Contemporary class structure at this level simply sees the steady gain of the white-collar group and its increasing ability to shake off old, shopkeeper-type norms. It seems pointless, indeed misleading, to call this a redefinition of class structure; it is a logical progression within the industrial framework. Much the same model, contrasting a transitional class structure of family-owned factories to the corporate hierarchy that was synonymous with industrialization itself, can be applied to middle-and upper-middle class history from at least the mid-nineteenth century onward. At the very top, the "new" upper class formed during the later nineteenth century in Europe was only partly new, precisely because traditional concepts of property and status still had such power; it was really a merger of new wealth with old aristocracy, and partly on the latter's terms. The twentieth century, and particularly recent decades, have seen a fuller working out of the implications of industrialization for the ruling class, with the growing interaction between property-owners and trained technocrats.

Thus the post-industrialists, including Bell, while correct on recent occupational trends, cannot build these into a really new society. They do not recognize how long it took for industrial society to shake off remnants of the older order. Bell's own figures for the United States suggest that what has really happened in the twentieth century is less the replacement of manufacturing workers by service workers, though this has occurred to an extent, than the replacement of agricultural labor (and for female workers, domestic service) by more modern service work. It simply makes no sense to view these important changes as the advent of a new order, rather than the elaboration, often surprisingly belated, of industrial social structure itself.

Bell's vision of the post-industrial society makes only a slight bow to protest. He sees the dilemma of a meritocracy confronting a mass of people excluded from decision-making, and thus touches base with the neo-Marxists, but he does not predict a high protest level. He also views the counterculture as a rather permanent feature of post-industrial life, which may already be questionable. Here too a bit of historical perspective would help, for a youth culture hostile to industrialization seems a recurrent phenomenon within industrial society (as in the agitation around the turn of the century, with its own back-to-nature motif). Bell is sure that the classic industrial protest is a thing of the past. Class conflict, with labor taking the combat role, is over; the "beast has been broken."

Neo-Marxist writers have gone farther in their definition of what will replace the classic industrial confrontations. They see those excluded from decision-making pitted against the decision-makers, with young people—notably students—who are partly outside the hierarchical system leading the way. Yet are we really entering a period capable of producing a new type of protest, as opposed to, possibly, a new rate and a slightly altered cast of characters? Student unrest of the late 1960's had many analogies with unrest of, say, the 1890's or even 1848 in terms of ideological inspiration, rigidified university institutions and sheer overcrowding in the schools and relevant postgraduate professions themselves. Social scientists have defined a general model of "industrial" or "modern" protest, applicable to the post-1850 period though only gradually gaining full hold over protest efforts. The model stresses organization, political action, class base and forward-looking goals. On the whole, working-class protest since 1950, including France's May 1968 protest seems to be evolving within this framework. To be sure, increasing numbers of white-collar workers are drawn into a similar kind of protest as well, reflecting their own evolution, but a fundamental redefinition of protest has occurred neither in goals nor in methods. If anything, we are simply drawing closer to the industrial model, particularly in the ability of increasing categories of protesters to seek genuinely progressive economic goals.

Finally, industrial protest from the first involved the problem of exclusion from decision-making. This was long intertwined with more immediate economic demands, a confusion which capitalist society and some impulses among workers themselves perpetuated. It is possible to trace the problem of organizational control back to protest of the mid-nineteenth-century at least. Even in the June Days during the French revolution of 1848, worker and artisan participants were drawn disproportionately from the largest companies, because of their reaction to their place in a big organization rather than any distinctive economic problems. Working-class unrest in the later nineteenth-century clearly sought new kinds of participation, in addition to more immediate economic goals. So, more obscurely, did lower middle-class protest against big business and big labor, though it anachronistically (because in part of the older property-owning element) turned against industrial society as a whole. In all this, including the fights for union recognition, it must be admitted that workers and others found it difficult to articulate their discontent over the lack of voice. They often turned against individual directors rather than asking for new rights. They often ended up modifying the control of one big organization only through another big organization. But the issue was there. One may hope that the contemporary protest movement improves its articulation, though the evidence is not yet clear. Again, we are dealing with evolution within the modern protest framework, not basic change.

On the evidence of Bell and others, we do not have a brand-new society or even the prospect of one. We are still trying to figure out what industrial society means, just as most of the world strives to adapt to the industrialization process in the first place. Of course, important changes have occurred in recent decades. We may, with Bell, share a "sense of a profound transformation in industrial society." But this is within the industrial framework. And one might even quibble about the "profound," given the familiarity of most of the topics Bell raises for any student of the course of industrial society since the late nineteenth century. The post-industrial terminology is too facile and misleading. Regrettably, given the nervous acceptance of change characteristic of industrial society—a realization that progress is inevitable but a sneaking fear that the next round may be catastrophic—it is probably too much to hope that the terminology will be quickly dropped. We must perhaps wait a generation, when a new round of social scientists, eager to prove that we are entering yet another decisive stage of human development, realize that they cannot handle a post-post-industrial concept and admit that we were industrial all along. But we can hope that serious students of society will even now recognize the questionable character of the whole concept. Certainly Professor Bell's approach, ultimately so limited by the horizons of the American university and science establishment, is inadequate to its claims.

The question ultimately is not one of terminology but basic perspective in the understanding of modern society and its future prospects. The post-industrialists are saying, implicitly, that we have no historical frame of reference for what is happening now. A study of even the recent past might turn up some origins of contemporary developments, but mainly it would reveal how different things were back then. We'd best examine the present alone; and then predict. A rather comfortless prospect, frankly, for the present alone yields little understanding. And it is simply not necessary in terms of the actual relationship of the present to the recent past. The post-industrialists engage heavily in a kind of utopian guesswork, which is why their various futures differ so radically. Professor Bell modifies this by discussing a number of topics now current, but this hardly qualifies as inspired forecasting; and he has his own utopia, in the future of the university meritocracy. Utopias are fun, of course, though this particular one is a bit bleak, but they are not scientific and are not necessary to an understanding of probable social trends.

We have in fact a large basis for the interpretation of the present and assessment of the future. We can trace important consistencies as well as contrasts in the social history of the industrial age, of which we remain a part. We must not neglect older structural problems in a quest for a new social order. If this dampens the ardor of some who would like to turn to new sources of victory, it can provide a realistic understanding of the conditions of protest in industrial society that need not trap us in the failures of the past. Certainly we should not be misled by claims of a brand-new governing elite in an assessment of where power actually lies in contemporary society. Even more, we should try to understand what industrial society is about whether we like it or not, so that we can determine when major change is taking place. The post-industrial approach, which rests so heavily on repeated assertion, can only distract from the kind of perspective we require.

Post-Industrial Society and the Welfare State

by Michael Harrington

In the *Communist Manifesto,* Marx and Engels described "conservative, or bourgeois, socialism."

> A part of the bourgeoisie [they wrote] wants to remedy *social grievances* in order to ensure the stability of bourgeois society.... They want to have the existing society, but without the revolutionary, transforming elements.

The function of this "socialism," they went on to say, was not

> the abolition of bourgeois relations of production, which is possible only in a revolutionary way, but administrative improvements, which can go forward on the basis of this mode of production, which thus alter nothing in the relationship of capital and labor, but in the best case lessen the cost of bourgeois domination and reduce its public budget.

It would be nonsense to suggest that this passing *aperçu* of Marx and Engels (which appears in a rich, but often unread, section of the *Manifesto*) anticipated all the developments of the welfare state. It would be equally silly to ignore the fact that it provides a remarkable organizing insight for the analysis of some of the events of the past century. Indeed, there is a contemporary example of the theory of "bourgeois socialism," which is one of the most influential sociological and political ideas of the times. It is the notion of industrial (or postindustrial) society associated with thinkers like Raymond Aron and Daniel Bell.

For Bell, three events led to the emergence of the postindustrial society. First, there was the Great Depression, which forced the recognition that the direction of the economy is "a central governmental task." Second, there was state subsidy of the new science-based technology, which became a decisive factor in the 1950s. And third, there was the response to the social demands of the '60s which, though "pell-mell and piecemeal," led the government to make a commitment "not only to the creation of a substantial welfare state *but to redress the impact of all economic and social inequalities as well."* This thesis, it will be noted, is essentially a generalization of the Keynesian experience. The other antecedents of planned capitalism are either briefly mentioned or ignored.

Bell introduced his analysis of this evolution in *The Coming of Post-Industrial Society* with a modest disclaimer. He wrote that he had resisted the impulse to make too large a generalization.

> Instead [he went on], I am dealing here with *tendencies,* and have sought to explore the meaning and consequences of those tendencies if the changes in social structure that I describe were to work themselves to their logical limits. But

there is no guarantee that they will. . . . Thus I am writing what Hans Vahinger called an "as if," a fiction, a logical construction of what *could* be, against which the future social reality can be compared in order to see what intervened to change society in the direction it did take.

The only problem with this humble agnosticism is that Bell does not act upon it. He continually makes assertions about facts, not tendencies, i.e., that the welfare state seeks *"to redress the impact of all economic and social inequalities."* That claim, as will be seen, is simply not true; but important at this moment is that the very fact that it is made indicates that Bell's "as if" image of his thesis is an escape clause, not a description of his work.

There are, Bell says, five "dimensions, or components" of the term, postindustrial society. In the economic sector there is a shift from goods-producing to a service economy; occupationally, there is the "pre-eminence" of the professional and technical class; the axial principle of the society is "the centrality of theoretical knowledge as the source of innovation and of policy formulation for the society"; there is technological forecasting; and decision-making takes place by means of a new " 'intellectual technology.' " All of this is clearly related to the growth of the welfare state, particularly in its role as manager of the economy. Bell writes, "A post-industrial society . . . is increasingly a communal society wherein public mechanisms rather than the market become the allocators of goods, and public choice, rather than individual demand, becomes the arbiter of services." So, ". . . if the major historic turn in the last quarter of a century has been the subordination of economic function to societal goals, the political order necessarily becomes the control system of society." Therefore, "what the traditional classes fought out in the economic realm . . . is now transferred to the political realm."

Although Bell does not make the point explicitly (he waffles on this count), these assertions add up to the theory that the postindustrial society is also postcapitalist. Indeed, if economic function has been subordinated to "societal" goals, that might even imply that it is socialist. But then, Bell would argue that the very terms "capitalist" and "socialist" have become, if not meaningless, not very useful and that he, and his colleagues, are inventing a new vocabulary to deal with a new reality. That is his and their right. If, however, the factual assertions that underpin the new definition—say, that economic function has been subordinated to "societal goals"—are inaccurate, then Bell's linguistic innovation is invalid too.

A critical point that allows one to check the worth of the postindustrial categories of analysis concerns the ruling class in contemporary society. "If the dominant figures of the past 100 years have been the entrepreneur, the businessman and the industrial executive," Bell argues,

> the "new men" are the scientists, the mathematicians, the economists and the engineers of the new intellectual technology . . . The basic values of society [prior to the postindustrial shift] have been focused on business institutions, the largest rewards have been found in business, and the strongest power has been held by the business community, although today that power is to some extent shared within the factory by the trade-union, and regulated within the society by the political order . . . In the post-industrial society, production and business de-

cisions will be subordinated to, or will derive from, other forces in society; the crucial decisions regarding the growth of the economy and its balance will come from government, but they will be based on the government's sponsorship of research and development.

This means, Bell holds, that "the long-run historical trend in Western society" is "the move away from governance by political economy to governance by political philosophy . . . a turn to non-capitalist modes of thought." But, if the experts are thus in the process of replacing the capitalists as decision-makers, surely the outcome of those decisions, made by new men on a new calculus, must be observably different from those of the old order. In fact, this is not the case. There are indeed changed structures; only they have an old, and quite capitalist content.

In the course of empirically challenging Bell's theory by showing that the results it predicts do not take place, not even incipiently, a basic proposition will begin to emerge. When the government intervenes into an economy dominated by private corporations to promote the common good, those corporations will normally be the prime beneficiaries of that intervention. The planners may be liberals, or even socialists, but they will not be able to carry out policies that run counter to the crucial institutions of the society unless they have the support of a determined mass movement willing to fight for structural change. Since this condition usually is fulfilled only in exceptional crisis circumstances, the normal tendency of the welfare state—even with the "new men" admittedly much more in evidence and conscious planning taking on a greater importance—is to follow the old capitalist priorities in a new, sophisticated way.

Marx and Engels glimpsed the essential mechanism of this phenomenon long ago (which is hardly to argue that they said the last word on it). Proudhon had proposed that the government provide cheap credit for cooperatives and small business. If that were done, Engels wrote to Marx, the workers' societies and small producers would not be able to qualify for credit at the state bank, but big business would. It would have the collateral to prove that it was a good risk and the expertise to take advantage of the cheap money. John Maynard Keynes understood this point in his own way. Businessmen, he said, must be treated more gently than politicians. "If you work them into the surly, obstinate, terrified mood, of which domestic animals, wrongly handled, are so capable, the nation's burden will not get carried to market; and in the end public opinion will veer their way."

John Kennedy was forced to learn this depressing fact during his brief presidency. He confronted this reality when he tried to deal with the balance-of-payments issue. "It's a ridiculous situation," he said, "for us to be squeezing down essential public activities in order not to touch private investment and tourist spending—but apparently that's life." That was not "life," but *life under capitalist conditions,* and the argument Kennedy faced— that government must sacrifice its priorities to profit in order to provide for investment—is still very much with us in the '70s.

The macroeconomic planning of the welfare state, then, follows, and must follow, capitalist priorities. The government and the "societal goals" that it articulates are subordinated to private purpose—not the other way around, as Bell thinks. This was, and is, clearly the case in energy policy. Here one sees vividly how the capitalist structure of the welfare state was the decisive reason for the great Inflation-Recession of the '70s.

It might be argued that oil is an exceptional case. Its giant American enterprises are vertically integrated and part of an international corporate conspiracy that has existed since the 1920s. Moreover, oil is the only instance in which there has been a dramatic increase in American overseas investment in the Third World; the more typical multinationals are involved in Europe and Canada. So, it would be well to outline how the patterns that are writ so large in energy policy apply to all big business in the United States.

First of all, there is the case of federal housing policy during the past 40 years. It too has followed corporate priorities. The migration of the middle class and the rich to the suburbs, as I documented in *Socialism,* has been subsidized by Washington. Over a period of three decades, the government helped build 10 million units for the better-off and 650,000 units of low-cost housing for the poor. In 1969, the *Wall Street Journal* reported that there were $2.5 billion in subsidies for the urban freeways, which facilitated the commuting of the privileged, and only $175 million for mass transit. All of this made good commercial sense even though it helped perpetrate the social disaster of the disintegration of the central cities, the consequent isolation of the racial and ethnic minorities, the subversion of the passenger rail system, and so forth.

As the Council of Economic Advisers put it in its 1969 report, "Investing in new housing for low-income families—particularly in big cities—is usually a losing proposition. Indeed the *most profitable investment* is often one that demolishes homes of low-income families to make room for business and high-income families." What did this government agency mean by "profitable" in this statement? It could not possibly have been referring to a social conception of increased benefits, since the process it was describing had exacted a high public cost in crime, welfare expenses and, above all, wrecked human lives.

The Council was, of course, talking about the private-profit criterion. And that was, not simply in theory but in fact, the one that the government had followed. Those billions of dollars had been assigned to the housing of the affluent on the grounds that their discarded dwellings would eventually "trickle down" to the poor. That did not happen; the central cities were turned into devastated regions instead.

A second case in point is food.

When one thinks of American agriculture, one usually envisions a mythic image of the yeoman farmer. In reality, it is a sector dominated by gigantic agribusinesses. Between 1960 and 1974, the number of farms in America decreased by 25 percent, but the larger units (with more than $20,000 a year in sales) went up by 80 percent. In 1971, the 21 percent of the largest farms received approximately 80 percent of the cash receipts from farming. Among the "farmers" in America, one finds I.T.T., the John Hancock Mutual Life Insurance Co., Tenneco (which used to be the Tennessee Gas and Transmission Co.), Gulf and Western, Boeing Aircraft, and other giant corporations. And the average investment in reproducible farm capital (machinery, livestock, etc.) in the United States was $18,000 in 1964. (In Latin America it is less than $500.)

These big businesses on the land have been the prime recipients of tens of billions of dollars in federal subsidy. In the '30s, when the Depression wreaked havoc on the farm, Washington embarked upon a program of planned, socialized scarcity, even though people were (and still are) hungry. It was an almost classic acting-out of the scenario described by Marx in Volume I of *Das Kapital*. Agricultural productivity had grown enormously and was "overproductive" for a society of restricted, maldistributed income. Therefore, the accomplishments of agricultural technology became, quite literally, a fetter upon the system. Farm animals were killed, farmers were paid for not growing crops. This latter policy benefited mainly the largest landowners and producers; it provided nothing for subsistence farmers and a pittance for small units. Thus, the trend toward agricultural concentration —the destruction of that sturdy, independent yeoman of the Jeffersonian myth and his replacement by a corporation—was expedited at enormous federal expense. It was, after all, "sensible"—without a capitalist definition of the term—to orient policy toward the most successful, and politically powerful, producers.

In 1974, a study carried out by the National Farmers Union documented the consequence of the government's pursuit of corporate priorities in the fields of America. Between 1968 and 1973—that is, in the five years immediately prior to an incredible inflation of food costs in America and the emergence of starvation as a reality in the poor countries—Washington paid $15.5 billion to farmers in return for their idling 233 million acres of land that would have produced an estimated grain crop of 23 million metric tons. "Assuming yields of only two thirds of the national average for the grain best suited to the various lands held out of production," the study said, "the five-year total would have reached the equivalent of 8,609 million bushels of wheat. This is nearly a billion bushels more than the actual total harvest of 7,669 million bushels of wheat in the U.S. during those five years."

It cost billions of dollars not to produce those bushels of wheat in a hungry, partly starving, world. As the Joint Congressional Committee staff computed the price for nonproduction in 1970, there were $5.2 billion in direct federal outlays to the farmers, and food cost the consumer an extra $4.5 billion in higher prices due to the scarcity he had already subsidized in his role as a taxpayer. So, the total cost in 1970 to the people of the United States was $10 billion to keep crops from being planted. This is perhaps the most obvious single case of how the business pursuit of profit is institutionalized in welfare-state policy and takes precedence over the most basic of all economic processes, the production of food. Moreover, as will be seen, these tens of billions of taxpayers' dollars made an important contribution to the inflation of the 1970s and helped limit America's ability to respond to the crime of global malnutrition.

The tax system in the United States is one of the most important instrumentalities of corporate values. It is utterly dominated by "political economy" (corporations) and not by "political philosophy" (liberal technocrats).

First of all, there has been no trend toward equality in the United States during the past generation (i.e., since 1945) and it is questionable whether there was any equality trend at all during the twentieth century. The relative shares of wealth are at least as maldistributed today as they were at the end of the Great Depression. The figures are difficult to pin down—this is after all the "dirty little secret" of American democracy—and some of the most reliable are more than ten years old. However, the basic and intolerable fact is not really in dispute; it was, for instance, admitted by Richard Nixon's Council of Economic Advisers in 1974. As the economist Lester Thurow assembled the data:

U.S. DISTRIBUTION OF FAMILY WEALTH 1962

	% of Total Families by Wealth	% of Total Family Wealth
Lowest	25.4	0.0
Next	31.5	6.6
Next	24.4	17.2
Top	18.7	76.2
(Top	7.5)	(59.1)
(Top	2.4)	(44.4)
(Top	.5)	(25.8)

So, the wealthiest Americans—0.5 percent of the families—own more (25.8 percent of the total) than the bottom 81.3 percent (who own 23.8 percent of the country).

In theory—and in the imagination of most Americans as well as in the propaganda of big business—the tax system is progressive. If this were indeed the case, one would expect that the trend toward the concentration of wealth would be offset by the various federal, state and local levies. In fact, the way in which taxes are collected is only most mildly progressive (if it is progressive at all); and the way in which tax expenditures are allocated favors the rich with billions and even tens of billions in subsidies a year. More to the point, the rationale whereby the government redistributes burdens from the wealthy to the working people is that it is necessary to make the capitalist system work.

Joseph Pechman and Benjamin Okner did a careful study of the tax burden in the United States. Before noting their conclusion, an important, but unfortunately abstruse, methodological point has to be made. Most government statistics omit capital gains as an element in family income; thus, the growth in the value of the equity held by the rich in boom years is not counted. (This is the *only* form of income that is not taxed when it is made, and this fact, along with the weakness of the inheritance laws, allows the rich to evade billions in taxes.) However, if capital gains are included, then the income inequality in the United States increases dramatically. Using the government's figures, the top 1 percent of the people get "only" 4.8 percent of the annual income; using the adjusted figures, their take goes up to 10.5 percent.[1]

Pechman's and Okner's point is recognized even by the conservatives in government, although they prefer, for obviously political reasons, to publish statistics that play down the maldistribution of income. If the adjusted figures are used, and if the reasonable assumption is made that corporation taxes are shifted, in whole or in part, to consumers, then the effective rate of taxation on the very rich is only 5 percent more than that paid by most families. The federal tax system is thus not progressive, but proportional "and therefore has little effect on the distribution of income."

It is a scandal that the tax system is not, as is so often claimed, progressive. One might infer that this is the case because of the political power of wealth in America. However, when one turns from the way in which taxes are collected to the manner in which tax expenditures are made, there is no need for inference. The government proudly and openly states that these are motivated by capitalist considerations.

A tax expenditure occurs when Washington decides that some particular class of taxpayers need pay no tax, or will be forgiven a portion of their tax. It has the same effect as a direct expenditure of government money, since lowering one group's rate effectively increases the rates of everyone else. For instance, realized capital gains are taxed at lower rates than any other form of income.[2] People with incomes of $20,000 to $25,000 a year, a Congressional Committee reported in 1972, receive $100 in benefits from this provision; while those with incomes of $1 million get $640,000 a year from it. More generally, the deductions—or tax expenditures—in the Internal Revenue Code provide 10 percent of the benefits for the 50 percent of the people at the bottom of the society and 15 percent of them for the 3 percent at the top.

In 1975, the projected federal budget for 1976 contained no less than $91.8 billion in tax expenditures. These figures, it should be noted, were computed on the basis of very conservative assumptions—the fact that imputed rental value of an owner-occupied house was not considered to be a tax expenditure and neither was the failure to count in the accrued value of capital gains during a tax year. But even with these definitions, which made the Internal Revenue code look fairer than it is, there were shocking notations. For instance, the deductibility of mortgage interest and property taxes yielded homeowners a tax subsidy of almost $13 billion—almost ten times as much as was spent on public housing assistance in 1975!

In 1975, the Treasury prepared, at the request of Senator Walter Mondale, an analysis of tax expenditures as they showed up in 1974 spending. In that year, the two-tenths of 1 percent of the taxpayers who had incomes of more than $100,000 a year received 12.6 percent of the subsidies in a number of major categories; the 46.9 percent of the taxpayers whose incomes ranged up to $10,000 that year, got a mere 16.6 percent. And the top 1.2 percent got a third more than the bottom 46.9 percent. In theory, such policies are supposed to stimulate business and individuals to act in a way that will promote the common good. In fact, as Senator William Proxmire pointed out when releasing a Joint Economic Committee analysis, "our studies have shown that many subsidy programs do not work well economically, they are often directed at out-moded or nonexistent objectives, they redistribute income to the affluent, and in many cases their costs far exceeded their benefits to the society as a whole."

So, in many cases the argument for a given deduction was clearly fallacious. The privileged treatment of the capital gains of the rich was worth $14 billion in 1971. The theory was that the government thereby encouraged people to save, which in turn provided investment funds for new jobs, and so on. In fact, as Benjamin Okner pointed out to the Joint Economic Committee, only a small and declining portion of corporate investment in 1971 came from external financing. So, most of the $14 billion was a handsome, if unconscious, gift to the wealthy from the less-well-off. But this systematic bias does not operate simply in this or that case. It informs all of macroeconomic governmental policy in the United States.

In this post-Keynesian era, the tax system is not conceived of as a mechanism for collecting and disbursing public revenues. Its prime function is to facilitate countercyclical policy, to expand demand when there is excess capacity and unemployment, to restrain it when the opposite is the case. Since corporations are the primary economic units in the society, such countercyclical tax policy must, as Keynes so well understood, be kind to executives. Over 30 years ago, Michael Kalecki shrewdly anticipated the problems that would arise in such an undertaking. Business, he said, is opposed to government spending for three reasons: a dislike of government intervention in the economy, as such; opposition to the direction of government spending (public investment and subsidizing competition); and fear of the undisciplined work force that would result from a full-employment economy.

One of the ways to deal with this corporate hostility to government intervention, Kalecki argued, was to have the state stimulate and subsidize *private* investment. That would make businessmen less grumpy about bureaucratic interference, since they would make money from it; and it would not put public money into public investments, nor would it underwrite the consumption of the masses. Kalecki's reading of the political dimensions of Keynesian policy in a capitalist economy proved prophetic, above all, in the United States.

Indeed, this point helps to explain the function of the warfare state within the welfare state. Military spending has the marvelous quality of conferring subsidized profits on inefficient corporations producing goods that do not, like the power generated by the Tennessee Valley Authority, compete with the output of other firms in the consumer market. It thus neatly synthesizes the worst potential of both capitalism and socialism. This does not, however, mean that a massive arms sector is a necessity for capitalism, a precondition for its continuing existence. As Seymour Melman has pointed out, Germany and Japan did quite well after World War II, even though defeat deprived them of the right and duty of wasting a good portion of their substance on the means of destruction. For that matter, the Pentagon's share of the Gross National Product has declined somewhat in recent years. Moreover, it is a mechanistic and silly economic determinism to try to reduce all of the complicated international politics of the postwar decades to a reflex of a militaristic economy. The tragic, unconscionable American intervention in Vietnam, to take but one case in point, was also senseless from a rationally calculated capitalist (or imperialist) point of view. The financiers and Wall Streeters who participated in considerable numbers in the antiwar campaigns of 1968 understood this even if some self-proclaimed Marxists did not.

And yet, if capitalism is not inevitably and intrinsically militarist, the great fact remains that arms spending is peculiarly congenial to it. The businessmen who refused to let Roosevelt engage in social spending at a rate that would have ended the Great Depression became patriotic "dollar a year" men as soon as war broke out. In part their reaction was sincere; in part, it expressed the knowledge (or, at the time, the *intuition*) that military "socialism" is profoundly antisocialist. But, then, even when the system adopts pacific measures of government intervention—and does so under liberal auspices—it has the same point of maintaining, and extending, the status quo. Military spending is only one instrument of capitalist survival, albeit an important and fearful one.

When, for instance, John Kennedy wanted to get the economy moving again in the early '60s, he could have done so, as Kenneth Galbraith and the AFL-CIO urged, by direct outlays for social investments. That, however, would have pitted him against the political power of business (and of reaction in general). So, just as Kalecki predicted, he opted for a tax cut that would benefit the corporations more than anyone else. In a speech defending his policy before the Economic Club of New York, he waxed so conservative that Galbraith said that he had given "the most Republican speech since McKinley," and *Time* Magazine noted that he sounded like the National Association of Manufacturers.

This did not mean, as many on the left would probably assume, that Kennedy had "sold out." It is much more profound than that, and one can concede Kennedy's *bona fides* without harm to the essential point. The President of the United States was bowing to the power relationships of an economy dominated by private corporations. In such a setting, he could—particularly if he had been much more powerful in the Congress than he was at that time—have acted otherwise; but all of the institutional, structural pressures in American society urged him to act as he did.

As a result of this general tendency of the political economy of a capitalist society, all of the tax reductions between 1964 and 1973 favored the rich. Some 16.1 percent of the tax returns in that period came from people with incomes under $3,000; they received 7.9 percent of the tax cuts. They were only 4.7 percent of the returns in the $20,000-to-$50,000 category, but they received 10.3 percent of the benefits; and the 0.6 percent of the people with incomes over $50,000 got 0.9 percent of the cuts. At the same time, the corporations got bonanzas in the form of investment tax credits. The economy of the United States was thus stimulated by pampering the rich and slighting the poor.

So macroeconomic policy is procorporate in two basic ways. First, it stimulates private investment and thereby allows the executives to determine the actual form that the public expenditure will take. Instead of direct outlays for health, mass transportation, education, and the like, there are tax cuts that allow the private sector to build and sell whatever it pleases without any reference to social usefulness. And second, the benefits of the public expenditures are assigned in inverse proportion to need, with the corporations and the rich getting most and the poor least.

A carefully documented and even ingenious study by an academic moderate, Harold Wilensky's *The Welfare State and Equality*, disputes the kind of argument I have made. The welfare state, Wilensky asserts, has an egalitarian effect, because the "pay out is typically more progressive than the financing is regressive." That conclusion is wrong, but Wilensky honestly arrived at it on the basis of a flawed, but revealing, method. In computing the regressivity of the financing, he excludes capital gains and expense accounts. But capital gains, as we have seen, are the most inequitable and massively subsidized source of the privilege of the wealthy. By one stroke of a statistical definition, Wilensky thus biases his cases. Second, he treats the welfare state narrowly, concentrating on social security programs, but ignoring the tens of billions paid out in the dole for the rich in the Internal Revenue Code as well as the gains made by the corporate class as a result of federal economic management. And finally, Wilensky is much too optimistic about the progressiveness of the welfare state "pay out." This is a point that deserves some attention in its own right.

Medicaid is the federal program designed to bring health care to the poor. It is financed by both Washington and by the individual states. Predictably, the richest states—New York, California, Massachusetts—take a maximum advantage of this law; the poorest states do the least. There are 46 percent of the poverty-stricken in the South, but only 17 percent of the Medicaid payments are made there, and the three affluent states disburse 50 percent of the funds. And even social security itself refracts the basic unfairness of America's class structure. It may well be that the poor do not get more benefits from it, because they die earlier and work longer than anyone else in the society. Moreover, we do know that whites use Medicaid more than blacks (because of the shortage of doctors in black areas) and that the elderly with a $15,000 income get twice as much from Medicare as those with less than $5,000 a year. Considerations like these led the Brookings Institution, a center of moderate, pragmatic liberalism, to conclude that there is no redistribution of wealth from federal programs for "transferring" income—theoretically, but only theoretically—from the rich to the poor.

All of these facts are at odds with Bell's theory of a postindustrial society. One of the quintessential domains of the "new men" was and is economic policy. This is an example of a new intellectual technology, of the rise of nonmarket forces and so on. And yet it turns out that, even under a liberal Administration like Kennedy's, those new men are forced, willy-nilly, to follow corporate priorities when they elaborate the government's program. And this is so because the macroeconomics of the welfare state, for all the momentous changes that have taken place, are still filled with a capitalist content. That welfare state, then, is not a new form of society, any more than Bismarckian "socialism" was; it is, rather, a new way of protecting the old order.

To be sure, the welfare state also contains contradictory tendencies, the seeds, not of one new order, but of two. As of now, however, it is primarily and fundamentally capitalist, and this is the key to the secret history of the great economic and social crisis of the '70s.

REFERENCES

1. Income, it will be noted, is less maldistributed than wealth; the top one percent have 10.5 percent of the income, but the top 0.5 percent have 25.8 percent of the wealth. This simply shows that the rich have most of their holdings in long-term assets, which are not subject to income tax, and that they have a positive incentive to minimize their income. Either figure is outrageous; both are only the different sides of the same golden coin.

2. When capital gains are realized—when stock is sold and a profit is taken—they are income. The capital gains that Pechman and Okner computed are "accrued"—that is, they include both gains that were turned into cash and those that were held as part of a continuing investment.

Second Thoughts on the Human Prospect

by Robert Heilbroner

Next to writing his own obituary, I suppose what every writer would most welcome is a chance to review his own books. To begin with, this would present an opportunity to voice those enthusiasms and extravaganzas the critics have unaccountably failed to express. But then there is also the possibility of criticising his own work from a truly privileged position—one that makes up for its obvious lack of objectivity by its special access to the writer's intentions, doubts, convictions.

Thus, I welcome a chance to review *An Inquiry into the Human Prospect* a little more than a year after it was written. This is particularly the case because I have no occasion to complain about the reception, or at least the notoriety, the book has received. Few things I have written have drawn the attention that was accorded *The Human Prospect*—a fact that should fill me with satisfaction, did I not believe it was largely the result of purely accidental factors.

I wrote my *Inquiry* between July 1972 and August 1973, during a time when, save for international monetary complications, a relative tranquillity characterised international relations and most domestic affairs. Then, like a thunderbolt, the Arab-Israeli war broke out in the fall of 1973, followed shortly thereafter by the imposition of the Arab oil embargo that literally convulsed the world.

Let me hasten to say that I was as surprised as everyone else by this turn of events. But the effect of the outbreak was radically to change the impact of my book. What had been intended as a distanced discussion of long-range events became a commentary on current affairs. A scenario not intended to be played out for many years was, so to speak, given a sneak preview in the headlines of every newspaper. The result was that quite without any intention on my part, *The Human Prospect* became uncannily prescient, and more than that, plausible. I had, for example, written about the possibility of nuclear blackmail initiated by the underdeveloped world as its economic situation deteriorated. This suggestion, advanced with great caution as a risk that might be encountered "within a generation," suddenly became an imminent possibility. On the one hand there was the unprecedented action by the Arab world against the industrial West; on the other, the detonation of an atom bomb by India.

In similar fashion, other events played into my hands. The grim Malthusian prognosis that I advanced was given credibility by a drought in the sub-Saharan zone that reportedly claimed six million victims. The Hobbesian struggle of each against all, which I had feared as the social consequence of a deceleration of economic growth, was made believable by the long lines of motorists queuing up to get "their" share of gasoline at the expense of everyone else. So, too, the rapid imposition of rationing measures and the immediate flurry of interest in legislation limiting energy use lent credence to my speculations about the resort to political authority in the face of domestic scarcity.

Thus, part of the sympathetic response given to *The Human Prospect* was simply due to a concatenation of events that made the book seem far more topical than I had intended it to be. As I now write these second thoughts, many of the immediate risks and dangers of early 1974 have receded, leaving only a small residue of caution in the midst of a general return to business as usual. Were my book to have been published last month instead of last year, I doubt very much that it would have caught public attention to the extent that it did. Yet if the somewhat calmer mood of today lessens the immediacy of my text, it restores a much needed perspective to what I intended—and still intend—to say. This was to present a reasoned and reasonable scenario of the major trends of history over an extended period of time—indeed, as far into the future as our very limited powers of foresight enable us to peer.

I must emphasize that this is a very different task from the prediction of short-run events. The near-random happenings that dominate the immediate future diminish in importance before the underlying trends and dynamics of things. Needless to say, this assumes that we can identify elements in the present that are so massive and deeply rooted that we can plausibly speak of their "trends and dynamics"—that is, plausibly investigate their influences over the general direction of human affairs. Obviously, I believe there are such elements, and that we can infer, however loosely, the pressures and constraints they will bring to bear.

Second, the long-term speculations and reasonings that lie at the heart of *The Human Prospect* differ from short-term forecasting in another way. When we make predictions about the immediate future, even dire predictions, we are almost always sounding a call for action. To predict the events of next week, month, year or even decade is to initiate a process of adaptation and counteraction. But that is not at all the intention or the rational response to "predictions" that stretch over a time span as long as that of my book. Now we are confronting events that seem likely to take place despite efforts to adapt or to change the course of things. The movement of history becomes—to the extent that we are persuaded that history has foreseeable movements—a process quite beyond our control. We are reduced to the impotence of astronomers watching the imperturbable mechanics of celestial objects. That may be a state of mind natural to astronomers, but it is surely not one that is natural to social observers. If the reviews and criticisms I have received during the past year have taught me anything, it is that a critical detachment from the historic future is the most difficult attitude to express or to defend. Accordingly, it is a problem to which I will return at the end of these second thoughts.

NEW ELEMENTS OF DANGER

Let me begin, however, by reviewing, with the benefit of a year's hindsight, the cogency of the initial premises on which the argument of *The Human Prospect* was based. They are so familiar they need only a word of exposition. The first was that population was expanding at unmanageable rates, especially in many parts of the underdeveloped world. The second was that the capability of waging nuclear war was moving into the hands of the underdeveloped world, radically altering the balance of power between rich and poor nations. And the third was that the process of industrial growth would become increasingly difficult to sustain because of resource limitations, and increasingly dangerous because of pollution problems, including the ultimate fatal pollution of an overheated atmosphere.

I have only minor additions to make to the first two of these fundamental premises. Demographic pressures do not change overnight. If I have any amendment to my previous position, it is a growing awareness of serious doubts among demographers as to the effectiveness of deliberate anti-natalist policies in curtailing population growth. There seems to be an increasing tendency to view population as an independant variable, susceptible to change only as a result of social and economic changes. I might add that this reinforces my conviction that the only means of bringing about a *rapid* diminution of population pressures is the use of educative and exhortative means along Chinese lines, although I am uncomfortably aware of how little we know about Chinese experience.[1]

I have equally little to add with regard to the nuclear problem. Immediately following the Indian detonation, there was much talk that it was only a matter of time before the bomb would be available to Iran, Brazil, Egypt and Pakistan; and there is a growing worry that nuclear explosives can be manufactured (or stolen) by private terrorist groups.[2] I will have a word to say later about the possible outcome of this changing balance of power, but that the balance *is* changing, perhaps even more rapidly than I had anticipated, does not seem in question.

This brings me to the last of my original triad of fundamental problems, namely economic growth. Here I do think that some emendation is in order, for there are aspects to the problem of resources and pollution of which I was not aware a year ago. To begin with, I would take a somewhat more hopeful view of the mineral resource problem. This is because I did not know when I wrote the book of the possibility of mining the seabeds for mineral nodules which are estimated to exist in the order of "hundreds of billions" of tons, promising supplies of manganese, copper, cobalt and nickel at significantly lower prices than today.[3] I do not know at what ocean depths these nodules lie or what period of development will be needed to bring the necessary technology into being, but on the basis of the information at hand, I would now assess the dangers of a "scarcity" of minerals less seriously than I did before.

But this more hopeful view of the possibilities for sustaining economic growth is at least counterbalanced and perhaps outweighed by two additional considerations of whose seriousness I have only recently become aware. The first has to do with the outlook for expanded food production.

World food stocks are today at their lowest points since World War II, and there is a general alarm concerning the possibility of unprecedented famines. Two eminent food technologists, Norman Borlaug and Raymond Ewell, have predicted horrendous famines within a very few years. Meanwhile, world fish harvests have levelled off, or actually declined, despite efforts to increase the catch, suggesting a limit to this important protein source, at least with current technologies and tastes. At the same time, there is concern expressed about the diminishing potential for increased acreage or yields of food crops, especially in the most fertile areas of the world. Finally, there appears to be no chance of building fertiliser plants rapidly enough to forestall a desperate food shortage in the underdeveloped world.[4]

We do not yet know whether the constraint on food production is a temporary or a permanent limitation on world output. Once again, technology becomes the *deus ex machina* that may yet rescue us from an otherwise intolerable situation. Nonetheless, until or unless technology makes its magic entrance, we must add the probability of food shortages to the list of difficulties that must be overcome if growth is to continue. And this added caution is given still greater weight by the ominous possibility that weather patterns may be changing, bringing the Sahelian disaster as their first consequence, and threatening the still more disruptive possibility of a North American drought or a Northern Hemispheric shortening of growing seasons.[5]

This new element of danger and uncertainty bears on my warnings with respect to an ultimate barrier on industrial expansion arising from heat pollution. I have seen nothing that challenges the calculations or data on which that warning was based. But I have become more aware of the extreme delicacy of the earth's climate mechanism, and of the possibility that even relatively small man-made changes may induce drastic alterations in the climate, long before a general overheating would threaten global viability. Alterations in local temperatures, in the earth's albedo (reflectivity), or in the concentration of particulate matter in the air, are all capable of inducing potentially disastrous and probably irreversible changes in weather patterns, rainfall, or global temperature gradients.[6]

These additional considerations diminish the specific threat of a world-wide thermal overload, but only in exchange for the much less clearly predictable but no less serious threat of inadvertent climatic change. Thus, my second thoughts greatly heighten the fear that global industrialisation, continued at the rates of the past and extended to all corners of the earth, is a process fraught with the gravest perils for mankind. The precise nature of that threat is more difficult to define with the clarity I perceived a year ago, but the gravity of the peril is, if anything, much greater.

CONTROLLED SPECULATIONS

The initial premises on which *The Inquiry* was based, chosen though they were with every effort to make them safe against what I called "the demolition of next year's research," have already been partly outmoded by next year's research. Yet here I find a curious thing. I had thought a year ago that I was moving step by step from very firm premises towards ever less secure conclusions. Today I am tempted to believe that the premises might be altered far more radically than I have found it necessary to do, without greatly altering the main conclusions to which the argument leads.

Moreover, I think I know why this is the case. *The Human Prospect* was not concerned only or even principally with the description of the central problems I have just reviewed. Its purpose was, rather, to engage in controlled speculations about the consequences of these massive facts. This led to a development of my historical scenario in what seemed like daring directions. From the facts of population pressure, I inferred the rise of "military-socialist" governments as the only kinds of regimes capable of establishing viable economic and social systems. From the proliferation of nuclear arms, I drew the conclusion that "wars of redistribution" would very possibly become a new, powerful shaping force for the future. And from the difficulties and dangers of continued economic growth in the industrial world, I anticipated a drift toward authoritarian measures as the only means by which a suicidal Hobbesian struggle could be avoided.

When I say that the conclusions of my book resist small changes in my premises, I do not mean to insist that the specific scenario I have just described is inherent in, or inexorably ordained by, the massive problems from which we begin. For example, I am not certain that revolutionary governments must emerge from the disorders produced by excessive population growth. As the Sahelian disaster has shown, millions can starve without creating an appreciable revolutionary ferment. It may well be that the outcome of the rural exodus and the urban disarray of India or Indonesia will be no more than social collapse, a condition that might last for a very long period, removing the affected parts of the world from the consciousness of the advanced areas and probably lessening the degree of international tension that seems likely to develop if determined revolutionary groups come into power.

I am equally unsure with regard to my frightening prognostications of nuclear blackmail. For one thing, I am now aware of a possibility I had not thought of a year ago, namely the use of economic (rather than military) power as a countervailing weapon in the hands of the underdeveloped world, as in the case of the Arab oil producers. What is difficult to foresee is the success with which other raw material producing countries will be able to concert their interests, or the long-term bargaining position of raw material producers and industrial users. Still another possibility has been suggested by Robert Tucker—the "decoupling" of the underdeveloped nations from their historic economic and political vassalage.[7] Such a trend towards autarky would have vast implications for world peace, for it would bring to a rapid halt the still incomplete internationalisation of capitalism. Among its possible consequences might be an intensification of intercapitalist wars of the 19th century kind, a matter about which we can only speculate.

Still less can I speak with certainty regarding the responses of industrial capitalism and industrial socialism to the slowly closing vice of environmental constraint. These long-term adaptive possibilities with which *The*

Human Prospect was concerned may remain only academic speculations if the warnings of a world depression or a worldwide credit collapse come to pass.[8] If indeed such a collapse occurs, it will greatly alter the problem of growth, at least in the short term, but I should think it would only accelerate the longterm conclusion to which the growth problem pointed—to wit, the centralisation of economic power and the assertion of more authoritarian rule.

CIVILISATION IN TRANSITION

Given these doubts and uncertainties, how can I maintain that my scenario is virtually independent of small changes in my premises? I think the answer is clear. What is important in these premises is not the particular avenues of the future that they suggest, but the fact that they indicate sustained and convulsive change as the inescapable lot of human society for a very long period to come. This overarching conclusion does indeed resist small changes in my premises. Nothing short of a total solution to the problem of population growth, nuclear danger, or economic growth would vitiate the larger anticipation of a rendezvous with forces that will subject human society to the buffets of a mighty storm.

It is in that sense that I find the overall conclusions of my book, however uncertain they may be in detail, stronger and more persuasive than I had originally supposed. Of course there is no way of proving such a statement. But here I would call attention to a matter of some significance. It is that even among my severest critics I have noted a surprising acquiescence in my diagnosis of the gravity of the human plight. Whatever my mistakes of fact, however fanciful my speculations, it has become plain that my vision of a major and protracted crisis—a crisis bound to deepen and intensify rather than to lessen or disappear—is a premonition shared by many.

The common, unspoken grounds for this agreement reflect that *malaise* of which I spoke early in *The Human Prospect*. There seems to be a widespread sense that we are living in a period of historic exhaustion, or perhaps more accurately, in a period of historic inflection from one dominant civilisational form to another. When I explore the nature of this feeling with its pervasive mood of exhaustion, I can do no more than repeat the diagnosis of *The Human Prospect*. The *malaise*, I have come more and more to believe, lies in the industrial basis on which our civilisation rests. Economic growth and technical achievement, the greatest triumphs of our epoch of history, have shown themselves to be inadequate sources for collective contentment and hope. Material advance, the most profoundly distinguishing attribute of industrial capitalism and socialism alike, has proved unable to satisfy the human spirit. Not only the quest for profit but the cult of efficiency have shown themselves ultimately corrosive for human well-being. A society dominated by the machine process, dependent on factory and office routine, celebrating itself in the act of individual consumption, is finally insufficient to retain our loyalty.

I am all too aware that there is an irritating flavour of bucolic utopianism in these thoughts. But I have no intention of urging a return to the simpler ways of rural community life. That route, alas, is blocked by the very forces that produce our civilisational climacteric. Until the forces of population growth, of nuclear danger, and above all, of a runaway industrial order have been brought under control, there is very little realistic likelihood of the establishment of the small kibbutz-like communities that many would urge as the most welcome alternative to the present order. For a very long period there will be no escape from the necessity of a centralised administration for our industrial world. There is no short-run possibility of dispersing our urban multitudes; no manner in which the immense military machines of the nation state can be disbanded; no substitute for state authority during the period of strain in which a redivision of wealth must be achieved within nations and among them.

Given these mighty pressures and constraints, we must think of alternatives to the present order in terms of social systems that offer a necessary degree of regimentation as well as a different set of motives and objectives. I must confess that I can picture only one such system. This is a social order that will blend a "religious" orientation and a "military" discipline. Such a monastic organisation of society may be repugnant to us, but I suspect it offers the greatest promise for bringing about the profound and painful adaptations that the coming generations must make.

It is likely that China comes closest today to representing this new civilisational form. No doubt the contemporary Chinese model is as specifically "Chinese" in its monastic form as, say, Sweden or Japan are in their "capitalist" forms or the Soviet Union in its "industrial socialist" form. But I think we can discern in Chinese society certain paradigmatic elements of the future—a careful control over industrialisation, an economic policy calculated to restrain rather than to whet individual consumptive appetites, and above all, an organising religiosity expressed through the credos and observances of a socialist "church."

These speculations, I would emphasise, are concerned with the long-term drift of affairs. They describe the general direction in which I see the societies of the world evolving, and do not offer any timetable for this general movement. For a considerable period it is possible that, as with the disintegration of the Roman Empire, world history will be characterised by a great variety of quite dissimilar states, some retaining many features of an individualist or capitalist social order, others displaying more marked tendencies toward collectivism in both culture and economic organisation. Yet, when I take the measure of the changes that must be accomplished, both within the underdeveloped world and in the industrialised nations, I cannot find a plausible alternative to the ideal-type of a monastery—a tightly disciplined, ascetic religious order—as the model to which the evolving societies of the world will gradually approximate.

CHANCES FOR THE PRESERVATION OF DEMOCRACY

No part of my book has aroused more expressions of unhappiness than the suggestion that authoritarianism will be necessary to cope with the exigencies of the future, and I do not doubt that my present harsher description of a monastic society will evoke even sharper feelings of dismay. Here I can only offer one softening suggestion. The line between coercion and co-operation, or between necessity and freedom, is not an easy one to draw; there are armies made up of conscripts and armies made up of volunteers, churches built on dogma and churches that rest on a commonality of freely expressed beliefs. The degree of harsh authority, in other words, depends on the extent of willing self-discipline. This offers the possibility that some nation states, endowed with unusual traditions of social unity or blessed with the good fortune of political genius, will be able to make the needed economic and social sacrifices and rearrangements with a minimum of repressive force.

This is where a faith in democracy—that is, in the public exercise of intelligence, good will, and self-restraint—must ultimately reside. As with many other aspects of the future, we have no "scientific" means of assessing the chances for the preservation of democracy—indeed, no means whatever other than an appeal to our intuitive judgments. Many critics have expressed a higher degree of faith than I in the resilience and adaptive capability of democratic institutions. Perhaps they are right and I am unduly pessimistic. But I do not find much evidence in history—especially in the history of nations organised under the materialistic and individualistic promptings of an industrial civilisation—to encourage expectations of an easy subordination of the private interest to the public weal.

For we must remember that the required adaptations are not heroic sacrifices that, however severe, are limited in duration and promise a return to normalcy thereafter. If indeed the industrial mode of civilisation is threatened from without, and exhausted from within, it will have to give way to new and unaccustomed patterns that must be permanently endured. I am not, therefore, sanguine that public understanding and co-operation will make unnecessary a considerable exercise of coercive power. But at least we can see the direction in which democracy must assert itself, if this coercion is to be minimised. The great adaptational effort that must be made during the next generation or two cannot be expected to arise from the undirected impulses of individuals, each guided only by his or her private understanding of the human plight. The preservation of democratic forms can only come about as a result of intellectually farsighted and politically gifted leadership. Paradoxically, it is only through leadership that authoritarian rule can be minimised, if not wholly avoided. Unhappily, we know nothing about how such leadership evolves, much less how it can be cultivated.

RECONCILIATION WITH HISTORY

There remains one last area in which "second thoughts" seem appropriate. This is the question raised at the beginning of this essay, when I discussed the difficulties of putting ourselves at a sufficient distance from the long-term perspective that the human prospect forces upon us. More specifically, it concerns the attitude of stoical disengagement, of rueful but removed commentary, with which I discuss matters whose advent fills me with dismay. Is this a responsible attitude to take? Is there not a more activist philosophy that would still be appropriate to the diagnosis of the text?

I must confess that I have worried over this aspect of *The Human Prospect* more than over any of its premises or conclusions. I have been concerned lest my attitude lead to a self-fulfilling prophecy of defeat, to a cowardly passivity, to an unbearable conflict of hopes and fears. Yet, after much self-search I find that I have not changed my mind on this central point, and in these last pages I must defend my position as best I can.

Let me begin by freely acknowledging the deep contradictions that my attitude seems to involve me in. As I examine the prospect ahead, I not only predict but I prescribe a centralisation of power as the only means by which our threatened and dangerous civilisation will make way for its successor. Yet I live at a time when I am profoundly suspicious of the further gathering of political power. So, too, my analysis leads me to place my hopes for the long-term survival of man on his susceptibility to appeals to national identity and to his willingness to accept authority. But my own beliefs incline me strongly in the opposite direction, detesting the claims of patriotism and mystical national unity, averse to hierarchies of sub- and super-ordination. Or take finally my judgments with respect to industrial civilisation itself. Am I not the child and beneficiary of this civilisation? Can I discuss its death throes unaware that I am talking about my own demise?

These and other contradictions are inextricably lodged in the human prospect as I have outlined it. Yet, curiously, I do not find myself unduly weighed down or paralysed by these conflicts. Perhaps this is because the human prospect involves us in considerations affecting the fairly distant future, and these considerations, both for better and for worse, do not greatly influence the decisions by which we live our daily lives. If this myopia weakens our ability to prepare for the future, it also saves us the agony of seeking to reconcile present behaviour with future requirement. For in my daily life I find that I do not have much difficulty in knowing what course to follow. As Thornton Wilder has written, I know that every good thing stands at the razor edge of danger and must be fought for at every moment. Within the scope of my daily life, I have few doubts as to what these good things are, or what steps I must take to preserve them from danger. (Let me add that I generally favour policies that would be called "democratic socialist.")

It is only when I look to the future and ask whether I can reconcile my daily life with the prospect ahead that I face the moral and existential problems I have described. For then indeed I experience the hollow recognition that perhaps no such reconciliation is possible and that I may live in a time in which no congruence can be established between the good things of the present and the necessary things of the future.

Such a point of view strikes us as "defeatist," intolerable, almost wicked. Is it? I mentioned in passing the disintegration of the Roman Empire; now I would like to take a moment to compare that period with ours. Certain analogues and correspondences are obvious. Then, as now, we find order giving way to disorder; self-confidence to self-doubt; moral certitude to moral disquiet. There are resemblances in the breakdowns of cumbersome economic systems, in the intransigence of privileged minorities. One is tempted to ask if revolutionary socialism is our Christianity; China and North Vietnam our Goths and Visigoths; the Soviet Union our Byzantium; the corporation and ministries our latifundia?

But the deeper parallel is encountered when we ask what consistent moral stance we could recommend to a person of good will who found himself or herself in the fourth century AD. Would we urge that he or she join the Christian sect, particularly if we had foreknowledge of the toll that Christianity would exact in lives and free spirit? Would we urge the defence of the intellectual heritage of Greece or republican Rome, when it was clear beyond doubt that these ideas had run their course and no longer had the power to conjure up belief and command action? Would we recommend a futile rear-guard effort to prop up a decadent Empire, or one last hopeless effort to persuade a dissolute upper class to carry out long overdue reforms? And finally, could we expect a cultivated citizen of Rome to go over to the Barbarians?

To ask such questions is to confront the fact that there are periods in history in which it is not possible to reconcile the hopes of the moment and the needs of the future, when a congruence between one's personal life and the collective direction of all mankind cannot be established without doing violence either to one's existence or to one's understanding. I believe that ours is such a time and that we must learn to live with its irreconcilable conflicts and contradictions. These conflicts and contradictions fill me with discomfort, but less so than any simpler or more consistent alternative that I can construct for myself.

This is the conclusion to which my analysis of the human prospect drove me a year ago, and it remains the conclusion to which it drives me today. I may complain at this state of affairs, but I cannot change it, just as Atlas, too, complained unendingly at the task that had been thrust upon him, but could not change that. To accept the limitation of our abilities, both as individuals and as a collectivity, seems to be the most difficult idea that Promethean man must learn. But learn it he must and learn it he will. The only question is whether the teacher will be history or ourselves.

REFERENCES

1. For a recent review of these problems see "The Human Population" by Freedman and Berelson, *Scientific American* (September 1974).

2. See John McPhee, *The Curve of Binding Energy* (1974).

3. See "Report on The Limits to Growth," Special Task Force of the World Bank, September 1972 (especially page 43); and *Science* (19 April 1974), especially articles by Landsberg, Berg and Hammond.

4. Borlaug and Ewell, *Ceres* (FAO), March-April 1974, pp. 55,56,60; also Lester Brown, *In the Human Interest* (1974) chap. 4; and *New York Times* (1 September 1974), pp. 1,34.

5. Borlaug and Ewell, *Ceres*, p. 61; also *Fortune*, "Ominous Changes in the World's Weather," (February 1974).

6. Reid A. Bryson, "A Perspective on Climatic Change," *Science* (17 May 1974), p. 753 ff.

7. Robert Tucker, "The Challenge to Inequality," unpublished paper presented at The Lehrman Institute (May 1974).

8. See Geoffrey Barraclough, "The Coming Depression," *New York Review of Books* (27 July 1974).

Futures Analysis

by Amitai Etzioni

Bridging the gap between the separate worlds of knowledge makers and policy makers is a problem at least as ancient as Plato, who sought to resolve it by integrating the two in a single individual: the philosopher-king. Yet even in the simpler and comparatively unchanging, hierarchical social order of the ancient Athenian city-state, Plato's proposed solution represents a "utopia" in the modern sense of something naively unworkable as well as in the sense of seeking the ideal. In our complex, advanced, industrial society, the problems of providing policy makers with a sufficient number of knowledge makers equipped with the necessary expertise and other prerequisites, as well as for appropriate articulation between knowledge makers and policy makers, are much more serious than those Plato faced, and more consequential as well. Indeed the treatment a modern society accords its experts on the future, i.e., the extent to which it solicits and attends to their forecasts and takes care to differentiate and reward those seers whose forecasts prove reliable as opposed to those whom future developments show to be faulty, deeply affects the society's capacity to exercise control over its own fate via deliberate guidance of societal processes.

Unhappily our society's treatment of its seers, by and large, takes the form of malignant—as opposed to benign—neglect, and a frequent reliance on experts chosen for irrelevant reasons rather than because of their proven wisdom. The result is chronic myopia of much of policy-making, seeing the nearby trees, but not the turns of the road.

Sound future-orientation requires:

1. *Futurology should be integrated rather than segregated from other forms of knowledge making.*

The best exploration of the future draws heavily on understanding the existing societal processes and their dynamics. For example, in seeking to anticipate the extent to which Americans might be likely or willing to adjust to *future* energy shortages and price rises by shifting to a less energy-intensive life-style, the responsible seer takes into account the conditions under which life-styles changed in the past, the extent to which previous life-styles adapted to new conditions, as well as changes which already occurred in the last two years, etc.

The trends discerned in these data are then interpreted in the light of some assumptions, such as an estimate of the likely persuasive power of a major public education campaign, in order to arrive at a projection of potential willingness of Americans to become more energy conserving. In contrast, the segregated futurologist is more likely to rely on projections founded on logic rather than experience, on "models" which are often mathematically neat but poor in reality-testing.

2. Deviation from data should be explicated.

Future-studies almost invariably require mixing data distilled from past trends, hypothetical assumptions about what might happen in the future, and drawing both on reasonable assumptions and on value preferences. Futurologists must be free to insert these add-ons because they provide horizon-broadening power. However, whenever they deviate from existing data, they should (a) explicitly state this fact, and (b) explicate the grounds for the deviation from straight-line projections of the past into the future. It is *not* that straight-line projections (i.e., assuming the future will mirror the past) are sensible, but that *un*accounted modifications open the door to wishful thinking. *Accountable* modifications are thus the responsible course.

Thus one may make a forecast based on the premise that the OPEC cartel will soon fall apart, despite the fact that many previous cartels, particularly in the oil field, survived for decades. In doing so, however, one ought to flag the deviation from expectations derived from past experience and explicate one's reasons for believing past patterns are unlikely to be maintained.

3. Heuristic futures and forecasts are to be carefully separated.

Heuristic futures are intellectual games or exercises offering insights into what *might* happen if a given set of circumstances were to come about, without necessarily making any claim that there are highly persuasive, let alone compelling reasons for believing these circumstances will indeed come about. Heuristic futures *do* serve to stimulate policy review and renovation by encouraging the exploration of alternatives not otherwise considered. Thus, a downtown area wholly closed to vehicular traffic might be contemplated, or a Zero Population Growth United States, or lunar settlements, to gauge, for instance, if the benefits might justify the costs, without predicting that any of these is on its way.

Similarly, forecasts which are highly *un*specific tend to be of primarily heuristic value. Thus, to say that the United States population by the year 2000 will either rise by 75 million or fall by 25 million, or be somewhere in between, provides an opportunity to contemplate alternative futures rather than a forecast of sufficient specificity to be of interest for most purposes.

In contrast, forecasts ought to be *relatively* specific, i.e., provide narrow ranges. In most areas, very specific forecasts cannot be expected because the world is too complex and the dynamics of most of its parts are still poorly understood. (Lunar eclipses are one of the exceptions.) Thus, it is more helpful to forecast that no major breakthrough of new energy sources can be expected to be available on a *mass* basis 8 to 10 years from now, than to be told that a major breakthrough is basically unpredictable and could be with us in the "near future."

4. Guidance intensity and heuristic futures vs. forecasting.

While both heuristic futures and forecasts are useful, the extent to which we should promote one as against the other depends on our assumption as to how knowable and malleable the world is, i.e., subject to our guidance. To put it first in extreme terms for illustrative purposes, if we assume we can know the world fully *and* mold it to our design, we can rely chiefly on heuristic futures because they tell us what it would be like *if* this *or* that "future" were to be brought about, in line with our preferences.

If on the other hand we believe the world to be relatively difficult to comprehend and to mold, we must rely more on forecasts as to what will happen. For reasons I detailed elsewhere, I hold that while the world—especially the social realm from crime to alcoholism, from education to welfare—is becoming more knowable and malleable, it is still largely unknown and above all very resistant to our efforts. Hence, we should rely more on forecasts and less on heuristic futures.

5. *Near- vs. long-run future forecasting.*

In some areas it is possible to forecast the relatively remote future (more than 10 years) and do so responsibly. Thus, the size of the 1986 fourth grade cohort can be quite well projected for the entire United States on the basis of the current birth rate, childhood mortality rates, and school attendance data. In many matters, however, experience suggests we cannot forecast with sufficient specificity to be useful beyond 5 to 10 years. It is not just that we incorrectly forecast the "readings" on the appropriate variables and, thus, they go down where we expected increases (e.g., in population) or rise where we expected declines (e.g., prices), but that major vectors often appear which were unanticipated (e.g., the energy crisis).

In any event, forecasters who want the ear of policy makers concerning the remote future, say the year 2000, may wish to use the next 3 to 6 years as a testing ground to validate their forecasting techniques.

Indeed the short-term future is problematic enough to predict and such predictions are often woefully wrong. In 1965 Thomas S. Power, Chief of the Strategic Air Command, wrote a book entitled *Design for Survival* in which he used the example of bombing North Vietnam as a hypothetical situation in which air strikes could deter a war. The aim would be to get the Communists out of South Vietnam. The United States would warn the North of an air attack, giving the enemy time to evacuate civilians, and then bomb. This should be done until the enemy agreed to remove its influence from the South. It would only take a *few days,* Power wrote; no ground troops or air reinforcements would be needed. In fact, the Communists would welcome this as an opportunity to pull out of the South. In the same vein, C. P. Snow said in 1960, on the likelihood of nuclear war: "Within ten years some of these bombs are going off. I am saying this as responsibly as I can. That is the certainty . . . a certainty of disaster."

Each year thousands of such predictions are made in all areas from inflation rates to cancer death rates, from traffic fatalities to interest rates. In most areas no record is kept of the predictive powers. When such studies are undertaken, as for instance in predicting the stock market or the prices of specific stocks, the difficulties in making specific predictions stand out.

As the short run (1 to 3 years) is more knowable than the intermediate run (3 to 10 years), let alone the year 2000 and beyond, we should concentrate relatively more on projects that promise near- vs. longer-run outcomes. E.g., in the energy field this suggests an emphasis on coal and nuclear power vs. shale oil, with the greatest payoffs to be expected from efforts to conserve energy, which can be implemented almost immediately.

Moreover, the likelihood that unexpected vectors will intervene to throw off our forecasts suggests that we should be ready to recommit our resources and efforts as we move into the future and find, alas, that we have again erred. (The Arabs will roll prices back? New unknown reserves will be found? A cheap way to milk the sun? An additive that stretches gas 40 percent or more?) We should not permit setups that lock us in, of the sort exemplified by the Highway Trust Fund which still pours billions into highway construction when clearly a higher priority should now go to public transit.

Similarly, we ought to favor those changes in homes, offices and factories which can be readily made and then unmade if necessary (e.g., taxes on gas and oil, which can be reduced by a stroke of a pen) rather than those which are difficult to reverse (e.g., conversion of home heating systems from gas to electricity, as the Project Independence report suggests).

Finally, because of the difficulties in making valid, sufficiently detailed predictions, let us also focus on those efforts which are desirable in themselves, or for reasons other than their elusive futuristic pay-offs. Thus, driving at lower speeds saves thousands of lives. We should maintain and enforce the lower speed limit even if we are not sure that there will be a shortage of gas in 1985 or that we shall run out of oil in the mid-1990's. Similarly, a commitment to developing solar energy seems a much sounder policy than a heavier reliance on nuclear reactors, from the viewpoint of public safety and harmony with the environment, even if we cannot tell which will produce cheaper electricity 10 years hence.

6. *Forecasting would benefit from systematic evaluation.*

Reliability ratings for bonds (i.e., predictions concerning the likelihood these securities will pay future dividends and return their principals) are regularly issued in terms of AAA, AA and so on. Restaurant guides award four or three or fewer stars according to the excellence of the cuisine and the likelihood future diners will be served comparable meals. Forecasts used by government agencies, the business community and the public are rarely rated. As this field knows its share of shamans, it is surprising how often one sees the fakers at the head tables, while the true prophets roam the streets. Thus, a leading designer of the war in Vietnam, author of a report which caused universities to shift billions from investments in bonds to stocks just before the stock market collapsed, and an advocate of a school decentralization plan which led to substantial anarchy, is still one of America's respected seers, while the editor of a major science magazine who correctly prophesized the energy crisis in great detail in 1971, is rarely invited to address the inner sanctum of policy making.

A computer retrieval system of forecasts and predictions made in the past combined with information on the events which followed, would help the forecasters to improve their work, and their clients to evaluate the advice they rely upon—or ignore. Too often we oscillate between blind faith and cynical contempt for futurologists. It might help to realize that like other professionals, their qualities vary; and while the more reputable ones are inevitably better than no help at all, no one owns a clear crystal ball.

7. *Policy makers' criteria for selection of forecasters.*

Particular seers come to be favored by policy makers for many reasons: in some instances because they favor a position the policy maker has already chosen; in others, because the seers chosen are dramatic and will "bring out the press and television"; or simply because they are witty, charming or pleasant company. Naturally, our capacity to deal with the future improves the more seers are listened to on the basis of the proven validity of their forecasts and disregarding their partisan, media, or "social" characteristics.

All in all, it cannot be stressed enough that to the extent that policy makers draw on futurology, the nation's business will improve. The extent of the improvement depends on using more forecasting, less heuristic futures; more near-term, less long-run forecasts; and drawing more on proven forecasters than on those whose forecasts are reassuring, convenient or dramatic.

PART

II

PROFESSIONALS IN POST-INDUSTRIAL SOCIETY

The Professional Regulation of Change

by John McKinlay

'The individuals composing the ruling class possess among other things consciousness, and therefore think. In so far, therefore, as they rule as a class and determine the whole extent of an epoch, it is self evident that they do this in their whole range and thus, among other things, rule also as thinkers, as producers of ideas, and regulate the production and distribution of the ideas of their age. Consequently, their ideas are the ruling ideas of the age.'

K. Marx, *The German Ideology* (1845-1846)

The twentieth century has witnessed a phenomenal expansion in the number and influence of the so-called professions. Those who call themselves 'professional' constitute an ever increasing proportion of the occupation structure, and the ideology or mythology of professionalism, is likewise more pervasive and sought after. So widespread and established is their influence in most western societies, and so successfully have their claims been accepted by the public that criticism of any aspect of the professions is met with the most vehement denunciations. It is almost as if the professions should be left, without scrutiny and criticism, to work out their good purposes for society.

Concern with the position occupied by professionals and their influence on society is, of course, not a new theme. Many writers have highlighted what they regard as the special functions they perform. Durkheim, for example, viewed the existence of professional organizations as a precondition of consensus in society.[1] For Tawney, professionalism was a forceful check against destructive individualism.[2] Carr-Saunders and Wilson saw the professions as among the most 'stable elements in society' which, above all, stand like rocks against which the waves raised by crude forces which threaten steady and peaceful evolution, beat in vain![3] This theme of stability has been expanded by Lynn who suggests that the professions indirectly help to maintain world order.[4] More recently, Halmos suggests that the 'personal service professions' are imparting a socially beneficial moral uniformity and that 'their interpretation of social realities and their formulation of social standards will continue to remain the authoritative and obvious guide to social change for all . . . '[5] Common to most discussions over the past two decades is the assumption that professionalism is in various ways beneficial for society. Partly as a consequence we have been innundated with studies of professional characteristics, images, socialization, careers and organizations —all of which fail to challenge this basic assumption.

There have of course been exceptions. Marx, for example, attempted to discern the secondary and derivative character of professional classes, particularly in terms of their negative contribution to surplus value.[6] Several economists have pointed to the harmful monopolistic practices of professional associations and call for reduction in their restrictive practices.[7] For Mills, the professions were succumbing to a 'managerial demiurge' and, rather than facilitating a desired expansion of liberal learned professions, were actually fostering narrow specialism.[8] Young claims that the fusion of knowledge and power has created a new professional-technocratic elite who will become more secure than any historical ruling class.[9] More recently, Freidson has argued that the professions are over-extending the moral and ethical boundaries of their autonomy.[10] He suggests that what may initially have been a public-oriented humanism has now become self-serving and totalitarian in everyday practice.

The author strongly agrees with Johnson who suggests that more recent theorists have departed from the problems and themes which informed the origins of the sociology of work.[11] Perhaps, with the principal exceptions of the recent work of Hughes and Freidson, writings on professionalism have excluded the one element which was constant in earlier approaches: *the attempt to understand professional occupations in terms of their power relations in society*–their sources of power and authority and the ways in which they are used. Such issues are the concern of this paper. In particular, consideration will focus on some of the means by which several dominant professions, having assumed a uniquely powerful position in society, influence the initiation, direction and rate of social change. It should, perhaps, be emphasized that the arguments in this paper are not invalidated by the exceptional technical competence of particular professionals. Rather they are intended to refer to the social category 'professionals' and their associations, and *their* influence on social change.

THE MYTHOLOGY OF PROFESSIONALISM

It may be useful at this point to elaborate briefly on this author's overall conception of professionalism, since it underlies most of the subsequent discussion regarding the ways in which aspects of professional behaviour influence social change. Much of the existing literature on the sociology of work assumes that there is a *qualitative difference* between professions and other occupations, and is devoted to describing and measuring along various dimensions, the nature of this supposed difference. Indeed, many university courses are currently offered on either professions *and* occupations, or on professions as distinct from other related aspects of occupational sociology. It is the author's contention that, despite the plethora of work utilizing this assumption, there is no *logical basis* for drawing such a distinction. This, of course, is not to suggest that the distinction does not exist in reality. It does exist simply because it is employed. However, the fact that the existing distinction, which primarily serves the interest of so-called 'professionals,' is fostered by their practices and the activities of the various associations which represent them, does not provide a rational basis for its continued use. Along with the public at large, many sociologists have 'swallowed' this assumption of the qualitative distinctiveness of so-called 'professionalism.' They have uncritically accepted the claims and assumptions of the subjects of their study to an extent which would be unforgiveable in most other areas of sociological enquiry. In a subsequent section of this paper, it will be argued that the extension of this uncritical acceptance in several ways constricts the possibilities for change.

There is, of course a voluminous literature, dating back to the beginning of this century, concerning the allegedly unique features of the professions, and the claims of various occupations to the sacred sanctuary of professionalism, and the elusive benefits that such membership brings. However, despite numerous attempts at definition, there remains little agreement on any essential attributes of a profession.[12] The continuing failure to reach some over-all consensus on defining characteristics may be indicative of the fact that, perhaps with the exception of their power position, they remain indistinguishable from most other occupations. It would be inappropriate here to engage in the seemingly endless argument over what makes an occupation a profession, or what makes one profession 'more professional' than another. The work of Goode is illustrative of the kind of issues involved. Goode's definition of professionalism, based on and taking into account the work of many authors, has been widely recognized and adopted. He considers that 'the two . . . core characteristics are a prolonged specialized training in a body of abstract knowledge and a . . . service orientation.'[13] As occupations become professionalized, they acquire several features reflective of these two core characteristics. According to Goode such features are: (a) the profession determines its own standards of education and training; (b) the student professional goes through a more far reaching adult socialization experience than the learner in other occupations; (c) professional practice is often legally recognized by some form of licensure; (d) licensing and admission boards are manned by members of the profession; (e) most legislation concerned with the profession is shaped by that profession; (f) the occupation gains in income, power, and prestige ranking and can demand higher calibre students; (g) the practitioner is relatively free from lay evaluation and control; (h) the norms of practice enforced by the profession are more stringent than legal control; (i) members are more strongly identified and affiliated with the profession than are members of other occupations with theirs; and (j) the profession is more likely to be a terminal occupation. Implicit in this conception and most other writings about professionals is the crucial role of professional autonomy which is held to be an essential dimension of professionalism.

Another influential proponent of this 'inventory' approach is Barber, who claims that 'A sociological definition of the professions should limit itself so far as possible to the *differentia specifica* of professional behaviour.' He claims that professions can be defined in terms of the following 'four essential attributes': (a) a high degree of generalized and systematic knowledge; (b) primary orientation to the community interest rather than to individual self-interest; (c) a high degree of self-control of behaviour through codes of ethics internalized in the process of work socialization and through voluntary associations organized and operated by the work specialists themselves; and (d) a system of rewards [monetary and honorary] that is primarily a set of symbols of work achievement and thus ends in themselves, not means to some end of individual self-interest.[14]

In a recent thorough critique of some of the more influential inventory approaches [including those by Goode and Barber] Johnson concludes that they are inadequate because: (a) they prematurely assume that there are or at least have been in the past, 'true professions' which exhibit to some degree all of the essential elements; (b) they often result from the pleading of a special cause relating to the claims of an occupation group which is striving for professional status; (c) many of the core characteristics are not exclusive of one another and some are derivative of each other; (d) there have been few attempts to articulate theoretically the relationship between the elements, or to distinguish between the levels of analysis used; (e) the decision to include or exclude elements is rather arbitrary and largely dependent on which occupations one wishes to endow with or deprive of professional status; (f) they too readily accept the professionals own definitions of themselves and their roles; (g) they are fundamentally ahistorical and largely ignore recent technological changes which have thrown up new occupations to challenge the hegemony of the old, have resulted in continuous occupational differentiation, and have been subject to new sources of external client authority which challenge existing power structures.[15] Johnson further argues that this confusion between these alleged essential characteristics of an occupation and the characteristics of a historically institutionalized form of its control is the most fundamental inadequacy of this inventory approach.

For the most illogical reasons the medical profession, and to a lesser extent law, have been employed either implicitly or explicitly as a basis for conceptualization. This tendency, combined with the inventory approach already discussed, has given rise to attempts to develop scaling procedures to measure an individual's or an occupation's professional standing.[16] Indeed, Barber explicitly states that his four essential attributes 'define a *scale* of professionalism, a way of measuring the extent to which it is present in different forms of occupational performance.'[17] The net effect then of the ever-increasing number of studies which utilize professionalism scales is not to determine the positional status and value of the labour of some individual or social group according to external criteria, but to measure the extent to which they approximate the claims of several self-appointed dominant professions.

To present a wholesale critique of the numerous inventories which are presently available would be clearly beyond the scope of this paper. Indeed, several useful critiques are already available.[18] While some criticisms will be directed at selected features of professionalism in the following sections, this will principally relate to aspects of social change. Suffice it to say that this author considers that there is no logical basis for distinguishing between so-called professions and other occupations, and that none of the inventories with which he is familiar facilitate such a distinction. Hughes may have been on a fruitful course when he stated:

> '. . . in my own studies I passed from the false question "Is this occupation a profession?" to the more fundamental one, "What are the circumstances in which people in an occupation attempt to turn it into a profession, and themselves into professional people?" '[19]

CAVEAT EMPTOR OR CREDAT EMPTOR?

A view that is subscribed to and publicly espoused by nearly every profession relates to their possession of, among other things, unique skills on the basis of which *they ought to be trusted in all things*. This claim to trust is almost universally accepted in Western societies and is regarded as an essential ingredient in any relationship with professionals, be it when individuals consult them as clients, or when their services are utilized by some group or community. The motto of the professions, unlike those of business where *caveat emptor* ('let the buyer beware') prevails is *credat emptor* ('let the taker believe in us').[20] On what grounds can those in the so-called professional occupations make a greater claim to trust than those in other occupations which have been unable to gain access to the elusive advantages offered by professionalization?

Firstly, it has been suggested that professionals ought to be accorded trust because they have been specially selected or 'called' to their particular occupation whereas those in other occupations simply chose it for themselves, for what appears, in comparison, mundane reasons. What is implied in this suggestion is *either* that professionals are specially selected by some higher authority, *or* that they respond to some higher idealism. Such claims were probably first advanced by the church in an effort to distance symbolically those who were supposedly in contact with God from those who were contaminated by evil. Several of the dominant professions were closely associated with the church during the early stages of their formation and gained legitimation largely through clerical sponsorship. Seemingly, the earliest meaning of the word 'professed' was 'that has taken the vows of a religious order.' The word was subsequently secularized to denote 'that professes to be duly qualified; professional.' Whereas the term 'professional' originally denoted an act of professing, it came to mean, as Hughes describes it: 'The occupation which one professes to be skilled in and to follow . . . A vocation in which professed knowledge of some branch of learning is used in its application to the affairs of others, or in the practice of an art based upon it.'[21] According to contemporary usage, professionals constitute a category of people, occupying a particularly favourable social position, who *profess* something. They profess to know more about certain matters than other people, and from this is *derived* their 'right' to exclusive practice, deference, prestige, trust, etc. What should perhaps be emphasized is that professionals only profess or claim x, they certainly *do not* necessarily know or perform x. Hence the possibility exists of 'professional rights' being accorded to individuals and groups whose public claims are either ill-founded, or perhaps even deliberately deceptive.

Vestiges of clericalism remain in the recruitment myths espoused by several of the dominant occupations. We are still told that people are 'called' to the ministry or priesthood, but suspect that no God called them. Similarly, in the field of law, we hear that people are 'called to the bar,' although again we know that nobody called them, and that the initiative was entirely theirs. To profess that one has been 'called' is probably the first claim by would be professionals which, along with all subsequent claims, does not lend itself to disproof. Additionally, the claim to calling provides a basis for subsequently derived rights by investing claimants with special qualities which distinguish them from those in 'lesser' self-chosen positions which are presumably entered for more mundane reasons. Since a disproportionate number of those in dominant occupations are from families with members already in or associated with them it would appear that whoever is doing the calling, is doing it in a highly biased and self-protective fashion! Clearly, many decide to enter the professions and other occupations for the purpose of maintaining existing life styles, or as a means of enhancing life chances.

A *second* argument advanced to support the accordance of an unusually high degree of trust to professionals relates to their supposed altruism and service orientation. They are commonly depicted as unlike other occupations in the extent of their selfless devotion to their clients in the pursuit of some higher ideal. Evidence for the existence of such self sacrificial behaviour is to be found in public spirited advertisements which professional associations sponsor in the news media. A gullible public tends to forget that these activities promote business of various kinds and may be generally unaware of the ways in which they are carefully engineered to perpetuate the myth of altruism.[22] It is indeed difficult to reconcile this supposed altruism to the ever increasing exposées of the backstage activities of the professions regarding fees and fee splitting, unnecessary referral and intervention, ritualistic procedures, or billing for work that was never undertaken, etc.[23]

Because they are insulated from observability, it is difficult to uncover these irregularities in the behaviour of professionals and disclosures are still uncommon enough to be newsworthy for the public. Those with backstage access to professional activities report however, that selflessness is not characteristic of professionals and these discrepancies, although often hidden, are in fact commonplace.[24] The argument concerning altruistic professionals bears many resemblances to Marx's discussion of the dispositions of individual capitalists.[25] The concern with the merits of particular individuals is somewhat misplaced. Rather, because they occupy a certain position within a social structure, they are required to act in certain ways. Their unique characterological features are overshadowed by these structurally based constraints. Generally speaking, the more access one gains to the backstage of the dominant professions the more nefarious their activities appear to be and the greater the disparity between them and front stage public conceptions.

As a *third* argument one often hears that professionals ought to be trusted because they, unlike those in 'regular' occupations, have undergone a *unique kind of training*. Again, that social scientists have been 'taken in' by this myth of uniqueness is reflected in the plethora of studies of 'professional socialization'—the term itself supposedly reflecting a belief that this type of socialization differs qualitatively from other types of socialization. Since there have been virtually no comparative studies of vocational training, there is little empirical support for such a belief. Additionally, it is difficult to conceive of any distinction in logic or theory between training for the so-called professions, or any other occupational category. In common with other types of vocational training their body of knowledge is shaped by prevailing entrepreneurial interests, they instill values and work orientations which engender continued business and they foster a perspective which protects the existence of related specialities. Compare, for example the orientations of pediatricians, obstetricians, and internists with those of plumbers, carpenters and electricians.

It is of course true that professional training typically takes a longer period to complete than that required for most other occupations. On this basis however, one obviously cannot argue for qualitative differences. It may be that during their longer period of training professionals are taught much the same kinds of rules and orientation as other occupations, but in a more sophisticated manner with more enduring and manifest consequences. One may also argue that a prolonged period of training enables those involved to acquire a relatively more specialized set of skills. While these skills, like those of the mechanic or the prostitute are specialized, they cannot be termed 'special.'[26] Perhaps an adequate distinction has never been made between *a* speciality, the *process* of specialization, and the *state* of being 'special.'

Fourthly, it is often held, particularly by those most affected, that trust ought to be accorded because the general public have no way of evaluating the esoteric activities of so-called professionals. In the absence of knowledge, or the means to obtain it, we must believe in their altruism, proficiency, etc. This argument also bears the vestiges of clericalism—in the absence of knowledge one must have ill-founded faith in the existence of God. While it may be difficult for outsiders to evaluate some of the more technical aspects of performance, many aspects of professional behaviour could be so evaluated. The principal difficulty lies not in the lack of an appropriate methodology, but in gaining access to the everyday activities of professionals. In opposition to professional claims it was recently shown that clients cannot only effectively evaluate the performance of physicians, but in doing so they utilize comparable criteria to physicians when they evaluate each other.[27] For at least these reasons it is suggested that the claim to trust on the basis of public ignorance of professional behaviour may in large part be without foundation and is employed to reduce any threatening evaluative activity which would jeopardize the claim to trust.

Bidwell, in a valuable discussion of professional trust relationships maintains that:

> 'For the professional, trust, as the sole basis of his moral authority, is essential for effective performance. Unless he enjoys his clients' confidence, he may be denied access to the client's person, or to the full range of necessary but often covert information about the client while the client may not follow the professional's directives or counsel. Hence the professional cannot fulfill his responsibilities to the client or to his peers for the client's welfare, unless the client trusts him. Thus the responsible professional must reject the client who will not trust him.'[28]

Since in many instances, trust is the only lever of social control that the professional has over the client, it must be carefully guarded and, if possible, enhanced. At the beginning of a relationship the client is usually prepared to trust on the basis of a professional role or reputation (a record of past success, insofar as it is publicly known). Once a professional commences work, he must maintain the client's trust, not only by virtue of reputational factors, but by demonstrable tangible signs, although, as Freidson reminds us, the professional need not always, in the absence of technical evidence, persuade his client that he is trustworthy.[29] The prestige and authority of his office may suffice independent of the esteem in which he is held by his clients and professional peers.

The relative importance of trust is not only dependent on the reputation of the professional's office, as is the esteem in which he is held by a client. It is also dependent on two additional factors which add some variation to the level of client trust. According to Bidwell these factors are: (a) *the client's technical familiarity* with the professional service (his access to purportedly esoteric knowledge and ability to assess the skillfulness of performance) and (b) *the client's need* for professional service (how urgent he perceives his situation to be).[30] The less knowledgeable the client, the more absolute his trust must be. The more the client stands in awe of the professional, the greater his tendency to accede to any demand made upon him for revelations or compliance to professional direction. The more he needs help, the more likely the client is to comply willingly with the professional's requests or orders.

THE MANUFACTURE OF ARTIFICIAL NEED

There is a widely held view in modern Western societies that most people are, (or if they are not, ought to be) free to choose whether to become involved in the activities of certain formal organizations and the people associated with them. Be it the military, government, church, education or whatever, freedom from unregulated intrusion into private life is generally held to be a cardinal value. Threats to this value are regarded as injurious to the basic social fabric and are vehemently repulsed. However, it appears that an erosion of this freedom is occurring in a number of key areas of social life, and it receives its impetus in large part from the unbridled activities of trusted professionals.

In the area of education for example, we see schools and colleges exceeding their appropriate bounds and attempting to act in *loco parentis*.[31] We have a social welfare system which in some cases appears overly keen to intervene and to initiate some morally degrading labelling process.[32] Many people, especially in the United States, are fearful of the insinuation of government agencies and departments into their private lives, and of the computer documentation of private activities.[33] The police and certain health agencies appear devoted to the location, apprehension and control of people who engage in supposedly 'deviant behaviour' or who display so-called idiosyncratic signs.[34] In many instances, such activities are actively supported by so-called professionals or are at least condoned by those who, if embodying the knowledge generally imputed to them, ought to respond quite differently. The examples cited involve fairly important social activities, and arouse considerable publicity when violations occur. Professionals must, therefore, be cautious in their public pronouncements and even in their backroom involvement. The recent activities of the American Bar Association regarding appointments to the Supreme court, and of the American Medical and Dental Associations in the obstruction of nation-alized health insurance schemes, reveal the extent of their influence and remain newsworthy.

There are, of course, many other areas of life, usually regarded as somewhat routine, but which nevertheless are being influenced by the activ-ities of professionals. Such everyday matters as taxation and insurance, with their complexity, increasingly require the services of so-called professionals. But the very complexity, which necessitates professional service, is due largely to the acceptance by administrators of the advice of the professional groups which will benefit. In other instances (e.g., the purchase of real estate), a professional is required by law to perform a routine procedure, even though the recipient of this 'service' may know everything there is to do and may even do a more competent job. The influence of professionals in such everyday areas of life is, of course, more insidious because they are usually overlooked until the particular service is required. A situation ap-pears to be arising then, in which services of professionals which are not actively desired, or are regarded as unwarranted, are being imposed on the public. Moreover, this situation of dependency seems to be carefully engi-neered by several of the dominant professions in collaboration with each other.

One should perhaps add that this dependency on professionals cannot be regarded as a natural outcome of technological development since the dominant professions usually do not have knowledge in these areas—it is only imputed to them. Having an established power base in society they manage those with expert knowledge of the technology.

Freidson discusses this manufacture of need in relation to the profes-sional's attempt to wield sanctions:

> 'What is characteristic of the profession's solution to this problem lies not only in its capture of exclusive control over the exercise of a particular skill but also in its capture of the exclusive right of access to goods and services the layman is likely to feel he needs to manage his own problem himself, independently of expert advice. By becoming a gatekeeper to what is popularly valued, the professional gains the additional sanction of being able to make taking his advice a prerequi-site for obtaining a good or service valued independently of his service.'[35]

INSULATION FROM EXTERNAL OBSERVABILITY AND EVALUATION

For any meaningful social change to occur there must be some open *observability* of the relevant social phenomena, an ability to *evaluate* these phenomena according to certain standards, freedom to *implement* various actions and *subsequently to evaluate* their effects. These factors appear as minimal prerequisites for any planned change. Typically however, such ingredients are not present with regard to the activities of the dominant professions who manage to insulate themselves from the observability with-out which the other essential ingredients for change cannot materialize.[36]

For any planned social change to occur there must also be *some basis for comparison*. Even to be aware of unintentional change, there must be such a basis. In the many broad areas covered by professionalism however, this appears difficult to achieve.

There have been many attempts to explain the secretive and insulative nature of much of professional behaviour. Some say it serves to enhance decision-making by removing the need for professionals to accommodate lay pressures, freeing them to adopt 'rational' criteria. Another suggestion is that it serves to disguise human mistakes which, if public knowledge, would jeopardize the credibility of professionals as a group. Perhaps there is more than a grain of truth in the saying that physicians are able to bury their mistakes! Despite evidence to the contrary, others maintain that insulation from observability is necessary because the public at large, lacking the requisite knowledge, are not in a position to understand the specialized procedures and activities, and therefore cannot properly evaluate them. In fact, it is claimed that their lay evaluations based on partial knowledge, may even be harmful and therefore should be avoided. Of course, the fact that secrecy, among other things enhances, or at least arrests the erosion of hard won social status should not go unnoticed as a reason for its careful enforcement among certain occupational groups.[37]

The so-called 'code of ethics', which consists of a body of rules to regulate performance in a way that will not jeopardize 'professional standing' also serves to minimize external observability.[38] Any violation of these rules in terms of public disclosure deems the offender *'unprofessional'* and places him in the category of 'untrustworthy' in the eyes of his colleagues. In those relatively rare situations where disclosure is absolutely essential, actions are either described in incomprehensible technical language, or surrounded with a magical mysticism—both of which are still insulative tactics.

The regulation of the observability of professional behaviour and the maintenance of secrecy is further facilitated by the close-knit social network which exists not only among members of the same profession, but between the members of different dominant professions. In an early paper, Freidson discussed some of the ways in which close-knit professional networks ('professional referral systems') regulate and control the activities of their members. Each new idea, technique or innovation can seldom be only personally acceptable to and adopted to solitary professionals. Rather, they must await the evaluation and approval of their professional network.[39]

Additionally, professionals may participate in extraprofessional networks whose activities or influence also remain essentially unobservable. While discussing the physician's status McClung Lee asserts that he:

> '. . . has usually—in fact, has almost always—identified himself socially and in the minds of the public with shopkeepers, bankers, lawyers, insurance salesmen, and realtors by joining with such persons in their Chambers of Commerce, Rotary Clubs, Lodges, and Tax Payers leagues. On the other hand, the physician has carefully avoided, in general, any intimate identification with such non-business organizations as trade unions, liberal political and economic movements seeking modifications in social policy and the like.'[40]

These informal social circles serve to link professionals with a particular set of powerful interests in the local community as well as to provide a potential reservoir of lucrative business. Social change may be impeded by the need for professionals to accommodate such networks, both in terms of the acceptance of sundry changes, and in various judgments the professionals may be required to render.

One serious consequence of this unobservability for social change lies in the fact that it is difficult to appraise the contingencies upon which insulated decisions are made. This difficulty is, of course, not only limited to the area of professional behaviour. It also plagues the work of political scientists who attempt to uncover the social origins of societal power and the actual basis of political decision making.[41] Because of the altruistic, self-sacrificial mythology espoused by the dominant professions however, sources of influence other than those manifestly presented to a gullible public tend to be overlooked. We often prematurely assume that professionals act in response to their acquired knowledge, forgetting that, as Horowitz and others have reminded us, knowledge itself is shaped by many quite unsavoury influences.[42] Even those professionals who respond only to knowledge (and their existence is doubtful) may be responding indirectly to influences which, if known, would be regarded as totally repugnant. The obstruction of change therefore by the newly emerging professional ruling class may not only occur in response to inadequate knowledge, but in response to forces whose unobservability protects them from exposure, public evaluation and removal.

PROFESSIONALS AS 'GENERALIZED WISE MEN'

While analyzing the various bases of authority in his classic essay 'Professions and Social Structure,' Parsons makes the claim that professional authority is limited to a particular technically defined sphere.[43] He elaborates as follows:

> 'It is only in matters touching health that the doctor is by definition more competent than his lay patient, only in matters touching his academic speciality that the professor is superior, by virtue of his status to his students. Professional authority like other elements of the professional pattern, is characterized by "specificity of function." The technical competence which is one of the principal defining characteristics of the professional status and role is always limited to a particular "field" of knowledge and skill.'[44]

This idealized account does not accord with the current social position and activities of several influential professions in Western society. So-called professionals today, rather than embodying only 'functionally specific technical competence,' claim, and are regarded as possessing, expertise in areas not directly related to their sphere of imputed competence. Increasingly it seems, key professionals are becoming generalized wise men and this tendency has profound effects on the possibilities for social change.

The numerous T.V., radio and cinema dramas devoted to the exploits of physicians and lawyers, for example, do not depict them as experts with 'functionally specific technical competence' so much as supportive friends and advisors to all and sundry on every conceivable problem. In the United States for example, there appears to be little difference in the 'work performance' of Marcus Welby M.D. and Owen Marshal, Attorney at Law. The activities of both appear to embrace and overlap with such fields as religion, business, education, ethics, psychology, welfare and employment, social movements, community organization, and to some extent politics.

That the public generally imputes expertise to professionals in a wide variety of spheres is borne out both by professional reports of the range of problems confronted, and their recognition of the need for training in areas not always regarded as directly pertinent to their 'speciality.' Medical students, for example, are now undergoing or are requesting formal instruction in legal medicine, economics, ethics, community oriented field activities and political science.[45] While not depreciating the importance of these concerns for a holistic perspective, in this case, on medical problems—one must be mindful of the unanticipated consequences of such training in terms of the eventual more formal acknowledgement of generalized wiseness in areas in which, at present, competence is only tentatively imputed. Their opinions, supported by myths regarding altruism, service orientation, and trust are given greater credibility and their activities more legitimacy than other 'lesser' specialists ('sub-professionals') who do not enjoy the same 'professional standing' and must repeatedly demonstrate the honesty of their intentions and continually establish themselves as qualified to even express opinions. In some cases, even advanced qualifications are thought to be incomparable, and the opinions of those possessing them non-authorative. After all, doctors of philosophy are not 'real' doctors. One danger then in the continued expansion of imputed competence to certain key professions is the excessive use of their select knowledge and experience to arbitrate on matters and opinions outside their sphere of actual competence.

It appears therefore that in Western societies several select occupations (especially medicine and law) are being permitted to claim a *licence* to carry out or have control over an ever increasing range of activities, and to *mandate* to define the proper behaviour of others toward the matters concerned with their work. Indeed, Hughes suggests that a profession is created when the presumption of a group to a broad mandate is explicitly or implicitly granted as legitimate.[46] He elaborates as follows:

> 'Professions also, perhaps more than other kinds of occupations, claim a legal, moral and intellectual mandate. Not merely do the practitioners, by virtue of gaining admission to the charmed circle of colleagues, individually exercise the licence to do things others do not do, but collectively they presume to tell society what is good or right for the individual and for society at large in some aspect of life. Indeed, they set the very terms in which people may think about this aspect of life.'[47]

One consequence of this trend in terms of social change is that we increasingly invest in select groups of inappropriately trained 'generalized wise men' the right to evaluate and pontificate on, among other things, ideas, techniques and behaviour, even though these may be outside their areas of imputed competence. Such judgments, supposedly based on generalized knowledge and altruism, made in the interests of others and guided by some vague code of ethics are prematurely adopted as authorative, assume a certain legitimacy and are difficult to remove. The burden of proof rests not with the wise men to reveal the evidential basis of their decision or claims, but with detracting experts and the public at large, who must establish the legitimacy of their interest and cite the conclusively contradictory evidence. In such a situation, double standards are clearly operating with regard to what constitutes evidence. For their part, experts must produce *scientific* and decidedly 'hard' evidence for their claims. Despite its conclusiveness on scientific grounds, such evidence can be dismissed by those with generalized wiseness as not according with their *experience,* while, in dealing with dominant professionals, experts and the public at large cannot employ experience as evidence in the same way.[48] Paradoxically, it is often the professional wise men whose decisions or activities are being questioned, who evaluate the credentials of their expert detractors, and the legitimacy of their interests. Such a situation is manifestly restrictive of social change both in terms of protecting the wise men from evaluation of erroneous judgments and by temporarily hindering experts in the pursuit of the consequences of their acquired knowledge.

The thesis that certain key professionals can act or are acting to impede social change may receive some support from a recent suggestion concerning the way in which physicians are losing their charisma and becoming culture heros.[49] Weber described this process of routinization in some detail and its consequences in terms of the possibilities for social change.[50] The authority of the charismatic hero rests initially on his dedication to his mission of precipitating social progress. As the crisis which gave rise to his power subsides, he is beset with the necessity of consolidating the changes wrought and with stabilizing the new order, and may in time become an enduring representative of the stability of the new social order—a culture hero. Thus a major difference between the charismatic and culture hero lies in the fact that the former are regarded as a force for social change, while the latter are regarded as the embodiment of tradition. In other words, the culture hero appears to serve as an agent of social control.[51]

Using the above distinction, Myerhoff and Lawson suggest that while the physician has been traditionally depicted as a charismatic hero, a harbinger of progress, and a self-sacrificing, uniquely gifted figure, this portrayal appears to be changing. He is losing his charisma and acquiring more of the attributes of a culture hero.[52] It is perhaps possible to argue that several other so-called professions are passing or will pass through a comparable process with the result that, rather than their influence dissipating, their generalized wiseness is more firmly established by being vested in offices to be occupied by anyone whose credentials are publicly acceptable.

PROFESSIONALISM AND CHANGE

It has been suggested in the preceding sections that several dominant occupations (especially medicine and law) have come to occupy uniquely powerful positions in Western societies from which they monopolistically initiate, direct and regulate widespread social change. Several of the mechanisms which have facilitated these developments have been identified and discussed. Principal among them are the emergence of a mythology concerning professionalism: the removal of certain activities from external observability and evaluation; a process by which professionals have become generalized wise men with an unwarranted mandate to challenge others; through the accordance of an unprecedented degree of trust based on ill-founded claims to altruism; and through the manufacture of artificial needs which render their services absolutely indispensible. Through such mechanisms it is suggested that professionals have been accorded almost dictatorial powers which appear to be cyclically re-employed to protect and even further enhance the power already vested in them.

Given that such a situation exists, some find it difficult to gauge the extent to which professionals have engineered a state of affairs conducive to the insinuation of their interests into various spheres of influence, *or* whether their power has been fostered by more widespread social changes, and by newly emerging client expectations. Many professionals seemingly agree that they now occupy a uniquely powerful social position, but quarrel over whether they deliberately engineered it—claiming instead they are responding to client requests and wider societal expectations engendered by the news and entertainment media. Such an apparent chicken and egg argument overlooks the possibility that professionals, and/or their representatives, have considerable input into the very media which shapes information and expectations regarding their activities. The professional engineering of client expectations and requests may then be indirect—clients responding to already manipulated media. Accordingly, professionals may continue to claim, quite legitimately, that they are simply responding to client requests and fulfilling widespread social needs.

It seems that, at least in terms of social change, the power and influence of several dominant occupations is approaching almost ruling class dimensions. Other social categories, groups and interests—although possibly numerically stronger but less organized and powerful—clearly cannot initiate social change to anything like the same extent, nor in the same manner.

For purposes of clarity it may be useful to distinguish between what this author calls *change from within* (professional action) and *change from without* (social action which, although possibly involving the professions in various ways emanates primarily from sources other than the professions). Change that is initiated by or sponsored from within a profession is nearly always, by definition, supported by members of that profession and usually by other associated professions. This type of change has been discussed in the preceding sections and requires no further elaboration except perhaps to re-iterate that a close examination of the self-interestedness of most of this change discloses the falsity of professional claims to altruism, service orientation and trust.

With regard to change initiated principally from an interest other than a profession, or group of professions, it may be useful to distinguish three general courses of action.

(1) *Apparent Support:* There are of course occasions (admittedly probably rare) when groups and interests other than the dominant professions

promulgate change which is identical with or so close to change which the professions themselves *could* propose that it is endorsed or perhaps even actively supported by them. In common with change initiated from within, such apparent support is likely to further reinforce or even enhance the unique position occupied by the professions in society, while the success of externally initiated change is clearly enhanced by some visible form of endorsement or active support by the dominant professions. The notion of 'apparent support' is introduced to allow for the possibility of a profession (almost against its own concerns, and perhaps even after active opposition) seeming eventually to support change when no other alternative remains open. Such a situation may, for example, occur in the United States with respect to some form of National Health Insurance. While the American Medical Association (and related professional groups) have vociferously opposed its introduction, various social movements and interested parties and an increasingly chaotic organizational structure may force the eventual acceptance of this professionally undesirable alternative.[53] Therefore, while *apparently* supporting some form of social change, professionals may *actually* prefer alternatives which, if publicly acknowledged, may place in jeopardy the myth concerning their altruism, trust, etc.

(2) *Passive Oversight:* There are clearly many occasions when social change—initiated from some source apart from the dominant professions— is thought to constitute neither a threat nor offer opportunities for an enhancement of influence. This calls forth what is probably the most commonly occurring general course of action—namely, ignoring or overlooking the change. It may be that social change is less likely to succeed through passive oversight by the dominant professions than if active obstruction were employed since this latter course of action involves public visibility and the possibility that oppositional forces may be mobilized. Passive oversight may also be a safe response to externally initiated change which is regarded as threatening because, by refraining from adopting a public position, other ill-founded related professional claims are not called into question.

(3) *Active Obstruction:* This third general response is employed when externally initiated change jeopardizes or is perceived as threatening the unique social position and power of professionals. Given the constraints imposed by the maintenance of the professional mythology, such obstruction is typically exercised indirectly—occuring through backstage committees, lobbying, etc. Of the three general responses, this active obstruction of change provides the clearest demonstration of naked power and its ramifications, and the falseness of professional claims to knowledge, trust, altruism and ethics. There are innumerable examples of proposed social policy and change whose failure can be legitimately attributed to such activities of professionals and their association.[54]

It is also in the obstructionist activities of professionals towards externally initiated change that we observe that so-called professionals are not qualitatively different from any other occupational category when it comes to self-interestedly protecting certain prerogatives. Although there may appear to be surface differences between say, manual workers and professionals in the actual tactics employed (e.g., workers openly strike, professionals usually engage in covert bargaining) there appears to be no difference in either party's self-interested motivation.

In general therefore it is suggested that several dominant occupations have insinuated themselves into a position where they have a mandate to question the propriety of and impede any social change initiated by or from any other source. It is perhaps paradoxical that a situation also exists in which—because of their general nonobservability, mythical claims to altruism and the false accordance of trust—it is now almost impossible to question the propriety of, or regulate, the professions' own attempts at social change.

REFERENCES

1. E. Durkheim, *Professional Ethics and Civic Morals* (London, 1957).

2. R. H. Tawney, *The Acquisitive Society* (London, 1921).

3. A. M. Carr-Saunders and P.A. Wilson, *The Professions* (Oxford: Claredon Press, 1933).

4. K. Lynn, "The Professions," *Daedalus* 92:4, 753 (1963).

5. P. Halmos, "The Personal Service Society," *British Journal of Sociology* 18:1 (March 1967), pp. 18-19. See also P. Halmos, *The Personal Service Society* (New York: Schocken, 1971).

6. K. Marx, *Theorien über den Mehrwert* 1:376-77, 384, 1905-10, in *Karl Marx, Selected Writings in Sociology and Social Philosophy*, trans. by T. B. Bottomore, (London: McGraw-Hill, 1964).

7. See for example S. Kuznets and M. Friedman, *Income from Independent Practice* (Washington: National Bureau of Economic Research, 1945). Also D. S. Lees, *The Economic Consequences of the Professions* (London: Institute of Economic Affairs, 1966).

8. C. W. Mills, *White Collar: The American Middle Classes* (New York: Oxford Univ. Press, 1951). In addition see C. W. Mills, *The Power Elite* (New York: Oxford Univ. Press, 1956), and particularly C. W. Mills, "The Professional Ideology of Social Pathologists," *American Journal of Sociology* 49:165-180 (1943).

9. M. Young, *The Rise of the Meritocracy* (London: Penguin, 1963).

10. E. Freidson, *Profession of Medicine* (New York: Dodd, 1970); also E. Freidson, *Professional Dominance* (New York: Atherton Press Inc., 1970).

11. For a useful introductory text see T. J. Johnson, *Professions and Power* (London: Macmillan Press, 1972). I would like to acknowledge my heavy reliance on this book for a variety of useful sources and my interest in the alternative framework provided by the author.

12. Illustrative of these attempts are A. Flexner, "Is Social Work a Profession?," *School and Society* 1:901-911 (June 1915); M. L. Cogan, "Toward a Definition of a Profession," *Harvard Educational Review* 23:33-50 (Winter 1953); E. Greenwood, "Attributes of a Profession," *Social Work* 2:3, 44-

55 (July 1957); G. Millerson, "Dilemmas of Professionalism," *New Society* 4:15 (June 1964); H. L. Wilensky, "The Professionalization of Everyone?," *American Journal of Sociology* 70:137-150 (September 1964); and B. J. Sherlock, and R. T. Morris, "The Evolution of the Professional: A Paradigm," *Sociological Inquiry* 37:27-46 (Winter 1967).

13. W. J. Goode, "Encroachment, Charlatanism and the Emerging Profession: Psychology, Sociology and Medicine," *American Sociological Review* 25:902-914 (December 1960).

14. B. Barber, "Some Problems in the Sociology of the Professions," *Daedalus* 92:4 (1963).

15. T. J. Johnson, "Professions and Power," (1972), pp. 23-32.

16. Some examples are to be found in R. H. Hall, "Professionalization and Bureaucratization," *American Sociological Review* 33:92-104 (February 1968); R. H. Hall, *Occupations and the Social Structure* (Englewood Cliffs, N.J.: Prentice-Hall, 1969); and D. J. Hickson and M. W. Thomas, "Professionalization in Britain: A Preliminary Measurement," *Sociology* 3, no. 1 (January 1969) pp. 37-53. Note also the empirical evaluation in W. E. Snizek, "Hall's Professionalism Scale: An Empirical Reassessment," *American Sociological Review* 37:109-114 (February 1972).

17. B. Barber, "Some Problems in the Sociology of the Professions," (1963), p. 671.

18. See T. J. Johnson, *Professions and Power*, chs. 1 and 2, and E. Freidson, *The Profession of Medicine* and *Professional Dominance*. Also, D. Rueschemeyer, "Doctors and Lawyers: A Comment on the Theory of the Professions," *Canadian Review of Sociology and Anthropology* 1:17-30 (February 1964).

19. E. C. Hughes, "Professions," *Daedalus* 92:4 (1963).

20. E. C. Hughes, "Education for a Profession," *The Library Quarterly* 31 (October 1961). Reprinted in E. C. Hughes, *The Sociological Eye* (New York: Aldine, 1971), pp. 387-396.

21. E. C. Hughes, *The Sociological Eye*, p. 375. See also H. Becker, "The Nature of a Profession," in N. B. Henry, ed., *Education for the Professions* (Chicago: Univ. of Chicago Pr., 1963), pp. 27-46.

22. The process is discussed in more detail in J. B. McKinlay, "Clients and Organizations," in J. B. McKinlay, ed., *Processing People–Studies of Organizational Behavior* (London: Holt, 1973). A similar case is argued in H. S. Becker, "The Nature of a Profession," in *Education for the Professions: Sixty-first Yearbook of the National Society for the Study of Education*, Part 2 (Chicago: Univ. of Chicago Press, 1962), pp. 27-46.

23. See for example E. Ranzal, "Kickbacks Found on Medical Tests," *New York Times* (11 January 1973); R. P. Bolande, "Ritualistic Surgery—Circumcision and Tonsillectomy," *New England Journal of Medicine* 280, no. 11 (March 1969), pp. 591-596; L. P. Williams, *How to Avoid Unnecessary Surgery* (Los Angeles: Nash Publishing Corp., 1971); and J. E. Carlin, *Lawyers Ethics: A Survey of the New York City Bar* (New York: Russell Sage, 1966).

24. This concept of front and backstage activities is developed in detail in relation to other areas of activity in E. Goffman, *The Presentation of Self in Everyday Life* (New York: Anchor, 1959).

25. This theme is reiterated several times in Karl Marx, *Capital, A Critical Analysis of Capitalist Production*, trans. by S. Moore and E. Aveling (Moscow: Foreign Languages Publishing House, 1959).

26. Evidence is accumulating which suggests that extensive training occurs even in allegedly "deviant occupations." For example, with regard to prostitution see J. H. Bryan, "Apprenticeships in Prostitution," *Social Problems* 12:3 (Winter 1965), pp. 287-297; J. H. Bryan, "Occupational Ideologies and Individual Attitudes of Call Girls," *Social Problems* 13:4 (Spring 1966), pp.441-450; and H. Greenwald, *The Call Girl: A Social and Psychological Study* (New York: Ballantine, 1958), pp. 8-23.

27. A. I. Kisch and L. G. Reeder, "Client Evaluation of Physician Performance," *Journal of Health and Social Behavior* 10:51-58 (March 1969).

28. C. E. Bidwell, "Students and Schools: Some Observations on Client Trust in Client-Serving Organizations," in W. R. Rosengren, and M. Lefton, eds., *Organizations and Clients* (Ohio: C. E. Merrill, 1970), pp. 37-69.

29. E. Freidson, "The Impurity of Professional Authority," in H. S. Becker, et al., eds., *Institutions and the Person* (Chicago: Aldine, 1968), pp. 25-34.

30. C. E. Bidwell, "Students and Schools: Some Observations on Client Trust in Client-Serving Organizations," p. 40.

31. M. Haug and M. B. Sussman, "Professional Autonomy and the Revolt of the Client," *Social Problems* 17:153-160 (Fall 1969).

32. Illustrative of several features of this process are H. Garfinkel, "Conditions of Successful Degradation Ceremonies," *American Journal of Sociology* 61:420-24 (March 1956); E. Cumming, *Systems of Social Regulation* (New York: Atherton, 1968); and R. A. Scott, *The Making of Blind Men* (New York: Russell Sage, 1969).

33. Probably the best analysis in this respect is in S. Wheeler, ed., *On Record: Files and Dossiers in American Life* (New York: Russell Sage, 1969). See also A. Westin, *Privacy and Freedom* (New York: Atheneum, 1967); H. Wilensky, *Organizational Intelligence: Knowledge and Policy in Government and Industry* (New York: Basic Books, 1967); and A. R. Miller, *The Assault on Privacy* (New York: Signet, 1972).

34. Many excellent studies of this and related activities appear in S. Dinitz, et al., eds., *Deviance* (New York: Oxford Univ. Press, 1969); and E. Rubington, and M. S. Weinberg, eds., *Deviance: The Interactionist Perspective* (New York: MacMillan, 1968).

35. E. Freidson, *Professional Dominance*, p. 117.

36. Durkheim was probably the first to discuss the impermeability of professional groups to outside attempts to control them. See E. Durkheim, *De la division du travail social*, Préface à la deuxième édition, Félix Alcan, Paris, "Quelques Remarques sur les groupements professionels," 1902.

Also relevant to this regard are A. W. Gouldner, "Organizational Analysis," in R. K. Merton, et al., eds., *Sociology Today* (New York: Basic Books, 1959); and R. L. Coser, "Insulation from Observability and Types of Social Conformity," *American Sociological Review* 25:28-39 (February 1961). Of more practical interest would be a study of the inexplicable asymetric backstage negotiations between the American Medical Association and Aetna Life and Casualty Company (the largest independent health insurance company in the United States). See B. Kramer and P. Meyer, "Doctors Gain more Control from Aetna Life over Disputed Payments on Medical Claims," *Wall Street Journal* (24 August 1972). See also C. L. Gilb, *Hidden Hierarchies: The Professions and Government* (New York: Harper, 1966).

37. Many of Simmel's ideas relating to the nature and uses of secrecy can be found in K. H. Wolff, ed., *The Sociology of George Simmel* (Glencoe: Free Press, 1950).

38. For a telling critique of professional ethics see A. K. Daniels, "Professionalism in Formal Organizations," in J. B. McKinlay, ed., *Processing People–Studies of Organizational Behavior*, (1973). Note also J. A. Roth, letter to the editor, *The American Sociologist* 4:159 (May 1969).

39. E. Freidson, "Client Control and Medical Practice," *American Journal of Sociology* 65:374-82 (January 1960). This process has some empirical support in J. Coleman, et al., *Medical Innovation, A Diffusion Study* (Indianapolis: Bobbs-Merrill, 1966); and J. B. McKinlay, "Social Networks, Lay Consultation and Help Seeking Behavior," *Social Forces* 52 (March 1973).

40. L. A. McClung, "The Social Dynamics of the Physician's Status," *Psychiatry* 7:372 (1964).

41. A number of these difficulties are discussed in P. Bachrach, and M.S. Baratz, *Power and Poverty* (New York: Oxford Univ. Press, 1970); C. W. Mills, *The Power Elite;* and G. W. Domhoff, *The Higher Circles* (New York: Vintage, 1970).

42. D. Horowitz, "Billion Dollar Brains: How Wealth Puts Knowledge in its Pocket," *Ramparts* (May 1969), pp. 36-44. A somewhat similar case is argued by J. O. Connar, "The University and the Political Economy," *Leviathan* 1:14-15 (March 1969).

43. T. Parsons, "The Professions and Social Structure," in *Essays in Sociological Theory* (Glencoe: Free Press, 1954), pp. 34-49.

44. T. Parsons, "The Professions and Social Structure," p. 38.

45. Report of the Royal Commission of Medical Education, 1965–68, (London: H.M.S.O.); A. Lepawsky, "Medical Science and Political Science," *Journal of Medical Education* 43:10 (1967), pp. 905-917; and J. R. Butler, "Sociology and Medical Education," *The Sociological Review* 15:87-96 (1969).

46. E. C. Hughes, "Licence and Mandate," chap. 6 in E. C. Hughes, *Men and Their Work* (Glencoe: Free Press, 1958), pp. 78-87.

47. E. C. Hughes, "Licence and Mandate," p. 79.

48. In his discussion of the "clinical mentality," Freidson depicts physicians as particularistic, pragmatic in the use of scientific knowledge, and inclined to employ personal first-hand experiences over scientific theory. See E. Freidson, *The Profession of Medicine,* chap. 8. There is no reason to assume that other dominant and related occupations do not have a comparable orientation.

49. B. G. Meyerhoff and W. R. Larson, "The Doctor as Culture Hero: The Routinization of Charisma," *Human Organizations* 17 (1958).

50. M. Weber, *The Theory of Social and Economic Organization,* trans. by A. M. Henderson and T. Parson (Glencoe: Free Press, 1947).

51. See for example O. Klapp, "Creation of Popular Heroes," *American Journal of Sociology* 54:135-141 (September 1948); H. D. Duncan, *Language and Literature in Society* (Chicago: Univ. of Chicago Press, 1953). Most of the research in this area to date concerns the position of the psychiatrist. See H. A. Ross, "Commitment of the Mentally Ill: Problems of Laws and Policy," *Michigan Law Review* 57:945-1018 (May 1959); D. L. Wegner, and C. R. Fletcher, "The Effects of Legal Counsel on Admissions to a State Mental Hospital: A Confrontation of Professions," *Journal of Health and Social Behavior* 10:66-72 (March 1969); and H. J. Steadman, "The Psychiatrist as a Conservative Agent of Social Control," *Social Problems* 20, no. 2 (Fall 1972), pp. 263-271.

52. B. G. Meyerhoff and W. R. Larson, "The Doctor as Culture Hero: The Routinization of Charisma," p. 189.

53. One recent example of the use of this alternative as a method of self preservation is discussed by H. B. Waldman, "The Response of the Dental Profession to Change in the Organization of Health Care—A Commentary," *American Journal of Public Health* 63, no. 1 (1973), pp. 17-29.

54. Many indicting illustrations from the field of medicine appear in B., and J. Ehrenreich, *The American Health Empire* (New York: Random House, 1970).

The Deprofessionalization of Everyone?

by Marie R. Haug

A little over ten years ago, in September 1964 to be exact, Harold Wilensky published a famous paper, "The Professionalization of Everyone?" Reacting in part to Nelson Foote's revival of old claims that *labor* was being professionalized and to the growing barrage of papers and books seeking to show that all occupations, and indeed the whole society, were on the professionalization kick, Wilensky tried to sound a note of warning. This caveat was based on both historical and definitional considerations. Professions, he noted, differed from other occupations in being based on esoteric knowledge acquired only through long training, and in having incumbents who adhere to the professional norm of a service ideal. The established professions, moreover, have gone through a process of professionalization involving, among other things, locating training within universities, forming professional associations, licensing, and the adoption of ethical codes. These characteristics and processes have combined to provide professions "extraordinary autonomy—the authority and freedom to regulate themselves and act within their spheres of competence."[1] Not all occupations, said Wilensky, can make the grade. Their members can try, but they are unlikely to be successful.

If all this sounds drearily familiar, it is because professions and professionalization have intrigued sociologists for generations, indeed ever since Durkheim. From Greenwood (1957)[2] to Goode (1969)[3] to Moore (1970)[4] to Freidson (1971)[5], discussions over definitions, lists, criteria, characteristics, catalogues and functions have engaged the attention of the discipline. It has been in the mode to argue that "profession" is really a continuum,[6] not a set of discrete categories, in which established professions are differentiated from semi-professions, and from occupations beyond the pale. Indices, it is claimed, can be constructed to place any occupation on the continuum, and give it its proper niche in the social hierarchy, be it mortician, sanitary engineer, real estate agent, or whatever. What all of this tended to boil down to was reliance on the "core characteristics" of specialized knowledge, a service ethic, and work autonomy. Only a few noticed that it was not knowledge per se, but the *monopolization* of knowledge that produced the autonomy. As Freidson[7] declared, "Knowledge itself does not give special power, only *exclusive* knowledge gives power to its possessors." And, as he might have added, the claimed monopoly of the professional over an area of expertise is productive of the aura of mystery which haloes professional tasks and of the myths about their difficulty and effectiveness.

Only a few have questioned the whole elaborate theoretical structure. One of the first was Becker,[8] who declared that profession is a folk concept, simply a word with good connotations, like motherhood and the flag. It is a semantic tool with which the members of an occupational group can win status, a better income, more privileges and fewer constraints. Julius Roth,[9] in one of his joyous jousts with establishment ideologies, calls professionalism "the sociologists' decoy." Instead of fiddling with attribute lists, sociologists should take a historical perspective and concern themselves with the processes professional groups employ to promote monopoly control of their turf and avoid accountability to the public for their actions.

The historical approach is indeed illuminating, particularly with respect to the status dimension. Elliot,[10] for example, in the British *New Perspectives in Sociology* series, distinguishes a concept of "status professional." He points out that in pre-industrial society in Britain, members of the established professions of the clergy, law and medicine were persons of high prestige, based on their political title, aristocratic connections, and inherited wealth, with negligible specialized knowledge but a general university training. Professions were "compatible with the social status of gentlemen" because they allowed a leisurely, independent life style, involving neither low-status manual labor nor vulgar commercial trade. In medicine, for instance, physicians' skills were "limited mainly to the art of writing complicated prescriptions. [They] might have extensive learning in classic literature and culture, but . . . depended on . . . gentlemanly manner, impressive behavior and . . . clients' ignorance to develop a medical practice."[11] A university degree from Oxford or Cambridge, which became a requirement for membership in the Royal College of Physicians when it was founded in 1518, was merely a mechanism for limiting membership to adherents of the Anglican church. Even by the end of the eighteenth century, examinations for physicians by the Royal College had little relationship to testing medical knowledge, but were concerned chiefly with determining the gentlemanly status qualifications of the aspirant. Examinations were brief, oral, in Latin, and focused on knowledge of the classical languages.

Historically, it would seem, in Great Britain status *preceded* other professional attributes, including specialized expertise and the service ethos, and autonomy flowed not from these claims, but from high position in the stratification system. Have sociologists been putting the cart before the horse? Status and autonomy, since they were prior conditions, could not have been a *consequence* of the acquisition of esoteric knowledge. On the contrary, exclusive knowledge and humanitarianism claims can be conceptualized as rationalizations developed to preserve antecedent privileges and power. Thus Elliott's phrase, "status profession," identifies a critical stage in the development of law, medicine and the clergy, permitting them to carry an indelible stamp of high position into the nineteenth century when they emerged as "occupational professions" in the context of an industrial society. This heritage of prestige has carried over to the present day.

In the United States, educational requirements were also used to preserve status differences, but in a somewhat different way. The Flexner Report of 1910, which revealed the deficiencies of proprietary medical schools, resulted in their being closed. While this eliminated a source of inadequate and ineffective training, it also shut off a gateway to the practice of medicine which had previously been open even to those with no status and little money. As a result, the wealthy medical elites, many of whom had trained abroad and came from prestigious New England families, were left in control of the field, using academic hurdles to preserve their own privileged position.[12] Historical data, in short, tends to be compatible with Becker's view of profession as a status symbol toward which occupational groups strive. The dismal lesson of history may be, however, that acquiring the trappings of high status, like a university-based fund of specialized knowledge, or a rhetoric of ethical motives, or even a legalized freedom from public control, cannot make a silk purse out of a sow's ear, or a gentleman out of a commoner. The evidence is right in our midst. Sociologists, architects, and real estate agents never quite seem to come up to the positions of power and prestige enjoyed by the former "status professions."

Although the historical view casts some doubt on the dominant themes of sociological analysis of profession, it can be countered by reference to the processes of social change which have accompanied industrialization, such as the primacy of technical knowledge, and the critical role of specialized expertise in dealing with the problems of individuals and the social order. Professions in the twentieth century cannot be fully understood in terms of work characteristics in the eighteenth. A different challenge is less easily dismissed, however, and that is the cross-cultural variation in the concept of profession, the insularity of English language writing on the subject, and the extent to which status and profession have been disjoined in other societies.

As Marc Maurice pointed out in a special issue of *Sociologie du Travail* on the professions[13] even the term "profession" is Anglo-Saxon, and it might be added that discussion of the concept has appeared to accept Western capitalism, and specifically the British-American social order, as typifying the industrial world. The fact is that sociological conceptualizations of this facet of the division of labor vary markedly across cultures and socio-economic systems. We model our thinking on the "learned," (or in Elliott's terms) the "status" professions of medicine, law and the clergy, highlighting monopoly of knowledge, service orientation and autonomy in work performance. The French, however, view the category much more broadly. In Michel Crozier's *World of the Office Worker*,[14] a series of clerical white collar occupations are classified as professions, and in general many non-manual work roles requiring training and skill are included in the concept. For the French, "profession" is very close to "*metier*," which translates as "trade." West German literature is in a different vein, equating profession with "*Beruf*," or "calling," which emphasizes an aspect of commitment and dedication derived from the socialization accompanying long academic training.

In eastern European societies, on the other hand, sociologists offer a somewhat different perspective. From the German Democratic Republic, for example, comes one paper which defines profession as an "ocupational activity for which certain capacities, knowledge and preparation through training are imperative,"[15] but then reports that such training is available in "389 professions," with 95 percent of all young people who complete their education planning to enter one of them. Among the "basic professions" are such job titles as specialized machinists and maintenance mechanics for data processing equipment, making it clear that "profession" is a term covering all skilled occupations, blue-collar as well as white-collar.

In the Soviet Union, the category appears more selectively defined, with the equivalence to professions in our terminology limited to those most highly qualified among non-manual occupations. There is no word for profession as such in the Russian language, "intelligentsia" being the closest semantic analogue. Thus, according to M. N. Rutkevich, the " 'intelligentsia' is usually understood to mean a very broad social stratum consisting of persons professionally engaged in intellectual work," such as "scientists, engineers, technicians, teachers, physicians and other experts."[16]

It is apparent that broadening the coverage of the category "profession" makes it less a unique component of the division of labor, and consequently tends to homogenize discrepancies in status and prestige.

Despite these cross-cultural and historical variations in the concept of profession, one recurring theme does emerge—the command of knowledge as setting the professional apart, whether it be a group of irrelevancies like classical Greek in Medieval England, or technical expertise in the inner tangles of a computer, as in contemporary Germany, or clerical proficiency as in France. Even Becker and Roth concur that professions gain power by convincing the public that their members have cornered their relevant knowledge market. And while Wilensky feels that not all occupations can "make it," it is only because as collectivities they are unable to claim exclusive jurisdiction over a theoretical knowledge base or a monopoly of practical skills.

Indeed it is the knowledge theme which undergirds the notion that ours is a professionalizing society. Daniel Bell defines the post-industrial society as one in which the professional and technical class will be preeminent, with theoretical knowlege a central source of power.[17] The scientific knowledge explosion and exponential growth in technology have produced a major shift in the distribution of the division of labor. Industrial production requires fewer workers, while the service-government sector commands an increasingly larger proportion of the work force. Thus the "post-industrial" tag. In this professionalized society of the future, Bell predicts that education, particularly university training, will become the "chief determinant of the stratification system."[18] The growth of the professional-technical class, with its control of scientific and theoretical information, will mean that property and political position will fade as bases of power, to be replaced by knowledge.[19]

Although this sounds very much like a rebirth of early ideas of technocracy, it need not be, as evidenced in the work of Halmos. This British sociologist echoes Bell in predicting a professionalized future, but sees professionalization as a "contemporary vehicle of integration in society and of moral renewal."[20] The values of the personal service professions—humanitarianism, selflessness, counseling, concern—will permeate the entire social structure and the relationships within it. The professions are a universal integrating moral force . . . shades of Durkheim!

This is the situation as we stand on the threshold of the twenty-first century. Undaunted by the rather poor record of sociologists as forecasters, a number of our colleagues, and foremost among these Bell, are predicting a "professionalized" means, except to suggest that a command, or a monopolized control, of scientific knowledge in the hands of an elite, humanitarian, minority, will lead to a new distribution of autonomy, privilege, power, and prestige. This hypothesis is quite consistent with Wilensky's estimate that not every occupation can become a profession. In Bell's projected future it is the *dominance* of the professional occupations, not their universality, which characterizes the professionalized society.

This paper presents a counter hypothesis, an alternative view, that runs against the tide of conventional sociological analysis and prediction. It projects a *de*professionalized future, and presents some preliminary evidence to indicate that this hypothesis may be tenable.

In doing so, only minor attention is given to bureaucratic power as a countervailing force to professional control. Much sociological theory has tended to put the two structures in conflict, but it appears that increasingly professionals are buttressed in their authority relations *by virtue* of their location in complex organization settings. The fact that professional practice is shifting from a fee-for-service to a salaried mode, and from solo to organization practice, has strengthened rather than weakened the experts' control. Professional power at the point of service delivery is power over *clients*. Location of practice in bureaucratic systems puts professionals in touch with authority structures which can be utilized to enforce their decision. If clients are disinclined to comply with the advice of the expert, legal or quasi-legal rules and regulations can bring them into line. The psychiatrist in the mental hospital is one dramatic example of this professional-bureaucratic power link.[21] The contradictory and complementary roles of organizational structures in relation to professional decision-making and implementation are complex, and this paper chooses to focus on other, perhaps more salient, features of the hypothesized deprofessionalization process.

For the first time in this discussion, it may be noticed, explicit reference has been made to clients. It is intriguing that clients are accorded so passive a role in the definitions and discussions about professions and professionalization. They are the recipients of service, far too often conceptualized as the silent, even grateful receivers of the beneficent professional's wisdom. The "competence gap" between clients and experts, to use Parson's terms,[22] justifies the norm of compliance. It would be a fascinating exercise in the sociology of knowledge to analyze why such a model of reality should have gained any sociological currency, even as an ideal type, but that enticing byway must also be foregone for the purposes of this paper.

Instead let us focus on the role of the client as the missing ingredient in the conceptualization of the professionalized future. Included in the discussion also must be some attention to technological change, the implications of which in interaction with the role of the client have been insufficiently considered as well. In the analysis which follows, medicine will be used as a major source of empirical example, for a number of reasons. It has been considered the prototype profession; it is subject to all the forces of historical, social and technical change which are ushering in the twenty-first century; and it happens to be a profession concerning which I have some first hand cross cultural empirical data as a result of recent sabbatical research.

With respect to medicine in particular and professions in general, I shall attempt to show the combined effects of client and technology in a counterprocess of *de*professionalization, involving erosion of monopoly over knowledge, undercutting of trust in the humanitarian ethos, questioning of autonomy and authority, as well as direct challenges to status position. The objective of the discussion is to cast doubt on the forecast of a professionalized future, and the projection of an alternative hypothesis to be tested against the data of unfolding history.

KNOWLEDGE MONOPOLY AND THE PUBLIC

The role of the educational system in protecting and perpetuating professional knowledge monopoly in the past is incontrovertible. Access to elite training has been blocked by various intellectual, social and financial hurdles, so that only a few were able to learn the mysteries. But this limitation on the acquisition of special information is relative to the diffusion of knowledge in the society as a whole, as symbolized by the rapidly changing general educational level of the public. Most high school graduates in the United States, where the median years of schooling is now more than twelve, know more about hygiene, health, and the human body than the gentlemen physicians of the Middle Ages. So far, however, scientific research has expanded medical knowledge sufficiently to keep health practitioners several lengths ahead in the information race. On the other hand, the expanding knowledge base puts new strains on monopolization. Knowledge growth has been of such proportions as to preclude its grasp by any one individual. Professional collectivities manage the proliferation of data by specialization; groups of individuals control the medical body of knowledge by a division of the expertise pie so that each group masters slices in depth instead of attempting to encompass the whole mass. But even this cannot serve to insulate the profession from the rising tide of general education and expanded public sophistication.

A more detailed consideration of the nature of professional knowledge will help to clarify the situation. If one accepts the fact that knowledge is based both on an academic and an experiential component, it is possible to discern two paths to weaken the practitioner's monopoly, even that of the medical specialist. To begin with, the experiential component is to a certain extent accessible to those without formal academic training. Medicine, as its practitioners like to remind us, is as much an art as it is an exact science, and cannot be learned simply from books. The unanticipated consequence of this stance is that some specialities, such as pediatrics, for example, share part of their knowledge with women who have extensive experience, such as the mother of a large family or the wise grandmother. Other specialities which treat some chronic diseases may be faced by patients whose long intimate acquaintance with their ailment has given them some knowledge of its typical processes and responses to treatment for them. The diabetic of many years duration is a typical instance of this phenomenon.

The whole concept of folk medicine for the management of everyday ailments like colds and rheumatism is based on experiential knowledge, or at least a claim to it. China is a prime example of the institutionalization of the contribution of folk medicine to health care, not only in the wide reliance on barefoot doctors in the countryside, but in the near-equal status accorded to "traditional medicine" and "scientific medicine" in the training of physicians.[23]

The point about experience is that it is widely distributed throughout the population, and is difficult to monopolize. Furthermore, although it can be argued that experience without an academic background will remain fragmented and incapable of integration into a conceptual framework, it is also possible that the elaborate academic obstacle course required for many professions goes beyond the real integrative need. High school and some college, available to ever larger segments of the public, should be sufficient in many instances to give meaning to experiences and observations.

The hue and cry against "credentialism" raised by those wanting to break into the charmed professional circle is based on some of this reasoning. "Credentialism" is the term used to denigrate the custom of admitting newcomers to professional practice simply by presentation of a university degree or other "credential" certifying to the completion of an academic sequence. The credential may be irrelevant to the real world requirements of service delivery: a diploma can be granted without the acquisition of the experience essential for successful performance. According to this viewpoint, experience informed by a general education may be more meaningful than an academic diploma without experience.

The effect of increased levels of schooling on professionalism gave pause, a decade ago, to Wilensky, who wondered about the paradox that education could result in greater utilization of professional services but could also produce "greater sophistication about matters professional, more skepticism about the certainties of practice, some actual sharing in professional knowledge (the mysteries lose their enchantment)." A series of unstructured interviews with general practitioners in Britain in the late winter of 1974 underscored the latter possibility, and made it clear that the professionals were not too happy with challenges from the more educated to their exclusive command over health care. Indeed the GP's tended to define questioning of their expertise as neurotic. "It's the neurotics with high IQ's who claim the doctor doesn't know," said one, and another: "Doctor's wives are difficult to treat, they always seem to think they have rare diseases," or, "Never take a teacher or university professor on your list."

The negative effect of public education on professional power also emerged in the U. S. S. R., where interviews with physicians in general practice in the Soviet polyclinic system produced answers similar to those which turned up in Britain. One remarked, "It is much easier to treat manual workers as patients. The intelligentsia and the non-manual workers are educated. They read books, literature, listen to radio, watch TV; when they speak of an illness they give not only the symptoms but also the diagnosis. It is easier for the doctor if the patient does not try to tell the doctor what to do." Another physician in a different polyclinic remarked that it is the neurotic patients who want to know everything and demand to have everything explained, while a colleague said only half in "jest" that if the time ever came when all Soviet citizens had a university education, "all patients will be neurotic, there will be much work for the doctor . . . lots of arguments."

General schooling which informs experience is not the only challenge to professional monopoly, however. Specific public education in domains of professional expertise is becoming more and more common. In this country as well as in Britain, there are books, magazines, articles, newspaper columns, and radio and TV programs, all in one way or another providing health education, discussion of danger signals, and ideas on appropriate regimen for various ailments as well as for general health maintenance. Do-it-yourself doctor books, such as the one published by the Boston Women's Collective, virtually leave the physician out altogether. Patients are now being given the right to see and correct their own medical records, an "idea whose time has come."[24] The American Civil Liberties Union handbook on *The Rights of Hospital Patients*[25] includes a glossary of medical abbreviations, so that patients can penetrate the mysteries of charts, records and conversations.

The patient-education trend is particularly marked in the Soviet Union. Every polyclinic visited by this author had a special office responsible for this function. Posters and displays in hallways and waiting rooms exhorted visitors about nutrition, care of chronic illness, hygiene, and human development, or explained medical equipment and disease processes. Every waiting room revealed colorful folders and pamphlets on specific ailments or health problems, often with detailed diagrams of various organs to explain how medical procedures work. The upshot of all this, however, is a certain amount of extra trouble for the doctor. As one explained, the most difficulty comes from the old folks, the retirees, particularly those without responsibility for care of grandchildren, who have time for all the pamphlets and all the media exposure and come to the polyclinic with complaints, demands, and requests for medication. Soviet physicians are aware of the dilemma faced by all physicians, who want their patients to be knowledge-able enough to make wise decisions about when it is appropriate to seek medical help and when it is not, but not so sophisticated as to be difficult to manage at the point of consultation.

Experiential knowledge and patient education clearly have their limits, and cannot substitute for the academic training dispersed in professional schools. Such knowledge, however, is not necessarily inaccessible. The information disseminated in text books and lectures is, almost by definition, technical, definable, and codifiable. Indeed Wilensky was one of the first to notice that narrowing the technical base of a profession made it vulnerable to codification into a set of rules and instructions that could be easily grasped by those with minimum training, and ripe for computerization. A similar point can be made about the computer storage and retrieval of the academic knowledge component of the professional's expertise.

Without reifying or deifying the computer, or attributing to it any magical properties, it is still possible to point out that the implications of this enormous combined storage file and adding machine have not yet been completely grasped. The invention of the printing press revolutionized knowledge dissemination in the Middle Ages by making duplication, preservation and accessibility of books enormously simpler than was the case with the old hand-written manuscripts. The electronic computer can again revolutionize knowledge availability and utilization by the geometric advances in the scale of its storage and the speed of its retrieval. No longer need knowledge be packed only in the professional's head or in a specialized library, where it is relatively inaccessible. It can be available not just to those who *know*, but also to those who *know how to get it.*

Medicine offers only one example of the radical changes in professional performance made possible by computer technology, developments discussed more fully in United States writings than elsewhere in the world.[26] Automated history taking and computerized physical examination devices, such as ultrasonic images and thermal sensors, are already in use. The hardware is presently available to develop a system capable of advising patients what treatment regimen to follow without the assistance of any medical staff. Computerization of the rapidly growing findings from medical research can overcome the recurrent problem of the obsolescence of professional knowledge; in this sense the computer will be more up to date than the average doctor. Education of the physician will be changed, with less focus on memorizing facts, and more on training in computer technology and personal counseling, two aspects of knowledge in which medicine will not be able to claim a monopoly because other occupational groups have already staked their own claims.

A third threat to professional exclusive information control, along with public education and computerization, are the new divisions of labor which are emerging in many professional domains. In the case of American medical practice there are the physician's assistant and the nurse practitioner, as well as the return of the midwife. Some of these occupations have long shared medical roles with doctors in other parts of the world. Midwives have successfully been delivering babies in much of Western Europe for many years. In Britain the health visitor carries out many pediatric duties having to do with well baby care. In the U. S. S. R. the *feldsher* provides first aid in rural areas, filling some of the functions of American hospital emergency room staff; in China the barefoot doctor takes care of everyday ailments of the patients and performs public health activities.

Even though the new occupations may be relegated to the less desirable "dirty work" aspects of the physician's tasks, the fact remains that by sharing some previously closely held responsibilities and expertise the medical professional opens the door to rivalry with other occupational groups, who can then make further claims on his exclusive turf. The full impact of these developments has not yet been felt here, because the physician still dominates the work of other staff in the medical division of labor,[27] both legally and normatively. And where the threat of lower echelon take-over appears, doctors have been able to assert their control over the situation.[28] What the future holds, however, is less clear. The relative independence of health visitors in Britain and *feldshers* in the U. S. S. R. may be explained in part by their geographical separation from physicians, and one can forecast that many health maintenance and chronic illness care activities may eventually slip from the physicians' hands. Knowledge is the more difficult to monopolize the more widely its assets are diffused.

TRUST AND THE HUMANITARIAN IMAGE

Public education, computerization, and the sharing of expertise in new divisions of labor undermine professional claims to being the sole repositories of esoteric knowledge useful to society and the individual. But what of another major claim, that the humanitarian ethos of the profession, the socialization to service which its incumbents undergo, and the ethical standards enforced by professional associations justify public trust in professional judgement? To ask the question is to realize to what extent trust has been eroded in an age of consumerism[29] and client revolt.[30]

One of the demands of the New Careers movement, which represented incumbents and advocates of new divisions of labor in professional fields,[31] has been that professionals should be held accountable for their actions, and to the public, not merely to their peers. This call for public accountability has been taken up by broader segments of the society, implying that the image of the professional as kindly, concerned and trustworthy is no longer widely shared. The various pieces of evidence for this trend in the United States include the rise of malpractice suits and limitations on medical experimentation. Malpractice suits, as any newspaper reader knows, have increased in number and amount of settlement. A recent special study by HEW has underscored the seriousness of the problem but also noted that breakdown in rapport and declining public regard for and trust in doctors are among the precipitating causes.[32] Patients who sue their doctors obviously have lost trust in them.

Another indicator of a decline in belief in the medical professional's humanitarianism is the wide-spread attack on the right to experimentation, and the controls and constraints now applied by governmental regulations on medical research.[33] As of this writing, research on the human fetus is prohibited altogether, and other types of research are hedged in by numerous requirements. For example, benefits must be shown in advance to be worth the risk of experimental procedures. Representatives of the community are required to participate in review of research proposals to determine if human subjects are properly protected. Politicization of the whole experimentation issue is undoubtedly a reflection of public skepticism concerning the researching physician's concern for his patient's welfare. Proof of this concern is required by the regulations, and demands for proof are incompatible with trust. Indeed, trust might be defined as belief without proof.

Similar trends are emerging in Great Britain. Although malpractice suits are much rarer, the complaint system attached to the National Health Service is increasingly being used to register disapproval with physicians, their attitudes to patients and their services.[34] The Patient's Association in London has recently mounted a successful campaign on hospital patients' rights to refuse to permit themselves to be used as teaching subjects. The only comparable developments noted in interviews in the U.S.S.R. referred to lack of trust of cancer patients in the reassurances of their physicians, along with references to the suspiciousness and skepticism of some of the elderly. On the other hand, a parallel trend is visible in reports from mainland China. Professionalism is criticized as breeding elitism and lack of concern, particularly in academia.[35] The requirement that medical school teachers and students spend time in the countryside is designed to eradicate elitism and disregard for the everyday troubles and hardships of the poor. Physicians are exhorted to lay aside "fame and fortune," no longer to "put professional work in command," and to identify instead with the people.[36] The implication is fairly clear. Ideological re-education is necessary because the incumbents have not demonstrated a fit with the service orientation model of their professional roles.

THE DECLINE OF AUTONOMY AND AUTHORITY

The logical and empirical consequence of the weakening of knowledge monopoly and decline of public belief in professional good will is that professional autonomy in work is undermined. For the physician, as with any professional dealing directly with clients, there are two faces of autonomy. It means freedom *from* superordinate power, the right to make decisions and judgments about practice without instructions or interferences from above. Peer review, by colleagues who understand the uncertainties and ambiguities of the application of an inexact science, does not occur at the point of production in terms of oversight or directions. It will occur, if it occurs at all, only later, and will evaluate causes, actions and outcomes in a colleague rather than an adversary mode. At the moment of service, when professional is interacting with client, no one is supposed to be standing over his shoulder, not even a colleague. That is one face of autonomy.

The other face involves freedom *to* exercise power over subordinates, the clients, who, moved by awe of superior knowledge and trust in good intentions, obey. Legitimation by clients of the right of the physician, or any professional, to direct their action constitutes a grant of authority. "Doctor knows best" justifies accepting "doctor's orders." In the folkways, indeed, "doctor's orders" are the highest authority. At least that has been the mythology.

In actual fact, patients have undoubtedly always challenged the authority of the physician, with the level of defiance geared to the power of the patient vis-a-vis the doctor. The British interviews with general practitioners made it quite clear that cultural patterns of deference to the upper class accounted at least in part for patients' attitudes and behavior towards physicians. For example, a symbolic rejection of the proper class stance—failure to address the physician as "Sir"—was reported as a contemporary mark of disrespect.[37] Johnson, in a little known British study, makes the point that only by sharing wider sources of power, such as membership in a dominant class, can occupations impose their "own definitions of the producer-consumer relationship," as occurs with the professions.[38] Even in medicine, as

Becker[39] has reminded us, "clients continually make judgments about the work and capabilities of the professionals they use. Medical patients often change doctors. . . ." Moreover, patients often bargain, argue, and wheedle their doctors into changing a medication or course of treatment. Indeed even the diagnosis may be the result of a negotiated agreement between the receiver and giver of service.[40]

If patients have never fully accepted the authority of the physician, or clients the authority of professionals, what makes current challenges so different from the past, one might legitimately ask. There are several things. One is the change in the normative environment. Past reality may have involved challenge, but challenge was deviant, individual, not the modal behavior accepted as the proper way to interact with the wise and kind professional. Indeed, this is the point of view that physicians express when they deplore too much questioning and too little acceptance by patients, and define it as neurotic. Arguments equal deviance, one recalls, in London as well as Moscow.

If there is a change, it is in the public's view of appropriate behavior for themselves as patients and for physicians as well. Both faces of autonomy are undermined by the demands for accountability, the pattern of consumerism, people's rights, and questioning of shibboleths which has characterized the 60's and 70's. The empirical sign that new norms are sprouting on physicians' freedom *from* oversight is the legitimation—even over the objections of some sectors of organized medicine—of the right to have health provider decisions checked on a massive scale. The Professional Standards Review Organizations (PSRO's) are in effect monitoring systems on doctors' standards of performance. The Malpractice Commission report[41] suggests that physicians should be re-examined and re-licensed every five years to make sure their knowledge has not grown out of date, and this proposal is surfacing in some state legislatures. One of the hazards of the computer to old-fashioned medical practice is the potential for mass ongoing evaluation of physicians' competence. In Ohio, review of medical charges by computer has already been proposed.[42]

Another well-spring of possible change is, paradoxically enough, the alliance being forged between medical care and bureaucratic structures. As medicine is more and more practiced in groups, clinics, health centers and other mass production locations, patients are aggregated on membership lists and in waiting rooms. The potential for interaction and the consequent development of "patient consciousness" exists. Marx argued that the aggregation of workers in the factory system was one basis for recognition of their common fate and the birth of class consciousness. A similar process is not inconceivable for patienthood. Bell suggests in his forecast that the struggles of the future will not take place over the control of material resources, between those who have them and those who do not, as in the past, but over the control of knowledge as a resource and as a basis of power and authority. The other face of physician autonomy, authority over clients, is clearly eroded when individual complaints and demands are transformed into organized group pressures.

The extent to which autonomy and authority have declined in other societies is not clear. In Britain the historical-cultural background is still strong. "Clinical Freedom," for example, is explicitly protected in the National Health Service Structure (National Health Service Reorganization, 1972). Appropriate inter-class habits of deference and compliance, do not seem to be diminishing. The Patients Association is a small, upper class group with little stomach for confronting the medical establishment, and it concerns itself chiefly with issues like comfort in hospitals. In the U. S. S. R., the historical-cultural heritage operates in a different fashion. Memories of the selfless services of many doctors during the destruction and death of World War II are a bank of good will and respect. Soviet law, which makes the maintenance of good health an explicit responsibility of all citizens, puts physicians in a quasi-legal position of authority; for example, keeping one's job is contingent on evidence of having had periodic health examinations. Moreover, the fact that most physicians are women produces an ambience of mothering which is not easy to pin down but can be felt—perhaps best by another woman. Health concern and regulation is pervasive in all areas of Russian life, and the female physician who oversees checkups, insists on clinic attendance, runs down no-shows, and makes frequent house visits is a kind of big mama. Although the image of the physician as the father figure may have faded in the United States, and although the duty to obey faded with it, my mother the doctor is still alive and well in the U. S. S. R.

STATUS—THE PRIZE AND THE PROBLEM

But suppose Becker is right after all, that the name of the game is status, and all this emphasis on knowledge and service is basically a ploy of old occupations wanting to hold on to the marbles history gave them, and of late-comers on the make for a piece of the prize. In a curious parallel, this is the implicit rationale both behind the early deprofessionalization objectives of the New Careers and similar movements in the United States, and the efforts of the Mao regime in Mainland China. As Gartner and Riessman[43] point out, "Chinese society has been struggling with the elitism of the old professionals; the protracted, seemingly unnecessarily long training provided for the acquisition of knowledge and skill." The goal has been to demystify medical knowledge, but more directly to minimize social distance between health care worker and patient, with the stated aim of "deprofessionalizing."[44] The logic is clearly that "professional" is a status term, and deprofessionalization a status-equalizing process.

The New Careers movement in its beginning stages, by downgrading academic knowledge, focusing on the experimental ingredient, and demanding a change in professional-client relationships, was perhaps seeking a short cut to status for previously disadvantaged groups. The blacks and the poor wanted dignity and respect for themselves, but rejected the pathways which others used to gain status, because they were closed to them, blocked by academic and financial mazes negotiable only by the middle class. The cry for deprofessionalization, however, lasted less than a decade. By 1974, some of the first leaders of New Careers were saying "we need not only a deprofessionalization, but a *re*professionalization combined with consumer involvement."[45] And in China, the medical schools, which had been closed while faculty and students were dispersed to the countryside, have been reopened. Degrees as such have been abolished, and training has a "vocational-technical" flavor,[46] but education in expertise has been reinstituted. The effect on restoration of a stratification system is not yet clear, however.

It has often been said that the status of physicians in the U.S.S.R. is lower than it is in this country, but while this is true, it obscures the more important reality that there are two very different status systems in the two societies. The more accurate assessment is that there has been a homogenizing of the statuses in the U.S.S.R., with medicine along with other professional occupations (the intelligentsia) grouped in the nonmanual stratum. The ideological object continues to be to erase distinctions within that nonmanual category and also between nonmanual and manual workers. To judge by the studies of Soviet sociologists on occupational aspirations of young people, however, value differences have persisted, and nonmanual jobs are still considered the more "attractive."[47]

Nevertheless in the U.S.S.R. as well as in China, the prestige-equalizing process is official policy. The difference, however, is in the effect of egalitarianism on the professionalization concept. Professional, or its equivalent "intelligentsia," is not a dirty word in the U.S.S.R. and it is in China. The Russian Medical Association as a power base was disestablished after the revolution,[48] but the notions of professional expertise based on academic knowledge and professional responsibility rooted in a service ideology were not. Medical deontology, defined as study of the history and philosophy of the profession, the duty of the physician, and the responsibility of the physician towards the patient, his family and to ancillary medical personnel, is a regular course in the Soviet medical curriculum.[49] The sense of being part of a special service elite is reinforced in the process.

Deprofessionalization by a direct assault on the status position of occupational incumbents remains problematic. Clearly, egalitarian ideology is a cross cultural trend, but it is less clear that the trend will succeed in diminishing the status of professions while leaving claims to autonomy, knowledge and service untouched. Occupational distinctions based on training and expertise are unlikely to fade. Perhaps the real question is whether these distinctions are to be conceptualized in terms of profession as a category of work, or on some other basis. Wilensky, in the article which opened this paper, was in effect declaring that occupations could not win high status and accompanying financial and honorific benefits without having the necessary prerequisites, including a scientific knowledge base and the rest. The obverse inquiry is whether the grant of status and the pattern of deference which are associated, historically and in contemporary terms, with the title of professional are necessary concomitant of expertise. Behind the questions about professionalization and deprofessionalization lie the classic sociological inquiries on the nature of societal stratifications, its causes, concomitants, and inevitability.

THE DEPROFESSIONALIZATION OF EVERYBODY

What then is the difference between a plumber and a urologist? Both require training, both deal with pipes. Neither works for nothing. It could be said that one deals with life and death matters and the other does not, but that evaluation depends on the nature of one's emergencies and one's sex. In the past do-it-yourself plumbing was considered less disastrous than do-it-yourself medicine, but in the past a plumber was just a worker and a doctor a gentleman, differentiated by college education and upper class family background. Nowadays do-it-yourself plumbing *and* do-it-yourself medicine are in vogue; the plumber may well have a college education, and the doctor be from a poverty background, or even a woman. Moreover, technology threatens the power and autonomy of both. Both are experts in their own fields. One might well ask, why should one be considered a professional and the other not?

This paper has been seeking to suggest that societal trends, both technological and ideological, are rendering the concept of profession obsolete. Wilensky argued that not every occupation can become a profession because it cannot claim a monopoly of scientific knowledge. This paper argues that presently designated professions are rapidly losing their control over their knowledge domain as a result of inroads from computerization, new occupations in the division of labor, and increasing public and client sophistication. As a result, their autonomy is challenged and demands for accountability and client rights are on the rise. The rhetoric or reality of service orientation has not stemmed the erosion of trust, or throttled the outcry for accountability to the consumer. The high prestige enjoyed by the old professions and yearned for by those striving for professional status has become an elusive prize, as a consequence not only of public challenges to knowledge monopoly and authority, but perhaps more importantly as an outcome of militant egalitarianism, whether it be a minority view, as in this country, or official doctrine, as in Eastern Europe.

The deprofessionalization of everyone, accordingly, would leave occupational incumbents without claims of mystery, authority, or deference. It does not, however, imply the utopian notion of the end of expertise. Elsewhere I have proposed a hypothesis that "The segments of the division of labor currently entitled 'professions' in the West are simply a range of occupations which require greater or lesser degrees of training and expertise, and in which clients, also with greater or lesser knowledge of the tasks the occupation performs, negotiate a course of action designed to accomplish some individually or socially desirable end. Factors affecting this negotiation are the bureaucratic structures in which the transactions occur, the ideological themes which place values on different transactional styles and outcomes, and the historical events and traditions which in various social and cultural settings have patterned practitioner and client beliefs and behaviors. The underlying model is one of expert and consumer, without moral and evaluative overtones of the professional model."[50]

In this sense Daniel Bell's "professionalized future" is faulty not because he has misread the fate of technology and expertise, but in the implication that expertise will carry with it the historical trappings of professionalism. The social compulsion to adhere to professional advice may give way to a new norm of critical evaluation of expert opinion in the light of personal concerns and knowledge. The deprofessionalization of everyone would usher in the age of the client as consumer, a consumer who is expected to question, compare, and treat all advice with a skeptical ear.

The varying implications of the expert and the professional role focus on the difference in the stance of the receiver of service vis-a-vis the provider of service. In the twenty-first century, now less than 25 years away, it seems very unlikely that nineteenth century patterns of obeisance, trust, and awe of superior knowledge will persist. But this is a hypothesis, not a prophecy. Like all hypotheses in social science, it can only be tested by history. We will have to check the findings 25 or 125 years from now.

REFERENCES

1. Harold Wilensky, "The Professionalization of Everyone?," *American Journal of Sociology* 70:137-158 (1974).

2. Ernest Greenwood, "Attributes of a Profession," *Social Work* 2:45-55 (July 1957).

3. William J. Goode, "The Theoretical Limits of Professionalization," in Amitai Etzioni, ed., *The Semi-Professions and Their Organizations* (New York: Free Pr., 1969), pp. 266-313.

4. Wilbert J. Moore, *The Professions: Roles and Rules* (New York: Russell Sage, 1970).

5. Eliot Freidson, "Professions and the Occupational Principle," in Eliot Friedson, ed., *Their Prospects* (Beverly Hills, Calif.: Sage Publications, 1971), pp. 19-38.

6. Marvin B. Susman, "Occupational Sociology and Rehabilitation," in Marvin B. Susman, ed., *Sociology and Rehabilitation* (Washington, D. C.: American Sociological Association and Vocational Rehabilitation Administration, 1965), pp. 179-222.

7. Freidson, "Professions and the Occupational Principle," pp. 19-38.

8. Howard S. Becker, "The Nature of a Profession," in *Sixty First Yearbook of the National Society for the Study of Education*, Part II (Chicago, 1962).

9. Julius A. Roth, "Professionalism: The Sociologist's Decoy," *Sociology of Work and Occupations* 1:6-23 (February 1974).

10. Philip Elliott, *The Sociology of Professions* (London: The Macmillan Press Ltd. 1972).

11. *Ibid.*

12. Stephen J. Kunitz, "Professionalism and Social Control in the Progressive Era: The Case of the Flexner Report," *Social Problems* 22:16-27 (1974).

13. Marc Maurice, "Propos sur la sociologie des professions," *Sociologie du Travail Treizieme Annee* 2/72:213-225 (Avril-Juin 1972).

14. Michel Crozier, *The World of the Office Worker* (Chicago: Univ. of Chicago Pr., 1971).

15. Gunther Bohring, "On the Role and Development of Profession in the Socialist Society," paper delivered at Working Group No. 6, Seventh World Congress of Sociology, Varna, Bulgaria, 1970.

16. M. N. Rutkevich, "Elimination of Class Differences and the Place of Non-manual Workers in the Social Structure of Soviet Society," as translated in *Soviet Sociology* 3:3-13 (Fall 1964).

17. Daniel Bell, "The Measurement of Knowledge and Technology," in Eleanor B. Sheldon and Wilbert E. Moore, eds., *Indicators of Social Change* (New York: Russell Sage, 1968).

18. *Ibid.*

19. Benjamin S. Kleinberg, *American Society in the Postindustrial Age: Technocracy, Power, and the End of Ideology* (Columbus, Ohio: Charles E. Merrill Publishing Co., 1973).

20. Paul Halmos, *The Personal Service Society* (New York: Schocken, 1970).

21. Arlene Kaplan Daniels, "Advisory and Coercive Functions in Psychiatry," *Sociology of Work and Occupations* 2:55-78 (February 1975).

22. Talcott Parsons, "Equality and Inequality in Modern Society, or Social Stratification Revisited," *Sociological Inquiry* 40:13-72 (Spring 1970).

23. Ruth and Victor W. Sidel, "The Human Services in China," *Social Policy* 2:25-34 (March/April 1972).

24. Fred Strassburger, "Problems Surrounding 'Informed Voluntary Consent' and Patient Access to Records," *Sandoz Psychiatric Spectator* 9:10-11 (March 1975).

25. George J. Annas, *The Rights of Hospital Patients: The Basic ACLU Guide to a Hospital Patient's Rights* (New York: Avon Books, 1975).

26. W. B. Schwartz, "Medicine and the Computer: The Promise and Problems of Change," *New England Journal of Medicine* 283:1257-64 (3 December 1970); and Ray M. and Mary Ann Antley, "Automation: Its Impact on the Delivery of Health Care," *Computers and Automation* 22:11-14 (April 1973).

27. Eliot Freidson, *Professional Dominance* (New York: Atherton Pr., 1970).

28. Jane Cassells Record and Merwyn R. Greenlock, "New Health Professionals at Kaiser: Role Ambiguity and Social Distance," paper presented at the American Sociological Association Meetings, New York, 1973.

29. Leo G. Reeder, "The Patient-client as Consumer: Some Observations on the Changing Professional-client Relationship," *Journal of Health and Human Behavior* 13:406-412 (1972).

30. Marie R. Haug and Marvin B. Susman, "Professional Autonomy and the Revolt of the Client," *Social Problems* 17:153-161 (Fall 1969).

31. Arthur Pearl and Frank Reissman, *New Careers for the Poor* (New York: Free Pr., 1965).

32. U. S. Department of Health, Education, and Welfare, *Report of the Secretary's Commission on Medical Malpractice* (Washington, D. C.: Govt. Print. Off., 1973).

33. Renee C. Fox, "Ethical and Existential Developments in Contemporaneous American Medicine: Their Implications for Culture and Society," *Milbank Memorial Fund Quarterly* 52:445-483 (Fall 1974).

34. Rudolf Klein, *Complaints Against Doctors* (London: Charles Knight and Co., 1973).

35. Ira Shor, "Education to the People: Higher Education in China," *Social Policy* 5:30-37 (November/December 1974).

36. Geoffrey Gibson, "Chinese Medical Practice and the Thoughts of Chairman Mao," paper presented to the Medical Sociology Section of the American Sociological Association Meetings, Washington, D. C., 1970.

37. Marie R. Haug, "The Erosion of Professional Autonomy: A Cross-cultural Inquiry on the Case of Medicine," paper presented at the American Sociological Association Meetings, Montreal, 1974.

38. Terence J. Johnson, *Professions and Power* (London: The Macmillan Press Ltd., 1972).

39. Becker, "The Nature of a Profession."

40. Elihu Katz et al, "Doctor-patient Exchanges: A Diagnostic Approach to Organizations and Professions," *Human Relations* 22:309-324 (August 1969); Michael Balint, *The Doctor, His Patient, and the Illness* (New York: International Universities Press, 1957); and Anselm Strauss et al, "The Hospital and its Negotiated Order," in Eliot Freidson, ed., *The Hospital in Modern Society* (New York: 1963).

41. Great Britain, Department of Health and Social Security, Management Study, *Steering Committee Management Arrangements for the Reorganized National Health Service* (London: Her Majesty's Stationery Office, 1972).

42. Fraser Kent, "Statewide Computer Bank Urged: MD Review of Changes Outlined," *Cleveland Plain Dealer*, July 28, 1971.

43. Alan Gartner and Frank Riessman, *The Service Society and the Consumer Vanguard* (New York: Harper, 1974).

44. Victor W. Sidel, "The Health Workers of the Fengsheng Neighborhood of Peking," *American Journal of Orthopsychiatry* 43:737-43 (October 1973).

45. Gartner and Riessman, *The Service Society and the Consumer Vanguard.*

46. Howard R. Swearer, "In Contemporary China," *The Key Reporter* 20:3 (Winter 1974-5).

47. V. N. Shubkin et al, "Quantitative Methods in Sociological Studies of Problems of Job Placement and Choice of Occupation," *Soviet Sociology* 7:3-24 (Summer 1968).

48. Mark Field, "Taming a Profession: Early Phases of Soviet Socialized Medicine," *Bulletin of the New York Academy of Medicine* 48:33-92 (January 1972).

49. Ralph Crawshaw, "Medical Deontology in the Soviet Union," *Archives of Internal Medicine* 134:592-594 (September 1974).

50. Haug, "The Erosion of Professional Autonomy."

The Licensing of Paraprofessionals

by Ivar Berg

The issues involved in licensing educational paraprofessionals are, in most instances, parallel to licensing issues in almost any occupation. The arguments of those who endorse occupational licensing reveal two sets of agendas. The first, which is typically made quite explicit, focuses on the alleged need to assure the public that the practitioner-members of an occupation are capable of maintaining the high standards of performance contemplated in well and conscientiously conceived licensing requirements.

The second, more "hidden" agenda, focuses on the economic utility of licensing arrangements that protect the work and therefore the income opportunities of those licensed and on the utility both to those licensed, and to practitioners of adjacent occupations as well, of a division of labor that restricts interoccupational movement while it enhances jurisdictional independence in the relationships among members of allied occupations. In the case of hidden agendas, the incumbents of some licensed occupations enjoy a kind of pseudo-occupational mobility into a sheltered or protected class, while the adjacent occupations' licensed incumbents are legally protected from what might otherwise be competent competitors.

My first purpose in this paper is to examine some of the complexities that are ignored in the explicit agenda of licensing advocates, an agenda in which the avowed focus is on the public's interests in "meritocratic" standards of entry to key occupations. My second objective is to examine some of the simplifications in the hidden agenda, in which the structure of our nation's employment opportunities is exploited in self-serving ways by these same advocates.

The assumptions that undergird this discussion are best identified at the outset. Thus, no discussion of licensing may sensibly overlook the fact that the matter of job requirements now involves a number of substantial *legal* questions pertaining to meritocratic standards. While technical questions about validity and reliability, in regard to job requirements in education, have always fascinated psychometricians, teacher trainees, educational examiners, and other involved parties, the focus of discussion has shifted from the laboratory and classroom, in which friendly antagonists debated the merits of screening requirements in the abstract, to the courtroom where a variety of interests are balanced off as matters of law and public policy.

At the same time that lawyers and judges have been accorded strategic roles in the occupational screening process (and closely related to that development), we have witnessed growing public concern over questions of equity in the allocation of jobs among an "excess" of applicants armed with traditionally valuable occupational credentials. Obviously, the present conditions of the American economy have considerably aggravated this public concern; future economic prospects will change these conditions only in marginal ways. Accordingly, no discussion of licensing can overlook these facts.

Thus, it is of fundamental significance that the number of routes to occupational success is larger when the economy is enjoying high levels of growth and high levels of employment than when it is enduring the constraints of secular and cyclical "adjustments." It ill-behooves educators who man the sluice gates that control manpower flows to exact illegitimate tolls of those who seek to pass through these gates. Yet it is precisely when "times are bad," as they clearly are today, that most of us in a position to do so begin to erect entry barriers to the positions in and around our occupations. And it is during such times that an occupation's clientele, no less than those who aspire to membership in it, will examine entry requirements with more critical eyes. Their understandable concern is that certification, licensing, and other job requirements have only little to do with the quality of performance, and much more to do with the effort of sundry occupational practitioners to shelter themselves from the chill winds of the marketplace. But the logic of the underlying assumptions is best constructed in the process of examining the visible and the hidden agendas of licensing, rather than in this brief, preliminary introduction.

THE VISIBLE AGENDA: THE PUBLIC'S INTERESTS

Let us allow that the work of many employed Americans is "affected by the public interest." Indeed, public regulation of a host of economic activities is made legitimate by exactly that principle: We fear to leave a large number of activities to the interactions of consumers and suppliers out of fears that even a competitive market would fail to assure acceptable standards of performance.

Few will contest the reality of such fears; even the most devoted free enterprisers among the ranks of neo-classical economists would wish that their loved ones receive medical treatments by duly licensed physicians. Similarly, the doings of dentists, apothecaries, lawyers—and teachers—have long, and virtually uncontestably, been held to be affected by the public's interest in quality, judgment, taste and, not least, in the adequacy of the practitioners' preparations for their callings.

While we might have *some* interests in a police officer's accuracy with his or her firearms, we have *highly developed* interests in his or her demonstrated familiarity with citizens' rights. And we clearly have an interest in the implications for safety of allowing unlicensed drivers of heavy trucks to move their ladings on busy, high speed turnpikes. So far, so good; no one doubts all that. The difficulties begin, as all can plainly recognize, when we move from sensible assertion to programmatic efforts to *specify performance criteria* and to *evaluate performance* in many areas in which licensing is routine.

A moment's reflection will persuade the reader that it is extraordinarily difficult to validate the criteria and standards applicable to most employments. Doubters may wish to peruse the details of testimony offered up in a randomly selected pair of medical malpractice cases in the jurisdictions in which they reside—a suggestion that is made, as the lawyers put it, "without prejudice" against the overriding majority of exceedingly well-intentioned physicians and surgeons in the nation. The fact of the matter is that many (though not all) malpractice cases have merit precisely because medical and surgical *performance* standards *are* problematical.

In this context, I might mention the results of a fairly extensive investigation published in 1970. The results showed that employers, even in instances in which performance data are collected, rarely seek to validate the performance criteria any more than they do the screening requirements with which they might usefully be juxtaposed. Even less often do employers seek to validate the kinds of experiences, educational or otherwise, that are typically taken to be potent predictors of valued performance profiles.

In this study we[1] examined the relationships between educational achievements, which are oft-used criteria in the selection, placement, and promotion of personnel. For a variety of occupations ranging from those of the upper reaches of the heavy electrical equipment industry (scientists and engineers), to unskilled and semi-skilled workers in the mills of two Mississippi textile corporations, we examined the relationships between educational achievement and performance on the job. We observed, in these data, almost no relationships at all, in occupations across the range that fits between these two occupational clusters, that could lead us confidently to use educational credentials as a prospectful indicator of potential performance.

This is not to suggest that there is anything wrong with education: the ultimate relevance of education for the well-being of individuals, their employers, or for that matter, for the well-being of the Republic need not be questioned. But the data do raise questions about the capacity we have, in a large number of occupations, for measuring performance. Nothing argues that we should give up our faith in education; we should be careful, however, that our faith in education as an object of both production and consumption aims is not confused with our faith in the devices used for examining performance and the validity of performance measures we can garner to meet the needs of employers or clients.

We need not dwell on the subtleties of the research except to say that the results are probably explicable by references to certain complicating facts. In occupational settings, individual efforts draw on the contribution of groups; individuals also draw on the contributions of sundry technical devices that facilitate the performance of those who bring diverse backgrounds to their work; and finally other factors, such as the quality and expertise of management and the intelligence of the client groups also operate on the individual performance.

In a parallel study, my colleague, Dr. Marcia K. Freedman of the Columbia University Conservation of Human Resources Project,[2] discovered similar patterns relating to the structure of occupations within an organization. She found, in assessments of five different occupational settings, that "nominal" occupational ladders are developed by employers and employees partly in response to the need to differentiate the positions of personnel of different seniority levels who earn differential incomes. These ladders do not reflect skill and related economically significant differences as much as they do simple desires to legitimize distinctions that are too finely drawn to stand up under rigorous examinations of skill differences.

These research findings are relevant to the present discussion because they point to the difficulties in identifying the precise skill requirements that apply to an occupational position or to a hierarchy of occupational positions. One does not need to be a critic of education to argue that it is probably no easier to identify performance standards for teachers than it is to identify performance standards for engineers and scientists. Thus, we are aware, and many of us have been arguing, that it is pointless to use pupil reading scores as a criterion of teacher effectiveness. Most readers will recognize, and may have argued, that young people are characterized by a series of traits and characteristics which facilitate learning in some instances and not in others.

Paralleling the studies mentioned is a Supreme Court decision that borrowed from their logic and results, and which bears even more significantly than research results on the question of whether performance on the job can be acceptably measured. Thus, in the case of Griggs v. Duke Power Company, decided in 1971, the Supreme Court held (by an eight-to-nothing vote) that it is illegal to elevate job requirements, in the form of test scores or educational achievements, that are not specifically and concretely related to job performance. The Court's holding in the Griggs case emphasizes the *consequence* that screening requirements may lead to the (statistical) "underrepresentation" from what the law now refers to as protected groups in our society. This consequence, in the Court's eyes, is more important than the *intentions*, even the best intentions, of those who develop and apply screening and credentialing measurements. Where the results in my study raised questions about the *rationality* of employer uses of tests and educational requirements, the Court redefined the issue as one of *equity, fairness,* and *justice*. It will not surprise some competent legal authorities to learn that a candidate for a regular teaching position who has been denied a teaching certificate for lack of an undergraduate degree or its equivalent has brought suit. When such a case comes before the courts, it will be interesting to see whether the judiciary will uphold the use of an undergraduate degree as a screening requirement in the absence of any concrete evidence that teachers without such degrees perform at lower levels of proficiency than those who do have such undergraduate degrees.

Major legal developments have accordingly reinforced widespread popular misgivings about the questionable character of occupational requirements. These developments are substantially subversive of arguments by well-intentioned defenders of performance standards as bulwarks protecting meritocracy in labor markets.

The simple but essential point is that we cannot disassociate our concerns regarding standards from the realities of the marketplace and the imperatives of legal developments. Both legal and economic developments underscore suspicions about the effects of licensing and credentialing requirements.

THE HIDDEN AGENDA

Turning now to the hidden agenda, we discover a set of concerns parallel to those involved in the visible agenda. Thus, in the invisible agenda we may list the concerns of the members of different occupational groups for their intra- and intermural protection from competition and from the "encroachments" of "outside interests."[3]

We might consider some of the reasons why these job concerns are paramount and help to explain efforts to require that jobs be licensed. Quite clearly, protectionist and exclusionary motives, as well as principled motives having to do with standards, are operative. We know, for example, that unemployment has been mounting in recent months; that enrollments in school are declining; that the age distribution of teachers finds us with a large concentration of teachers in the younger age cohorts; and that there are problems concerning the division of labor among the members of the work forces in educational settings.

In quest of information relevant to this paper, I was informed, by a Teachers College staff member that paraprofessionals have tended to become the instructors of so-called "problem" children. Paradoxically, such teaching is becoming an area of specialization and the preparation of people to work in this area is supposed to facilitate the work of "regular" teachers who work with less difficult children. We may also be mindful of the interests of teacher-training institutions which will have their own hidden agenda in troubled economic times. *Paraprofessional* aspirants, could take, after all, the vacant places of *teacher* candidates at a time when job opportunities for teachers reduce teacher candidate enrollments.

Finally, there is a concern on the part of the parents of many children that our educational personnel be used in more flexible ways in the interests of improving and enhancing the learning experiences of their children. Such a public interest would allegedly be served by the more extended use of adult community members whose understanding of the subcultures of children in heterogeneous urban centers could be mobilized for educational purposes. While such community concerns do little to enhance the pride of teachers, they constitute a serious attack on their occupational security.

In fine, we can list the pros and cons of licensing, keeping in mind the distinction between the visible and the invisible agenda. The latter agenda relates to job security, job shelters, and job protection. To the extent that the *hidden* agenda reflects a genuine and deep-seated concern about job security, the public will inevitably have its doubts as to the real basis for the alleged concern for meritocratic *standards* expressed in the visible agenda.

In connection with licensing and certification arrangements, we ought to be concerned about the implications of the growing extension of state laws to a variety of enterprises, including the education enterprise. In a most intriguing article, Reich[4] has developed a theory of occupational licensing as a kind of "property creation," by government largess. The difficulty is that government largess of this type involves employees, managers, and clients (both pupils and their parents) in a dependency relationship with those who are charged with responsibility for the conduct of licensing, certification examinations, and screening procedures.

At the same time, the mobility for paraprofessionals presumably assured by licensing arrangements may be a kind of pseudomobility. These arrangements will ultimately involve paraprofessionals, teachers, teachers' unions, and educational managers in mounting concerns about the possibility of shifting standards and the difficulties of determining, from one jurisdiction to another, who the credentialing agents should be, how they should be chosen, and the standards and research findings that should inform *their* decisions. These questions *always* develop where wealth is created, and let us not forget that when we introduce certification procedures that block the entrances of some to an occupation, we create a form of wealth.

The crucial question to be addressed is how much do we really want further involvements of the state in what amounts to *regulatory* procedures. The history of regulatory procedures in many jurisdictions and on many issues, both nationally and statewide, suggests that regulation generates at least as many problems as it solves.

There is, of course, a partial alternative to the increasing involvement of public agencies in the day-to-day, week-to-week, month-to-month, and year-to-year comings and goings of the parties to a working relationship between professionals and their employers. Thus, we may strive to settle as many problems as we can through *bargaining* and thus to reduce, rather than to increase, the scope of problematic regulation. Regulation too often involves the systematic displacement of concerns from those most capably and intimately involved in the issues, and therefore most competent to resolve them, in favor of a delegation of these issues to public agencies to resolve. Note that it is difficult to read a newspaper these days without running into the extraordinary difficulties that have resulted from the fact that we have enshrined, in legally binding *contracts*, arrangements such as seniority clauses which now must be juxtaposed with legal requirements regarding equal opportunity. The result is a nightmarish mixture of court decisions, some of which support seniority arrangements and others which support equal opportunity arrangements. The upshot is that judges, rather than the parties involved in a day-to-day occupational relationship, are ultimately making decisions affecting the well-being of bargaining units and individuals, the well-being of clients and the work process, and the interests of concerned parties and much more, in those instances in which the parties to a labor agreement fail to bargain in inventive ways over the seniority-equal opportunity question.

We might well join Archibald Cox, who years ago wrote a marvelous piece entitled "Danger: Judges at Work" in the *Harvard Law Review,* regarding the need to uphold arbitrators' awards. When we fail to bargain ourselves a set of occupational arrangements that have built into them the kinds of flexibilities that bargaining over multiple issues almost certainly assures, we become beholden to a state licensing or other regulatory apparatus and the judges who are obligated to adjust disagreements about enforcement. One may compare the advantages to the parties and to society of a "50–50 chance," in a law case, with the bargaining situation in which the parties can avoid a so-called "zero-sum game" and in which context it is possible to work out arrangements that will avoid, for example, freezing the jurisdictional claims of teachers and other educational personnel.

In New York City such arrangements, in fact, have developed. Thus, paraprofessionals can move from the paraprofessional category, after achieving additional educational and related types of experiences, into the teaching ranks, and one might wish to applaud such flexible results of thoughtful bargaining.

One might also wish to recognize, however, that the unemployed younger alumni of teacher-training programs are not likely to continue to look with equanimity on arrangements whereby the jobs for which they prepare themselves are being "coopted" by those who enter the educational apparatus as paraprofessionals while teachers were attending college in order to earn certificates. The problems attending the division of educational labors are complicated enough without adding the rigidities that, in some jurisdictions, are almost certain to develop in connection with the extension of licensing procedures. One may have great confidence that in many jurisdictions the hidden agenda will lead to immobilizing arrangements, despite the fact that, in New York, the United Federation of Teachers, the licensing agencies, and presumably state legislators have been persuaded to do all this in a reasonable and sensible way.

CONCLUSION

To the degree to which the orders of flexibility that occur within the educational enterprise are protected, to that extent faith is kept with those "outside" who view licensing skeptically. There is a need for unions, whether they be AFT or NEA, and for education managers to keep such faith with clients by avoiding the development of any certification and licensing agreements that are problematic with respect to performance measures on the one side, and with respect to needed flexibility in the utilization of educational personnel on the other. The facts that there are inherent and intractable difficulties in assuring clients about the role of "competence" and the needs for one or another kind of background experience as requirements for appointments argue tellingly for the caution urged in this analysis.

It will occur to some that it is possible to use "second" and "third order" performance criteria. It will be suggested, as it was at the outset, for example, that while it may not be necessary to screen every policeman in respect of how straight he shoots his gun, it may be important to appoint policemen who are knowledgeable in the laws pertaining to civil rights. By analogy, one might argue, we in fact can measure the capability and the competency of teachers on *broad* issues, such as their knowledge of subject matter, as contrasted with their capacity to impart knowledge. I would argue that this is a necessary condition for conscientious licensing procedure, but, in the face of the decision in Griggs v. Duke Power, it may well *not* be a sufficient legal rationale!

One may fondly hope, however, that bargaining procedures can be developed that will assure the safeguarding of meritocratic standards, on the one side, and flexibilities and options, on the other, that avoid both legal problems and community reactions stemming from rigid requirements that cannot be clearly related to performance.

In conclusion, let me say that I am relatively sanguine about the problems outlined in this discussion. It seems to me that the economy is so messy and damnable, in many respects depending on your ideology, that it supports very little effort, right now, to secure the interests identified in the hidden agenda as I have described it. Our "social contract" in the United States is clearly "up for grabs." This social contract is fragile enough in good times; it is even more vulnerable during troubled economic times. It would be difficult to view with equanimity any kinds of licensing procedures that further pit groups against each other, as licensing and certification arrangements predictably will.

Next, I am sanguine that we will avoid many of these problems over the longer haul because of the changes in legal arrangements that compel performance justifications for the application of standards in many occupations, including occupations in the educational sector. Furthermore, declining enrollments will create significant difficulties for anyone who would move in the direction of additional licensing arrangements. Thus, it would surprise me if declining enrollments did not lead school boards to be supersensitive to the costs of adding supernumerary personnel to the classroom. On the other hand, it would surprise me to discover that declining enrollments did not lead to a recognition among younger teachers, particularly young unemployed teachers, that the sharing of classroom responsibilities with paraprofessionals would simply reduce by some margin the access they would have to teaching-level jobs. The declining average age of teachers, both employed and unemployed, who will be concerned about the degree to which their colleges are involved in training paraprofessional competitors, must also be considered among the factors weighing against more licensing.

In short, one may readily identify forces which will have the effect of constraining easy opportunities for teachers to segregate themselves from paraprofessionals against whose economic encroachments licensing and credentialing procedures might be useful. These constraints will also act on paraprofessionals who seek to protect *their* accesses, either to paraprofessional jobs or to opportunities to move up from paraprofessional to teaching roles, from constraints that guarantee only pseudomobility of the type discussed earlier.

By way of summary, the forces in favor of licensing will be slowed down to the extent that licensing: (1) subverts whatever goodwill educational professionals and their representative agencies already enjoy with the public by emphasis on "ritual" requirements and irrelevant performance criteria; (2) "bureaucratizes" and further "legalizes" the educational system by creating more dependency on state agencies and what Reich called their largess; (3) raises more questions about performance than are already asked in a world in which performance measures are becoming increasingly the subject of client interest and legal review; (4) adds to the number or intensity of battles along the jurisdictional lines within the educational apparatus; (5) creates, out of good intentions at one point in time, nominal and pseudoskill hierarchies rather than real skill hierarchies over a larger time period; and (6) reinforces the "sellers' market" in teacher training by giving teacher-training institutions new paraprofessional student client populations, thereby reducing incentives to improve the quality of teacher training.

REFERENCES

1. Ivar Berg, *Education and Jobs: The Great Training Robbery* (New York: Praeger, 1970).
2. M. K. Freedman, *Good Jobs and Bad Jobs: The Search for Shelters* (New York: Columbia Univ. Conservation of Human Resources Project, forthcoming).
3. An MIT scholar has developed a very interesting line of analysis of this agenda, in a recent issue of *Public Interest* (L. Thurow, "Toward a definition of economic justice," *Public Interest* 31:56–80 [Spring 1973]), that parallels one developed by my colleague Dr. Freedman to the effect that members of the American labor force are as much engaged in job competition as they are engaged in wage competition.
4. C. A. Reich, "The new property," *Yale Law Journal* 73:5 (April 1964).

ACKNOWLEDGEMENT

"The Licensing of Paraprofessionals: The 'Visible and Hidden Agendas,'" by Ivar Berg is reprinted from *Education and Urban Society* Vol. VIII, No. 1 (November 1975) pp. 104–118 by permission of the Publisher, Sage Publications, Inc.

Professional Employees
Turn to Unions

by Dennis Chamot

In March 1975, the nation witnessed a relatively minor, but rather dramatic event. More than 2,000 doctors in New York City went on strike for four days. In the best tradition of more conventional trade unionists, they walked picket lines and demanded improvements in pay, hours, and working conditions. It should be noted that this was an honest-to-goodness labor dispute and not the increasingly common but, in union terms, less significant protest of malpractice insurance problems by established doctors.

This action (and similar, more recent ones in Washington, D. C., Chicago, and Los Angeles) caught many people by surprise. After all, who needs a union less than a doctor? When put in proper perspective, however, these developments are neither strange nor unexpected, and they have important implications far beyond the medical community.

In fact, the men and women who participated in these strikes, and the many more doctors who are currently in unions, are not the highly paid, independent practitioners one usually thinks of. They are, instead, hospital interns and residents, *employees* of large bureaucratic organizations. Thus the similarities between them and other employed professionals are far greater than the more obvious differences.

There are currently almost 3 million members of unions and employee associations who are classified as professional and technical.[1] They include public schoolteachers, college professors, musicians, actors, journalists, engineers, nurses, and doctors, among others.

The American work force as a whole is changing. "White collar" now describes one half of all working people, and this figure has been increasing steadily (see *Exhibit I*). The fastest-growing segment, professional and technical employees, currently accounts for one seventh of the total work force, and is expected to increase to one sixth within ten years (see *Exhibit II*). Paralleling these changes has been the upsurge in white-collar union membership, which, in the past decade and a half, increased by over 1 million (to 3.8 million), and now accounts for 17.4% of all union membership; another 2 million employees are in state and professional associations that engage in collective bargaining (see *Exhibit III*).

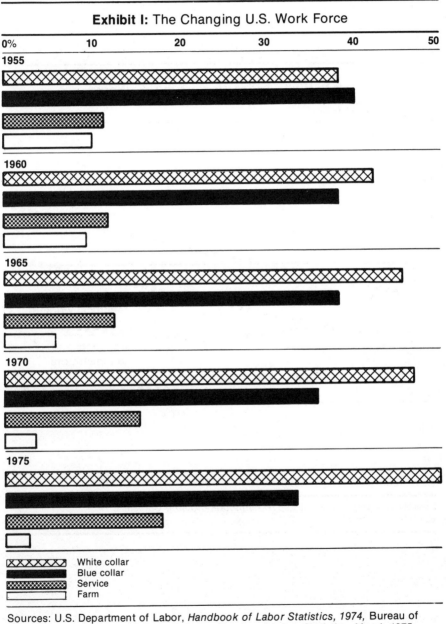

Exhibit I: The Changing U.S. Work Force

Sources: U.S. Department of Labor, *Handbook of Labor Statistics, 1974,* Bureau of Labor Statistics, 1974, and Press Release, Bureau of Labor Statistics, March 1975.

Exhibit II: White-Collar Workers in U.S. Work Force

Percent of work force

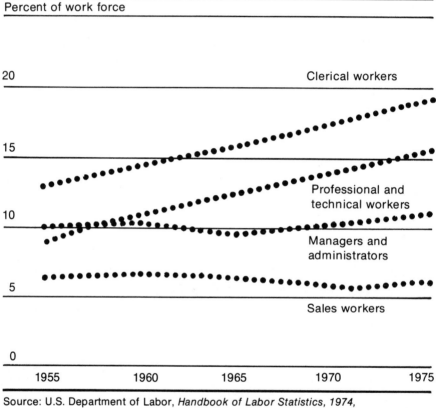

20   Clerical workers

15

10

Professional and
technical workers

Managers and
administrators

5

Sales workers

0

| 1955 | 1960 | 1965 | 1970 | 1975 |

Source: U.S. Department of Labor, *Handbook of Labor Statistics, 1974,*
Bureau of Labor Statistics, 1974

EXHIBIT III
UNION MEMBERSHIP GROWTH (RELATIVE TO 1963)

Year	AFT	AFSCME	AFGE	CWA	SEIU	UAW	Teamsters	Carpenters
1963	1.00	1.00	1.00	1.00	1.00	1.00	1.00	1.00
1965	1.41	1.07	1.31	1.05	1.09	1.09	1.03	1.03
1967	1.76	1.28	1.88	1.15	1.18	1.31	1.13	1.08
1969	2.33	1.66	2.78	1.28	1.32	1.37	1.20	1.07
1971	2.90	2.02	3.07	1.51	1.48	1.38	1.26	1.11
1973	3.51	2.40	2.76	1.59	1.64	1.30	1.27	1.11
1973	249	529	293	443	484	1,394	1,855	820

(by thousands)

AFT: American Federation of Teachers
AFSCME: American Federation of State, County and Municipal Employees
AFGE: American Federation of Government Employees
CWA: Communications Workers of America
SEIU: Service Employees' International Union
UAW: United Automobile, Aerospace, and Agricultural Implement Workers of America
Teamsters: International Brotherhood of Teamsters, Chauffeurs, Warehousemen, and
  Helpers of America
Carpenters: United Brotherhood of Carpenters and Joiners of America

Source: U.S. Department of Labor, *Directory of National Unions and Employee Associations*, Bureau of Labor Statistics, 1963–1973.

WHITE-COLLAR UNION GROWTH

Several white-collar unions have experienced spectacular growth over the past few years, with much of the increase occurring in the public sector. For example, by mid-1975, the American Federation of Teachers (AFT) claimed 450,000 members, 4½ times its 1963 membership. Furthermore, 1 in 10 AFT members is on a college faculty. If the professors belonging to other unions are added, it appears that 20% of the American professoriat, on over 420 campuses, have been organized—virtually all within the past decade.

Similarly, the American Federation of State, County, and Municipal Employees (AFSCME) and the American Federation of Government Employees (AFGE) each tripled its membership between 1963 and 1975. It should be noted that many unions represent for collective bargaining purposes more people than are indicated by membership figures, e.g., AFGE has about 325,000 members but represents over 600,000 federal employees.

By contrast, the United Brotherhood of Carpenters and Joiners' membership expanded by only 11% in the decade 1963-1973. Both the Autoworkers (UAW) and Teamsters, mostly blue-collar unions that are trying to increase white-collar membership, did only slightly better (about 30%, although from a larger base).

Growth is not the only measure of success when one is dealing with a finite system. Organization is proceeding slowly in some areas because most eligible workers in these fields are already in unions. This is true, for example, in the performing arts, where union membership is the accepted norm among professional and supporting personnel.

Historically, unions have been most successful among blue-collar workers. Why the rapid and sustained increase in white-collar interest? In the public sector, at least, the situation was helped by changes in the appropriate laws. The Wagner Act, passed in 1935, applied only to workers in the private sector. However, under President Kennedy's Executive Order 10988 in 1962, followed by new laws in state after state during the 1960s, collective bargaining rights were granted to government employees. Many were quick to use them.

This is only a part of the answer, however, since the laws could not have been changed if there had not been a good deal of pressure already for the changes. Furthermore, union interest has increased in the private sector, too, and here the legal framework has been available for decades, permitting, if not mandating, organization.

At the heart of the matter is the nature of modern employment, which is likely to consist of very routine, nonchallenging jobs. Here the problem for nonprofessional white-collar employees is in many ways identical to that of their blue-collar colleagues. It is only natural, then, that they should choose similar means to solve those problems. As the white-collar work force rapidly expands, union successes continue apace.

SPECIAL PROBLEMS OF PROFESSIONALS

The large number of professional employees presents a more complex situation. Although it is beyond the scope of this article to examine in detail individual professions or industries (which differ from group to group even within the same profession), several important generalizations may be drawn.

It might be useful at this point to note that the word *professional* has two rather different connotations. The first emphasizes the external, economic aspect of the job. A person is a professional because he or she is paid for services rendered. This is one of the differences between Arnold Palmer and a weekend golfer. It is this definition I use in discussing problems with salaries, termination policies, and the like.

The complementary definition involves an internal, psychological view. The professional sees himself as a member of a special group to which admission is gained only after advanced or specialized study. He seeks recognition among his peers and takes great pride in the knowledge he has acquired and the opportunity to use it.

One of the big differences between professional employees and all other nonmanagement workers is that the professional expects that he will have a major role to play in deciding how to perform his job. Unlike a production worker or a secretary, the professional expects to help determine the problems he will work on and the approaches toward their solution. All too often, his expectations fall far short of reality. Dissatisfaction may result from inadequate technical support, insufficient opportunity to pursue interesting ideas, excessive interference by superiors, lack of sufficient input to project assignment decisions, and so on. Whether or not there are overriding economic considerations behind these decisions, the professional employee frequently feels he is not treated with the respect he deserves.

Back in the "good old days," the individual professional enjoyed a one-to-one relationship with his client. He experienced a great deal of autonomy both in making decisions and in determining work assignments and conditions. Further, he had sufficient control to effectively determine adequate compensation.

The professional-client relationship today has been radically altered. Today's professionals are no longer self-employed, independent practitioners, but are instead employees of ever-larger organizations. No matter what the nature of the employing institution—corporation, university, or government agency—few individuals within it feel they have sufficient personal bargaining power to effectively control their careers or their jobs.

The problem is that we are dealing with two very different viewpoints. As Archie Kleingartner of the University of California at Los Angeles put it some years ago in a discussion of industrial engineers, "Management equates professionalism with loyalty to management, and perceives unions as threatening the loyalty of engineers. Any engineer who joins a union is perceived as disloyal, and by extension as behaving unprofessionally. [However,] management opposition to engineer unionism reflects purely managerial interests more than a concern for high professional standards. I would guess that management opposition would be just as strong if professional societies attempted to bargain."[2]

Authority and Decision Making

Discussion with representatives of several unions that are active in organizing professionals confirms that dissatisfaction with policies relating to authority and decision making is a major issue. For example, at most campuses where faculties have unionized in recent years, the primary concerns were job security and the somewhat related but much broader subject of university governance. Colleges and universities are moving away from the old system of collegiality and are increasingly employing full-time administrators who exercise considerable authority. Attempts to impose business practices (e.g., measurement of faculty "productivity") by people who are perceived, at least, as having insufficient teaching experience, threaten established notions of professional responsibilities, duties, and prerogatives. Unionization is looked on as a way for a faculty to improve its bargaining position with an administration that has grown too powerful in areas that have been traditionally the domain of the educators.

Current union contracts have provisions safeguarding these areas:

- The contract between the Southeastern Massachusetts University Faculty Federation (AFT Local 1895) and the university trustees states:

"The faculty shall have the responsibility to determine course content and texts."

- A recent contract between the faculty union (AFT Local 1600) and trustees of Cook County Community College, District No. 508, has sections limiting class size and teaching loads.
- The Rhode Island College Chapter of the AFT apparently felt that more basic problems existed, because the contract it negotiated in 1972 with the Rhode Island Board of Regents declared: "Each full-time faculty member shall be assigned office space."

In these, and in many other cases, the faculty felt it needed a union to secure rights in areas that are at the heart of its ability to properly perform its professional duties.

Salary and Work Schedules

Where unions have been active in organizing employees of hospitals and other health care facilities, it has been found that issues involving quality of patient care (e.g., the number of doctors in clinics or emergency rooms, the improvement of nursing and technician staffs, the improvement of X-ray services, the availability of physical therapists, and so on) are of great concern at all professional levels. Salary is the other major issue, although this is far less important at the higher pay levels. Nurses, for example, are much more interested in salary improvement than the better paid pharmacists, but both groups seek greater impact on institutional decision making.

In many cases, concerns overlap: interns demanding shorter schedules will work fewer hours, but they will also provide better care if they get proper sleep; professors fighting enlargement of classes (or elimination of some) are protecting their jobs, but they are also vitally concerned with the effects of proposed changes on the quality of education.

In the federal sector, salary cannot be an issue because the unions are forbidden by law to bargain over congressionally set pay levels. In 1973, NASA engineers at Huntsville, Alabama joined the International Federation of Professional and Technical Engineers (AFL-CIO). A key issue in the campaign was employee disgruntlement over an extremely complex and rigid organizational structure, which they felt would be changed by a union. One might note that, even before they organized, these engineers were earning an average salary of about $20,000 a year. Engineers in federal, state, and municipal agencies have turned to unions in large part because of a strong desire to have greater impact on managerial decisions.[3]

Although the general concerns noted here seem to be fairly universal, the details of every organizing campaign or bargaining session are different. We are, after all, dealing with groups of *employees,* and, professional or not, they worry about wages, hours, and working conditions.

Furthermore, since professional employees are only human, they do not like to be taken advantage of. For example, they are exempt from the maximum hours provisions of the Fair Labor Standards Act. In other words, they are entitled to work overtime for free. As Robert Stedfeld, editor of the magazine *Machine Design,* wrote a few years ago, "Some companies have discovered a new cost-cutting gimmick—force engineers to work overtime without pay. The company saves money. Engineers can be laid off, and the regular work load is imposed on the remaining engineers. The engineers being unfairly exploited are afraid they will lose their jobs if they protest, so they take it."[4]

This situation is still fairly widespread, especially in R & D. Hours are set for the nonexempt clerical and support staff, but the professional employees —scientists, engineers, computer people, and the like—are expected to begin work at least as early as the secretaries and feel a great deal of indirect pressure to stay quite a bit later each day than the official quitting time. The worst offenders are those employers who offer services to others. Here, the pressures can be quite intense as contract proposal or termination deadlines approach.

It should be noted that these pressures are applied to all members of the professional staff, not just to those who are eager to get ahead. Some companies formalize the system by offering compensatory time off, but this is not the norm. Even where this option does exist, it is often abused. For example, one plant has some restrictions on how the compensatory time is taken, limiting it to days approved by the supervisor, and to no more than one day at a time. The rules may be bent a bit, but, in fact, a large part of the overtime put in by those engineers is never paid for in any way.

A recent study of overtime trends by the U. S. Bureau of Labor Statistics shows that nearly a quarter of all professional and technical employees regularly work more than 40 hours a week, but only 18% are paid for overtime.[5] Furthermore, one half of all workers on extended workweeks are white collar, and this number has continually increased, even though over-time for blue-collar workers has fluctuated with changes in general economic conditions.

The reader, especially one in a managerial or executive position, may see nothing wrong with this. The point, though, is that affected employees do. They do not like being required to work overtime routinely. This is particularly true when nonexempt assistants draw premium pay while their professional colleagues get only titles.

Grievance Procedures

Another serious problem for the employed nonunion professional is the lack of a realistic grievance procedure. If problems arise, as they invariably do, he is encouraged to complain to his immediate supervisor or perhaps to the personnel department.

Both the supervisor and the personnel people are representatives of the employer; further, their future careers and rewards are in the hands of that same employer. Should the disagreement between the professional and the employer be a serious one that cannot be easily resolved without cost to the company (either in dollars or in "managerial prerogative"), then the employee probably will not get satisfaction through the only channels open to him. His only choice is to accept the unilateral decision of the employer or resign. In neither case is the employee able to demonstrate sufficient professional status to influence the outcome. This can be very discouraging.

It should be emphasized that lists of specific grievances are not as important as are the deficiencies of the system for dealing with them. To be sure, the complaint may be very serious to the individual involved (e.g., dismissal, involuntary transfer, insufficient salary increase, improper job assignment). But, whatever the nature of the specific dispute, a modern organization is not set up to deal directly with individuals. Authority for settling disputes is usually much higher up in the hierarchy than the immediate supervisor or personnel person with whom the complainant tries to bargain.

Frequently, policies are too inflexible in any case, as the following examples show:

- A few years ago a physicist at a major corporation was offered a 10% salary increase. He asked if he could have instead an additional week of vacation (which was worth much less in dollar terms). He was refused.

- Sometimes a clash may occur over issues of quality of work rather than individual benefits, as in the case of three professional employees of the Bay Area Rapid Transit (BART) in San Francisco. The three, a systems engineer, a programmer analyst, and an electrical engineer, became increasingly concerned with defects in the automated train control system being developed by a contractor and with the manner in which the installation and testing of this system was being carried out. When their supervisors continued to disregard their warnings, they complained to the BART board of directors. After a public hearing, the board voted to support management. Shortly thereafter, the three engineers were fired.[6]

Several months later, a BART train overran the station at Fremont, injuring several passengers. Other failures of the automatic system occurred frequently. These three engineers were never rehired by BART and have instituted a court suit.

Whatever the nature of the grievance, if refusal defies common sense, the professional employee in particular feels slighted, impotent, and unsatisfied. Moreover, as the BART engineers found, he may discover that bucking the system invites catastrophe.

Job Security

The fear of layoffs among white-collar and professional employees has increased greatly in recent years. There are many contributing factors, but the most important are probably the widespread layoffs of engineers and other white-collar workers that occurred in the early 1970s and the continually poor job market for (and, hence, oversupply of) recent college graduates.

Employees at professional levels used to be encouraged to believe they were a valuable talent pool and a part of the management team. It has come as a shock to them to realize that they are no longer as sheltered from the effects of general economic declines as they once were. They can be fired for any reason (except, ironically, for union activities—these are protected by law). Notice, severance pay, continuation of company-paid health and life insurance after separation, company assistance in locating new employment, all of these benefits are conferred solely at the discretion of the company. Frequently, policies in these areas are inadequate. And unlike laid-off blue-collar workers, professional employees have virtually no chance of being recalled.

This situation is unfortunate even if the person who is fired is professionally incompetent. But when incompetence is the excuse given for terminations in cases of personality clashes, square pegs in round holes, and economic exigency, then a reasonably sophisticated labor pool can determine for themselves that a colleague is being shafted. It takes only a few clear-cut examples to do a great deal of psychological damage. A union, while it could not prevent a layoff, would eliminate much of the arbitrariness otherwise possible.

A case in point is provided by the American Federation of Musicians, which represents symphony orchestra members, among others. For example, the union at the Detroit Symphony recently won a demand that dismissal proposals be submitted to a committee consisting of 15 musicians elected by the orchestra members. At least 10 must give their approval before management can dismiss a player. Furthermore, a union can negotiate the right of recall, a right that is virtually nonexistent for nonunion professionals.

REASONS FOR RELUCTANCE

There certainly seem to be a lot of reasons for professionals to join unions, and many have. How, then, can we explain the reluctance of some segments (e.g., scientists and engineers) to do so?

A major reason is that unorganized professionals frequently have rather limited knowledge of what unions are and what they can do. They tend to think of unions in terms of not too accurate blue-collar stereotypes: complex and rigid work rules, excessive reliance on seniority, narrow jurisdictional lines, dictatorial power in the hands of union leaders, and so on. They are unaware of the flexibility of collective bargaining and the legal safeguards that exist for protecting their right to influence internal union policies. In short, they need realistic models for professional unions.

No one group's problems are unique, even among professional employees. The questions that are being asked today were asked and answered years ago by other professionals; it is an ongoing, evolutionary process. The renowned educator John Dewey held membership card No. 1 in the American Federation of Teachers, and the highly respected journalist Heywood Broun helped found the Newspaper Guild.

More recently, such professionals as Theodore Bikel, Charlton Heston, Walter Cronkite, and Ed Sullivan have been very active in the affairs of their unions. In the technical world, Albert Einstein spoke in favor of unions for "intellectual workers" 30 years ago. Nobel laureates Linus Pauling and Harold Urey recently wrote in support of unionization among scientists.

Unionization of a particular group may be delayed, but the general outcome is inevitable. There are, after all, inherent differences of interest between employers and those they employ. While they have a common general goal—the success of the business—they often have very different views on specific issues. A prime example should suffice: a major source of income for the employee, his salary, is an expense for the employer. The latter will want to minimize the same flow of dollars that the employee seeks to increase. No matter how enlightened the compensation policy, one is ultimately faced with the basic decision of how to divide limited available dollars between employees and stockholders.

There are only two ways to reconcile the differences, economic and otherwise: either unilateral management decision making or some kind of bilateral, employer-employee system for reaching compromises. (Individual bargaining, philosophically most acceptable to professionals, is totally unrealistic for most employees of large organizations.) It is inevitable that management decisions will not always parallel the personal interests of affected employees. Since employees lack strength as individuals, the logical approach is to join together to support each other.

RESULTS OF UNIONIZATION

Let's take the bad news first. At the very least, and perhaps most important, management flexibility will be reduced. The union will quickly seek to negotiate a contract, and the company is bound by law to bargain with it in good faith. In the course of such negotiations, many areas that were formerly in the exclusive domain of management will become negotiable.

It is probably worthwhile to stress my major caveat—one must not overgeneralize, especially when dealing with unions of professionals. It is fair to say that such unions will be concerned with salaries and fringe benefits. However, in some cases, these may already be at satisfactory levels, so that the main emphasis will be on other areas. In still other instances, the general level of benefits may be satisfactory, but the distribution may be at issue (e.g., a desire for more vacation with very little pressure for major salary increases). In any event, the union's priorities will vary tremendously from place to place, depending almost entirely on local conditions.

The biggest noneconomic change would probably be the establishment of a bilateral grievance system. Quite obviously, this would significantly affect management flexibility. It might require a major overhaul of personnel practices. The union becomes the official representative of that group of employees, and as such, the union, not the individual employee, must be dealt with. Indeed, it could be illegal to make a deal with a particular employee without the knowledge and acquiescence of the union.

Where abuses were rampant in the past, the union might be interested in having the contract contain sections dealing with overtime (number of hours, as well as extra pay), type of allowable work, relocation policies, and the like.

Uniquely professional concerns will be of interest to the union, too, reflecting the desires of the members. These will vary from one group to another but might include requests for additional technical or supporting staff, tuition refund plans (or improvements thereto), formal peer input to promotion or termination decisions, and the like.

Besides less flexibility in dealing with professional staff, management will probably also face higher costs. In addition, time will have to be spent on contract negotiation and administration. Still, all of the changes can be (and have been) adjusted to.

Unionization need not be all bad for management. A few years ago, the Conference Board surveyed several companies that had recently been involved in successful organizing drives.[7] About 40% saw some advantage to the company as a result of the unionization of their white-collar employees. Some of their comments are indicative:

- "The presence of the union has made the company much more sensitive in the handling of employee relations matters."
- "[It] forced us to formalize and administer properly a merit review program."
- "We gained insight into a group of dissatisfied employees. . . ."[8]

Improved worker morale may be the biggest benefit. The union helps employees regain the professional stature and pride that in recent decades were submerged beneath the corporate monolith. The individual union member does not have the freedom enjoyed by members of the learned professions in years past, but, by joining with his peers, he can once again participate meaningfully in decisions that affect his professional life. The result should be more productive, less dissatisfied employees.

CONCLUSIONS

We are dealing here with several rather fundamental assumptions:

1. The fraction of professionals who are employed by others will continue to grow.
2. In spite of similarities in educational backgrounds and mores, professional employees and those who employ them have inherently different viewpoints about many aspects of the job situation.
3. White-collar and professional employees will continue to be attracted to unions in ever-growing numbers.

There should be little disagreement with the first two points. As to the third, all trends point to the increasing organization of professionals. The most important factor is the growing size and impersonality of employing organizations. This will make the professional ever more remote from the center of decision making and will inevitably increase his frustrations. It is this professional malaise, rather than strictly monetary considerations, that in the long run will result in a union.

A progressive management will recognize that a unionization attempt at the very least indicates widespread employee discontent with existing conditions and that professional employees in particular desire a stronger voice in solving their problems. The union provides the employees with such a voice.

Should management be less than enlightened, then the union will at least fight to obtain for its members a greater measure of dignity and a larger share of the economic rewards.

REFERENCES

1. U. S. Bureau of Labor Statistics, *Directory of National Unions and Employee Associations 1973* (Washington, D. C.: Govt. Print. Off., 1974).

2. Archie Kleingartner, "Professionalism and Engineering Unionism," *Industrial Relations*, (May 1969), p. 235.

3. For a more general look at scientists and engineers, see Dennis Chamot, "Scientists and Engineers: The New Reality," *American Federationist*, (September 1974), p. 8.

4. Robert Stedfeld, editorial, *Machine Design*, (April 15, 1971), p. 65.

5. Diane M. Westcott, "Trends in Overtime Hours and Pay, 1969–74," *Monthly Labor Review*, (February 1975), p. 45.

6. See John T. Edsall, *Scientific Freedom and Responsibility* (Washington, D. C.: American Association for the Advancement of Science, 1975), p. 37.

7. Edward R. Curtin, *White-Collar Unionization* (Personnel Policy Study No. 220 [New York: The National Industrial Conference Board, Inc., 1970]).

8. *Ibid.,* p. 66.

New Roles for Professional Women

by N. R. Hooyman
and J. S. Kaplan

"There's this clever maneuver you have to watch for. At the beginning of a meeting, men will hug and kiss you hello. Then they greet each other with a handshake. The kiss means 'Hiya Honey.' The handshake means 'Let's get down to business.' There's nothing particularly friendly about those business meetings and that kiss never has had any real personal feeling. It diminishes a woman."

Governor's Staff Assistant[1]

"In meetings, I noticed that my voice was a problem. Men just didn't tune into my higher pitched voice. I had to compensate by coming on stronger and talking faster."

Lawyer[2]

"It's lonely being the only woman planner. The secretaries are uncomfortable, the men are uncomfortable."

Human Services Planner

INTRODUCTION

Everyday, in both informal and formal ways, women's influence within the human service professions is minimized. This article describes the concentration of women in lower-level positions and suggests changes necessary to enable women to assume higher-level administrative or planning jobs. It is assumed that even if—and when—systemic changes provide full opportunity for women to advance, internal and interpersonal barriers that derive primarily from women's socialization can prevent them from fully utilizing such opportunities. In other words, even when women occupy a formal authority position, they may face internal, interpersonal, and structural obstacles to exerting influence.

The authors have implemented a training program as one means to begin to remove such barriers to women's participation in upper-echelon decision-making processes. The training model deals with values, skills, and knowledge within internal, interpersonal, and organizational contexts. While it focuses upon women in the human services, the model is relevant to women attempting to increase their power in a variety of professions.

HISTORY OF THE PROBLEM

Human service professions, such as teaching, nursing, and social work, have generally been defined as appropriate for women because they involve expressive, person-oriented tasks and require the skills of helping, nurturing, and empathizing.[3] Women, however, did not enter human services simply because they had the unique skills or desire to do so; until recently, that was one of the few areas open to women in any large numbers.

Sex stratification has, in turn, occurred within such professions.[4] While women predominate in lower-level positions, changes in the human services have increased the number of positions in management, administration, research, policy, and planning that have attracted men. Many of the recent job openings are assumed to require qualities traditionally associated with men, such as detachment, analytic objectivity, and the effective exercise of power—qualities which women often lack because of their socialization not to be ambitious or aggressive.[5]

When the administrative component of a female profession expands, the increasing demand for administrators enhances the tendency of men to move relatively quickly into authority positions.[6] In social work, for example, men form a higher percentage of administrators, researchers, consultants, and university teachers than women do.[7] Men are thus concentrated at the top of human service organizations, implementing plans, administering programs, and contributing to the profession's knowledge development through publications and presentations at professional conferences.[8]

Admittedly, structural changes regarding admissions to professional schools and promotion and hiring for women have occurred. While necessary, these changes are not sufficient as strategies to maximize women's influence within the human services. Any strategy must take account of women's values, self-concepts, and attitudes, as well as the institutional factors that have minimized their influence. For example, women are socialized to believe that they do not belong among those who make important decisions;[9] such beliefs constitute a strong internal barrier to entering or to being effective after attaining a higher-level position of responsibility. Women's power in the past has generally been confined to their private lives and their ability to please men.[10] Women have not been socialized to be comfortable with exerting the authority of upper-echelon positions that can involve substantial resources or have negative repercussions on others.[11]

Women's lack of confidence, fear of acting aggressively, and desire to smooth away difficulties and to meet others' needs are societally taught norms. Once internalized, these become formidable psychological obstacles buttressing structural barriers. Therefore, both subtle, built-in psychological resistances and social-structural conditions within agencies and professional schools need to be altered.

A TRAINING MODEL

The authors have developed a training program as one means of modifying such barriers. The model focuses upon training women for upper-level positions in planning, administration/management, and policy formulation. These positions require the abilities to set long-range goals and develop the plans to attain them, to make and implement significant decisions that affect others, to negotiate and resolve conflict, to develop proposals and grants, to influence and mobilize others, to form coalitions, and to run meetings efficiently. The authors have identified internal, interpersonal, and structural barriers to women's acquiring these skills.

Internal Barriers to High-Level Positions

Internal barriers, or the forces originating from within women, may be the most difficult to change because of the years devoted to learning them. Women are socialized to perform a "stroking" function which disqualifies them from competitive, challenging jobs and deflects them from their highest potential achievement.[12] Horner's study of women's fear of succeeding suggests strong internal barriers.[13] Socialized to meet others' needs, women generally are not taught intellectual aggression or problem-solving abilities. Women grow up thinking of a career as a contingency plan; until recently, many women entered a profession idiosyncratically rather than as a result of deliberate planning.[14] Women who are promoted to high-level administrative positions often experience ambivalence and inner conflict with their role of mother and wife.[15] One way to resolve such conflicts is to leave an upper-level position in order to return home or to a lower-level position that requires nurturing qualities more consistent with the role of wife and mother. Another means of resolution is to attempt to become a "superwoman" to perform both roles more adequately than is expected of either a male administrator or a full-time housewife.

Interpersonal Barriers to High-Level Positions

Such role relationship barriers refer to the manner in which women are defined—or not defined—by others in their interactions. Women who enter upper-echelon jobs or administration/planning sequences in professional schools do not have many other women with whom to identify, either as successful role models or as support systems. For the woman administrator, the loneliness of being a "pioneer" can often interfere with her competency.

Women face the added burden of not being able to garner respect as competent decision makers from most other women. This lack of respect stems from being socialized to define their lives in terms of being the "other half" of a man, to compete with other women for men, and to use power covertly. Those who have "made it" in male-dominated functions such as administration may mistrust and exclude other women. Women need to develop the skills for working effectively and supportively with each other.

Men's attitudes and behaviors toward women administrators or planners are another interpersonal barrier. Women's appearance in collegial networks as co-professionals often confuses men, because these women no longer fit their role definitions as being sweet, pretty, passive, and nurturing. Past standards for interaction are no longer appropriate or are ambiguous. In meetings, attention often becomes focused on the uneasiness which everyone feels and on the need to define new ground rules for the situation rather than on carrying out the business at hand. Men frequently resort to humor as one way to deal with their uneasiness. Unable to engage in a collegial relationship with women, men may fall back on the traditional norms of male-female interactions or attempt to compensate by being overly solicitous, congenial, underdemanding, or overdemanding. Thus, men may respond to a woman agency director as a woman and secondly as director. Women are then confronted with the dilemma of how to respond to male colleagues in a way that will preserve their dignity and influence.

Structural Barriers to High-Level Positions

Structural barriers refer to organizational patterns and practices; these include discrimination in hiring and promotion, nepotism, full-time work requirements, lack of child care facilities, and maternity-paternity leaves. While federal laws and administrative rules have brought about organizational changes that benefit women, relationships and opportunities have been formally and informally structured to minimize women's influence after they enter such organizations.

Sexism is manifested in the organizational atmosphere primarily through informal interactions, unstated norms, and casual exchanges. Clubs, cliques, the "culture" of a profession, even the golf game and handball courts for men are structured to exclude women.[16] A woman in a position of formal power may often be denied the informal signs of belonging and recognition, such as having lunch with the other agency directors, stopping for a drink after work with her male colleagues, or being able to share in "locker room talk." Use of titles, especially in an academic setting, becomes a way of bestowing—or withholding—recognition and thereby power; for example, a male administrator may use all the appropriate titles when referring to other men, but call a woman Mrs. or Miss rather than Doctor. Men can diminish a woman's influence by referring to her as a girl or gal, particularly if she is the one female member in an agency or committee. Secretaries, socialized to defer to men, may fail to inform women of meetings, phone calls, or appointments. In addition to the debilitating effects such experiences have upon professional women day after day, they deny women access to information and other kinds of resources essential for effective decision-making. Without such resources, women's power may be marginal at best.

Another effect of these structural barriers is that women have to invest considerable time, energy, and skills in changing their organization and in gaining access to informal channels of influence. Yet their resources could be put to better use in planning and administering programs. In addition, such demands of fighting organizational constraints can simply wear a person out. In fact, women may oftentimes choose to leave an organization rather than attempt to join the "old boys club." Thus, women need the organizational, analytical, and research skills to understand and to change their organizational settings from within.

THE TRAINING PROGRAM

The training model deals with the three areas both sequentially and simultaneously. The initial training stage focuses on the individual woman's values, goals, and attitudes. This component leads into the interpersonal sphere in which role relations are explored in terms of communication, assertion, problem-solving skills, and team development. In the organizational stage, the awareness and skill attainment resulting from the previous components form the basis for developing techniques of conflict resolution, coalition formation, and mobilizing others. The authors have found the greatest success conducting a one-day session to provide an overview and then having women complete the process described below for one evening a week for five or six weeks. This extended time period enables women to approach each skill exercise in depth.

Internal Skills

Women need to increase their own personal power to be most effective in higher-level positions. A series of tools are used for this purpose. Life scripting aids women in understanding the effects of their upbringing on their current decisions.[17] Through an internal dialogue exercise, women can focus on their strengths, weaknesses, fears, and hopes about exercising responsibility. Life planning and skills assessment exercises enable women to explore a range of career possibilities and examine them in relation to a detailed inventory.[18]

Interpersonal Skills

Learning how to develop effective working relationships with both men and other women is the focus of the model's second stage. Early in the program, women are asked to find a partner with whom they feel comfortable sharing their thoughts and ideas. From working in pairs, they move into small groups. Such small group interaction begins to build some of the necessary interpersonal skills in communication, problem solving, and decision-making. Techniques such as values clarification and assertion training help individuals develop a well-thought-out set of value concepts consistent with their own needs and then to express those needs (along with their feelings) comfortably and honestly.[19] Videotaped case situations allow women to practice interpersonal skills.

Organizational Skills

To overcome some of the structural obstacles facing them, women need skills in conflict resolution, organizing others, and leading groups. They must be able to increase their own effectiveness by learning when, where, and how to intervene in organizations. Simulations, role plays, and games are used to learn skills of lobbying, grant-writing, coalition formation, and planning.[20] Videotaped role plays and trigger films of conflict situations and of how to be effective as the "token" woman are also included.

Women need to expand their knowledge base in order to be well prepared when they appear at legislative hearings, in committee meetings, or on the media. They need a firm grasp of substantive areas such as the law, computer terminology, research, management information systems, and political processes. Women need to know where to attain information and how to use it. Through lectures and mimeo handouts, women are informed of the availability of abstracts and directories for such purposes. Likewise, lectures and tapes are used to transfer information about how to write a grant, read legislation, or write reports.

Much of the knowledge base cannot be communicated in a short-term training program, but is best developed through professional education. In other words, formal education provides a woman with the credentials required to enter an institution; the training program can help her develop additional skills required to function as effectively as possible, despite the constraints of existing institutional sexism. A woman formally trained in administration still needs to learn to be comfortable with conflict among her staff, to make decisions when the proverbial buck stops at her desk, to deal with being a token, or to fire someone when it becomes necessary. Her socialization, even her formal education, may not have adequately prepared her for such daily experiences.

CONCLUSION

The training program is adaptable to formats such as seminars, workshops, regularized small group meetings, and continuing education and extension programs. Ideally, the authors would like to see such training built into staff development programs within human service agencies and the curriculum of professional schools. The provision of this training will be a social change in and of itself, which will lead to further social change initiated by women who have the necessary decision-making, reinforcement, and implementation power to bring about changes from within.

REFERENCES

1. Letty Cottin Pogrebin, "The Intimate Politics of Working with Men," *Ms.*, vol. 4 (October 1975), pp. 48–52.

2. *Ibid.*

3. Margaret Adams, "The Compassion Trap," in Vivian Gornick and Barbara Moran, eds., *Women in Sexist Society* (New York: Basic Books, 1971), p. 404.

4. C. Bernard Scotch, "Sex Status in Social Work: Grist for Women's Liberation," *Social Work*, vol. 16 (July 1971), pp. 5–12; Martha Williams, Liz Ho, and Lucy Felder, "Career Patterns: More Grist for Women's Liberation," *Social Work*, vol. 19 (July 1974), pp. 463–467; Janet Saltzmen Chafetz, "Women in Social Work," *Social Work*, vol. 17 (September 1972), pp. 12–19; Jessie Bernard, *Women and the Public Interest* (Chicago:

Aldine-Atherton, 1971); Florence Howe, "Women and the Power to Change," in Florence Howe, ed., *Women and the Power to Change* (New York: McGraw-Hill, 1975), p. 166; and Cynthia F. Epstein, "Encountering the Male Establishment: Sex-Status Limits on Women's Careers in the Professions," in Athena Theodore, ed., *The Professional Woman* (Boston: The Schenkman Publishing Company, Inc., 1971), p. 52.

5. Winifred Bolen, *Feminism, Reform and Social Services: A History of Women in Social Work* (The Minnesota Resource Center for Social Work Education, July 1973), p. 18; Edward Gross, "Plus Ca Change? . . . The Sexual Structure of Occupations Over Time," in Athena Theodore, ed., *The Professional Woman*, p. 49; and Aaron Rosenblatt, Eileen Turner, Adalene Peterson, and Clare Rollesson, "Predominance of Male Authors in Social Work Publications," in Athena Theodore, ed., *The Professional Woman*, pp. 103–115.

6. James W. Grimm and Robert N. Stern, "Sex Roles and Internal Labor Market Structures: The Female Semi-Professions," *Social Problems*, vol. 21, no. 5 (June 1974), p. 702.

7. *Ibid.*, p. 703.

8. Bolen, *Feminism, Reform and Social Services*, p. 18.

9. Pamela Robey, "Structural and Internalized Barriers to Women in Higher Education," in Jo Freeman, ed., *Women: A Feminist Perspective* (New York: Mayfield Publishing Co., 1970), p. 178; and Sandra L. Bem and Daryl J. Bem, "Training the Woman to Know Her Place: The Power of a Nonconscious Ideology," in *Women's Role in Contemporary Society* (Avon Books, 1972), pp. 101–115.

10. Howe, *Women and the Power to Change*, p. 134.

11. Adams, "The Compassion Trap," p. 404.

12. Bernard, *Women and the Public Interest*, pp. 88, 126.

13. Matina Horner, "Fail Bright Women," in Athena Theodore, ed., *The Professional Woman*, pp. 252–260.

14. Cynthia Epstein, *Woman's Place* (Berkeley: Univ. of California Pr., 1971), p. 29.

15. *Ibid.*, p. 20.

16. Epstein, "Encountering the Male Establishment," in *Woman's Place*, p. 55.

17. Claude M. Steiner, *Scripts People Live* (New York: Grove Press, 1974).

18. George A. Ford and Gordon L. Lippitt, *A Life Planning Workbook* (Rosslyn, Va.: NTL Learning Resource Corporation, 1972).

19. Sidney Simon, et al., *Values Clarification* (New York: Hart, 1971); Robert E. Alberti and Michael L. Emmons, *Your Perfect Right* (Impact, 1970).

20. Armand Lauffer at the University of Michigan has produced *Lobbying, Compacts, and Shoot for Marbles* for practicing skills necessary for higher-level positions.

PART

III

ORGANIZATIONS IN POST-INDUSTRIAL SOCIETY

On Work and Authority

by Kenneth O. Alexander

Historical and contemporary concepts of work are marked to a greater degree by contradiction than by consensus. On the one hand, it has been viewed as fit only for slaves and social subordinates. On the other, it has been held to be God's calling on earth. It has been seen as the source of man's degradation; it has been exalted as the source of man's dignity and identity.

Adam Smith, in first setting out the intellectual rationale for the market system, claimed productive advantage from the division of work into narrower, more specialized components but also saw specialization and subdivision of work as demeaning the worker. After less than a century of continued industrialization, Karl Marx saw the system as inevitably engendering massive worker alienation through large-scale capitalistic production, factory discipline, propertyless labor uprooted from the land, the workers' divorce from ownership, etc.

The relative significance of productivity and alienation, and the relative weight society should give to each, remain unresolved to this day. This is so in spite of an enormous amount of research and literature. Work and what it means in terms of output and also what it means in terms of the well-being of the input, have been focal points for study in the older disciplines of economics, sociology, anthropology and psychology. More recently, they have become major issues in the newer, applied fields of management, organization theory, and industrial relations.[1]

I

There is a major thrust, a persistent theme, that runs through this vast literature.[2] In one way or another, that theme maintains that society suffers significant losses through the organization of work within the typical authoritarian, hierarchical bureaucracy. The losses are in terms of both output and input; on the one hand through resultant lower labor productivity in the traditional sense, and on the other through increased disutility of work for the worker. The explicitly subordinate worker is denied the opportunity to make productive changes in the work process. In large measure, those who are most experienced and most familiar with the daily details of the work are organizationally prohibited from contributing to its improvement. The worker has become the child in a system in which there is general acceptance of the dictum that father knows best. In some work situations the process of specialization and subdivision of tasks continues in the best traditions of Adam Smith and Henry Ford, with the also-traditional result of boring, repetitive, monotonous and stultifying jobs.

The worker must accept the position of a subordinate. But more than that, he must accept the position of a functional inferior. As such, he is denied satisfaction of what have come to be called his higher needs on the job.[3] In the typical work situation he cannot seek, let alone fulfill, self-expression, recognition by co-workers, or personal challenge by way of his contributions to work. His drives in these directions cannot be denied. But they can be and are diverted away from work and toward leisure activities and an attendant variety of consumption activities. His substitutions in these areas are then regarded as his reward for enduring the work experience; they enter our national income accounts as proof of our high material standard of living. The accounts contain no adjustment for the disutility of work, whose quantification would pose more problems than the negatives of externalities in the recent attempts to devise new measures of net social welfare to complement Gross National Product (GNP). So economists continue with work disutility at the core of labor supply theory in microeconomics, while ignoring it completely in macroeconomics.

Manpower specialists frequently express concern over permanently recruiting into the labor force elements of the hardcore unemployed, the young of urban ghettos, the members of minority groups, etc. Perhaps more attention should be paid to the great contradiction entailed in entering the American labor force, which these groups find particularly difficult to hurdle. We live in a society which pays massive informal homage to individualism. We have structured an educational system which formally imbues our youth, year after year, with the social values of freedom, liberty and individual expression. Then they learn that they are expected to spend a lifetime on a job while explicitly submitting to authority. Even for those new labor force entrants from the mainstream of society, it may take some time before the leisure time substitution is made and accepted. And the rising educational level of the labor force makes the contradiction steadily more severe. But the significant point is that the contradiction itself is not only unnecessary but costly.

The results of theory, of work experiments since the Hawthorne studies of the 1920's, and of various forms of shared authority in the workplace both abroad and in a few firms in the U.S. all indicate a vast potential through task-oriented worker participation for both enhancing workers' job satisfaction and increasing labor productivity in the traditional sense. If the worker is granted equal status in the approach to production problems, if merit and respect could emanate from functional contribution rather than hierarchical position, if individual ingenuities could be harnessed to common work problems, then work, the single biggest activity in life, could become challenging, meaningful, and stimulating, rather than the degrading, boring, and burdensome activity it so often is today. The motivations of the worker can indeed mesh with the goals of the firm. In the process the worker, the firm, and society can gain.

Of course it must be accepted that decreased authoritarianism may not mean greater job satisfaction for all workers and increased labor productivity in all work situations. Individual differences must leave room for the worker who prefers authority to participation; the sometimes-delicate task of attempting a relative transfer from authority to participation may be botched. But these points basically deal with the size of the potential for increased satisfaction and productivity, not with the existence of that potential.

In this connection, worker response to surveys and questionnaires, sometimes used to document individual differences, tends to be biased in favor of prevalent authoritarianism. The worker typically is not a visionary. The response will be out of perceived practical alternatives and implications, not out of the preferred dimensions of basic changes he has neither experienced nor contemplated. In brief, authority breeds authoritarianism. The results of the status quo can be used to justify the status quo.

So too for management. The management operating out of Theory X, viewing workers as unknowing, uncooperative, and unwilling, who must be forced to contribute to the goals of the firm through the carrot of wages and fringes and the stick of discipline, will breed a work force which meshes with its beliefs. Their managerial philosophy is self-reinforcing and self-justifying.

II

It is in the United States that one finds what is probably the sharpest contradiction between cultural respect for the individual, on the one hand, and the submergence of the individual in a starkly authoritarian work hierarchy, on the other. Occasionally, the contradiction and resultant worker dissatisfactions become topics for the public media, as in recent treatments of the particularly severe symptoms at the Lordstown plant of General Motors. Now and then the issue crops up in political discussion. But the nature of work in society is of much lesser national concern than it is in, say, France.

As a generalization, developments toward worker participation and shared authority in production have gone much further in other industrialized countries than they have in the U.S. The kibbutz of Israel, the "workers' management" of Yugoslavia, the co-determination of Germany, the rapid developments toward worker participation in management in Scandinavia—these and other developments abroad far exceed the pace of change in the United States. This is so in spite of the fact that in the relatively few American cases of shared authority with workers, as under the Scanlon Plan,[4] the results in terms of both worker satisfaction and worker productivity can be impressive. A projection into the future of these relative rates of change among nations leaves open the very real possibility that in the future the United States economy may be marked by a work force relatively less satisfied and relatively less productive than that of other countries, with serious implications for our position in world trade and our balance of payments. History and culture may allow the Soviet Union and Japan to retain relatively authoritarian managements while suffering less by way of social stress and reduced productivity.

Historic evolution in the U.S. helps to explain the current slow movement toward shared authority in the productive process. We too are here because of where we've been. The owners and managers of American enterprise have faced explicit challenge to their authority in the not too distant past. In the 19th and into the 20th centuries it came via ideological, political, and labor opposition to their position. Their response to what was often viewed as threats to their very survival was widespread and effective, ranging from powerful political influence, to the American Plan of the 1920's, to persistent and pervasive opposition to organized labor.

The response was based on a philosophy of elitism. The American system was one in which all could run for the prizes. It was a system in which the best would rise to the top. Their authority was then wielded legitimately out of functional superiority. Father indeed knows best; indeed, that's why he is father. There is no contradiction between our ideological respect for the individual, on the one hand, and his subordination to authority in the production process, on the other. Rather, the latter is the logical extension of the former.

Of course, this view is open to serious challenge. A good deal of empirical evidence can be mustered to point out that the race is not run fairly, that individuals run it while carrying unjustifiable handicaps or advantages, that elitism was more appropriate to the earlier American economy of the entrepreneur than it is for a world of corporate bureaucracy, etc. But the validity of the doctrine of elitism is not the point.

In fact, one could argue that the failure of American management to realize the potential gains in worker satisfaction and productivity that lie in systems of shared authority with workers must in itself indicate that we certainly do not get the best possible managers out of the existing system. The point of relevance here lies in the fact that some form of elitism is so widely accepted not only by management but by the general public. Management authority is legitimate authority. It then is asking a great deal of the individual manager when he is expected to voluntarily seek change which would reduce his own authority, with its attendant presumption of functional superiority, perquisites of office and formalized respect of subordinates.

III

Possessing legitimate authority, and coming out of a recent past in which that authority was used to fight radical attack against the basic system of private enterprise, American management has the tendency to link preservation of its authority with preservation of private enterprise. The continued preservation of "management rights" becomes part of a patriotic duty to preserve the American way. But this represents a form of social lag in management thinking, convenient and comforting, but more appropriate to the past out of which it grew than to the present and future.

The manner in which human beings are organized to perform productive tasks stands in no necessary relationship to the particular ism which describes the economic system within which production takes place. A Soviet Union and a Mainland China may have similar centrally-directed economies and differ widely in how they view the role of the individual in the productive process. A Britain can find that the nationalization of industry leaves the same and intensified problems of worker performance and productivity. Those relatively few American firms which have initiated programs of greater worker participation and shared authority pose no threat to private enterprise. Indeed, history may well record that it is they who led the way toward strengthening and preserving it.

But if the sharing of authority over production decisions with workers can yield increased labor productivity and consequently lower production cost, shouldn't the market force management to share authority? Yes, but only under the assumptions that markets are competitive and at least some managements initiate change. If no managements initiate change, even a purely competitive market will operate at that efficiency level.

Even if some managements initiate change, markets which are less than purely competitive need not force other managements to change. And of course the vast majority of American product markets do not approach the model of pure competition. Enough has been written about "X inefficiency" (with appropriate double meaning),[5] "satisficing" managements, etc., to document that neither the marketplace nor stockholders need force management either to maximize profit or minimize cost.

Desperate economic circumstances for the firm may prompt management to abandon traditional ways and allow genuine worker participation in the production process, sometimes out of a quest for survival. This is why serious economic difficulties are part of the background of so many Scanlon Plan firms. It is not the economic difficulties which are necessary for the success of the Scanlon Plan. But management readiness genuinely to share authority, prompted by those difficulties, *is* indispensable to success of the Scanlon Plan.

A management imbued with elitism but aware of the growing evidence of worker dissatisfaction can easily ignore any relationship between the two. Rather, changing problems of worker motivation and performance conveniently can be viewed as another challenge to the superior expertise of management. It is really quite simple. If worker performance depends upon the opportunity to satisfy higher needs on the job, then management can enlarge and enrich jobs to contain such opportunity. While comfortable in conforming with the past, such an approach of retaining the authoritarian hierarchy will result in job enlargement and enrichment evolving as another phase of the "human relations" of twenty years ago, with the attendant criticism of Pavlovian manipulation of workers.

Perhaps more important, strict retention of elitism contains a false functional presumption that marked time and motion study in the scientific management movement of fifty years ago. Before the pace of work can be established through time study, management will first find the single best method of performing the work. In this instance, before a worker can be fully motivated, management will find the optimum definition of the job. The presumption is even more untenable in the current context, for the presumption itself will tend to undermine worker motivation.

Job enlargement and job enrichment are relatively new terms which can mean different things in different specific applications. They may indeed be a modern form of more sophisticated managerial manipulation of subordinates. Even then, they can result in improved worker performance and job interest through reductions in monotony, repetition, etc. But any such results are likely to be short-run, the reaction to "shot in the arm" therapy, with the future bringing a new plateau of worker performance and attempts to develop a new bag of manipulative tools for management.

On the other hand, they may be applied to instances of genuine sharing of authority by management, in which workers and managers approach production problems as equals. It is the latter which holds an enduring and long-run potential for improvement in both job satisfaction and performance. Results may even be somewhat cumulative in the long run, as workers become accustomed to self-fulfillment within the organization and as lesser authority breeds fewer authority-prone workers. Should such change in the organization for work gain momentum, the old elitist managers will face relatively more difficulty in retaining a work force during periods of tight labor markets.

In summary, the salutary results of job enlargement and job enrichment are more dependent upon how they are viewed by management than on the specifics of changes in job content.

IV

Powerful forces of inertia hold back any development toward greater worker participation and shared managerial authority. After struggling for generations to protect management "prerogatives," or "residual rights," it would be quick turnabout indeed if management were to begin voluntarily to yield authority on any appreciable scale. An elitist philosophy rationalizes and legitimizes that authority. On a more practical level, it is simpler and more ego-satisfying to administer a productive organization from a position of authority than from a position where one is left open to continuing and explicit challenge and debate. Even assuming management willingness to share authority, implementing policies likely would be met with typical fear of change on the part of employees, and hostility, suspicion, and resistance by unions. So aside from philosophy, management faces significant threats to the organization's goals if its administration while entering new and uncertain terrain is found wanting. A reversal of policy, once an attempt at shared authority failed, would not simply undo the damage.

One may legitimately ask why the expected resistance by unions. With evidence of job dissatisfaction, and with evidence that participation in production can diminish that dissatisfaction, should not unions, as institutions whose *raison d'etre* is the welfare of workers, be a significant force pressing for such participation?

Quite the contrary. For just as history and inertia deny the logic of management voluntarily sharing authority, so also do they deny the logic of unions pressing for it. A contemporary paraphrase of the view of American labor unionism is that management authority is to be contained, restricted and regulated by the union under formal and legal arrangements, and not shared with workers under informal arrangements and with unpredictable results.

After all, unions themselves are the result of the traditional wielding of authority in the production process by management. Unions arose as a countervailing force to that authority. The powerful desire of American workers to "be their own boss" is well known. Denied this by the institutional facts of industrial evolution, they substituted the "desire to tell the boss to go to hell." Historically, management authority was not infrequently used arbitrarily, unjustly, frivolously, etc. The desire of American workers to challenge and regulate that authority probably stands as a single more powerful explanation for the growth of American unionism than the desire for higher wages.

American unions grew and remain today as a *response* to managerial authority. To some degree, a diminishing of managerial authority will result in a concomitant diminishing of their historic and contemporary role. Today's issues of job content and job dissatisfaction are quite understandably interpreted by unions in a manner which legitimizes and supports their position as a formal adversary to management. They simply document that the union's basic task continues unabated. Management, as holder of authority, is responsible for worker discontent. The union, as usual, must restrict management and wring new concessions from it for the welfare of the worker.[6]

Attempts at job enlargement, job enrichment, worker participation and shared authority will meet union opposition through traditional contractual restraints of work rules, job classifications, seniority, etc. Unions will tend to view management initiatives in these areas as new gimmicks, as new forms of "scientific management," designed to lure the workers into a greater contribution to management goals. They can muster ample justification for their posture from out of the past. A typical elitist management will reinforce and validate their posture in the present. The traditional confrontation continues; the adversary relationship is reinforced.

Unions can and do support their traditionalist approach with evidence that workers continue to be concerned with the traditional "wages, hours, and working conditions." But this classic trio includes conditions both on and off the job and worker concern is inevitable and does not thereby mandate an inevitable adversary union-management relationship. That adversary relationship typically treats wages, hours, and working conditions as compensating issues in collective bargaining. One issue will be traded for another. A gain in one area can be achieved by concession in another. It is the adversary relationship and not the nature of the issues that makes this so. For the whole thrust of research and experience indicates that improvement in working conditions by way of worker participation and shared managerial authority can also improve productivity and the material benefits of the workers.

But shared production authority is a continuous, largely-informal, day-to-day and unpredictable process. As such, it threatens to deny the union one of its major roles: that of bureaucratic, formal, legalistic, contractual restraint of managerial supervision of production. The union focuses on the basic divergence of interests between workers and management over the share of value added by the enterprise that will be received by labor and the share that will be received by property. The question is the split of the pie. It is a legitimate struggle.

But workers and management have a harmony of interest in the economic health and viability of the enterprise; in the size of the pie. If the union retreats from its bureaucratic restraint of management in the production process, if it goes along with shared worker-management authority and effort in achieving a bigger pie, will it thereby undermine its effectiveness in representing the worker in the legitimate struggle over sharing that pie? If the worker gains greater job satisfaction through cooperating with management as an equal on production problems, will that same worker become less militant, less of an adversary, in the continuing process of dividing the pie?

Union fears about worker participation in production go beyond the concern that its effectiveness in contract negotiations over interests may be weakened. They extend to the possibility of weakening the basic strength and viability of the American labor movement. The worker, drawn closer to management, may become not only less militant in supporting the union in contract negotiations but also less militant in basic support of the union itself.

There is some threat to institutional health and survival for unions, a powerful motivator for defensive actions. For American unionism has a continuing concern with its own survival, strength and growth. Even today it only has about one-quarter of the work force organized. It views its struggle for survival and growth as a continuing one. Current leaders come out of a history in which this was *the* issue during their careers. Anything which threatens their institution, to which their beliefs, careers, and lives are so closely tied, will be viewed with deep suspicion and hostility.

V

The situation today is one in which the two major institutional power centers, management and unions, have deep suspicions and fears about worker participation in the production process. An observer can argue that the fears are largely unfounded. Participation is a challenge to management ingenuity, not to management. So too for unions, whose basic task of negotiating labor's share will continue, with added questions of whether and how that share shall be tied to cost, productivity or profit improvements resulting from worker contributions.

But nobody could deny that participation will involve changes in the traditional roles of both unions and management. And their fears stem from the desire to protect their traditional roles. In that sense they are well-founded. From the viewpoint of the observer, however, as a drag upon progress toward achieving the multiple gains of worker participation, such fears are lacking in logical sanction.

In all this, the worker loses, caught between two bureaucracies with fears out of the past and inertia. But the worker too is carrying some of the fears that trouble management, the union, or both. And he too fears change and is much less the visionary than the man of practical, short-run improvement.

Left without a vehicle for expression, he is unlikely to accelerate movement toward worker participation in any significant way. The Lordstowns will continue here and there, when a juxtaposition of conditions makes work dissatisfaction particularly severe so that some degree of revolt against both management and the union is prompted. But this is nothing really new and reaction can continue to be the traditional one: formal, contractual change in rules within the union-management adversary relationship.

Finally, conditions of work and worker participation do not seem destined to become significant political issues in the U.S., as they have in some European countries. They can too easily be transferred into the language of old ideological and power struggles, and as such are dangerous to the politician. We will continue to get some vague and general political expressions of concern. Furthermore, there is doubt about what could be accomplished politically.

The daily, informal tasks of shared production authority, the tapping of the best productive ideas among all those involved, is a process not easily prompted by political edict. As already mentioned, even a basic change in ideology, basic change in ownership or management of enterprise, warrants no presumptions about the position of the individual and his motivation and opportunity to contribute to the productive effort in which he is involved.

In all these dimensions, the past weighs heavily on the future. Progress toward the potential of increased labor productivity and worker satisfaction via participation and shared authority promises to be slow. But the promise is there. And progress may be accelerated as we learn from developments abroad and as more American firms, unions and workers demonstrate that change is feasible and experience benefits therefrom.

The issues of work and authority, long discussed in a number of disciplines, are beginning to be discussed in the public media, a hopeful sign that experimentation eventually may be transferred to reality. The future may see us more rapidly approaching a society in which individualism in our culture and democracy in our politics become consistent with the daily work lives of our citizenry.

As we move toward the potential that awaits, the institutions of management and union will change. In academia, the applied fields of business and industrial relations will change, and almost every issue within their purview, from organizational structure to leadership skills, from collective bargaining to early retirement, will change in its dimensions.

As labor productivity increases concomitant with increased satisfaction from work, traditional economics will find inadequate its micro theory of labor supply, founded as it is on the "disutility" of work, as well as its macro attempts to quantify social welfare.

REFERENCES

1. Three recent books continue and expand the concern over the nature of work and its consequences: Harold L. Sheppard, and Neal Q. Herrick, *Where Have All the Robots Gone?* (New York: Free Pr., 1972); David Jenkins, *Job Power* (New York: Doubleday, 1973); and *Work in America*,

Report of a Special Task Force to the Secretary of Health, Education, and Welfare (Cambridge, Mass.: The MIT Press, 1973). Extensive footnoting will be avoided in this summary article. An appreciation for the duration, scope, and volume of research and writing on the nature of work and its consequences can be gained by reference to the sources, notes, and bibliographies in these books.

2. Blumberg summarizes as follows: "There is hardly a study in the entire literature which fails to demonstrate that satisfaction in work is enhanced or that generally acknowledged beneficial consequences accrue from a genuine increase in workers' decision-making power. Such consistency of findings, I submit, is rare in social research." Paul Blumberg, *Industrial Democracy, The Sociology of Participation* (New York: Schocken, 1969), p. 123.

3. Abraham Maslow, *Motivation and Personality* (New York: Harper, 1954).

4. Frederick G. Lesieur, ed., *The Scanlon Plan: A Frontier in Labor-Management Cooperation* (New York and Cambridge: Wiley and The Technology Press, 1958).

5. In the sense of management acceptance of McGregor's Theory X as contributing to Leibenstein X inefficiency. Douglas McGregor, *The Human Side of Enterprise* (New York: McGraw-Hill, 1960). Harvey Leibenstein, "Allocative Efficiency vs. 'X-Efficiency,'" *American Economic Review*, vol. 56, no. 3 (June 1966), p. 392.

6. "If you want to enrich the job, enrich the pay check. . . . If you want to enrich the job, begin to decrease the number of hours a worker has to labor in order to earn a decent standard of living." William W. Winpisinger, "Job Enrichment—Another Part of the Forest," *Proceedings of the Twenty-Fifth Anniversary Meeting*, Industrial Relations Research Association, edited by Gerald G. Somers, 1973. But at the same time unions appreciate that worker subordination within an authoritarian bureaucracy is a powerful unionizing force. See Jack Golodner, "Professionals Go Union," *The American Federationist*, AFL-CIO, vol. 80, no. 10 (October 1973).

The Changing Character of the Public Service and the Administrator of the 1980's

by Richard L. Chapman
and Frederick N. Cleaveland

In 1971 the National Academy of Public Administration conducted a Delphi exercise on developments affecting the public service, 1971-1980. It was sponsored by a Ford Foundation grant, and its purpose was to bring together the collective views of a group (approximately 100) of well-informed leaders in public affairs regarding the changing character of the public service in the United States over the next decade. The results were expected to be helpful to both practitioners and educators, and to constitute an important element in the Academy's study of programs to prepare people for careers in public administration.[1]

The discussion which follows is based upon an analysis of the results of the Academy's Delphi exercise, conducted in three rounds from September to December 1971. Frederic N. Cleaveland directed the study and conducted the analysis jointly with Richard L. Chapman.

FORCES OF CHANGE AFFECTING THE PUBLIC SERVICE

Four major trends are seen as challenges to the public service today, and as important determinants of the public service in the next decade: (1) pressures for centralization *and* for decentralization; (2) unionization of the public service; (3) increased citizen involvement; and (4) the impact of technological change.

Pressures for Centralization and Decentralization

The pressure for greater centralization is fueled by the demands for national solutions to complex public problems, for national policy determination built upon uniform standards, and the demand for effective control. Widespread citizen interest in such issues as consumer rights, environmental protection and improvement, economic well-being, and access to medical care will strengthen the trend to seek national, centralized solutions. The pace of citizen intervention in public decision making, especially in local government, adds to pressures for centralization in those policy areas where intractable local conflicts seem to require transfer of the locus of decision to a more distant regional, state, or national level if a decision—any decision—is to become politically feasible.

The thrust of technology and the kinds of changes in government induced by technological development also strengthen centralizing forces. As effective performance in managerial and decision-making roles calls for greater scientific and technical competence and for adopting a systems perspective, the responsibility and authority for design and performance of public programs tend to move to higher levels of government closer to the chief executive. The complex technology required for information and control functions and the use of temporary problem-solving groups which require sophisticated direction and coordination (and which are less accessible to local political forces) further centralization. In similar fashion, the press for greater uniformity to insure equality in the way government deals with people, the expansion of legislative oversight over administrative actions, and the tendency toward judicialization of administrative decision making as a by-product of citizen intervention all encourage centralization.

What of the countervailing trend toward decentralization, toward returning governmental functions to government which is closer to the people? These pressures toward decentralization are reinforced by a number of trends, some of which contribute to centralization as well. For example, the move toward revenue sharing to help finance state and local government operations will stimulate further decentralization. Increasing experimentation with ways to organize regionally to cope with the problems of the complex metropolitan areas and the emergence of regional political processes and regional political leadership contribute to the growing interest in decentralization.

Greater emphasis on local control is not totally incompatible with the trend toward centralization. Efforts to decentralize have been concentrated in the areas of the delivery of services and the collection and analysis of information (including citizen advice and opinion). Both forces can be accommodated by redefining the role of the higher level of government as: (1) determining broad policy, (2) defining uniform national standards and program guidelines, and (3) evaluating information generated at the level of program execution and service delivery. By contrast, the local government would be engaged directly in managing the delivery of services for a unique local area with all the principles of decentralization met by: (1) regular feedback from those receiving the service, (2) opportunity to develop appropriate neighborhood delivery units, and (3) emphasis on fitting quality of service to recipient needs—recognizing the value of diversity in program, policy, and even objectives.

Unionization in the Public Service

A second major trend is the spread of employee unionism in the public sector. Within the next 10 years a large majority of clerical and blue collar employees in government probably will be members of unions, and many, if not a majority, of those in middle management will be active in labor organizations. Without question this trend will have a significant impact upon the functioning of the public service.

In some places a professional association rather than an existing trade union has organized employees within an agency and is representing them in discussions with agency management. This suggests that the character of unions and union activity within the public service is likely to vary at least as widely as it does among labor organizations in the private sector. Some unions of public servants undoubtedly will manifest the values, objectives, and patterns of behavior characteristic of militant craft-type unions seeking to limit freedom of managerial decision, control entry into the trade or profession, and press for more emphasis upon seniority and compliance with formal union rules in hiring, promotion, and dismissal. Larger, more militant employee unions will reinforce the movement toward centralization noted above. Just as organization for collective bargaining in the private sector has been a centralizing force increasing the power of top union leadership and its industrial counterpart, so union activity in the public service may lead to greater concentration of authority.

The parallel growth of unionism among government employees and citizen participation in the processes of public decision making poses a double threat to the traditional power and authority of agency managers. If employee union leaders, representatives of the clients whom the agency is intended to serve, and militant public interest groups are all pressing the administrator simultaneously for some action (or inaction), the inevitable result will be to slow down the administrative processes and to force a retreat into more formal rule making. The potential competition for employee loyalty should also be noted. Whereas the public service in the United States has prided itself on the dedication of public employees to the public interest, the prospect for the 1970's and beyond is for a public servant who must respond to pulls and tugs in at least three directions:

1. Union pressures will be directed toward serving the special needs of its members and extending its influence.
2. Professional pressure will be exerted upon the public servant to encourage that behavior which will enhance the stature of the profession and extend its control over vital work processes.
3. The agency will continue its efforts to build a loyal and dedicated work force committed to the public service ethic and to *its* view of the public interest.

Increasing Citizen Involvement

The involved citizen is the ideal of a democratic society, and, according to democratic political theory, is the *sine qua non* of a working democratic political system. Yet the thrust of citizen participation today goes well beyond the well-informed, voting citizen. Now citizens regularly are challenging government decision makers about denial of equal rights in employment, about failure to consider all environmental impacts before locating a public facility, and so on. The growth of consumer power put together through the challenges to government and to large-scale private interests by the public interest lobby, as symbolized by Ralph Nader, has added alternatives of citizen participation and built a whole range of new norms and behavior patterns into the conception of citizen activism.

The mutually reinforcing thrusts of unionism among public employees and activism among citizens who are clients of public agencies will further politicize the administrative process. Agency managers will become more vulnerable to pressures, both from outside and from within. A further judicialization of administrative processes will result since the legal process continues to offer an appropriate weapon to both disaffected agency employees and disgruntled citizens among those affected by its proposed actions. As the process of government decision making becomes further politicized and judicialized, the role of professionals in the public service will be subtly altered. Citizen activism may affect the nature of the public service, both by modifying the nature of the administrative process and by altering the reward structure, making it more difficult to attract and retain competent people in the public service.

The Impact of Technological Change

The pervasive influence of past technological developments can be observed readily in the creation of new professions or career fields—for example, in the area of computer science and automatic data processing, or in the emergence of systems analysis as essential to adequate perspective. Systems analysis appears especially relevant in the public service since so many contemporary issues in American politics involve trying to understand the relationships among parts of what is assumed to be a complex, yet single entity. Technology works first on the nature of the tasks to be performed and then on the requisite training, experience, and orientation of public servants, affecting their capacity to perform these tasks. Increased emphasis will be placed upon a public manager having the capability to use the product of quantitative analysis and upon managers whose backgrounds are interdisciplinary in character.

Developing technology has reinforced trends to loosen hierarchical organizations, making them more flexible, open systems. The very structure and operating style of some agencies have proved conducive to innovation and an open, experimental approach. Working groups have been organized around clearly defined tasks but given only a temporary life, to be broken up and regrouped once the task is performed.

The effect of new technology upon the mix of, and the boundaries between, public and private sector roles in American society is another important consideration. There is ample evidence that the distinctions between private and public sector are disappearing or becoming blurred. Private corporations, both profit and not-for-profit, are engaged in performing public functions. The implications for the nature of the public service—mobility between private and public sector, and potential areas of competition—are relevant issues for exploration.

THE PUBLIC SERVICE OF THE 1980's

The foregoing trends are viewed as affecting four important components of the public service of the future: the organization of executive functions, the work force of the public service, the administrative process, and the administrator.

Organization of Executive Functions

First, one can expect flatter organizations with shorter chains of authority but a broader network for providing information and advice. More employees at all levels of government will be engaged in sophisticated data collection and analysis, program evaluation, and similar decision-supporting or participating tasks.

Second, greater use will be made of temporary groups which pull together a team of specially qualified people to do a job, and who, upon completion of the task, return to their parent organizations or become members of new temporary groups. Such assignments will stimulate creativity and provide a sense of participation and accomplishment. But such assignments also will cause anxiety about future assignments, requiring employees constantly to upgrade their knowledge and skills. Managing an organization of such teams presents challenging balancing and control problems to the agency leadership.

Third, the trends toward decentralization and wider participation make the control of public programs more difficult and more complex for top management. The agency director becomes more dependent upon a wider variety of people for information and analysis and faces more points of potential intervention by those outside of the agency (e.g., citizen activists using the courts). There is greater potential for vetoes by citizen groups—or at least delay—but project organization and more structured, rapid systems of communication promise the potential of quicker response once a decision is reached. In terms of authority and control, the political executive may be the loser unless he can use citizen intervention as a lever within the bureaucracy. The power of the professional, who will have to be very knowledgeable about the system, can be enhanced considerably. Conversely, there will also be influences at work associated with increasing politicization which can weaken the influence of professionals.

Fourth, greater attention will be given to planning. This will include long-range planning and the more systematic use of forecasting. Closer operating relationships will develop between those responsible for planning and those responsible for program execution.

Fifth, accountability will become more difficult because of the larger number of actors in the advisory-decision process (even though there may be fewer actual decision points) and because of the progressive blurring of the public and private sectors in the planning and conduct of public programs.

The Public Service Work Force

The term "work force" designates the people—generally career civilians—who constitute the public service. They include the classified civil service, wage boards, and members of special systems outside civilian classified service such as public school teachers and administrators, foreign service officers, Public Health Service physicians and nurses, and police and firemen.

An important result of trends described above will be much greater emphasis upon the development of new skills and knowledge by public employees at all levels. The need for post-entry training and a changing emphasis on the content of pre-entry education is evident. Increased participation by both citizens and the work force, more centralization in control and information but decentralization in the delivery of services, together call for administrators with considerably improved interpersonal, intergroup, and leadership skills. The increased use of systems analysis and quantitative measurement will require more employees with these skills or with the ability to use the product of such analyses. Both technical and organizational changes will place greater importance on the continuing nature of education —no longer can one complete a degree program with the comforting assumption that it will be sufficient to see one through a decade, much less a full career.

Public employees will have greater opportunity for self-expression and self-actualization with fewer restrictions in their roles as public servants. Wider participation is opening the public service to currents of opinion and ideas that used to be ignored or considered inappropriate. The public service is beginning to be more representative of the heterogeneity of American society. The use of project teams and more temporary types of organizations, and better education, broaden the opportunities for members of the work force.

There will be greater mobility in the public service, both within levels of government and between levels. More specific transferable skills and the use of temporary team groups will facilitate movement among agencies or subelements within agencies. The increasingly federated nature of public programs, where control and policy are centralized but services are decentralized, will require closer ties among federal, state, and local governments. In order to upgrade state and local capabilities, there will have to be more joint efforts to tap resources for education.

Employees will pay less obeisance to their agency. A better educated work force will not automatically follow agency policy if it is seen as in error, unjust, or unresponsive to the needs of the time. To the extent that "rebellion" hinges on strictly personal predispositions or on narrow, perhaps professional, self-interest, it can be seriously destructive of the public service by undermining political executives, the legislative process, and public confidence in the ability of the public service to serve the public interest. A decline in the public service ethic can be expected if classical unionization sweeps the work force or if professional and peer loyalties grow stronger than the larger sense of the public interest. Such a decline probably will carry with it a noticeable reduction in effectiveness.

Pressures toward politicizing the public service will have a direct impact on the work force. Citizen intervention in the administrative process will encourage employees to become active advocates for or against particular policies or programs. Strong unionization or professional associations may have the same effect, reducing the neutrality of the employee in the discharge of his program responsibilities. This can lead to considerable friction within an organization and to action against programs or individuals by legislators and political executives. Politicization will lead to greater conflict, more anxiety, less continuity, and less action.

The Administrative Process

Three tendencies clearly are identifiable—the first two of which are directly at odds: increasing flexibility and increasing rigidity. A number of trends reinforce increasing flexibility: (1) the increase in temporary organizations with better ability to shift resources to meet changing needs; (2) more reliance on state and local governments with greater attention to diversity; (3) greater use of private enterprise in performing public services, providing more options for the delivery of services; (4) more emphasis on a systems perspective, stimulating consideration of more options; and (5) the greater involvement of citizens and more intense focus upon local problems, promoting closer responsiveness to citizen-defined needs.

On the other hand, there are a number of developments which tend to promote rigidity more than flexibility. For example, although citizen participation (or intervention) in the administrative process can force a new look at old premises, it can also politicize the process, bring the intervention of the courts and the legislatures, and surround the process with a quasi-judicial context—ultimately more rigid and less responsive to change. Militant industrial unionism will tend to debase whatever flexibility now exists in the personnel system and erode management flexibility as well. Where employee dissent or citizen intervention reaches a pathological state, the administrative process will be forced into highly structured channels in order to act at all.

A third significant influence is that of increasing complexity in the administrative process. There will be more participants and a heavier representation of those who have played lesser roles in the past: consumers, conservationists, welfare recipients—even prison inmates—plus legislative committees and the courts. The use of sophisticated analyses in program evaluation and planning will demand systematic procedures incorporating a wider variety of skilled people. Greater attention to state and local problems, but from a national perspective and using national resources, will give an intergovernmental cast to more public programs, requiring better liaison and coordination. The blurring of the distinction between private and public enterprise, and the greater use of contractual services to perform public functions also will contribute to the complexity of the administrative process.

Four changes can be expected to have significant effects upon the future administrative processes. First, new standards for effectiveness and for accountability will be developed. "Least cost" was disposed of some time ago as the most important criterion for measuring program success. Even "most services for the money" is considered less than adequate. There is increasing concern about related or secondary impacts of services delivered and the nature of their delivery, as well as the process by which public program decisions are reached.

Second, the administrative process will be much more open—available for observation or participation by a wider variety of people, groups, and institutions. Decision points should be more easily identified. But there will be a tendency for the process to slow down as the number of observers or intervenors increases. As is the case now, it will be easier to block action than to push it through. The processes of participation and intervention will have to be structured carefully in order to preserve their purpose, yet permit timely action.

Third, where complex public issues involve many groups and strongly diverse opinion, there will be a decline in the ability of the public service to deliver. This will be the price of wider access by both citizens and the work force in the administrative process. The likely intervention of the courts will force administrators into the habit, perhaps unconsciously, of developing a record which can be used in judicial proceedings.

Fourth, there will be a significant expansion in the planning function, which will be tied more closely to, and with more emphasis upon, program evaluation and assessment, program execution, and attention to program purposes. There will be greater emphasis upon comprehensiveness, responsiveness to and integration with both the management and political considerations that are part and parcel of program operations.

THE PUBLIC ADMINISTRATOR OF THE 1980's

The cumulative effect of these trends is most important in terms of how they affect the administrator, the man who as agency head, program director, or branch chief must make organizations perform. His role has been the traditional focus of public administration. The individual administrator will face considerable change in: (1) how he leads and directs his agency; (2) how he handles relations with other organizations, other levels of government, the public, the legislature, the judiciary, and his executive superiors; (3) maintaining his own competence and some sense of direction without being submerged in change; and (4) the personal and ethical challenges to him as a professional administrator.

Coordinator and Facilitator

The adminstrator of the future will be more of a moral leader, broker, and coordinator than he will be an issuer of orders. Several factors will force more of a leadership and collegial role upon the administrator. Hierarchical authority already has been on the decline for several decades, as authority based upon position has become less synonymous with the requisite skills or knowledge needed for decision and leadership. Contributing further to this change will be the improved education of the work force, tied closely to increased specialization and the rise of authority based upon knowledge or skill.

Another factor facilitating this change in roles will be the increased interdependency within the administrator's organization. Increased applications of technology, greater use of temporary organizations, and more complex organizations to deal with the variety of interrelated programs combine to require an improved capability for meshing specialists in a productive fashion. The fact that specialists will be vital to the agency's operations, that employees or their organization representatives will exercise more authority within the organization, and that a wide collection of diverse people (frequently without any substantial loyalty to the agency itself) must be orchestrated in order for programs to function, all demand this change in role of the administrator.

Bargainer and Politician

The public administrator of the 1980's will be subject to vastly increased political pressures. The institutionalization of citizen intervention in the administrative process will make the administrator more visible publicly, and he will be pressed to adopt an advocacy role by citizen and political activists. In a simpler time the administrator could concern himself with accountability principally to one or two congressional committees and a few well-recognized clientele groups. In the future he is more likely to face competing groups of citizens working at cross purposes. Competing interests will stimulate increased attention from legislators and their committees, as well as from the judiciary, when competing interests seek court intervention to block or stimulate action.

Administrators in the future will work with a much greater array of organizations than has been true in the past. Increasingly, programs cut across levels of government so that an administrator must work effectively, not only with sister organizations, but with counterpart organizations at federal, state, local, or regional levels. Revenue sharing and other forces of decentralization (as well as the trends toward centralization) will tend to blur what once were considered clear lines of authority and responsibility, so that programs must be cooperative in nature—strengthening the demand for administrative roles of a bargaining and political nature.

An Agent of Change

The pace of change, the increased complexity of institutional arrangements, and the demise of traditional hierarchy will require the public administrator of the future to be adaptable, knowledgeable about changing trends and new developments, and perceptive in his judgment about which trends to exploit and which to resist or ignore. Personal and organizational relationships will be less permanent, making it necessary for administrators to adapt to constantly changing organizations and shifting personnel. The administrator will be able to reap substantial benefits, as can his subordinates, through increased mobility and the opportunity to learn new skills through new job assignments. There will be greater need for advanced planning, forecasting of trends, and evaluation of future alternatives. Both technical and social change will force the adminstrator constantly to upgrade his own skills, as well as to provide means for developing the skills of his staff. Education will be viewed as a continuing process involving informal, personal, and graduate refresher education as an integral part of keeping fit for the job.

Personal Challenges

Among the changes which will mold the public service are several which will challenge the public administrator personally as a professional: (1) a decline in the public service ethic, (2) erosion of loyalty to an employee's organization, and (3) greater political activism by employees, directed at policy changes. In the face of rapid change, increased complexity, and mounting pressure to produce results, these challenges weaken an administrator's ability to meet, responsibly, more substantive problems by diverting his time and attention.

As part of the Delphi exercise, participants were asked to assess changes in key attributes of the public service from 1961 to 1971. The results reflect a current pessimism about the adequacy of public institutions and public leadership to deal effectively with major problems (See Table 1). The same attitudes were revealed by the recent study *Hopes and Fears of the American People*.[2]

Of 12 attributes rated, eight were judged to have improved since 1961. When viewed as a composite, the change was positive (and statistically significant). But the four attributes rated as most important in 1961 declined:

- "honesty and impartiality in the conduct of assigned responsibilities,"
- "public confidence in the capacity and integrity of the public service,"
- "committed to merit principles in appointments and promotions," and
- "fully responsive to political leadership established by the electorate."

At the very time when one can foresee the need for professional leadership in the public service, the base upon which it and a professional public service must rest appears to be weakening. The public administrator of tomorrow will be sorely tested.

The future promises to be extraordinarily challenging to those who pursue careers in the public service over the next decade. In many respects, public administrators will have to be more adaptable, knowledgeable, patient, tenacious, and perceptive than ever before. Yet they will have new tools of management, analysis, information, and control. Managing public programs will be even more demanding than it is today, but those challenges can be met if today's adminstrators take the lead in anticipating the future and preparing to meet it.

REFERENCES

1. See Richard L. Chapman and Frederic N. Cleaveland, *Meeting the Needs of Tomorrow's Public Service: Guidelines for Professional Education in Public Administration* (Washington, D.C.: National Academy of Public Administration, 1973).

2. Albert H. Cantril, and Charles W. Roll, Jr., *Hopes and Fears of the American People* (Washington, D.C.: Potomac Associates, 1971).

ATTRIBUTES OF THE PUBLIC SERVICE:
THEIR RELATIVE ATTAINMENT, 1961–1971

(using a 10 point scale, 0 = completely failed to attain,
10 = completely attained)

Respondents were given 12 attributes significant in judging the quality of the public service. They were asked to select the 6 most important and to assess where the U.S. public service was in 1971 and where it was a decade earlier on each attribute:

	Means		
	1961	1971	Calculated t
1. Honesty and impartiality in the conduct of assigned responsibilities.	6.70	6.60	−.59
2. Cognizant of, and responsive to, the desires and wishes of the public.	5.22	6.19	+3.23*
3. Encouraging organizational innovation and experimentation with new ways of conducting the public business.	4.26	4.95	+2.62*
4. Emphasizing value and worth of individuals, both in government and outside, and need to respect dignity and worth.	5.08	6.08	+3.65*
5. Employing a reward and incentive system that attracts the highest quality personnel and retains them for long careers.	4.97	5.81	+2.77*
6. Public confidence in the capacity and integrity of the public service.	5.90	4.50	−5.83*
7. Committed to merit principles in appointments and promotions throughout the system.	6.72	6.33	−1.00
8. Maintaining strong, progressive manpower planning and career development programs.	4.37	5.59	+5.55*
9. Responsive to changing needs and sufficiently flexible to move in new directions rapidly.	4.62	5.05	+1.65
10. Fully responsive to political leadership established by the electorate.	6.05	6.02	−.18
11. Able to adapt to technological change and take maximum advantage of technological innovation.	5.00	5.95	+3.65*
12. At all administrative levels, broadly representative of the heterogeneity of American society as a whole.	3.57	4.39	+2.73*

*Calculated t is significant at the .05 level using the repeated measures formula.

	Means		
	1961	1971	Calculated t
Composite of the 12 attributes	5.18	5.53	+2.58*

Bureaucracies and Community Planning

by Paul Mott

The purpose of this article is to discuss four propositions about public bureaucracies and their effects on the efforts of communities to mobilize themselves for community action.

1. Public bureaucracies, which are often portrayed as monolithic intruders in a pluralist American society, are in fact usually pluralistically organized themselves.
2. Vested with the diffusion of power that accompanies pluralist organization, bureaucracies have greater difficulty initiating collective action and bringing it to a successful conclusion than they do preventing such action.
3. Given these difficulties in achieving collective action, public bureaucracies are almost incapable institutionally of solving the problems of communities, which intrinsically require holistic solutions.
4. If comprehensive solutions to community problems are to be implemented, then major modifications must be made in the ways the American public bureaucracies function.

BUREAUCRACY AND SOCIAL PLURALISM

Whenever the subject of bureaucracy comes up in courses in sociology, it is begun, almost inevitably, with a discussion of Weber's[1] definition of that concept. Except that it was not a definition: it was what Weber called an ideal type. Ideal types are logical constructs which, like the Ideal Gas Law, do not necessarily exist in the real world. They are analytical tools, and Weber constructed his ideal type as a model against which to compare existing bureaucracies. It was in the comparison that insights could be gained about the social forces that molded bureaucracies into the various structures actually found in societies. But, nonetheless, Weber's ideal type is often confused with a definition which, in the case of worldly objects, is an attempt to denote as accurately as possible something that actually exists. Perhaps people equated this ideal type with a definition of bureaucracies because it seemed so similar to the German bureaucracies of his time or because the current, popular conception of bureaucracies share so much with Weber's construct. At any rate, the important point is that the equation, where it occurs, is unfortunate, because public bureaucracies in the United States seldom bear more than a superficial resemblance to the ideal type. Perhaps these differences can best be summarized by the following table:

Weber's Ideal Type	Bureaucracies in the United States
The higher the role is in the hierarchy, the greater the authority it contains.	The authority vested in roles may be little more than a paper statement. People lower in the hierarchy may have greater power than those higher up.
The units or offices in the hierarchy are welded into an integrated structure by rules, procedures, and discipline.	The units or offices are very commonly autonomous with few close ties with each other.
The major forms of influence are giving advice up the hierarchy and giving orders down.	Bargaining and coalition formation are the most common methods of exercising influence.
Rationality governs the selection of efficient means to achieve ends.	Inefficient means are frequently preferred to achieve ends.

It is not difficult to support with abundant examples the statements on the right-hand side of the table. For example, while the Secretary of a federal department has greater authority on paper than his agency heads, the latter can very often nullify his policies and even get him removed from office. The well-known autonomy of the FBI under J. Edgar Hoover was so great that that agency could defy the Attorney General even when he was the brother of the President of the United States. What is less well known is that this autonomy of the agencies in departments is more the rule than the exception. Examples abound. It is very difficult for a Secretary of HUD to give orders to the Federal Housing Administration even though it reports to him on paper, because the FHA has powerful allies in Congress and in the banking community. The ability of each of the Armed Services to control Secretaries of the Department of Defense is well known. In DHEW the health and education components have considerable ability to pursue their own courses of action because of the strength of their constituencies and their relationships with Congress. But even within the health and education agencies there are subunits (bureaus) that have the power to control their own actions at the expense of agency heads and Secretaries, again largely because of personal ties with the President, powerful constituencies, or members of Congress.

This autonomy also has a horizontal dimension in that cooperative efforts between bureaus is the exception rather than the rule, even though they may be dealing with common clients and common problems. For example, there are over a dozen programs for child health in government agencies. Some are in the health section of DHEW, but others are in the Office of Education, Social Security Administration, the Social and Rehabilitation Service (SRS), or outside of DHEW altogether in such agencies as the Office of Economic Opportunity. Despite enormous overlaps in these programs, there has been little effort to coordinate them or to engage in joint projects. The Administration on Aging, which has a legal mandate to coordinate the efforts of departments and agencies to help senior citizens, has experienced great difficulty in obtaining the cooperation it needs from other agencies to assure that they give adequate expression to the needs of the aged in their programs.

The problem exists at all levels of government, not just at the national level. Stoloff[2] reports the difficulties that the East New York Model Cities planning group experienced getting the cooperation of established agencies in planning for services in the selected model city area. The Board of Education said that it could not guarantee the number of schools the planners wanted for the area and also that it would not support any innovative curricular programs unless they were the ones with which the Board itself was experimenting. The Department of Social Services refused to engage in joint planning for day care facilities in the model area, noting that it was developing its own plan.

Dahl and Lindblom[3] once defined a pluralist organization as one in which there is a diversity of groups or organizations that have a large measure of autonomy over which no unified body of leaders exerts control. This definition applies very nicely to public bureaucracies in the United States. Each is best described as a collection of relatively autonomous groups whose relationships with each other are more nearly bargaining than they are hierarchical. Some of the groups in the bureaucracies have strong permanent relationships with each other while others have none at all, and a great many of them form only temporary coalitions with each other around specific issues. But the strongest relationships are likely to exist with groups outside of the bureaucracy: with the committees of Congress that control their appropriations and with associations in the private sector for whom their program has relevance.

It is this intimate relationship with Congress and groups in the private sector that causes the pluralism of the bureaucracy. Congress was conceived and still functions as an area in which pluralist forces can vie with each other.[4] Members of Congress very often prefer categoric legislation—legislation that is directed to specific groups in the population—because they hope to attract the votes of those groups. Consequently, they would rather write legislation for the aged, the construction of highways, or the handicapped than to include these interests in more general legislation like revenue sharing under which the States or localities are simply given money for very generally stated purposes. Interest groups usually share this penchant, because it is a lot less chancy to have their own categoric legislation and appropriations that they can lobby for periodically with their own categoric, but probably friendly, committees—a lot less chancy than competing with other pressure groups for money made available through revenue sharing.

By designating a new agency to implement a categoric law, pluralism is transmitted to the Executive Branch. Attempting to find its place in the power system of administrative agencies, mindful of its prerogatives, and necessarily jealous of its territory, the new agency quickly learns that it is easier to build its own program than it is to weave together the resources of other mindful, jealous agencies. Besides, the pragmatic agency head knows that his career hinges on his success at satisfying the special interests represented in the legislation he administers. Joint program action with other agencies consumes energies better devoted to his own program, and it is less likely to make him politically visible than is solo action. Consequently, the federal government is really a congeries of agencies, each of which is devoted to carrying out a rather narrowly defined legislative mission.

This diffusion of power has another dimension that extends beyond the federal government that makes it difficult for even a categoric agency to fulfill its narrow mission, much less cooperate with other agencies to achieve broader ones. I am referring to the pluralist nature of federal, state, local, and private sector relationships. In addition to being categoric, federal programs usually allocate funds to States or communities on a formula basis, which means that the federal agency is expected to provide each State or city with the proportion of appropriated funds that the formula in the law provides. By this means Congress assures that the agencies will have very little to say about whether or not a State receives money or how it actually uses it. Sometimes this formula money has few, if any, strings attached to it: the agencies refer to it as "stump and run" money. ("We just leave it on a stump and run.") In this case the agency is little more than a check writing office. Other times some constraints are written into the law which give the agency some control over how the States use the money. But federal efforts to enforce these laws usually lead to the countermobilization of political power by irate mayors and governors who seek to neutralize the agency's actions. For instance, in 1971, when SRS sought to make California comply with the welfare regulations, it was eventually forced to back down when the State appealed successfully to President Nixon. The very powerful States like New York and California and powerful mayors like Richard Daley of Chicago routinely circumvent the bureaucracy and make their cases directly with the political leadership.

But the State bureaucracies are not monolithic either, because the same forces are at work in them to assure that they will exhibit the virtues of social pluralism. And county and city organizations are similarly molded (or riven) by our pluralist culture.

We add only one more complicating dimension—the existence of hundreds of private agencies and foundations, often with missions identical to those of public bureaucracies and each other, and often separated by strong associational and professional jealousies—to complete our Gordian picture. Whatever service or problem one cares to look at, whether it is health care for the poor or police protection, the picture of federal, state, local, and voluntary bureaucracies is uncomprehendingly complex both internally to each bureaucracy and externally in their relationships to each other. Internally or externally they are usually the epitomes of the concept of social pluralism.

It would be a mistake to label the resulting picture "fragmented" or "segmented" rather than pluralistic. Fragmentation or segmentation exists, but that is only a part of the picture. Strong alliances and coalitions also exist. In the vocational rehabilitation field, for example, strong ties bind some friendly members of Congress with the federal, state, local, and private sector rehabilitation agencies. They are easily coalesced against outsiders like governors or state welfare directors who might intrude on their prerogatives, and yet they are very sensitive to the locations of drift fences among their own prerogatives. Occasional expediency might even dictate temporary alliances with the American Medical Association, the Manpower Administration of the Department of Labor, or some other momentarily convenient political bedfellow. It is this middle ground between the mono- lithic and the anarchic models that offers the most accurate picture of American bureaucracies.

A natural reaction to such complexity of pluralist bureaucratic systems would be to throw up one's hands and wish a pox on their unintegrated houses, but it is our purpose here, rather, to describe the consequences of bureaucratic pluralism for collective social action, particularly community problem solving. Our point is essentially that the pluralist nature of public bureaucracies seriously undercuts the willingness and ability of their manag- ers to help solve the problems of communities, which, by their multifaceted and comprehensive nature, require holistic, collective solutions.

COMMUNITY NEEDS AND BUREAUCRATIC STRUCTURE

The antithetical character of bureaucracies and communities has been discussed many times in the literature in sociology, but most recently by Litwak and his colleagues.[5] They start with the same premise used by earlier theorists[6] that the structures and cultures of bureaucracies and communities are so different from each other that they have great difficulty developing mutually beneficial interfaces. Litwak *et al* went on to identify the seemingly incompatible characteristics of each of these types of groups. Bureaucratic emphasis on expertise, pragmatic, highly focused relationships, im- personality, and rules is opposite to a community's emphasis on open, diffuse, affective relationships, and informality. Where the community wants the bureaucrat to be concerned about the plight of human beings like those suffering from black lung disease or living in inadequate housing, the bureaucrat is concerned about whether the people are eligible for the services that they are seeking. Where the community would like prompt action based on a minimum of formalized procedures, the bureaucrat pre- fers deliberation and adherence to established procedures. The conflict was succinctly illustrated for this writer during a training session that OEO sponsored to equip community leaders to do community planning and write grant applications. The instructor was discussing the meaning and impor- tance of cost/benefit analyses to an increasingly restive group when one community leader who had become particularly angry stood up and shouted, "To hell with the costs, we just want the benefits!"

The cultural and structural differences between communities and bu- reaucracies are very real, and they do make it extremely difficult for them to work together. But pointing to the classic characteristics of bureaucracies as the sources of the problem is only partially accurate for two reasons. First, we have already suggested that the characteristics in Weber's ideal type often bear little resemblance to the realities of American bureaucracies. Some- times bureaucracies make their decisions based on impersonal criteria, but at other times they are extremely concerned about who made the request or who the decision will affect and are quite willing to find a way to bend the rules to assure that favored or feared people receive what they want. A research proposal coming from the congressional district of the chairman of their appropriations committee usually will receive favored treatment; at the very least it will not be set aside lightly without a few inquiries being made. In some areas the expertise of the bureaucracy, as in the cases of disease control or criminal detection, is obvious. In others it is not. For example, an agency may require that proposals be based on social planning yet not have any people in it who really know what social planning is or how to do it.

Second, very often bureaucrats invoke the letter of the rules or adhere to impersonal standards as a defense against much deeper problems. For example, if a community's proposal required the agency to deliver resources in new, unaccustomed ways, the evaluators are likely to couch their rejection in terms of the ineligibility of the applicants, errors in the proposal, or some similar reason. In other words, bureaucrats often assume the appearance of the Weberian ideal-type bureaucracy when it is convenient for them to do so in order to avoid some more serious problem, and it is those more serious problems that concern us here.

Therefore, while we accept the notion that bureaucracies and communities have many antithetical elements and that many of them have to do with the formal characteristics of bureaucracies, we propose that a more fundamental reason communities and bureaucracies have difficulties engaging in joint action has to do with the pluralist character of most bureaucracies and the inappropriateness of that form of organization for dealing with many community problems.

Problems are invariably embedded intimately into the fabric of a community, which means that they cannot be treated in isolation from other aspects of community life. Arresting drug abusers will not solve a community drug problem, because the practice may be the result of many other factors—unemployment, poor housing, discrimination, psychological depression, or alienation—which are likely to generate new drug users. Unless the attack on the problem is fairly broad, it is unlikely to be solved. Given their categoric bases, bureaucracies are not geared to make sufficiently comprehensive attacks on community problems. Consider, for instance, the problem of providing adequate health care in a poor inner-city neighborhood. Health facilities have to be developed, people enrolled in programs for which they are eligible, and information about services and transportation to them must be provided. Yet because of their categoric character, no single agency can provide for all of these needs. The Medicaid agency can accept for enrollment all of the people in the neighborhood who are eligible for that program, but it does not build health facilities or provide transportation. Facilities can be obtained via a project grant under Title V of the Social Security Act which is administered by a different agency. And transportation to the health facility can be arranged by social service caseworkers. Outreach workers who would go out into the neighborhood and get eligible people into the program are unlikely to be available in any of these agencies, but the OEO program might have them. In other words, the problems are integrated, but the resources to deal with them are not. Furthermore, we have already suggested that attempts to aggregate resources and bring them to bear on problems must struggle against the pluralist characteristics of bureaucracies. Even among the best intentioned managers it is very difficult to put together a joint project. Eligibility standards in the different programs do not match; rules and standards block action; distrust and suspicion are easily aroused. And since they are so seldom practiced, the techniques of managing projects that cut across agencies often are little understood and poorly used by program managers.

But more commonly, and for reasons developed earlier, agency personnel are not inclined to work on joint projects with people from other agencies. They get their rewards for performance within their own programs and not for their contributions to other programs, and resources devoted to joint projects must be taken from other program areas that may be more highly valued by the agency or its client groups. In the earlier example of the East New York Model City area, the Board of Education's reluctance to meet the demand of the Model City planning group was based on real concerns. Meeting the requests of the planning group would mean diverting resources from other areas of the city and other potentially powerful and vocal interest groups.

Categoric bureaucracies can have a second, subtler impact on communities, one that erodes the ability of the latter to organize themselves for social action. By sticking to their categoric programs and delivering their services or money to clients on an individual basis, bureaucracies can be an individuating influence in communities. A veteran confined to a wheelchair may receive job training and income support but be unable to visit others in his neighborhood because architectural barriers have not been removed. The economic well-being of the aged may be improved through Social Security payments, but their social well-being may inadvertently be lessened because they live alone, isolated from the community. Since the government takes care of the aged, there is no apparent need for community action; neighbors don't stop by to see if the person is well—that is the job of the public health nurse. Marriages are often precluded by the potential loss of welfare payments or Social Security checks. Ironically, the more effective bureaucracies are at delivering their categoric services, the more they are likely to sap the community's will to organize itself and, without community organization, the more organic problems of community life are likely to go unsolved.

BUREAUCRATIC RESPONSES TO COMMUNITY ACTION

Usually aware that the pluralist design of their organizations is not very appropriate for dealing effectively with community problems, agency leaders have responded to community action in a variety of ways, not all of them constructive.

Traditional bureaucratic responses have been commonplace. Community grant applicants were required to use the usual procedures to obtain a grant: an almost hopeless task unless aid could be obtained from knowledgeable people or institutions. Or when community groups attempted direct action with political or bureaucratic leaders, they found it easier to get their attention than to get some follow-up action on their demands. In one scenario, the top agency leaders would appear at the petitioners' rallies or meetings and suggest strategies for helping them that involved meetings between representatives of the agencies and the community. In those meetings and under the guise of cooperation, the agency representatives would gradually lead the community people into the game of bureaucratic procedures. Solving the community's problems was posed as a series of hurdles to be jumped, but jumping those hurdles would prove to be such a long and complicated process that little was ever likely to occur. Nonetheless, it was important for the community people to think that success was just around the corner.

Another almost opposite approach was to give the community a planning grant. Very often these grants were little more than bribes to the community leaders, since many of them would receive salaries from them. These grants might actually be followed by other grants to demonstrate one service or another in the community, but rarely did they touch the mainstream of money that the agencies administered. By placating the community somewhat, the agencies protected themselves from the grim prospect of diverting money from the traditional channels or increasing the demand for the programs that they administered.

Especially galling to local political leaders were the programs of OEO. These programs struck at the very core of the political apparatus of the city, if there was such a core. In some areas the activist efforts at community organization competed with the traditional ward organization of the city. Where the ward organizations were used to maintain the status quo while gathering votes, the new organizations proposed radical change that undercut the power of the ward organization. In many areas the new organizations supplanted or captured the older ward organizations. Communities also learned to use the courts to force city leaders to act, and they did it via lawyers supported on grants from OEO. It took a while, but eventually the countermobilization of the city leadership proved effective, and the OEO programs were brought under greater control by the city leaders. This is the situation today.

Other responses have been more constructive. They center around increased consumer involvement in planning either by informal or legislated mechanisms. Some agencies have begun involving consumer groups systematically in their planning. Since 1970, the Social and Rehabilitation Service, for example, has gotten the advice of the National Welfare Rights Organization and many other organizations on new regulations governing its programs. That same agency also consulted with a wide variety of client groups in its planning for future programs. But these efforts are few in number, seldom institutionalized, and do not exist at all levels of government. If community involvement in bureaucratic planning and operations is to become more prevalent and institutionalized, legislative action is required.

This line of reasoning led to the insertion of consumer or client participation articles in various laws. Usually these insertions took the form of simple statements that consumers must be involved in the planning for a program. Because of the genuine difficulties involved, specific criteria rarely were established for the types of consumer groups that should be included or what constituted adequate participation. Therefore, actual practice usually varied greatly from the intent of these laws. The planners would involve representatives from the establishment client groups rather than the more militant, unpredictable ones. Or they would brief client groups on the finished proposals, rather than involve them in the construction of those proposals. Legislative draftsmen have been aware of these potential abuses but reluctant to write stronger, more concise language into their laws. There are several reasons for this reluctance. First, many lawmakers believe that specific criteria should appear in administrative regulations and not in laws. Second, there is a valid opinion that it is impossible to write such criteria because of the complexity of the problems and the ultimate ability of anyone who really wishes to circumvent the intention of the law to do just that. Third, there is the more typically bureaucratic reason that having stated there should be consumer participation, responsibility for what occurs is shifted elsewhere—the bureaucracy has done what it could.

Perhaps the most comprehensive and imaginative effort to deal with the problems that have been discussed above has been the Allied Services Act, which was drafted by the Department of Health, Education, and Welfare and submitted to the 92nd Congress and again to the 93rd. This bill would put greater power in the hands of governors or any agent designated by the state to focus aggregated services on particular problems. It also would give the governor or other state designee the power to transfer significant sums of money from one program to another. At the local level the bill required that local planning groups include client representatives in the planning process and that every planning effort begin with a careful study of actual community needs. While the bill would restore the power of governors and mayors and increase the role of community groups in community planning, it would also force categoric agencies and professional groups to foresake some of their territorial imperatives to achieve some collective objectives. For example, a community planning group could determine that one of its major priorities was providing adequate health care for the poor. It would then design a service plan that pulled together the services of several local agencies. If a particular service were in inadequate supply, the plan might recommend that funds be transferred from another, less valued program to strengthen the valued one. The Allied Services Act would not eliminate the categoric character of bureaucracies, but it would remove some of the barriers to collective action. However, because it is limited to DHEW programs, this proposal is not the ultimate answer to the problems raised in this paper.

Currently, revenue sharing is being posed by the Administration as the ultimate answer. Under revenue sharing the states or localities are given formula grant money to achieve a variety of generally stated purposes. The difference from the usual formula grant money is the generality of the objectives listed in the legislation; they can range from no stated objectives to lists of relatively generic categories like family planning, interurban transportation systems, or secondary education. The theory is that by being given such unfettered money local governments can determine what their major problems are and solve them directly without the intervention of several federal agencies.

However, in this case, theory and practice are little likely to be related. While the encroachments of the federal bureaucracy are eliminated, pluralism still exists and state and local agencies and pressure groups still exist. These social forces and groups can be expected to operate when revenue-shared funds are allocated, and, therefore, it is quite likely that the money will be divided among existing agencies. In other words, the categoric programs and agencies would probably still exist at the local level, doing business in the same way as prior to revenue sharing and still no more capable of serving comprehensive community needs.

Revenue sharing will not be a strategy readily accepted by many groups, because it undercuts their roles in the pluralist system. Many members of Congress are concerned that revenue sharing might undercut their prerogatives to specify the uses of funds: to develop priorities of their own. And they recognize that a vote for revenue sharing is not as politically useful as a vote for a veterans' bill or a senior citizens' project. Many federal agency managers see revenue sharing as a further erosion of their control over their programs. They argue for a larger federal role to prevent the states from misusing the funds.

The greatest potential advantage to revenue sharing is that the states and localities can use the pooled money to attack problems more comprehensively. If a state already has a good interurban transportation system, it can put more of its money in some other area where the need is greater. This is precisely what worries the representatives of various pressure groups: that they will have to compete with each other for rather limited noncategoric money. More of them are realizing the security of their older categoric programs. Whether revenue sharing will become increasingly popular is problematic. Whether such funds will be used for comprehensive attacks on community problems is even more problematic.

CONCLUSIONS

Overcoming the pluralism of American bureaucracies in order to deal comprehensively with the problem of communities will not be easily or readily accomplished. But more people are recognizing the problem, and articles are being included in legislation that require studies of community needs and the development of plans that are responsive to those needs. The Allied Services Act is one example, but the Older Americans Act and the Developmental Disabilities Act are others. Unfortunately, these laws are relatively narrowly focused in terms of the clients they serve and the problems they deal with.

As we saw, revenue sharing is unlikely to solve the problem, because although it eliminates one source of categoric activity—the federal bureaucracy—it does not eliminate the others. Once the money reaches the states and moves from there to the local level, it is most likely to travel well-worn paths through existing agencies.

Perhaps one useful long-term solution would be to combine the philosophy built into the Allied Services Act with revenue sharing. Allied Services proposes a balanced power relationship among governments at the federal, state and local level. Much of the debate over how to allocate power in the American system has focused on centralization versus decentralization, as if these were the only options. The Allied Services Act vests power in general purpose governments, rather than trying to avoid them, and says that each level of government has an important and different set of functions to perform in solving human problems. Unlike revenue sharing, Allied Services says that the Congress has a major role in the establishment of societal priorities. If it states these priorities very generally—family planning, crime control—it does not fulfill its function, because the money would then be stump and run money. If, on the other hand, it is too specific in its priorities —provide maternity care for 750,000 poor, pregnant women by the following means—it has moved beyond priority setting to doing the job for the states and local governments. Allied Services recognizes that every state and every community is in some ways unique, each possessing its own particular combination of problems. Therefore, the task of determining how much emphasis to give each federal priority or how to implement it is best managed at those levels. Power is balanced then in the sense that all levels are involved in social policy formulation and implementation, with each level having different functions in that process. At the local level a representative planning group would be able to develop a comprehensive plan to deal with community problems. In its plan it would have to show the contributions of the different agencies to the implementation of the plan and how the revenue-shared money would be allocated among them. The planning group could also make proposals to integrate the agencies or some agency functions, like developing a common intake function for all of them.

This proposal is not new or untested. Other countries have recognized the conflict and the needs of communities and have been more successful than we in dealing with them. Yugoslavia has used the system of nationally set priorities around which communities develop their plans. That system also allocates some funds for nonpriority items, thus recognizing that communities are bound to have some unique problems that they want very much to have solved. Great Britain has used the local features of this model in its planning for services to children. Local councils composed of public and private sector agencies and citizens plan for the services needed in the community. Then each of the representatives on the planning group indicates its contribution toward the achievement of the plan. For example, if the plan involves the development of a dozen day care centers, the national government may contribute teachers and psychologists, a charitable organization may volunteer transportation services for the children, and so on. Rather than having several different agencies working in unconcerted fashion on the same or overlapping problems, a single plan is created to which they all contribute systematically.

It would not be necessary, therefore, to start from scratch to reshape American bureaucracies. Most of the elements of necessary law exist. There is ample experience in other countries and in some American programs to suggest which practices work and which do not. What seems to be required is broader recognition and acceptance of the problem among decision makers at the national level and a willingness among them to solve it.

REFERENCES

1. Max Weber, *The Theory of Social and Economic Organization*, A. M. Henderson and Talcott Parsons, trans., 2nd ed. (New York: Wiley, 1947), pp. 329–341.

2. David Stoloff, "Model cities: model for failure," *The Architectural Forum* 132:101–115 (January–February 1970), pp. 101–114.

3. Robert A. Dahl and C. E. Lindblom, *Politics, Economics and Welfare: Planning and Politico-Economic Systems Resolved into Basic Social Processes* (New York: Harper, 1963), pp. 302–6.

4. David B. Truman, *The Governmental Process* (New York: Knopf, 1951).

5. Eugene Litwak and Henry Meyer, "A Balance Theory of Coordination Between Bureaucratic Organizations and Community Primary Groups," *Administrative Science Quarterly* 11:35–38 (June 1966–March 1967), and Eugene Litwak et al., "Community participation in bureaucratic organizations: principles and strategies," *Interchange* 1:44–60 (1970).

6. Ferdinand Tonnies,*Fundamental Concepts of Sociology* (New York: American Book Company, 1940) pp. 18–28; and Weber, *The Theory of Social and Economic Organization*, pp. 354–358.

School Decentralization in the Context of Community Control

by Daniel Elazar

The demand for community control of schools is usually understood as a demand by blacks and other racial or quasi-racial minorities for greater control over the institutions within their inner-city "ghettos."[1] In fact, it is, in one form or another, a well-nigh universal demand in the United States today, one that transcends the immediate interests of inner-city residents, important as those interests are. Indeed, the demand for community control is not a new demand but simply a restatement of one as American as mother's proverbial apple pie.[2] It has been brought back into the public eye by the militancy of blacks, Puerto Ricans, and Chinese in the country's great central cities in their search for a right common to most Americans but which they have never been able to exercise.

The demand for decentralization of big city school systems, which includes the demand for control over the personnel responsible for the schools within them, is the most widely recognized element in the quest for community control but is not the only aspect of that quest. The desires of suburban residents to maintain relatively small independent school districts is of the same order except that because the suburban school systems were constituted in that way from the first, their demand does not involve a militant campaign for the attainment of the objective. Still, suburbanites must wage more subdued campaigns to maintain their version of community control. Their situation generally goes unrecognized for what it is and, worse than that, is usually attacked for what it is not. One additional dimension has now been added to the suburban interest in community control. It was in the suburbs that the notion that education was somehow "not political" reached its peak. With the erosion of that idea, one finds growing demands in the suburbs for moderating the control of professional educators over the schools and injecting greater citizen participation at least in the shaping of educational policy. This, too, is part of the demand for community control, one that is no different in its essentials from that of the inner-city minorities.[3]

Finally, the demand for community control of schools still flickers in the "peripheral" areas of the United States, in those small town and rural communities which have borne the brunt of the consolidation movement of the past generation and were the first to lose control at the immediate community level for the sake of principles of administrative and organizational efficiency widespread in educational circles beginning a generation ago. While the reduction in the number of school districts from a high of approximately 125,000 some 30 years ago to the present 16,000 or so has virtually eliminated the question in its original form for many communities;

the reshaping of the communities themselves in light of technological changes connected with the metropolitan frontier has no doubt revived it in the new, consolidated districts. In these districts there is the added problem of how to maintain community control while at the same time maintaining a sufficiently comprehensive educational program manned by personnel of sufficiently high caliber.

All three situations described above reflect different but equally meaningful dimensions of the quest for community control. In all three, two other problems remain crucial factors in the quest: school finance and racial segregation. Virtually no school system today is immune from budgetary problems while the demand for equalization of fiscal resources, whether on a metropolitan, statewide, or national level, has become an insistent one. Regardless of the level of political interest in community control, the fiscal problems must be solved if such control is to be a viable arrangement. At the same time, political decisions can be taken that will adequately deal with the fiscal issues within a context that provides for community control, if such should be the will of those who shape the political decisions involved.[4]

Racial segregation as an issue is intimately tied to the entire question of community control, especially since the argument of whites for segregated schools generally has been couched in those terms. There are even strong hints of it in the black militants' present demands for the same in their areas. By its very existence as an issue, it raises questions about the limits and possibilities of the demand within a national society such as that of the United States.[5]

The question that is placed before those concerned with education and politics is precisely to determine the possibilities, limits, and likely consequences of community control of the schools or its alternatives. This is essentially a political question, that is to say, there are no extrapolitical considerations that will automatically determine how the decisions on community control should go. Rather, by taking particular political decisions it will be possible to shape the other factors so as either to enhance or to limit the possibilities for real and realistic community control.

THE PERSPECTIVE

While the concern here is with the demand for community control of schools, any inquiry into the meaning and likely consequences of that demand must begin with the understanding that it is part of a larger demand for community self-government.[6] Again, as in the case of schools, the suburban experience is especially useful in defining the meaning of this demand.

Originally, people sought suburbanization for essentially private purposes, revolving around better living conditions. The same people then sought suburbs with independent local governments of their own for essentially public ones, namely the ability to maintain those conditions by joining with like-minded neighbors to preserve those life styles which they sought in suburbanization. They soon discovered that control of three functions was necessary to provide a solid foundation for local self-government: (a) control of zoning to maintain the physical and social character of their surroundings; (b) control of the police to protect their property and to maintain the public aspects of their common value system; and (c) control of their schools to develop an educational program for their children that met their perceived needs and pocketbooks. It has become evident over and over again that suburbanites will fight to retain control over these functions as long as they see them threatened by "outsiders" who would change them in such a way as to alter the life styles of their communities.[7] The suburbanites' instincts were quite correct in all this. Despite the thrust toward centralization in American society, control over these three functions in most cases maintains the kind of local control which they desire.[8]

The functions that suburbanites will fight to retain as "close to home" as possible are essentially the same as those presently being demanded by blacks in the great cities who wish the same rights as their suburban countrymen for their neighborhoods (most of which are not really neighborhoods at all but congeries of neighborhoods with populations as great as those of the more substantial suburbs, if not of large cities). They, too, justify those demands on the grounds that it is necessary for them to control their destiny in these public matters in order to be able to achieve their private and public goals. Given the premises from which they began, they are indeed correct. The same reasons lie behind the efforts of peripheral communities outside of metropolitan America to maintain their institutions of self-government.

The struggle over community control is necessarily conducted within the context of the American political system and is accordingly bound by that system. Thus it is not a struggle for the re-creation of the sovereign *polis* (except perhaps in the minds of the most extreme militants) but for the achievement of maximum local control over vital public functions in a properly scaled locality. Most Americans of whatever race, creed, or ethnic origin share common values and goals. What they seek are not separate ways so much as variations on the "American way of life." Thus they strive for the kind of local control that makes the maintenance of those variations possible, and moreover, within the context of a meaningfully sized place, the definition of which has changed periodically throughout American history.

The most pronounced characteristic of the American system, from this perspective, is its federal character and the precise nature of that federalism. In the first place, the very existence of federalism offers the possibility of legitimately achieving a very substantial degree of community self-government; indeed, one might say that it creates the conditions and stimulates the demand for community self-government. Secondly, the highly intertwined system of cooperative relationships linking governments on each plane—federal, state, and local—shapes the limits and the possibilities for community self-government. Both of these aspects will be further treated below.[9]

THE SCHOOLS AND THE CIVIL COMMUNITY

An understanding of the problem of community control must begin with the exploration of two questions: how is the community to be delineated, and what is the place of the schools within it? In the United States, communities are essentially artificial creations purposely founded and organized in the course of the country's development by people with immediate common interests, often of the most narrow economic character or for the most limited social purposes. With some rare exceptions, they have not been organic entities embracing all forms of human life and linking the same families over generations, nor were they ever conceived to be. Rather, their residents are linked by the need to commonly pursue certain interests that thereby take on a political or civil character. Hence they are best understood as civil communities, people living in a common territory bound together for political or civil purposes. The maintenance of common political goals provides the basis for community and the existence of institutions designed to pursue those goals provides its framework.[10]

Given the nature of the American political system which tends to encourage what is often called "fragmentation" of government on the local plane, responsibility for the maintenance of those goals is usually entrusted to many different institutions which can be grouped in sets. Taken together, they create the institutional "bundle" that gives shape to a particular civil community, defines its limits and character, and serves its needs. The sets are (1) the formally established local governments serving a particular locality, such as the municipal governments, the county, the school districts, and the like; (2) the local agencies of the state and federal governments insofar as they are adjuncts of the local community existing primarily to serve it, such as the local branches of the state employment office and the post office; (3) the public non-governmental bodies serving local governmental or quasi-governmental purposes, such as the chamber of commerce and the community welfare council; (4) the political parties or factions functioning within the civil community to organize political competition; (5) the system of interest groups functioning in the local political area to represent the various local interests; and (6) the body of written constitutional material and unwritten tradition serving as a framework within which sanctioned political action must take place and as a check against unsanctioned political behavior. The foregoing governmental, public non-governmental, and quasi-governmental institutions are linked with each other and with the local citizenry through a congeries of "games" (the "education game" is a major one), any of which will involve some or all of them. These in turn create "complexes" which represent the institutionalized relationships between the governmental and non-governmental, public and private participants. These "games" and the "complexes" which participate in and manage them reflect the political dynamics of community in each locality.[11]

In a very real sense a civil community consists of the sum of the politically relevant complexes and games which function in a given locality and which are tied together in a single bundle of governmental activities and services. This bundle of governmental activities and services is manipulated in the locality to serve the local political value system. There is no standard set of political jurisdictions that can be used to delineate the individual civil community. Each civil community must be delineated in its own terms. In any particular, the territorial basis of the civil community may consist of a city or township, an entire county or other regional political entity, a school district, a regional planning district, or the like.

Schools and games which surround them are subsumed under one or more of the foregoing categories. Public schools are among the local governments while parochial and perhaps even private schools can be counted among the public non-governmental institutions.

Not every entity with its own local government is, willy-nilly, a civil community. Some entities are too small, some are too large and some are too fragmented. In the case of the first (a category that embraces quite a few suburbs and some of the country's peripheral cities or towns), their governmental and other institutions may simply mask the fact that they are really no more than neighborhoods, capable of political expression but not really capable of self-government, even in the limited sense used here.

In the case of the second (a category which embraces every city of over 500,000 population in the United States and some smaller ones), the mere fact of a common government does not create community. In fact, those cities are generally less fragmented governmentally than the smaller ones but are more likely to be congeries of subcommunities that have few if any common civil goals of a local character and which may indeed have conflicting local interests. Nominally local governments, the governments of these cities, are in fact neither local nor supralocal. More often than not, they impede true local government without being able to provide the kind of general government provided by the states or the federal government.

The third category consists of localities otherwise capable of functioning as civil communities whose residents are for some reason unable to pull together sufficiently to do so. Unable to successfully pursue any common ends, they remain without political form regardless of their formal structures.

The question of community control is directly related to the problem of civil community. Thus it may be that in any particular locality there are good convergences among all the appropriate elements or sets in existing civil communities, that there are better convergences in potential civil communities than in actual political jurisdictions, or that, particularly in the case of the biggest cities, local government exists but not civil community.

The conclusions to be derived from determining what happens to be the case in particular localities must necessarily assist us in dealing with the problem of community control of the schools within real or potential civil communities. What are the likely or possible effects of community control on the schools and on the community itself? Will the schools' educational program be substantially changed? In what ways? To what effect? Will community control of the schools serve as a rallying point for the community? Assist in the development of its self-image as a community? Change its composition or character by encouraging particular kinds of immigration or out-migration? These are only a few of the questions that must be raised.

EDUCATIONAL OPTIONS AND COMMUNITY CONTROL

The sheer complexity of American society today places the foregoing questions in a radically different context than they were in the days of the "community school" debate a generation ago. Then it was generally assumed that schools would be serving homogeneous territorial communities and, properly run, would find no particular difficulty in serving the educational needs of the great bulk of the community's members. Whether that view was correct or not even then (it entirely ignored the existence of parochial schools and minority groups, for example), it is not now. Today part of the study of the possibilities, limits, and consequences of community control of the schools must be a study of the provision of options, both within the civil community as defined and in determining the definition of the community.

One choice of options that immediately presents itself for investigation is that of the neighborhood versus the regional or specialized school. The neighborhood school principle is based on the view of the civil community as a relatively homogeneous whole that can be effectively subdivided into smaller units that are equally or even more homogeneous internally, for even closer relationships as well as for sheer convenience of the citizenry and their children. The idea is, in essence, that children will go to public school within the same geo-social framework in which they live and play. This leads to a number of questions. What is a neighborhood for school purposes? To what extent are regional schools something other than devices to achieve the breakdown of certain kinds of neighborhoods or communities? To what extent is schooling a means of creating or maintaining neighborhoods? All these are questions that must be explored.

More recently, a new view of the civil community has begun to emerge which sees its primary components as social or cultural groups that function in place of or within neighborhoods rather than homogeneous neighborhoods as such.[12] Heterogeneity in such communities either cuts across all potential neighborhood lines or is manifested in symbiotic rather than homogeneous neighborhoods where two or more such groups live together for reasons of mutual advantage. This emerging view is manifested in a second set of options which consider non-public as well as public schools as parts of the civil community's overall educational system. The non-public sector used to consist exclusively of parochial schools and a few upper-class academies. Today not only has the variety of parochial schools increased to include more Jewish and Protestant schools as well as Catholic, but private schools catering to a widening variety of middle-class interests have begun to emerge as well.

Study of the role of non-public schools in the overall framework of the local community has been substantially neglected. Today such neglect is no longer possible, particularly as Americans begin to seriously consider options, such as the issuance of educational scrip to every family so that each may choose the kind of schooling it wants for its children, that would drastically change or even eliminate the present system of public education as we know it.

Clearly, such factors as the size of a particular civil community or the composition of its citizenry would influence the impact of such changes and the changes themselves would clearly affect the character of the community. In very large cities, for example, the proliferation of freedom of choice schools not built on any neighborhood principle might very likely exacerbate the already fragmented character of the community, while in small and medium size civil communities the very lack of distinctive neighborhoods and the availability of other opportunities for inter-group contact might lead to very different consequences. All the options involving non-public education—for example, religious (or parochial) day schools, private day schools for special purposes or interests, and shared time programs that combine public and non-public education—should be examined in this context.

In this connection, the contents of the educational program in public schools should also be examined as a third option. Under the system of territorial democracy practiced in the United States until well into the twentieth century, local school systems (which were usually quite small) determined their own educational programs including the religious, cultural, and social values they attempted to transmit as representing the "American way of life." The major thrust of the twentieth century, at least until recently, was away from such local decision-making and toward the imposition of common national standards of what could or could not be taught. The rise of black and other militants with their demands for an education that would strengthen their peoples' search for a common identity has opened the possibility for a new version of the older approach toward the use of the school as a medium for transmitting different versions of the "American way of life" rather than any single one. Consequently, even the maintenance of public schools as we know them may bring local curricular changes of a very distinctive character for neighborhoods, for whole civil communities, or for neighborhoods on their way to becoming civil communities.

Determinations as to the use of any or all of these options must be treated as major political questions, not simply as educational ones, since it is at precisely this point that education and politics meet. Viewed from this perspective, education is, indeed, the handmaiden of politics in the highest sense.

THE MOBILIZATION OF EDUCATIONAL RESOURCES[13]

It has already been pointed out that the question of community control can only be considered in the context of the American political system as a federal one in which the political units are bound together in cooperative relationships. Consequently, a significant aspect of the study of the question must involve inquiry into the roles to be played by the extra-local governments in any system of locally controlled education. In other words, what can a community actually control and what can it not, politically, administratively, and economically must be asked. Under what conditions can it exercise control? What resources must be made available to it? By whom? Under what conditions? Are there any extra-local units, forces, or actions that will particularly advance or deter community control? Why?

Studies of intergovernmental relations have repeatedly confirmed that, while participation in the provision of resources for given programs virtually guarantees the donor a role in shaping those programs, it does not by any means guarantee a level of influence commensurate with the resources provided. Thus most states have rarely exercised control over education commensurate with the amount of money they provide their school districts. Conversely, some states exercise more control than contributions might call for. In essence, the provision of resources and the exercise of influence represent separate political decisions which are related only when the decision-makers wish to relate them. Consequently, they may be treated as separate decisions, potentially related, when they are considered in the context of support or opposition to community control in one form or another.

While the roles of all the extra-local governments or authorities in the United States—state, federal, and regional—are potentially significant in determining the outcome of the community control issue, the role of the states will in all likelihood be the most significant. The states begin by having authoritative custody over the organization of education within their boundaries, the development of educational standards and requirements, and the determination of the mode and character of financing educational systems. More than that, they have final authority over the legitimation of the civil communities themselves. In both connections they are bound to affect the school systems within their boundaries. Theoretically, at least, they have the ability to make true community control possible by creating the legal framework for it and by "backstopping" their communities with technical assistance, financial resources, and proper standard-setting so that community control becomes feasible. On the other hand, the existence of conditions or interests supporting the status quo with power in the state house could render the possibilities for achieving real community control remote.[14]

The federal role in education has been growing again in recent years, not only in the provision of support for certain educational endeavors but in the stimulation of educational innovation. An activist federal government can operate so as to lend its support to the movement for community control or work against it. Today federal influence operates in both directions, supporting black ghetto efforts on one hand and seeking the metropolitanization of local educational systems on the other, encouraging local innovation in educational techniques and restricting local policy-making on religious questions. The very existence of any clear-cut federal policy is doubtful. Indeed, given our knowledge of the complexities of policy-making and administration on the federal plane, we may conclude that it is unlikely that any clear-cut policy will ever emerge from Washington. (We may even reflect on whether such a policy should emerge.)

The relationship between federal aid and the educational establishment must be viewed from this perspective as well. The various federal programs can be examined individually in terms of their effects on the community control issue. Since "community control" works both ways and is often used as an argument to maintain racial segregation, federal policies should be examined in this regard as well.

Finally, the growing (if still small) influence of regional arrangements on the educational scene also has its bearing on the community control issue. Regional arrangements are presently of two kinds: there are interstate arrangements such as Education Commission of the States which serves over 40 states primarily in a research and advisory capacity and others such as the

Appalachian Regional Commission which provides both funds and a forum for political tradeoffs among the member states for educational purposes related to regional economic development. The first has yet to demonstrate any direct impact on the community control issue but is important for its efforts to reintroduce the country's political leadership into the educational picture. The second has already had an effect on the peripheral communities in its region, strengthening the educational systems of those it considers promising from an economic perspective and weakening others by denying them additional resources for growth. There are also intrastate regional relationships, usually but not exclusively in metropolitan areas. To date, these, too, are essentially coordinating or research relationships but areawide structures to create a new fiscal base for financing education in the region by available funds are under serious discussion in many quarters. They, too, can be supportive of or detrimental to the community control principle, depending upon the goals set for them politically and the way these goals are implemented.

In the end, the question of community control of schools will remain tied to the larger system of community control in general. We will have to choose what path we wish to follow in an age in which centralization is not only taken for granted but is considered right and proper by those who fear that the diffusion of power will interfere with the achievement of goals which they espouse. The residents of the inner city, no more than 20 percent of the population, have done all Americans a service by reviving the issue of community control as a meaningful one; but their success or failure in the pursuit of that goal will also hinge upon the success or failure of the other 80 percent in the pursuit of similar goals. Local self-government is a fundamental aspect of the American dream. Whether it will remain a realistic one depends less on the objective factors usually cited to justify continued centralization than on the political decisions of American citizens desirous of shaping the world in which they live.

REFERENCES

1. See, for example, Milton Kotler, *Neighborhood Government* (Indianapolis, 1969); Donna Shalala, *Neighborhood Governance: Proposals and Issues* (New York, 1971); and Marilyn Gittell, "Saving City Schools" in *National Civic Review*, LVII (January 1968), pp. 21–26.

2. Alan Altschuler makes this point, in part, in *Community Control* (New York: Pegasus, 1970). See also, Daniel J. Elazar, "Community Self-Government and the Crisis of American Politics," *Ethics*, LXXXI, no. 2 (January 1971), pp. 91–106.

3. Thomas H. Eliot dismisses this in "Toward an Understanding of Public School Politics," *American Political Science Review*, LIII, no. 4 (December 1959), 1032–1051.

4. Advisory Commission on Intergovernmental Relations, *State Aid to Local Government*, Lois Pelekoudas, ed. Chap. III (Urbana, 1961).

5. See, for example, Charles Abrams, *Forbidden Neighbors* (New York, 1956).

6. Alvin Toffler, ed., *The Schoolhouse in the City* (New York, 1968), contains a number of essays relevant to this point.

7. Elazar, "Community Self-Government."

8. See Morton Grodzins, *The American System* (Chicago, 1966), particularly Part Two.

9. *Ibid.;* Daniel J. Elazar, "Local Government in Intergovernmental Perspective" in *Illinois Local Government* (Urbana, 1961), pp. 36–48.

10. Roland Warren describes the character of the American Community in *The Community in America* (Chicago, 1963).

11. Norton Long sets forth a similar idea in "The Local Community as an Ecology of Games" in *American Journal of Sociology*, LXIV, no. 3 (November 1968), pp. 251–61.

12. See, for example, Nathan Glazer and Daniel Patrick Moynihan, *Beyond the Melting Pot* (Cambridge, Mass., 1963); and Raymond E. Wolfinger, "The Development and Persistence of Ethnic Voting," *American Political Science Review*, LIX, no. 4 (December 1965), pp. 896–908.

13. See Thomas N. Dye, *Politics, Economics and the Public* (Chicago, 1966) Chap. IV, "Educational Policy"; and Philip Meranto, *The Politics of Federal Aid to Education* (Syracuse, 1967).

14. See, for example, Robert H. Salisbury, "State Politics and Education" in Herbert Jacobs and Kenneth N. Vines, eds., *Politics in the American States* (Boston, 1965); and Paul Mort, Walter Reusser, and John Polley, *Public School Finance* (New York, 1960).

The Careers of Clients and Organizations

by William R. Rosengren

It is popular to say that formal organizations are ubiquitous and salient in the lives of people. The so-called "organizational" society may well distinguish contemporary modernized societies from the "Gemeinschaft"-"Gesellschaft" typology which preoccupied social scientists for so long. To borrow Earl S. Johnson's words:[1]

> With Gemeinschaft I associate *natural, sentimental, kinship,* and personal; with Gesellschaft I associate fabricated, rational, contrived, and impersonal. We must, and likely do, understand that the Community Chest, the Red Cross, the Peace Corps and other institutional agencies we now use at home and overseas lack, in significant ways, the warmth and intimacy of the simple face-to-face and private charitable devices of the parish.

That, perhaps, is the profound issue in service organizations: how to strike a working balance between the rational structures of bureaucracy, and the ethic of conviction which tends to make all organizations something less than bureaucratic.

But rationally fabricated organizations are more than the meeting place of Gemeinschaft and Gesellschaft. They are the ground upon which the individual as a person confronts his social institutions and his social structure.

Some might even argue that large scale organized efforts are *the* distinctive earmark of modern societies—signaling their historic drift, shaping the lives of people in all of their facets whether workers or clients, and bearing the prevalent values which inform relations between persons and their social institutions.

To say this, however, fails to give much of a clue to four main problems with which organizations—service organizations in particular—are now confronted.

The first has to do with Weber's wise observation that the bureaucratic organization represents efficiency and effectiveness par excellence. But at the same time it arises out of conditions of democratization and egalitarianism and hence is pressed to serve humanely and effectively. Michel Crozier's fine analysis of the French bureaucratic system could be turned to this theme to the extent that the members of that system attempt to eke out a sphere of personal autonomy in opposition to the system; the American system leans more toward favoritism and the growth of informal cliques which may subvert the system; British bureaucracy retains an element of elitism which harks back to an earlier era of traditional authority.[2] Each cultural setting, in its own way, seems to manage some degree of accommodation between the ethics Gemeinschaft and Gesellschaft.

The second problem I want to explore has to do with the ways and extent to which organizations change over time. Although the empirical evidence is scanty, I entertain the idea that organizations—like people—live out a career which has discernible stages from beginning to end even though the larger social order may remain very much the same throughout. Hence we must ask what the career followed by service organizations is; to what social forces turning points in the organizational career may be traced; and what the posture of an organization is likely to be as it passes through its career-cycle towards those with whom it is involved, especially in regard to technical imperatives on the one hand, and humanistic expectations on the other.

Thirdly, there is a related set of issues which springs from the second general theme of this symposium—inter-organizational collaboration, and especially organizations as "members" of other organizations. Organizations of all kinds are presently forced to respond not only to the demands of client groups, but are also called upon to alter their historic patterns of isolation from one another and established loyalties to special segments of the communities in which they exist. The question that I wish to pursue here is the following: if organizations change in discernible ways as they age, what consequences may this have for the *kind* of inter-membership activity of which they are capable?

Finally, I want to mention just briefly one last aspect of organizations. That has to do with the degree to which clients are "taken-in" to organizations more or less as full participants. In recent years service organizations of all kinds have "invited" clients to take a more active part in organizational life. The fact that this democratization of bureaucracy has in some cases opened Pandora's Box is hardly surprising: mental hospitals, for example, through devices such as patient government, family visitation, community advisory groups, and others have drawn the patient (and other quasi-members) into the organizational system in quite real and sometimes authoritative ways. Schools—universities especially—seem well along the way to transforming student power into student authority in ways which can wrought significant changes in the functioning of educational institutions. Welfare agencies—largely through OEO—have taken welfare recipients *directly* into their membership, thus breaking through the hallowed crust traditionally separating staff from clients. Prisons also have been toying for a long time with ways of engaging inmates in the work of the organization.

In short, client-serving organizations may well be quite far along the road to becoming—at least in an approximate sense—*voluntary associations*—in the sense that the needs and expectations of the "clients" become the goals of the organization staff and the determinants of the patterns of work which develop. As a result they are likely to contain many of the processes that Charles Perrow has described.

So by way of introduction, these four issues are certain to constitute a rich mix: (1) the dual demands for efficiency and humanism; (2) the possible presence of quite inexorable organizational careers; (3) the increasing demand for—under various names—inter-organizational contact and collaboration; and (4) the increasingly flirtatious relationship between organizations and their clients.

ORGANIZATIONAL CAREERS AND ORIENTATIONS TOWARD CLIENTS

A first task is the labeling process itself—how shall organizations be referred to at each stage of their growth and development? These labels are not totally arbitrary, for they obviously must be ones that I can work with, and which can be of some utility in addressing the four issues just posed. I draw upon what has, by Mark Lefton and myself, been called the "client-biography" model.[3] This derives from the proposition that the internal structure and dynamics of organizations are closely related to the manner by which organizations intervene in the life course of their clients—both present and future. To re-cap this perspective simply: organizations may choose to interrupt the contemporary lifespace of their clients in either a highly focused, specific way, or more diffusely and broadly in an attempt to alter—if you will—the whole person. Mark Lefton and I (in stubborn opposition to the pleas of friends and colleagues) persist in referring to this social space dimension of the client biography as "laterality." A general hospital might typify the "non-lateral" specific focus, while a family counseling agency is called to mind as a more "laterally" or broadly oriented institution.

Organizations may also choose to intervene in the lives of their clients in either the short or long run. Those which attempt to attach themselves, perhaps even permanently, to their clients' future lives are termed "longitudinal." Those which detach themselves from clients after but a truncated period of time are called "non-longitudinal." Hence, such a perspective yields four analytic types of organizations, each expressing a distinctive orientation towards its clientele. Using these types as the bench-marks, I wish to pursue—in turn—the following questions: (1) What type are organizations likely to be when they are new, and toward what type are they likely to drift as they age? (2) What are some of the internal features of new and old organizations? (3) With what kinds of collaborative activity are old and new organizations most compatible, and what implications may this have for present-day preoccupations with service programs predicated upon interorganizational membership?

ON NEWNESS

I want to pursue the argument that organizations of the "service" variety are likely to begin with a broadly focused and short-term style of intervention. In doing this, I thoroughly expect to be making a number of inferences, some of which may not be totally justified.

Contending with Liabilities of Newness

In his discussion of the "liabilities of newness" Stinchcombe makes the point that new organizations must rely heavily on establishing social relationships with strangers, and that their initial relationships with strangers tend to be highly unstable and subject to change.[4] The aim is to standardize and routinize these relationships and—in the interests of economy and efficiency—to reduce these relationships to the smallest possible number. (This is not unlike the point made by James Thompson that organizations, when operating under norms of rationality, attempt to seal off their "core-technologies" from environmental influences.)[5]

One manner by which organizations may overcome this initial liability and establish tentative and temporary ties with strangers is to offer services of a broad-based kind, addressing as it were multiple sectors of the community by focusing upon multiple aspects of the client's life space. This will serve not only to attract a heterogeneous clientele, hopefully one large enough to sustain the new organization as an economy, but will also serve to link the new institution to a large organizational set. As some of these strangers come to be colleagues, associations with others are terminated. With this comes a more specific focus in the organizations' orientations towards its clients: the stabilization process has begun.

At the same time, during the early unstable period, the organization is unlikely to adopt a long-term orientation precisely because of the tentative nature of its external linkages. Over time, however, and in accompaniment to its drift toward a specific orientation, the institution is likely to attempt to retain a continuity of clientele through intervening for a long period of time in the client's biographical career. This is consistent with what Thompson has called "smoothing" out-puts in an effort to reduce uncertainties. For as the organization's focus becomes more specific, it reduces its alternatives, becomes less capable of shifting its goals, and can reduce some of the organizational uncertainties produced by these facts by retaining clients as organizational property for longer periods of time. As Stinchcombe says, "One of the main resources of old organizations is a set of stable ties (*lateral/ longitudinal,* italics mine) to those who use organizational services."[6] And, "the stronger the ties between old organizations and the people they serve . . . the tougher the job of establishing a new organization."[7] One way by which new organizations may break into the existing organizational set is by altering the customary pattern and codifying their relationships in accord with the prevailing specific and long-term pattern.

A further contingency of newness has to do with the fact that clients can sometimes be attracted away from existing old organizations by holding out the appeal of full organizational membership and participation to them. Hence, new organizations may initially begin by becoming, in Charles Bidwell's terms, "Moral-Associational" in nature, with clientele acquired by being "inducted" into the institution on a quasi full-membership basis.[8] However, at least some students, David Mechanic, for example,[9] argue that lower level participants may be quite effectively insulated from organizational effectiveness and authority, and these organizations take the form of what Bidwell terms "Technical-Communal." In short, the new organization may achieve this ultimate effect by beginning in a broad lateral fashion, and then later effectively limiting the participation of lower-member-clients by focusing more specifically upon them and for a longer period of time. Hence, the initial contract between the client and the organization may be normative, turning later into a technical imperative.

Stinchcombe also points out that new organizations arise out of an effort to meet needs which are presently unmet and to introduce a technology, or series of technologies, not currently being made available.[10] Perhaps as a result of this, new organizations are likely to begin life with a relatively untried and untested technology, the efficacy of which is yet to be demonstrated. In the absence of a viable and specific technological repertoire (already achieved by more stable and mature organizations) an intensive technology is likely to form the basis of organizational operation—the utilization of multiple and uncoordinated efforts to achieve through *scope*, what cannot yet be achieved through *depth*. Hence, services are likely to be offered initially on a broad lateral basis. One can only speculate that the original short-term orientation may also arise because of an awareness of the temporary character of the first "technology" and the likelihood of its radical reduction in scope of kind as the organization ages.

There is yet another factor which might account for an early broad orientation toward clients. This has to do with the need for new service organizations to acquire both a clientele and a patronage. The relation of both of these imperatives to the kind of service credo that develops has been suggested by both Eisenstadt and Perrow.[11]

One way by which new service organizations can attract clients and patrons is to offer services on a broad lateral basis. This serves not only to attract the attention—and potential support—of multiple groups in the community with rich and varied interests at stake, but it also serves to present a unique cluster-appeal to clients who may already be the property of organizations with more routine service patterns.[12]

In short, new organizations must somehow break through the crust of the existing organizational set. They can do this best by offering "novel" combinations of services to clients. But the economies of newness invite a tentativeness about this, and hence result in a short-term orientation toward clients.

With a beginning such as this, I want to turn now to the question of the factors—both internal and external to the organization—which might account for a subsequent drift toward a specifically focused and long-term orientation toward clients.

Some Processes of Organizational Change

Let us assume once again that organizations—especially as they mature —increasingly come to pay homage to the "norms of rationality," not only for economic reasons but for organizational control purposes as well. In this sense (and as Thompson has pointed out) organizations attempt to seal-off their core technologies from environmental contingencies. The laterally oriented organization is acutely vulnerable to environmental contingencies. This is due largely to three structures which tend to accompany a broad focus toward clients. First, a multiple technology system demands the presence of multiple professionals with varied technical and varied ideological persuasions. Secondly, the lateral organization inducts more of the client's social personality into the organization. This institutionalization of client latent roles is potentially disruptive to the organization. Thirdly, a broad lateral orientation normally means that the organization draws support from many different groups in the community. This is potentially a divisive pattern because it leads to competitive processes among supporters, with the organization itself as the target for manipulation and control. So, factors such as these will tend to reduce the organization's broad scope orientation and give rise to a more specific and delimited service ideology.

In addition, and drawing once again upon Stinchcombe's discussion, one characteristic of formal organization is an effort to "achieve" predictability of future benefits or outcomes. This, according to Stinchcombe, is consistent with Weber's repeated emphasis upon calculable law, calculable taxation, etc., in the growth of rational enterprise. So a presumed penchant for predictability will not only reduce the organization's scope of interest in the client, but will tend to stretch it out in time as well. A single technological focus is more easily calculable than are several, and a long-term attachment to the client more easily assures that calculability will be realized. At the same time, as an organization becomes more stable, i.e., ages successfully, it may calculate its own "survival" in terms of long-time spans, while the young and unstable organization is more likely to seek for measures of adequacy more immediately in the here-and-now. Furthermore, a drift toward a more specific and long-term orientation allows an accommodation of standardized routines, while a broader and short-term perspective mitigates against a "norm of rationality" such as this.

I mention only parenthetically the fact that an increase in organizational age cannot help but be accompanied by increased urbanization of the environment in which the organization undergoes the aging-process. And it is now axiomatic that urbanization is equivalent to population density, and that population density is equivalent to functional specialization.[13] One can only add that functional specialization is consistent with a differentiation among organizations along the non-lateral dimension.

A not unrelated argument stems from the proposition that organizations of all kinds attempt to effect some kind of *change* upon the people whom they serve. Organizations are instruments of alteration, and *service* organizations attempt to alter materials which are highly reactive—people. On the whole, "technical" changes are more easily wrought than are changes in ways of life; the first involves the manipulation of some specific aspect of the human material, while the latter must engage the material's conscious desire and cooperation in altering himself.[14] The broadly oriented *lateral* organization, as a matter of fact, attempts to bring about these ways of life-changes, while the specifically focused *non-lateral* organization addresses itself to the problem of technical change. And to bring to fruition changes in the total configuration of people is more difficult organizationally, more costly in terms of resources, and less conducive to organizational stability and permanence, than are those interventions which elect to change some specific part of the human resource. As a result, surviving new organizations will tend to renounce their original broad focus and zero-in on a specific mechanism, a technologically accessible aspect of their materials. Changing human persons also demands that the alteration be made more or less permanent: hence as the organization becomes more stable in terms of its own survival capacity, it will elongate its specific orientation toward the client in an attempt to make its technical change as irreversible as possible.

As the new organization enters the set, resource scarcity (or the perception of its presence) becomes increasingly an issue. As a result, organizations which become set members—that is as they age and survive—must compete at two levels.

Inter-organizational competition first occurs for what Levine and White have called goals-priorities—laying down some special claim or service or competence which shall insure a source of clients and a support fund: hence a drift toward a specific non-lateral focus once the initial survival problem is overcome.[15] Secondly, competition develops over set domination—how directly to effect the relations among the set members so that the distribution of set resources is not left either to the whims of the present dominant nor to the mysteries of *deus ex machina*. One good way to achieve set domination is for the organization to extend itself in the "social time" of its clientele, thus achieving some leverage in the organizations which may later be held responsible for departed clients. This arena of set domination competition may also account for the fact that the long-term oriented institution tends to be one which contains a large number of discretionary job-holders at the administrative level called upon to alter their conduct depending upon the existing pattern of power relationships amongst set members. Younger short-term oriented organizations are often ignored in this pattern, thus allowing them to become full participating members in the organizational set.

These are but some of the external processes and forces which move new organizations from a plus-lateral/minus-longitudinal to a minus-lateral/plus-longitudinal service orientation. Some internal forces may also be at work leading to a similar result: the first has to do with the ambiguities for staff roles which accompany a broad orientation toward clients as reflected in the unspecialized division of labor which such an organization usually contains. Role expectations are ambiguous and poorly defined. Tasks are highly discretionary, demanding creativity, imagination, and commitment, especially on the part of lower level personnel. In Caplow's terms,[16] new organizations of this type tend to have too little stratification, too high interaction, ambiguity, loss of autonomy for the individual, and too much flexibility and goal deflection as far as the organizational system is concerned.

In addition, new multiple-technology organizations face serious coordination problems. Priorities are competitive at best and unclear at worst. Criteria as to final results are similarly confused and perhaps in conflict. Due partially to this, the organization is likely to drift to a more specific orientation toward clients, hence solving problems deriving from an initial broad orientation toward clients.

Problems of control are yet a further issue faced by the new plus-lateral organization. Specifically, the new broadly oriented institution is unable to achieve worker compliancy through its structural division of labor. Rather, it turns to supervisory management tactics to achieve through styles of leadership what its unspecialized division of labor has failed to achieve.[17] This, in turn, means that much administrative time and effort must be devoted to overseeing and supervising the work of operative personnel. Parenthetically, it may be in this early stage of organizational life that the oft noted conflict between operatives and administrators is most acute and disruptive to the organization. On the other hand, a more specifically focused orientation obviates the need for direct supervisory controls, hence mitigating, to some extent, potential conflict between operatives and administrators. At the same time, the development of a longer-run interest in the client requires that administrators devote more of their time and energies to "future" contingencies rather than to work-a-day routines. Hence, a drift towards a minus-lateral/longitudinal orientation helps to resolve both internal conflict and external contingencies.

Some Characteristics of End-State Organizations

At a general level, I think that old organizations of the type discussed—specifically and long-term oriented—contain quite contrasting ideologies in the operational as compared with the administrative sphere. Indeed, this kind of terminal organization is likely to contain classic rational bureaucratic (Gesellschaft) elements at the operational level, but more Gemeinschaft characteristics at the administrative level. Operative activities are likely to be informed by rationalization while the latter by humanism. Operations are likely to be integrated through specialization, while administration by means of esprit de corps;[18] control of operative personnel is likely to be accomplished by means of structural authority while compliancy of administrators is likely to be achieved through strategies of managerial supervision;[19] the day-to-day routines of the operative wing are likely to be conducted on the basis of rules and regulations, while the administration is likely to be oriented more towards incalculable contingencies uncovered by pre-existing rules. Finally, the face-to-face relationships between operative workers are likely to have the impersonality signaled by Weber, but the administrative wing will be permeated by the pressures of latent cultures and the demands of many latent roles. In sum, the old organization has a specific focus on the client, and from this can devise a single technology around which it can organize a rational and bureaucratic division of labor. But, on the other hand, it has also a long-term, perhaps incalculable time-interest in future contingencies and must therefore conduct its administrative work more in terms of the ethic of commitment, rather than of rational calculation. In short, the specific focus of the mature organization permits the structures of bureaucracy to develop within the operational line, while the diffuse and long-term commitment to future unknown contingencies results in a more de-bureaucratized administrative system.

Furthermore, under the assumption that age leads to a specific and long-term orientation towards clients, it might also follow that the old organization is characterized by *member involvement* of an "exchange" variety at the operational level, but to "commitment" at the administrative level.[20] If the exchange bargain which is struck is adequately negotiated and satisfactory, then the organization can probably anticipate "efficient but personally detached" work. It is more likely to be the case however, that old and specifically focused organizations will increasingly contain "early-ceiling" occupations in which the economic structure of the larger social order will rather effectively mitigate *against* continually altering the bargain to raise levels of worker satisfaction. In short, the old organization is—in Caplow's terms—likely to result in high stratification and low salience, hence boredom and low productivity, alienation and sabotage, anomie and apathy, coercion and rebellion.[21]

This pattern is generally consistent with Udy's comparison of *bureaucratic* and *associational* production systems.[22] In this sense, the older organization is likely to contain what Udy refers to as technical salience at the operational level, but to organization membership in the administration. Hence, the specifically focused and long-term organization will be technically integrated—and its operatives technically motivated, but it will be normatively integrated at the administrative levels, and its administrators more subject to ideological values. Let me emphasize that later I hope to argue the importance of these patterns for inter-organizational relationships.

Assuming, furthermore, that the old organization does become specifically and long-term focused, it is also likely to develop what Thompson refers to as a "long-linked" technology with *certain inputs* (a controlled predictable source of clients) but with uncertain out-puts.[23] In some sense, this kind of organization receives its human materials usable in their presenting form, but the long-term intervention which is intended may well mean that the organization is seldom fully satisfied that it knows when the job is finished. Hence, tremendous concern for and ambivalence about moving clients *out* of the organization while still retaining some degree of interest in or even control over them. What is involved here is probably better said by suggesting that the new organization is not quite sure what it's doing, but it knows when its job is finished; the old organization is more certain about what it's doing, but not quite sure when the job is over.

In addition, the old organization, with its specific and long-term orientation, has little difficulty in inducting its clients into the organization, but must devote much staff effort and organizational resources to "out-ducting" them. Not only must they contend with the problem of delineating the precise time at which clients ought to be discharged—they must also determine the suitable places to which clients ought to be sent. All of these problems are essentially administrative in nature and result in judgments which may be more system maintenance in nature than service oriented. For example, in an organizational "set," in which the members mature to the end state, the out-put needs of one can very easily come to be resolved by input needs of another institution.

There are, undoubtedly, many other characteristics of old organizations which are worth pursuing: (1) a focused and single technology exists at the operational level, but multiple and uncoordinated technologies exist at the administrative level; (2) authority informs staff relations at the operational level, but power and attractiveness is the bench-mark at the administrative level; (3) clienteles are regarded as exclusively the organization's own at the operational level, while there is great awareness of overlapping clienteles at the administrative levels. In short, the new organization is likely to be preoccupied with *perfecting* its core technology more than with accommodating large inter-organizational problems. On the other hand, the aged organization is more likely to preoccupy itself with accommodating its administrative melange to the power setting, having already settled on its technological tour de force.

If these patterns are true, it could be argued that they hold important implications for present programs in the fields of human welfare which currently press upon us. I turn lastly to this issue.

Current Demands Upon Service Organizations

I want to indicate what I understand to be five aspects of recent federally inspired programs in health and welfare: *First,* such programs call for innovations, departures from the present practices in both operational and administrative spheres. *Second,* most federal programs ask for rather dramatic alteration in the work load of existing organizations. Inducements are offered, of course, but these must be balanced against out-puts. *Third,* the success of these programs demands a minimum of conflict between organizations. *Fourth,* and perhaps the base issue, these opportunities usually call for broad based and long-term engagement of multiple organizations in the community—a collectivized plus-lateral/plus-longitudinal orientation. *Fifth,* and finally, many of the new programs seem to be moving in the direction of renouncing the traditional organizational complexes in favor of those which can enhance inter-agency collaboration.

On the whole, I think it is fair to say that new collaborative programs tend to be initiated through the established, i.e. old, organizations in a community. It is the dominant, viable, large, and visible institutions to which funding agencies normally turn. As a result, local community mobilization for new programs tends to fall in the hands of those organizations which have certain structural limitations as far as adequate implementation is concerned.

One cannot ignore Caplow's contention that decisive innovations tend to be introduced into the organizational set by organizations of intermediate prestige and power—those which are younger, less firmly established, less visible, and otherwise less established in the total organizational complex. We are talking, of course, about technical as well as ideological innovation, and in this sense a prime dilemma is posed: the old organization with its specifically focused interest *is* capable of accommodating technical changes, but its extensive external administrative linkages to an established organizational set tend to prohibit dramatic ideological changes. On the other hand, new "zealot" organizations are often founded on the problem of perfecting their core technologies, but are fertile ground for ideological transformation. Hence, the old and the new: the first capable of and in a set position to innovate at one level, the second capable of another kind of innovation but not in a set position to do it.

I think it is also fair to say that as organizations age and mature, they tend toward a stabilization of work roles and work loads. This occurs not only through rationalization and formalization processes, but also as a result of collective negotiation between workers and management which, over time, come to acquire the character of precedents. In old organizations, the answers to questions such as who shall do what work, at what pace, for what rewards, and even for what purpose tend to be quite inflexible. The reverse is the case in the new laterally oriented organization. The problem, of course, is that most of the new programs in health and welfare—if *properly* implemented—demand drastic alterations in work role and work loads. Paradoxically, perhaps, it seems that new organizations, broadly oriented toward the client's biographical career, *are* capable of conducting the work called for by the new programs, but incapable of effectively engaging themselves.

On the other hand, the old and established organizations are capable of mobilizing the necessary inter-agency contact and dialogue, but least capable of responding meaningfully to the appeal for a more diffuse orientation toward clients.

Thirdly, an obvious component of most federally inspired programs— explicit in some cases—is a renunciation of inter-agency conflict and divisiveness in the interests of mobilizing the collective energies of multiple agencies toward common problems. Organizations, however, especially mature ones with a specific and long-term interest in their clienteles are probably less capable than others may be of responding to this call. I would entertain the hypothesis that as organizations become specifically focused they increase their inter-agency competition for scarce operational resources. And as organizations attempt to maintain an interest in their clients for a longer period of time, they compete for dominance in the set concerning what the final or long-term goals ought to be.[24] Moreover, established organizational sets in a community tend to constitute prestige sets as well— some organizations are thought to be more desirable to work in and to be serviced in than are others. As Caplow has pointed out, this self-aggrandizing tendency of set members effectively mitigates against precisely the kind of inter-agency "rank-equality" which full collaboration calls for:[25] it also minimizes the likelihood of sharing of scarce personnel, a process often regarded as critical to the success of forward-looking programs. In fact, one might suppose that the very enunciation of the principle of non-conflict has itself brought to the fore aspects of intra-set conflict which were before only occasionally visible when the barriers to inter-agency isolation were not challenged.

Fourth, most of the new programs call for what we have termed a lateral and longitudinal orientation toward clients. Yet the dominant and mature members and those to which granting agencies usually turn for leadership for some of the reasons set forth here have a structural incapacity to deal with client problems in this global way.

An alternative, of course, and one that has been followed in many communities, is to allow the aged organizations to go their own way and construct new organizations to deal with the clients in the broad fashion desired. The difficulty here, of course, is that new organizations are hardly able to break through the hard-crust of the organizational set and fulfill the constituent demands for inter-agency collaboration and integration. The effect can be only that of introducing *another* service sector into communities which are already encumbered by the presence of multiple-organizational sets, the members of which engage in prestige ranking with their co-members, and are effectively insulated from other sets which deal with the similar clients and similar client problems.

One outcome of this embroglio has been to give the burden of responsibility to the least mature zealot new organizations without anchorage or leverage in the total organizational complex, and even more poignant, to turn to the clients themselves as a resource. And in this sense, new organizations, and even the clarion call of the new community programs themselves, tend toward voluntary associations in which the desires of those served become the goals of those who serve, and determine final organizational structure. The present trap in all of this, of course, is that the new organizational systems will themselves age. If they do so in the directions which I have suggested they will move toward a specific and long-term interest in their clients, a codification of their position within existing organizational sets, and all of the other patterns which I believe inhibit effective inter-agency contact and collaboration.

SOME SPECIFIC PROBLEMS OF OLD ORGANIZATIONS AS EFFECTING INTER-AGENCY COLLABORATION

Let me mention just briefly and in propositional form a few specific characteristics of specifically focused and long-term oriented organizations as they bear upon collaborative demand, not *all* of which are as gloomy in outlook as what has previously been said.

First, age leads to non-discretionary jobs at the operational level and to highly discretionary jobs at the administrative level. Persons in discretionary jobs—in this case administrators charged with the responsibility for giving direction to inter-agency collaboration—attempt to maintain power over others in the task environment. This will lead to the development of coalition arrangements to maintain the status quo as persons in discretionary jobs in multiple-organizations seek, to coalesce their powers in the face of threatening forces from outside.[26]

In addition age leads to the development of precarious values at the administrative level and to stabilized values at the operational level. Persons in organizational sets subject to precarious values tend to become partners in organizational coalitions in an effort to codify their values and make them acceptable to the environment. On the other hand, inter-organizational coalitions can easily develop into "hold-actions" until the environmental heat is off.

Also, age results in an organizational occupational structure which involves up-grading through negotiation and collective action at the operational level, but through work visibility and prestige at the administrative level. Most new community programs, however, are of such a type as to be enhanced through prestige and work visibility at the operational level and through rational negotiation at the administrative level. The conflict presented is obvious.

A final reference to Starbuck probably sums up in a global fashion much of what has been said:[27] the older an organization becomes the more resistant is its social structure to change. Demands for collaboration call for great changes in the structural arrangements of service organizations.

Let me sum up briefly my argument before a final remark on the Gemeinschaft-Gesellschaft distinction with which I began:

1. Many service organizations begin life with a broadly focused but short-term interest in their clients. This occurs because of the need to collect clients, garner community support, and to survive initially without access to the prevalent organizational set.

2. As they age, they tend toward a specific and long-term orientation toward clients. This happens because of the press of norms of rationality, perfection of technology, membership in the organizational set, and the need to retain a hold on clienteles in order to sustain relationships with other organizations in the environment.

3. Current federal programs call for a broadly focused and long-term commitment to clients. New organizations are operationally able to provide the first, but their weak set membership prevents them from accomplishing the second. Old organizations are incapable of shifting from a specific to a broad orientation toward clients, but *are* able to sustain their set dominance.

4. An alternative, represented in some of the CAP programs and which can easily be read as an admission of organizational defeat, is to turn to the clients themselves and ask them what to do and how to do it—to become voluntary in nature. Charles Perrow writes more authoritatively about the limits and possibilities of this strategy of making clients full participants in service organizations.

OLD ORGANIZATIONS AND THE CONFRONTATION OF GEMEINSCHAFT AND GESELLSCHAFT

In Earl Johnson's words, for an organization to be natural, sentimental, kin-like, and personal it must be lateral in its orientation toward clients. The taking-in of the total person in milieu psychiatric hospitals, in collegiate educational institutions, and in other such broadly oriented institutions represents an effort to inject these *kinds* of relationships between clients and the formal organizations which periodically touch the lives of people.

On the other hand, the technically elaborate and specifically focused minus-lateral organization more closely represents a Gesellschaft context—fabricated, rational, contrived, and impersonal.

But both Gemeinschaft and Gesellschaft must deal in their own unique terms with the person not only as he *now* is, but as what he shall be. Hence, the short-term minus-longitudinal organization opts for gesellschaft in the long-haul: the client—treated either personally or impersonally in the here and now—is soon cast off as a person as if he were never a member of the organization. In the long-term plus-longitudinal organization, however, the ethics of sentiment, natural, personal, and kinship follow him about from organization to organization for a very long time.

Perhaps with the enthusiasm of the Great Society, the new programs in human welfare call for the organization to deliver Gemeinschaft in both the present and future tenses—organizations are asked to be sentimental and natural with regard both to the clients' contemporary life space and future life course. This may be too much to ask. Old organizations may be able to deliver Gemeinschaft in the long-haul because of their established linkages with other organizations which can deal with the client later on. New organizations may be able to give a context of Gemeinschaft in the short run because of their zealot character. Unfortunately, I see no real evidence that Gemeinschaft in the present as well as in the future can easily be accomplished for clients without more drastic organizational transformation than has as yet taken place. It will be very hard indeed to reconstruct the parish in the presence of bureaucracy.

But in spite of the obstacles to achieving the kinds of inter-organizational memberships presently thought to be desirable by many, it is clear that there are systematic relationships between organizations. The analysis of these relationships as they are found to occur at the local community level is taken up in the following chapter.

REFERENCES

1. Earl S. Johnson, "Gemeinschaft-Gesellschaft Perspectives on the Human Experience," Kermit Eby Memorial Lecture, Manchester College, January 15, 1968, p. 1.

2. See for example, Michel Crozier, *The Bureaucratic Phenomenon* (Chicago: Univ. of Chicago Press, 1964); Talcott Parsons, "Definitions of Health and Illness in the Light of American Values and Social Structure," in E. Gartly Jaco, ed., *Patients, Physicians, and Illness* (Glencoe: Free Press, 1958), pp. 165–187; and Monroe Berger, *Bureaucracy and Society in Modern Egypt* (Princeton: Princeton Univ. Press, 1967).

3. Mark Lefton and William R. Rosengren, "Organizations and Clients: Lateral and Longitudinal Dimensions," *American Sociological Review* 31:802–810 (December 1966); William R. Rosengren, "Organizational Age, Structure, and Orientations Toward Clients," *Social Forces* 47:1–11 (September 1968); William R. Rosengren and Mark Lefton, *Hospitals and Patients* (New York: Atherton Press, 1969); and Carl Gersuny, "Servitude and Expropriation as Dimensions of Clienthood," paper presented at the Annual Meetings of the Eastern Sociological Society (April 1969).

4. Arthur L. Stinchcombe, "Social Structure and Organizations," in James G. March, ed., *Handbook of Organizations* (Chicago: Rand-McNally, 1965), pp. 142–193.

5. James D. Thompson, *Organizations in Action* (New York: McGraw-Hill, 1967).

6. Stinchcombe, "Social Structure and Organizations," p. 149.

7. *Ibid.*, p. 150.

8. Charles E. Bidwell and Rebecca S. Vreeland, "College Education and Moral Orientations," *Administrative Science Quarterly* 8:166–191 (September 1963).

9. David Mechanic, "Organization Power of Lower Participants," *Administrative Science Quarterly* 7:349–364 (December 1962).

10. Stinchcombe, "Social Structure and Organizations."

11. See for example, Ray Elling, "Organizational Support and Community Power Structure," *Journal of Health and Human Behavior* 3:257–269 (Winter 1962); Charles Perrow, "Goals and Power Structures," in *The Hospital in Modern Society*, E. Freidson, ed., (New York: Free Press, 1963); and S. N. Eisenstadt, "Bureaucracy, Bureaucratization, and Debureaucratization," in *Complex Organizations*, A. Etzioni, ed., (New York: Holt, 1961), pp. 268–277.

12. Elaine Cumming, *Systems of Social Regulation* (New York: Atherton Press, 1968).

13. The Durkheimian axiom is too frequently neglected.

14. Oliver P. Williams and others, *Suburban Differences and Metropolitan Policies: A Philadelphia Story* (Philadelphia: Univ. of Pennsylvania Press, 1965).

15. Rosengren, "Organizational Age, Structure, and Orientations Toward Clients."

16. Theodore Caplow, *Principles of Organization* (New York: Harcourt, 1964).

17. William R. Rosengren, "Structure, Policy, and Style: Strategies or Organizational Control," *Administrative Science Quarterly* 12:140–164 (June 1967).

18. Peter M. Blau, *Bureaucracy in Modern Society* (New York: Random House, 1956).

19. Herbert C. Kelman, "Compliance, Identification, and Internalization," *Journal of Conflict Resolution* 11:51–60 (March 1958).

20. This is not inconsistent with Etzioni's "compliancy theory": Amitai Etzioni, *A Comparative Analysis of Complex Organizations* (New York: Free Press, 1961).

21. Caplow, *Principles of Organization.*

22. Stanley Udy, Jr., *Organizations of Work* (New Haven: Human Relations Area Files Press, 1959).

23. Thompson, *Organizations in Action.*

24. For a discussion of the "set" concept see William M. Evan, "The Organization Set: Toward a Theory of Interorganizational Relations," in *Approaches to Organizational Design*, James D. Thompson, ed. (Pittsburgh: Univ. of Pittsburgh Press, 1966), pp. 173-191.

25. Caplow, *Principles of Organization.*

26. Thompson, *Organizations in Action.*

27. William H. Starbuck, "Organizational Growth and Development," in *Handbook of Organizations*, pp. 451-533.

Knowledge Management

by Nicholas Henry

It has become a commencement address cliché in technological societies that knowledge really *is* power. Lynton K. Caldwell has spoken of the "techno-scientific superculture," Jean Meynaud has labelled it "technocracy," Bertram Gross has called it "technipol," Allan Schick speaks of "systems politics," Aaron Katz refers to America's "high information-level culture," Jacques Ellul addresses our "technological society," Kenneth Boulding forecasts a science-based "postcivilization," Robert E. Lane considers the political implications of a "knowledgeable society," James D. Carroll focuses on "administration as a clockwork orange," Pierre Teilhard de Chardin embraces the "Noosphere" with its god-like qualities, while Robert Boguslaw warns of the "new utopians" spawned by science. The discipline of political science and the profession of public administration, largely in the last decade, have devoted entire subfields to the study of science, technology, and public policy.

All these concepts and developments reflect the concern of scholars about the impact of information and technology on public policies and on public policy making. On the one hand, we must grapple with the problem of how new uses of data, both human and technological uses, alter policy outcomes. On the other hand, we must confront the question of whether these new informational uses signify change for the ways and styles in which policy makers actually make policy. The academicians just cited, for example, share the broad conviction that new patterns of information and new information technologies (1) can change the content and quality of public policies, and (2) may cultivate a new strain of politics and policy making, one that is based less on the bargaining/negotiating/compromising/disjointed incrementalist paradigm favored by most political scientists, and more on scientific information and systems analysis.

In this article I shall address the new roles of information, particularly scientific and social scientific information, and of new information technologies in the public policy-making process. I shall contend that these new roles have changed and may change further not only public policy outcomes but the policy-making process itself. Consequently, public administrators and administrationists must confront and design new metapolicies for knowledge management in our highly technological society. Finally, I shall review current American policies for knowledge management, and indicate their deficiencies.

INFORMATION, DATA, AND THE POLITY

By *information* and *knowledge,* I mean *data that change us.* This distinguishes information from *data,* which are merely raw facts that do not change us. By *knowledge management,* I mean *public policy for the production, dissemination, accessibility, and use of information as it applies to public policy formulation.* In this sense, knowledge management constitutes what Yehezkel Dror calls "metapolicy"; that is, policy for policy-making procedures.[1]

Knowledge is everywhere central in the polity. Consider: policies toward government secrecy, the cry for "participatory democracy," the privacy of individual citizens, the need for a "social report" as a more accurate indicator than gross national product of America's quality of life, the question of whether managerial computers and clerical automation will induce less or more responsive government, the significance of our educational institutions to society—these and other issues are related directly to the necessity of having information that possesses political utility. The inseparable phenomenon of new information technologies is equally pertinent to policy outcomes and changing policy-making styles. Many of the most ambitious public policies and programs of the last two decades simply would not have been feasible without computer-based information storage and retrieval systems, and, at a deeper level, computers and their programs are beginning to shape even our beliefs about reality and the possibilities and methods of effecting social change. In brief, to understand the dimensions of knowledge management, we must first appreciate the role of knowledge in affecting public policy outcomes and, second, the potential of new uses of knowledge and information technology in altering the paradigm of public policy formulation itself.

INFORMATION AND PUBLIC POLICY OUTCOMES

A number of analysts have tried to trace explicitly how the possession of information alters public outcomes, and in most of these expositions certain overriding themes are outstanding.[2] One is that our increased reliance on information in order to make decisions bodes ill for presently accepted paradigms of politics. The political pressures engendered by knowledge, or "truth," displaces the traditional pressures emanating from interest groups. The rise of such information-based governmental agencies as the General Accounting Office, the General Services Administration, and the Council of Economic Advisers, as well as the cerebral decision-making style of the National Aeronautics and Space Administration, the growing importance of the Congressional Research Service in the Library of Congress, and the recent emergence of the Office of Management and the Budget, the Environmental Protection Agency, and the President's Council on Environmental Quality (together with the extremely far-reaching National Environmental Policy Act) attest to the validation of the notion that knowledge *qua* knowledge does seem to exert its own pressure for political and social change.

Of course, there are many kinds of knowledge, and reality can be distorted in many directions during the acquisition of those information bits we call data. A second theme addresses itself to this problem and asks: How does the structure of bureaucracies distort information, and how do these distortions affect political outcomes? Knowledge may indeed exert its own pressure, but that pressure does not necessarily signal the end of ideology; beliefs, myths, and patterns of communication will affect the presentation of the most unbiased knowledge to decision makers. Organization theorists, in considering the problem of information distortion, have indicated how bureaucratic decentralization, bureaucratic centralization, and even bureaucratic size apparently have resulted in policy fiascos of monumental proportions.[3]

Finally, a third theme argues that what the public bureaucracy does with its information, whether distorted or intact, affects quite a few people other than members of the bureaucracy. Information—particularly freedom of information on a massive scale—has been instrumental in the democratization of international politics.

It is an increasingly plausible proposition that the historic tradition of elitism surrounding international diplomacy may be disintegrating because elites no longer possess the monopoly on political knowledge that they once had. (The example of *The Pentagon Papers* comes to mind.) The international press and other media have slimmed the walls of mutual political and cultural ignorance between nations, as well as democratizing foreign affairs. Freedom of information on a meaningful scale not only has altered fundamentally political science's paradigm of international relations, but the reality of diplomacy between states as well. A French social commentator goes so far as to call this phenomenon "the new American revolution," which has global implications. Because of freedom of information in this country, the American populace has been able to pressure policy makers to execute a transition from democracy in internal affairs to democracy in external affairs as well—notably, the extreme domestic resistance to the war in Vietnam, a resistance spawned in large part by media.

INFORMATION AND PUBLIC POLICY FORMULATION

Apart from policy outcomes, however, and perhaps more significantly, new styles of using information may well result in new styles of public policy making that differ radically from the usual incrementalist model. Precisely what forms these new policy-making processes might take is unknown, but analysis of social "futures" offers us two extremes along similar analytical continua, which emphasize the pervasiveness of information usage and technologies in the policy-making process. One extreme I shall call "new utopianism": the other I shall entitle "noetic politics."[4]

New utopianism amounts to a comprehensive explanation of how new informational patterns and technologies can yield greater decision-making autonomy to policy makers in a democratic context. The reasoning is that the systems designers, engineers, city planners, some social scientists, operations researchers, and the computer boys in general are the "new utopians," since they are working for a society in which all is uniform and human error is omitted. The new utopians are discomforting in that people problems are not their bag. Nevertheless, as people-centered social complexities arise, the need for planned public policies will grow, and the new utopians will be the planners. Their expertise, their professionalism, their disinterest in people problems, will isolate them from democratic considerations in the designing of public policy. Politicians, in turn, can use the educated expertise of their professional planners as a defense against or a lever for change: What the experts say is right must in fact be right because they are the experts. Information is the basis of expertise, and control of "relevant data" through the use of new information technologies should yield the controllers more "expertise" (i.e., arguments that can be marshalled in support of policies favored by the controllers) than they ever have enjoyed in the past.

Nevertheless, information technology also has tremendous potential for making government more responsive to social crises, if in a sense that connotes participatory democracy only indirectly. It gives policy makers the knowledge they need before they can apply solutions. Such, at least, is the contention of those who urge the advent of "noetic politics." They argue that new ways of relying on and using information should make noetic politics— that is, policy decisions based on social and factual knowledge that has been gleaned in a matter approximating the scientific method, rather than on deals between interest groups—a far more feasible proposition than it now is. Policy makers can get the information they need for the problems with which they are confronted, and in a considerably more economical and parsimonious way.

There are overtones of benevolent despotism (or, at least of benign neglect) to noetic politics that are unavoidable. The essential difference between new utopianism and noetic politics, however, is one of people-problem sensitivity. With the former we are confronted with an engineering mentality at the helm. With the latter we are captained by a social scientist. In both, we are concerned with governance by officially certified experts in an increasingly complex society, "the public interest" defined as the systems approach, and the denigration of democratic values in favor of elitist values.

THE NEED FOR KNOWLEDGE MANAGEMENT

If new knowledge and new uses of knowledge have profound implications for the policy-making process, it would seem apparent that a new policy or policies are needed for the management of knowledge, if for no other reason than to assure that information is applied intelligently in the analysis and rectification of public problems. Innovative knowledge management policies are increasingly critical in a high information-level culture such as ours, in which old laws and new technologies scrape side by side in an increasingly dysfunctional fashion.

These informational dysfunctions occur along at least two dimensions. One is the sheer glut of raw data inundating decision makers. When data swamp us, they are not information, because they are not capable of changing us. Information and potential information thus are converted into data, which are, at best, noise in the decision-making system.

The second dimension concerns information technologies. Information technologies, such as photocopying, microreproduction, cable television, and especially computer-based information storage and retrieval systems, are designed to maximize the knowledge of decision makers and minimize data, or noise, which can only blur the focus and diffuse the impact of public policy formulation and output.

CURRENT ATTEMPTS AT MANAGING KNOWLEDGE

These dysfunctions of too many data and too little information have arisen in the absence of knowledge-managing metapolicies to deal with them. Aside from the general constitutional principle of freedom of the press, the United States has three major policies concerning knowledge management.[5] Two of them are children of the times: the Fair Credit Reporting Act of 1970 and the Freedom of Information Act of 1966. The third policy is more than 250 years old in concept, although the present policy was enacted by Congress in 1909: Copyright Law.

The first two policies, while steps in the right direction, have been less than successful. The Fair Credit Reporting Act reflects a public concern over the uses of new information technologies and private information, and is intended to permit a citizen to examine his credit files and similar records, record objections to data in them that he considers inaccurate, and demand a rechecking and correcting of objectionable data. While the law does represent a form of knowledge management, it concerns information not especially germane to the policy-making process: personal, private data that would be pertinent only to limited spheres of public-policy formulation, and then only under peculiar circumstances.

The Freedom of Information Act is considerably more relevant, although it broaches problems that are centuries old: the pathologies innate to aging bureaucracies, in this case, excessive secrecy. The law attempts to let the public read public records assembled by public servants. Suffice it to say that, with few exceptions, the Freedom of Information Act has met with entrenched and effective resistance from public bureaucrats. By way of indication a 1972 survey by the American Society of Newspaper Editors found that 19 of 28 leading Washington correspondents believed government secrecy had increased.[6]

Copyright law, while the oldest of the three policies, deals with information in the polity on the most systemic scale. Copyright has received virtually no attention from persons concerned with public policy making, yet copyright represents the only knowledge management policy for the kinds of information that ultimately may have the greatest significance for public policy formation in a technological society.

Information may assume many forms in the polity: news, propaganda, blackmail, opinions, exposés, ideas, and findings from science and social science are only some of them. Informational forms may be classified, in turn, along a variety of dimensions: secret and public information, personal and societal information, factual and fictional information, information that can be labelled according to particular academic disciplines, and copyrighted and uncopyrighted information. These classifications are less than neat; they overlap a great deal. For instance, copyrighted information often (but not always) is public, fictional (in the sense of *belles lettres*), academic, and societal in character, while uncopyrighted information often (but not always) is secret, factual, and personal.

It can be argued that copyrighted information is considerably less crucial to the political process than the uncopyrighted, secret, or private knowledge that we, the public, seldom see. Perhaps this is so; no doubt, secret knowledge has swayed policy decisions radically one way or the other. But even these decisions must be made in a milieu which is saturated by information that is read, heard, or seen by the public at large, or by various publics peculiarly pertinent to particular political issues. From another perspective, the uses of private, uncopyrighted knowledge pose questions of greater immediacy to the individual citizen in this country than do the uses of accessible, copyrighted information. Clumsy political surveillance and irresponsible credit checks are facts of American life that affect us all at the most personal levels.

In the long run, however, information that is designed to transmit ideas is the kind of knowledge that invariably is associated with social "progress." This is true no matter how progress is defined, whether as the attainment of industrial growth, environmental preservation, or spiritual fulfillment. Information, after all, is what changes us. The kind of information that changes society, that is, educational, scientific, and social scientific knowledge, often is subject to copyright law.

Moreover, developments in the technology of information dissemination and access would seem to indicate that public information (as identified, for convenience here, by its copyright status) will become increasingly significant in political policy making. While knowledge was always power, today it is the central force in technological societies and the indispensable resource in public policy formulation. This new dimension of knowledge has made academics and universities—which deal almost exclusively in publicly accessible and copyrighted information—far more powerful in terms of social development, at least in technological cultures, than industrialists and generals, factories and armies. In an age in which biologists discuss the possibility of "cloning" 23 Mozarts (or half-a-dozen Hitlers) through new discoveries in genetics, and in which *Esquire* magazine tells us how to build a nuclear bomb in terminology readily comprehensible by any nine-year-old, the preceding assertion does not seem at all far-fetched. Nor, by implication, does the hypothesis seem unreasonable that the copyrighted information on which academicians and the rest of the public chiefly rely for developing their scientific, political, and social perspectives is at least as vital to the political process as secret and uncopyrighted information.

Copyright law, then, affects an extremely significant portion of information which has public policy ramifications. Adding to its significance, however, is the fact that, because of peculiarities innate to the copyright concept and because copyright is indeed a metapolicy, national knowledge management policy spills over into other spheres of social importance as well. Copyright law articulates not only a national policy toward freedom of information and its related function of freedom to research, but expresses significant public policies concerning innovation in society and the citizen's right to own property—specifically, intellectual property. Information, research, innovation, and property are fields of some importance in any society.

Unfortunately, the copyright concept seems an increasingly inadequate basis on which to form new knowledge management policies for the use of information in public policy making. This is true principally because of the new information technologies. Although copyright does provide the originators of data (authors, researchers, and publishers) with a motivation to produce information (royalty checks), it ignores those new technologies that allow the users of knowledge (policy makers, researchers, and the public generally) to acquire knowledge essential for public policy formulation and execution.

To ignore information technologies produces at least two dysfunctions, both of which already are visible in the American polity. First, widespread use of "neo-publishing" technologies eventually may undermine the economic incentive of information producers to produce information under the arrangements provided by copyright law. Second, the reactions of information producers against the new technologies, precisely because popular use of them may reduce their income via copyright arrangements, in turn may inhibit the increasingly necessary use of information technologies by decision makers—an inhibition that may be intensified by the uncertainties of copyright law relative to the new technologies.[7] In such a situation, no one wins, neither the producers of knowledge, the users of knowledge, nor the public.

MANAGING KNOWLEDGE FOR FUTURE NEEDS

Any new policy for managing knowledge must confront these contradictions as well as those policies that we already have. Moreover, in light of radically new ways of gathering and processing data, a knowledge management policy must be extraordinarily well-planned, comprehensive, and different from what now exists. Planned because we are dealing with a policy for the framing of virtually all other policies, and the utmost care must be taken; comprehensive because information is an autonomous system that pervades and links all other systems in our society; different because the Fair Credit Reporting Act, the Freedom of Information Act, and the Copyright Act are inadequate as knowledge management policies in our increasingly interrelated and complex techno-scientific super-culture.

Steps are being taken in the direction of recognizing the problems of knowledge management. A National Commission on New Technological Uses of Copyrighted Works has been proposed in Congress, and the Ad Hoc Task Group on Scientific and Technical Information of the Organization for Economic Cooperation and Development has recommended points to be considered in the formulation of national metapolicies for knowledge management. While such steps are encouraging, they also are inadequate, particularly in light of the enormity and complexity of the knowledge/society interface.

Obviously, it is beyond the scope of this article to recommend a detailed public policy for knowledge management. What is within its scope, however, is to call attention not only to the need for a comprehensive knowledge management policy, but to indicate those institutions and organizations that already are groping toward its formulation and expression. Of special note in this regard are the President's Office of Telecommunications Policy, the Educational Research Information Center of the U.S. Office of Education, the Copyright Office and the recently expanded Congressional Research Service (particularly its Science Policy Research Division) of the Library of Congress, the Federal Communications Commission, the Office of Science Information Services of the National Science Foundation, the National Technical Information Service of the Department of Commerce, and the Medical Library Analysis and Retrieval System of the National Institutes of Health, although there are others. Additionally, certain quasi-official and private bodies exist that have considerable significance in the knowledge system, such as the International Council of Scientific Unions, the Committee on Scientific and Technical Communication of the National Academy of Sciences, the United Nations Educational, Scientific, and Cultural Organization, the American Society for Information Science, the American Federation of Information Processing Societies, and special committees of numerous scholarly associations, although, again, there are others.

The efforts presented by these agencies and organizations in terms of thinking about (if not formulating) knowledge management policies stand in acute need of conceptual and administrative coordination. Until very recently, the agency that possessed the greatest likelihood of providing such coordination was the Committee on Scientific and Technical Information of the Federal Council for Science and Technology. The committee had recognized at an unusually early phase the problems posed by the relationships between new information technologies, traditional knowledge management policies, and public policy making. Moreover, its members once had White House access. Now, however, the futures of the committee and the council are in doubt. So, for that matter, are the futures of the Office of Science and Technology, the President's Science Advisory Committee, and the President's science adviser, which also were important in terms of knowledge management; all have been relegated severely (or eliminated officially) in their influence and activity as the result of a recent White House "reorganization."

The proposed National Commission on New Technological Uses of Copyrighted Works has the potential for being not only a successor to the Committee on Scientific and Technical Information, but it possibly could become a more viable organization for coordinating the efforts of various public and private agencies in formulating knowledge management policies. Its structure and purpose, as currently conceived, would require alteration and expansion, but this would not be an insuperable task at this stage. In any case, a coordinated analysis of the knowledge/society interface by the institutions of government, education, science, communications, and information is essential if the American technoculture is to avoid miring down in its own data. Coordinating present analytical activities in this direction under a single organizational umbrella would represent a needed beginning.

Knowledge management is a vital, if unfamiliar, field; the profession and discipline of public administration would do well to recognize its implications and, presumably, future knowledge management policies also would benefit by such recognition. Both public administration and knowledge management present dynamic dilemmas that never can be ultimately "solved," and both mandate the concern of people with synthesizing intellectual capacities. Both enterprises stand to gain from the attention of the other, but, more importantly, the society stands to gain the overriding benefit of a government that is more responsive to the governed.

REFERENCES

1. Yehezkel Dror, *Public Policymaking Reexamined* (San Francisco: Chandler, 1968), p. 8.

2. For examples of these themes, I would suggest: Robert E. Lane, "The Decline of Politics and Ideology in a Knowledgeable Society," *American Sociological Review,* vol. 31 (October 1966), pp. 649–662; Harold L. Wilensky, *Organizational Intelligence: Knowledge and Policy in Government and Industry* (New York: Basic Books, 1967); Richard E. Neustadt, *Alliance Politics* (New York: Columbia Univ. Pr., 1970); and Karl W. Deutsch, *The Nerves of Government: Models of Political Communication and Control* (New York: Free Pr., 1963).

3. To briefly elaborate, Wilensky (*Organizational Intelligence*) has explained how the surprise of American forces at Pearl Harbor during the Japanese attack can be attributed to the extensive and chaotic decentralization of military information, while the Cuban Bay of Pigs blunder may be attributed to the extensive and rigid centralization of intelligence (in the form of the aptly dubbed Central Intelligence Agency—itself an effort to avoid the informational pathologies inherent to decentralization). In this regard, James G. March and Herbert A. Simon in *Organizations* (New York: Wiley, 1958) have delineated the useful concept of "uncertainty absorption," or the phenomenon whereby each successive layer of the bureaucratic hierarchy tends to "harden" information that is initially "soft." Thus, data that may be highly tentative when first gathered, become concrete and unencumbered by doubt as higher organization officials see them. Poor decisions can be a function of uncertainty absorption. Gordon Tullock's *The Politics of Bureaucracy* (Washington, D.C.: Public Affairs Pr., 1965), and Anthony Downs' *Inside Bureaucracy* (Boston: Little, 1967) both argue that organizational size is the chief reason why information is changed as it moves through bureaucracy. Tullock offers an arithmetical "model of hierarchical distortion" (late adopted by Downs), designed to show that information is increasingly mauled as organizations grow. Both scholars conclude that bureaucracies must be radically reduced in size in order to cope with informational complexity.

4. Examples are plentiful for both extremes, but two writers who have influenced the following paragraphs are: Robert Boguslaw, *The New*

Utopians, A Study of Systems Design and Social Change (Englewood Cliffs, N.J.: Prentice-Hall, 1965), and James D. Carroll, "Noetic Authority," *Public Administration Review*, vol. 29 (September/October 1969), pp. 492–500.

5. Rather than review all the knowledge management policies and semi-policies extant in the American polity today, I have chosen only those that strike me as being "major" in the sense that they may have long-range social and administrative effects. There are, of course, others. Worth mentioning, I think, are the sundry promulgations of the various agencies and organizations listed in the concluding section of this article; government research, development, and data dissemination policies; government citizen surveillance policies; agency dossiers on individual citizens; and sections of the Administrative Procedures Act.

6. Allen Schick, "Let the Sun Shine In," *The Bureaucrat*, vol. 1 (Summer 1972), p. 160.

7. Already there are indications of information users being inhibited in their use of information by information "owners." Notable in this regard is the recent suit against the National Library of Medicine and the National Institutes of Health by Williams and Wilkins Company, a small publisher in the biomedical field. The company won its case in the U.S. Court of Claims, arguing that the large-scale and unauthorized photocopying of its publications by the Library infringed the company's copyright registrations. More broadly, and more significantly in terms of the relationship between information uses and information technologies, is the ongoing and extensive politicking over copyright law revision, which is well into its second decade of intense debate. Involved are interest groups representing the fields of television, radio, recording, design, music, education, entertainment, publishing, library services, science, research, computer and photocopier manufacturing, film-making, and authorship, indicating the widespread character of formulating meta-policies for knowledge management.

IV

SERVICES IN POST-INDUSTRIAL SOCIETY

On the Impact of the Computer on Society

by Joseph Weizenbaum

The structure of the typical essay on "The impact of computers on society" is as follows: First there is an "on the one hand" statement. It tells all the good things computers have already done for society and often even attempts to argue that the social order would already have collapsed were it not for the "computer revolution." This is usually followed by an "on the other hand" caution which tells of certain problems the introduction of computers brings in its wake. The threat posed to individual privacy by large data banks and the danger of large-scale unemployment induced by industrial automation are usually mentioned. Finally, the glorious present and prospective achievements of the computer are applauded, while the dangers alluded to in the second part are shown to be capable of being alleviated by sophisticated technological fixes. The closing paragraph consists of a plea for generous societal support for more, and more large-scale, computer research and development. This is usually coupled to the more or less subtle assertion that only computer science, hence only the computer scientist, can guard the world against the admittedly hazardous fallout of applied computer technology.

In fact, the computer has had very considerably less societal impact than the mass media would lead us to believe. Certainly, there are enterprises like space travel that could not have been undertaken without computers. Certainly the computer industry, and with it the computer education industry, has grown to enormous proportions. But much of the industry is self-serving. It is rather like an island economy in which the natives make a living by taking in each other's laundry. The part that is not self-serving is largely supported by government agencies and other gigantic enterprises that know the value of everything but the price of nothing, that is, that know the short-range utility of computer systems but have no idea of their ultimate social cost. In any case, airline reservation systems and computerized hospitals serve only a tiny, largely the most affluent, fraction of society. Such things cannot be said to have an impact on society generally.

SIDE EFFECTS OF TECHNOLOGY

The more important reason that I dismiss the argument which I have caricatured is that the direct societal effects of any pervasive new technology are as nothing compared to its much more subtle and ultimately much more important side effects. In that sense, the societal impact of the computer has not yet been felt.

To help firmly fix the idea of the importance of subtle indirect effects of technology, consider the impact on society of the invention of the microscope. When it was invented in the middle of the 17th century, the dominant commonsense theory of disease was fundamentally that disease was a punishment visited upon an individual by God. The sinner's body was thought to be inhabited by various so-called humors brought into disequilibrium in accordance with divine justice. The cure for disease was therefore to be found first in penance and second in the balancing of humors as, for example, by bleeding. Bleeding was, after all, both painful, hence punishment and penance, and potentially balancing in that it actually removed substance from the body. The microscope enabled man to see microorganisms and thus paved the way for the germ theory of disease. The enormously surprising discovery of extremely small living organisms also induced the idea of a continuous chain of life which, in turn, was a necessary intellectual precondition for the emergence of Darwinism. Both the germ theory of disease and the theory of evolution profoundly altered man's conception of his contract with God and consequently his self-image. Politically these ideas served to help diminish the power of the Church and, more generally, to legitimize the questioning of the basis of hitherto unchallenged authority. I do not say that the microscope alone was responsible for the enormous social changes that followed its invention. Only that it made possible the kind of paradigm shift, even on the commonsense level, without which these changes might have been impossible.

Is it reasonable to ask whether the computer will induce similar changes in man's image of himself and whether that influence will prove to be its most important effect on society? I think so, although I hasten to add that I don't believe the computer has yet told us much about man and his nature. To come to grips with the question, we must first ask in what way the computer is different from man's many other machines. Man has built two fundamentally different kinds of machines, nonautonomous and autonomous. An autonomous machine is one that operates for long periods of time, not on the basis of inputs from the real world, for example from sensors or from human drivers, but on the basis of internalized models of some aspect of the real world. Clocks are examples of autonomous machines in that they operate on the basis of an internalized model of the planetary system. The computer is, of course, the example par excellence. It is able to internalize models of essentially unlimited complexity and of a fidelity limited only by the genius of man.

It is the autonomy of the computer we value. When, for example, we speak of the power of computers as increasing with each new hardware and software development, we mean that, because of their increasing speed and storage capacity, and possibly thanks to new programming tricks, the new computers can internalize ever more complex and ever more faithful models of ever larger slices of reality. It seems strange then that, just when we exhibit virtually an idolatry of autonomy with respect to machines, serious thinkers in respected academies [I have in mind B. F. Skinner of Harvard University[1]] can rise to question autonomy as a fact for man. I do not think that the appearance of this paradox at this time is accidental. To understand it, we must realize that man's commitment to science has always had a masochistic component.

Time after time science has led us to insights that, at least when seen superficially, diminish man. Thus Galileo removed man from the center of the universe, Darwin removed him from his place separate from the animals, and Freud showed his rationality to be an illusion. Yet man pushes his inquiries further and deeper. I cannot help but think that there is an analogy between man's pursuit of scientific knowledge and an individual's commitment to psychoanalytic therapy. Both are undertaken in the full realization that what the inquirer may find may well damage his self-esteem. Both may reflect his determination to find meaning in his existence through struggle in truth, however painful that may be, rather than to live without meaning in a world of ill-disguised illusion. However, I am also aware that sometimes people enter psychoanalysis unwilling to put their illusions at risk, not searching for a deeper reality but in order to convert the insights they hope to gain to personal power. The analogy to man's pursuit of science does not break down with that observation.

Each time a scientific discovery shatters a hitherto fundamental cornerstone of the edifice on which man's self-esteem is built, there is an enormous reaction, just as is the case under similar circumstances in psychoanalytic therapy. Powerful defense mechanisms, beginning with denial and usually terminating in rationalization, are brought to bear. Indeed, the psychoanalyst suspects that, when a patient appears to accept a soul-shattering insight without resistance, his very casualness may well mask his refusal to allow that insight truly operational status in his self-image. But what is the psychoanalyst to think about the patient who positively embraces tentatively proffered, profoundly humiliating self-knowledge, when he embraces it and instantly converts it to a new foundation of his life? Surely such an event is symptomatic of a major crisis in the mental life of the patient.

I believe we are now at the beginning of just such a crisis in the mental life of our civilization. The microscope, I have argued, brought in its train a revision of man's image of himself. But no one in the mid-17th century could have foreseen that. The possibility that the computer will, one way or another, demonstrate that, in the inimitable phrase of one of my esteemed colleagues, "the brain is merely a meat machine" is one that engages academicians, industrialists, and journalists in the here and now. How has the computer contributed to bringing about this very sad state of affairs? It must be said right away that the computer alone is not the chief causative agent. It is merely an extreme extrapolation of technology. When seen as an inducer of philosophical dogma, it is merely the reductio ad absurdum of a technological ideology. But how does it come to be regarded as a source of philosophic dogma?

THEORY VERSUS PERFORMANCE

We must be clear about the fact that a computer is nothing without a program. A program is fundamentally a transformation of one computer into another that has autonomy and that, in a very real sense, behaves. Programming languages describe dynamic processes. And, most importantly, the processes they describe can be actually carried out. Thus we can build models of any aspect of the real world that interests us and that we understand. And we can make our models work. But we must be careful to remember that a computer model is a description that works. Ordinarily, when we speak of A being a model of B, we mean that a theory about some aspects of the behavior of B is also a theory of the same aspects of the behavior of A. It follows that when, for example, we consider a computer model of paranoia, like that published by Colby *et al.*,[2] we must not be persuaded that it tells us anything about paranoia on the grounds that it, in some sense, mirrors the behavior of a paranoiac. After all, a plain typewriter in some sense mirrors the behavior of an autistic child (one types a question and gets no response whatever), but it does not help us to understand autism. A model must be made to stand or fall on the basis of its theory. Thus, while programming languages may have put a new power in the hands of social scientists in that this new notation may have freed them from the vagueness of discursive descriptions, their obligation to build defensible theories is in no way diminished. Even errors can be pronounced with utmost formality and eloquence. But they are not thereby transmuted to truth.

The failure to make distinctions between descriptions, even those that "work," and theories accounts in large part for the fact that those who refuse to accept the view of man as machine have been put on the defensive. Recent advances in computer understanding of natural language offer an excellent case in point. Halle and Chomsky, to mention only the two with whom I am most familiar, have long labored on a theory of language which any model of language behavior must satisfy.[3] Their aim is like that of the physicist who writes a set of differential equations that anyone riding a bicycle must satisfy. No physicist claims that a person need know, let alone be able to solve, such differential equations in order to become a competent cyclist. Neither do Halle and Chomsky claim that humans know or knowingly obey the rules they believe to govern language behavior. Halle and Chomsky also strive, as do physical theorists, to identify the constants and parameters of their theories with components of reality. They hypothesize that their rules constitute a kind of projective description of certain aspects of the structure of the human mind. Their problem is thus not merely to discover economical rules to account for language behavior, but also to infer economic mechanisms which determine that precisely those rules are to be preferred over all others. Since they are in this way forced to attend to the human mind, not only that of speakers of English, they must necessarily be concerned with all human language behavior—not just that related to the understanding of English.

The enormous scope of their task is illustrated by their observation that in all human languages declarative sentences are often transformed into questions by a permutation of two of their words. (John is here → Is John here?) It is one thing to describe rules that transform declarative sentences into questions—a simple permutation rule is clearly insufficient—but another thing to describe a "machine" that necessitates those rules when others would, all else being equal, be simpler. Why, for example, is it not so that declarative sentences read backward transform those sentences into questions? The answer must be that other constraints on the "machine" combine against this local simplicity in favor of a more nearly global economy. Such examples illustrate the depth of the level of explanation that Halle and Chomsky are trying to achieve. No wonder that they stand in awe of their subject matter.

Workers in computer comprehension of natural language operate in what is usually called performance mode. It is as if they are building machines that can ride bicycles by following heuristics like "if you feel a displacement to the left, move your weight to the left." There can be, and often is, a strong interaction between the development of theory and the empirical task of engineering systems whose theory is not yet thoroughly understood. Witness the synergistic cooperation between aerodynamics and aircraft design in the first quarter of the present century. Still, what counts in performance mode is not the elaboration of theory but the performance of systems. And the systems being hammered together by the new crop of computer semanticists are beginning (just beginning) to perform.

Since computer scientists have recognized the importance of the interplay of syntax, semantics, and pragmatics, and with it the importance of computer-manipulable knowledge, they have made progress. Perhaps by the end of the present decade, computer systems will exist with which specialists, such as physicians and chemists and mathematicians, will converse in natural language. And surely some part of such achievements will have been based on other successes in, for example, computer simulation of cognitive processes. It is understandable that any success in this area, even if won empirically and without accompanying enrichments of theory, can easily lead to certain delusions being planted. Is it, after all, not terribly tempting to believe that a computer that understands natural language at all, however narrow the context, has captured something of the essence of man? Descartes himself might have believed it. Indeed, by way of this very understandable seduction, the computer comes to be a source of philosophical dogma.

I am tempted to recite how performance programs are composed and how things that don't work quite correctly are made to work via all sorts of stratagems which do not even pretend to have any theoretical foundation. But the very asking of the question, "Has the computer captured the essence of man?" is a diversion and, in that sense, a trap. For the real question "Does man understand the essence of man?" cannot be answered by technology and hence certainly not by any technological instrument.

THE TECHNOLOGICAL METAPHOR

I asked earlier what the psychoanalyst is to think when a patient grasps a tentatively proffered deeply humiliating interpretation and attempts to convert it immediately to a new foundation of his life. I now think I phrased that question too weakly. What if the psychoanalyst merely coughed and the cough entrained the consequences of which I speak? That is our situation today. Computer science, particularly its artificial intelligence branch, has coughed. Perhaps the press has unduly amplified that cough—but it is only a cough nevertheless. I cannot help but think that the eagerness to believe that man's whole nature has suddenly been exposed by that cough, and that it has been shown to be a clockwork, is a symptom of something terribly wrong.

What is wrong, I think, is that we have permitted technological metaphors, what Mumford[4] calls the "Myth of the Machine," and technique itself to so thoroughly pervade our thought processes that we have finally abdicated to technology the very duty to formulate questions. Thus sensible men correctly perceive that large data banks and enormous networks of computers threaten man. But they leave it to technology to formulate the corresponding question. Where a simple man might ask: "Do we need these things?", technology asks "What electronic wizardry will make them safe?" Where a simple man will ask "Is it good?", technology asks "Will it work?" Thus science, even wisdom, becomes what technology and most of all computers can handle. Lest this be thought to be an exaggeration, I quote from the work of H. A. Simon, one of the most senior of American computer scientists:[5]

> As we succeed in broadening and deepening our knowledge—theoretical and empirical—about computers, we shall discover that in large part their behavior is governed by simple general laws, that what appeared as complexity in the computer program was, to a considerable extent, complexity of the environment to which the program was seeking to adapt its behavior.
>
> To the extent that this prospect can be realized, it opens up an exceedingly important role for computer simulation as a tool for achieving a deeper understanding of human behavior. For if it is the organization of components, and not their physical properties, that largely determines behavior, and if computers are organized somewhat in the image of man, then the computer becomes an obvious device for exploring the consequences of alternative organizational assumptions for human behavior.

and

> A man, viewed as a behaving system, is quite simple. The apparent complexity of his behavior over time is largely a reflection of the complexity of the environment in which he finds himself.
>
> . . . I believe that this hypothesis holds even for the whole man.

We already know that those aspects of the behavior of computers which cannot be attributed to the complexity of their programs is governed by simple general laws—ultimately by the laws of Boolean algebra. And of course the physical properties of the computer's components are nearly irrelevant to its behavior. Mechanical relays are logically equivalent to tubes and to transistors and to artificial neurons. And of course the complexity of computer programs is due to the complexity of the environments, including the computing environments themselves, with which they were designed to deal. To what else could it possibly be due? So, what Simon sees as prospective is already realized. But does this collection of obvious and simple facts lead to the conclusion that man is as simple as are computers? When Simon leaps to that conclusion and then formulates the issue as he has done here, that is, when he suggests that the behavior of *the whole man* may be understood in terms of the behavior of computers as governed by simple general laws, then the very possibility of understanding man as an autonomous being, as an individual with deeply internalized values, that very possibility is excluded. How does one insult a machine?

The question "Is the brain merely a meat machine?", which Simon puts in a so much more sophisticated form, is typical of the kind of question formulated by, indeed formulatable only by, a technological mentality. Once it is accepted as legitimate, arguments as to what a computer can or cannot do "in principle" begin to rage and themselves become legitimate. But the legitimacy of the technological question—for example, is human behavior to be understood either in terms of the organization or of the physical properties of "components"—need not be admitted in the first instance. A human question can be asked instead. Indeed, we might begin by asking what has already become of "the whole man" when he can conceive of computers organized in his own image.

The success of technique and of some technological explanations has, as I've suggested, tricked us into permitting technology to formulate important questions for us—questions whose very forms severely diminish the number of degrees of freedom in our range of decision-making. Whoever dictates the questions in large part determines the answers. In that sense, technology, and especially computer technology, has become a self-fulfilling nightmare reminiscent of that of the lady who dreams of being raped and begs her attacker to be kind to her. He answers "it's your dream, lady." We must come to see that technology is our dream and that we must ultimately decide how it is to end.

I have suggested that the computer revolution need not and ought not to call man's dignity and autonomy into question, that it is a kind of pathology that moves men to wring from it unwarranted, enormously damaging interpretations. Is then the computer less threatening than we might have thought? Once we realize that our visions, possibly nightmarish visions, determine the effect of our own creations on us and on our society, their threat to us is surely diminished. But that is not to say that this realization alone will wipe out all danger. For example, apart from the erosive effect of a technological mentality on man's self-image, there are practical attacks on the freedom and dignity of man in which computer technology plays a critical role.

I mentioned earlier that computer science has come to recognize the importance of building knowledge into machines. We already have a machine—Dendral—[6] that commands more chemistry than do many Ph.D. chemists, and another—Mathlab—[7] that commands more applied mathematics than do many applied mathematicians. Both Dendral and Mathlab contain knowledge that can be evaluated in terms of the explicit theories from which it was derived. If the user believes that a result Mathlab delivers is wrong, then, apart from possible program errors, he must be in disagreement, not with the machine or its programmer, but with a specific mathematical theory. But what about the many programs on which management, most particularly the government and the military, rely, programs which can in no sense be said to rest on explicable theories but are instead enormous patchworks of programming techniques strung together to make them work?

INCOMPREHENSIBLE SYSTEMS

In our eagerness to exploit every advance in technique we quickly incorporate the lessons learned from machine manipulation of knowledge in theory-based systems into such patchworks. They then "work" better. I have in mind systems like target selection systems used in Vietnam and war games used in the Pentagon, and so on. These often gigantic systems are put together by teams of programmers, often working over a time span of many years. But by the time the systems come into use, most of the original programmers have left or turned their attention to other pursuits. It is precisely when gigantic systems begin to be used that their inner workings can no longer be understood by any single person or by a small team of individuals. Norbert Wiener, the father of cybernetics, foretold this phenomenon in a remarkably prescient article[8] published more than a decade ago. He said there:

> It may well be that in principle we cannot make any machine the elements of whose behavior we cannot comprehend sooner or later. This does not mean in any way that we shall be able to comprehend these elements in substantially less time than the time required for operation of the machine, or even within any given number of years or generations.
>
> An intelligent understanding of [machines'] mode of performance may be delayed until long after the task which they have been set has been completed. This means that though machines are theoretically subject to human criticism, such criticism may be ineffective until long after it is relevant.

This situation, which is now upon us, has two consequences: first that decisions are made on the basis of rules and criteria no one knows explicitly, and second that the system of rules and criteria becomes immune to change. This is so because, in the absence of detailed understanding of the inner workings of a system, any substantial modification is very likely to render the system altogether inoperable. The threshold of complexity beyond which this phenomenon occurs has already been crossed by many existing systems, including some compiling and computer operating systems. For example, no one likes the operating systems for certain large computers, but they cannot be substantially changed nor can they be done away with. Too many people have become dependent on them.

An awkward operating system is inconvenient. That is not too bad. But the growing reliance on supersystems that were perhaps designed to help people make analyses and decisions, but which have since surpassed the understanding of their users while at the same time becoming indispensable to them, is another matter. In modern war it is common for the soldier, say the bomber pilot, to operate at an enormous psychological distance from his victims. He is not responsible for burned children because he never sees their village, his bombs, and certainly not the flaming children themselves.

Modern technological rationalizations of war, diplomacy, politics, and commerce such as computer games have an even more insidious effect on the making of policy. Not only have policy makers abdicated their decision-making responsibility to a technology they don't understand, all the while maintaining the illusion that they, the policy makers, are formulating policy questions and answering them, but responsibility has altogether evaporated. No human is any longer responsible for "what the machine says." Thus there can be neither right nor wrong, no question of justice, no theory with which one can agree or disagree, and finally no basis on which one can challenge "what the machine says." My father used to invoke the ultimate authority by saying to me, "it is written." But then I could read what was written, imagine a human author, infer his values, and finally agree or disagree. The systems in the Pentagon, and their counterparts elsewhere in our culture, have in a very real sense no authors. They therefore do not admit of exercises of imagination that may ultimately lead to human judgment. No wonder that men who live day in and out with such machines and become dependent on them begin to believe that men are merely machines. They are reflecting what they themselves have become.

The potentially tragic impact on society that may ensue from the use of systems such as I have just discussed is greater than might at first be imagined. Again it is side effects, not direct effects, that matter most. First, of course, there is the psychological impact on individuals living in a society in which anonymous, hence irresponsible, forces formulate the large questions of the day and circumscribe the range of possible answers. It cannot be surprising that large numbers of perceptive individuals living in such a society experience a kind of impotence and fall victim to the mindless rage that often accompanies such experiences. But even worse, since computer-based knowledge systems become essentially unmodifiable except in that they can grow, and since they induce dependence and cannot, after a certain threshold is crossed, be abandoned, there is an enormous risk that they will be passed from one generation to another, always growing. Man too passes knowledge from one generation to another. But because man is mortal, his transmission of knowledge over the generations is at once a process of filtering and accrual. Man doesn't merely pass knowledge, he rather regenerates it continuously. Much as we may mourn the crumbling of ancient civilizations, we know nevertheless that the glory of man resides as much in the evolution of his cultures as in that of his brain. The unwise use of ever larger and ever more complex computer systems may well bring this process to a halt. It could well replace the ebb and flow of culture with a world without values, a world in which what counts for a fact has long ago been determined and forever fixed.

POSITIVE EFFECTS

I've spoken of some potentially dangerous effects of present computing trends. Is there nothing positive to be said? Yes, but it must be said with caution. Again, side effects are more important than direct effects. In particular, the idea of computation and of programming languages is beginning to become an important metaphor which, in the long run, may well prove to be responsible for paradigm shifts in many fields. Most of the common-sense paradigms in terms of which much of mankind interprets the phenomena of the everyday world, both physical and social, are still deeply rooted in fundamentally mechanistic metaphors. Marx's dynamics as well as those of Freud are, for example, basically equilibrium systems. Any hydrodynamicist could come to understand them without leaving the jargon of his field. Languages capable of describing ongoing processes, particularly in terms of modular subprocesses, have already had an enormous effect on the way computer people think of every aspect of their worlds, not merely those directly related to their work. The information-processing view of the world so engendered qualifies as a genuine metaphor. This is attested to by the fact that it (1) constitutes an intellectual framework that permits new questions to be asked about a wide-ranging set of phenomena, and (2) that it itself provides criteria for the adequacy of proffered answers. A new metaphor is important not in that it may be better than existing ones, but rather in that it may enlarge man's vision by giving him yet another perspective on his world. Indeed, the very effectiveness of a new metaphor may seduce lazy minds to adopt it as a basis for universal explanations and as a source of panaceas. Computer simulation of social processes has already been advanced by single-minded generalists as leading to general solutions of all of mankind's problems.

The metaphors given us by religion, the poets, and by thinkers like Darwin, Newton, Freud, and Einstein have rather quickly penetrated to the language of ordinary people. These metaphors have thus been instrumental in shaping our entire civilization's imaginative reconstruction of our world. The computing metaphor is as yet available to only an extremely small set of people. Its acquisition and internalization, hopefully as only one of many ways to see the world, seems to require experience in program composition, a kind of computing literacy. Perhaps such literacy will become very widespread in the advanced societal sectors of the advanced countries. But, should it become a dominant mode of thinking and be restricted to certain social classes, it will prove not merely repressive in the ordinary sense, but an enormously divisive societal force. For then classes which do and do not have access to the metaphor will, in an important sense, lose their ability to communicate with one another. We know already how difficult it is for the poor and the oppressed to communicate with the rest of the society in which they are embedded. We know how difficult it is for the world of science to communicate with that of the arts and of the humanities. In both instances the communication difficulties, which have grave consequences, are very largely due to the fact that the respective communities have unsharable experiences out of which unsharable metaphors have grown.

RESPONSIBILITY

Given these dismal possibilities, what is the responsibility of the computer scientist? First I should say that most of the harm computers can potentially entrain is much more a function of properties people attribute to computers than of what a computer can or cannot actually be made to do. The nonprofessional has little choice but to make his attributions of properties to computers on the basis of the propaganda emanating from the computer community and amplified by the press. The computer professional therefore has an enormously important responsibility to be modest in his claims. This advice would not even have to be voiced if computer science had a tradition of scholarship and of self-criticism such as that which characterizes the established sciences. The mature scientist stands in awe before the depth of his subject matter. His very humility is the wellspring of his strength. I regard the instilling of just this kind of humility, chiefly by the example set by teachers, to be one of the most important missions of every university department of computer science.

The computer scientist must be aware constantly that his instruments are capable of having gigantic direct and indirect amplifying effects. An error in a program, for example, could have grievous direct results, including most certainly the loss of much human life. On 11 September 1971, to cite just one example, a computer programming error caused the simultaneous destruction of 117 high-altitude weather balloons whose instruments were being monitored by an earth satellite.[9] A similar error in a military command and control system could launch a fleet of nuclear tipped missiles. Only censorship prevents us from knowing how many such events involving non-nuclear weapons have already occurred. Clearly then, the computer scientist has a heavy responsibility to make the fallibility and limitations of the systems he is capable of designing brilliantly clear. The very power of his systems should serve to inhibit the advice he is ready to give and to constrain the range of work he is willing to undertake.

Of course, the computer scientist, like everyone else, is responsible for his actions and their consequences. Sometimes that responsibility is hard to accept because the corresponding authority to decide what is and what is not to be done appears to rest with distant and anonymous forces. That technology itself determines what is to be done by a process of extrapolation and that individuals are powerless to intervene in that determination is precisely the kind of self-fulfilling dream from which we must awaken.

Consider gigantic computer systems. They are, of course, natural extrapolations of the large systems we already have. Computer networks are another point on the same curve extrapolated once more. One may ask whether such systems can be used by anybody except by governments and very large corporations and whether such organizations will not use them mainly for antihuman purposes. Or consider speech recognition systems. Will they not be used primarily to spy on private communications? To answer such questions by saying that big computer systems, computer networks, and speech recognition systems are inevitable is to surrender one's humanity. For such an answer must be based either on one's profound conviction that society has already lost control over its technology or on the thoroughly immoral position that "if I don't do it, someone else will."

I don't say that systems such as I have mentioned are necessarily evil— only that they may be and, what is most important, that their inevitability cannot be accepted by individuals claiming autonomy, freedom, and dignity. The individual computer scientist can and must decide. The determination of what the impact of computers on society is to be is, at least in part, in his hands.

Finally, the fundamental question the computer scientist must ask himself is the one that every scientist, indeed every human, must ask. It is not "what shall I do?" but rather "what shall I be?" I cannot answer that for anyone save myself. But I will say again that if technology is a nightmare that appears to have its own inevitable logic, it is our nightmare. It is possible, given courage and insight, for man to deny technology the prerogative to formulate man's questions. It is possible to ask human questions and to find humane answers.

REFERENCES

1. B. F. Skinner, *Beyond Freedom and Dignity* (New York: Knopf, 1971).

2. K. M. Colby, S. Weber, F. D. Hilf, *Artificial Intelligence* I, no. 1 (1971).

3. N. Chomsky, *Aspects of the Theory of Syntax* (Cambridge, Mass.: MIT Press, 1965); N. Chomsky and M. Halle, *The Sound Pattern of English* (New York: Harper, 1968).

4. L. Mumford, *The Pentagon of Power* (New York: Harcourt, 1970).

5. H. A. Simon, *The Sciences of the Artificial* (Cambridge, Mass.: MIT Press, 1969), pp. 22–25.

6. B. Buchanan, G. Sutherland, E. A. Feigenbaum, in *Machine Intelligence*, B. Meltzer, ed. (New York: American Elsevier, 1969).

7. W. A. Martin and R. J. Fateman, "The Macsyma system" in *Proceedings of the 2nd Symposium on Symbolic and Algebraic Manipulation* (New York: Association for Computer Machines, 1971); J. Moses, *Commun. Assoc. Computer Mach.* 14, no. 8 (1971), p. 548.

8. N. Wiener, *Science* 131 (1960), p. 1355.

9. R. Gillette, *Science* 174 (1971), p. 477.

Information Technology: Its Social Potential

by Edwin B. Parker
and Donald A. Dunn

Broadcast television is like the passenger railroad, taking people to scheduled places at scheduled times. Cable television has the potential of becoming like a highway network, permitting people to use their television sets in the way they use their personal automobiles; they may be able to select information, education, and entertainment at times and places of their own choosing.

The technologies of cable television (especially two-way cable television), video cassettes, computer information systems, and communication satellites are now at a stage that could permit the creation of an "information utility" for the purpose of fostering equal social opportunity in the United States. The unit costs of public access to information could be reduced so much that the total expenditure on information services would probably increase substantially. In the same way that the automobile led to greatly increased expenditure on transportation, and the printing press led to greater expenditure on production and distribution of information, so the newly developing technology of information accessibility will have broad social effects. The main difference between the present period of technological change and the earlier periods is that our society now has a greater opportunity to direct the development of the technology to meet positive social goals, instead of becoming the beneficiary (or victim) of uncontrolled technological change.

The greatest single potential of an information utility might be the opportunity to reduce the unit cost of education to the point where our society could afford to provide open and equal access to learning opportunities for all members throughout their lives. Total expenditures for education are unlikely to be reduced, but an information utility could make possible the provision of quality education at an economical rate to those not adequately served by the present educational system. Significant gains in economic productivity as a result of education may be the most promising way to stimulate general economic development. Denison's analysis of past sources of per capita economic growth in the United States supports such a conclusion.[1]

The benefits of an information utility will not be attained quickly, or be guaranteed, unless there are major federal expenditures on the research and development needed for their accomplishment and some measure of coordinated planning and management of the overall system. The federal government has the continuing challenge of providing equal social opportunity for all citizens; this includes the provision of equal access to education and information, as well as the maintenance of an economy that provides equal opportunity of employment.

An information utility could be made available to every urban home and rural community in the United States by 1985. Such a national goal would, like the goals of the space program, have the glamor of new technology. It would differ from national space goals in two respects. One is that an information utility would be built largely by private enterprise with private capital; federal planning, research, and development funds could provide the additional incentives to ensure that the needs of education and other public services are met. The other difference is that instead of the information utility being justified in terms of national prestige and "spin-off" benefits, it would be designed to serve people directly in a way they could understand.

Before such a national goal could be adopted or have wide political appeal, the launching of a first "Sputnik" would be required in the form of credible pilot projects demonstrating the technical and social feasibility of the larger goal. By means of these pilot projects, it would be possible for the government to determine the combination of factors needed to guarantee the social, political, and economic success of the venture while still reserving the option of not proceeding further. In this article we present arguments that support the idea of financing pilot projects and coordinated planning that will test the technical and social feasibility of a national information utility.

PRESENT CABLE TELEVISION SYSTEMS

As of January 1971, there were 60 million households with television sets, 5.3 million of which were served by cable.[2] In Figure 1, the projected curves for 1971 to 1980 are based on an assumption that growth will continue for the next 5 years at the same rate as it has done for the past 5 years; it is also assumed that there will be a saturation effect in the number of households with cable television starting in 1976.

The typical cable television system now has a capacity for 12 or fewer channels, all of which are used primarily for retransmission of television programs broadcast over the air. Revenue for the cable system is obtained by selling (at rates of about $5 per month) better quality television signals than those available over the air, or by selling reception of distant signals not locally available. Some cable systems are also being used to provide local television service directly over the cable without broadcast transmission. Growth of cable television has been slowed by Federal Communications Commission (FCC) regulations preventing the importation of distant signals into the top 100 markets (the larger metropolitan areas containing more than 85 percent of the nation's homes). There is a general discussion of cable television policy issues in the recent report of the Sloan Commission of Cable Communications.[3] New FCC rules that went into effect in April 1972 permit at least two distant television signals to be imported by each cable system, although copyright rules make that option less attractive in the top 50 markets than in the second 50.[4]

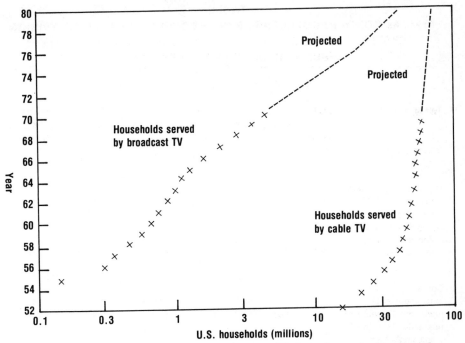

FIG. 1. The number of U.S. households served by broadcast television and the number of households served by cable TV. Figures projected for 1971 to 1980. [From *Television Factbook (2)*]

A single television cable has the capacity for many more than 12 channels because the cable amplifiers now available can amplify frequencies from near zero to about 300 megahertz; a band-width of 6 megahertz is required for each color television signal. If there were economic incentives, the number of cable channels could be increased indefinitely by laying more cable. The older cable systems can be made to supply more than 12 channels by changing the amplifiers that are spaced throughout the system.

Television and radio signals, and digital communication signals, can be transmitted directly over a cable without the necessity of allocating broadcast frequencies. Charges to those wishing to transmit signals over the cable can be much less than for broadcasting over the air for two reasons. First, charges can be closer to actual cost because access to a cable does not require payment of the opportunity cost associated with preempting a scarce resource. Second, it is not necessary to pay for larger audiences than the originator wants to reach, because cable systems can serve groups of 10,000 (or fewer) subscribers instead of entire regions with populations on the order of millions.

To estimate the cost of the hardware for a 24-channel system (and of more complex systems discussed below) the capital cost of a complete cable system is first calculated. The capital cost is then converted to a monthly cost and then to a cost per terminal hour that a user would expect to pay and a cost per channel hour that would have to be paid by any group or individual making exclusive use of a channel. These calculations are summarized in Table 1.[5]

TABLE 1

TYPICAL COSTS IN DOLLARS FOR THREE TYPES OF CABLE TELEVISION
SYSTEMS (NOT INCLUDING COST OF TELEVISION SETS); SRS,
SUBSCRIBER-RESPONSE SYSTEMS.

Type of system	Cost category (dollars)					Maximum numbers of	
	Capital (per sub-scriber)	Monthly (per sub-scriber)	Per terminal hour	Per channel hour	Simultaneous users	User terminals per channel	Pictures simultaneously displayed
National average costs for underground cables							
Conventional 24-channel one-way TV	110	2.29	0.03	2.38	10,000	10,000	24
Interactive TV with SRS	320	6.67	0.07	6.95	10,000	10,000	24
Interactive TV with SRS and single frame local storage	520	10.82	0.14	11.26*	720 to 7,200	30 to 300	720 to 7,200
Typical costs for underground trunk cable in central city locations							
Conventional 24-channel one-way TV	250	5.20	0.07	5.44	10,000	10,000	24
Interactive TV with SRS	460	9.60	0.12	10.00	10,000	10,000	24
Interactive TV with SRS and single frame local storage	660	13.75	0.17	14.32†	720 to 7,200	30 to 300	720 to 7,200

*Cost per subscriber sharing a channel is $0.04 to $0.37.
†Cost per subscriber sharing a channel is $0.05 to $0.48.

TWO-WAY COMMUNICATION

Many of the new cable television systems now being installed have sufficient channels to enable subscribers to communicate data back to a computer at the head-end of the cable system.[8] Such systems, referred to as subscriber-response systems (SRS), now permit a single computer to collect information from as many as 10,000 subscribers in less than 2 seconds.[9] These same systems can automatically record whether the television set is on and what channel it is tuned to. Figure 2 shows the network configuration for this type of system.

The terminal configuration at the subscriber's end of such a system will probably have the form shown in Figure 3, if it is built during the next few years. In this configuration, the lines leading from the trunk cable to the house (house-drops) are connected to a unit containing a modulator-demodulator (modem) and a digital memory. The signal received in any one of the regular television channels may be passed directly to the television set. Alternatively, a separate tuner and channel selector may be included. When a signal is received from the computer in the data channel it is demodulated and, if the address is that of this terminal, the data signal stored in the memory is read out, modulated, and transmitted upstream to the computer. Messages from the subscriber are written into the memory through a 12-

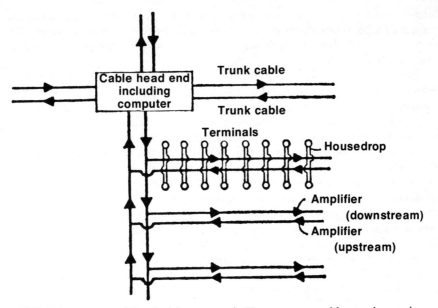

FIG. 2. A two-way cable television network. Two separate cables can be used to carry downstream and upstream signals, as shown here, or two separate frequency bands in the same cable may be used.

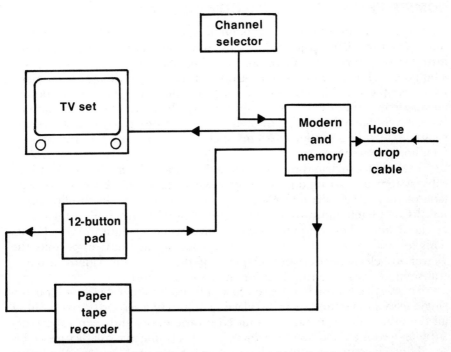

FIG. 3. Terminal configuration of a two-way cable television system. A 12-button pad allows subscriber responses to be entered into the system and a paper tape recorder gives the subscriber a record of his transactions.

button pad. A paper tape recorder may be used to record the subscriber's messages as he types them or to record acknowledging signals from the computer. The 12-button pad could be replaced with a teletype keyboard at a cost of about $100.

The cost of a terminal configuration of this type, apart from the television set, is in the range of $100 to $300, depending on the detailed design requirements and the quantity produced. We have estimated $200 for all items in Figure 3 except the television set. The production of large quantities, on the order of tens of thousands of terminals per year, is assumed. Additional costs for a two-way system of this type include the cost of a return cable or of upstream amplifiers in the existing cable, plus the cost of a computer at the head-end for polling and for storing and processing data. We estimate $10 per subscriber for these items in a 10,000-subscriber system of the type and density considered above. When these costs are added to the costs of a one-way system, the total capital cost per subscriber becomes $320. The costs for this type of system are summarized in Table 1. It should be emphasized that the costs are based on the present state of the technology. Systems built 5 to 10 years from now will probably have improved performance at lower costs than those estimated here.

COMPUTER AND SATELLITE COMMUNICATION

Cable television may turn out to be the most economical way to provide some kinds of digital communications to homes, such as computer-aided instruction, information retrieval, and time-shared computer services.[10] The potential of time division multiplexing (sending messages from many users over the same channel at different times) on polled systems may permit cheaper communication from computers to individual remote terminals on the shared "party line" type of system than on dedicated (space division multiplex) communications systems such as that provided by the present telephone network.

Techniques such as those recently demonstrated in the Reston, Virginia, cable system also permit time-sharing of particular channels for analog data (still pictures), with the television set becoming a computer display terminal.[11] Completely individualized computer-aided instruction, information retrieval, and other computer services can thus be brought to every home. This technique, with the aid of a local video storage device, permits the viewer to select, on demand, displays of digital or still video messages transmitted from a central location at reasonable cost.

This device is usually referred to as a frame-grabber, because it takes a single televison picture (or frame) lasting 1/30th of a second, grabs it out of all the other frames being transmitted on the cable, and then repeatedly supplies it to the set so that the viewer sees this frame as a still picture on his set. The key component of such a system is the unit that stores the frame locally. For the system demonstrated in Reston, a commercially available video tape recorder was used as the local storage unit. Other methods of storage are possible, such as the plasma display tube,[12] silicon storage tube,[13] or delay line systems in which the delays may be 1/30 second or more.

A critical cost parameter in such a system is the number of subscribers that can share a channel. If the average time between frames for each user is 1 second, then the maximum number of subscribers per channel is 30. If the average time is 10 seconds, 300 subscribers can share the channel. We have estimated $200 per terminal for a frame-grabber that could be integrated with the subscriber-response system in which the 12-button pad or keyboard is used. The total costs for this type of system that we summarize in Table 1 are less accurate than the other cost estimates given here because the technology is still in a state of rapid change. The cost per channel hour is given in Table 1, first for this system as a cost for the channel as a whole and then as a cost for an individual using the channel either 1/300th or 1/30th of the time, corresponding to an average time between frames of 10 seconds or 1 second.

To provide instructional or other services via such systems, additional computer hardware, computer software, and program production would be required. Hardware costs are likely to be small compared with other costs. Nevertheless, the costs of communication hardware can be critical to a decision as to what type of information system should ultimately be used. Costs as low as those indicated may be sufficient to make the costs of information distribution in this form cheaper than other forms, such as classroom instruction or printed newspapers delivered by truck and bicycle.

Schemes for providing individual homes with direct access to centrally stored motion video on demand do not appear to be economically viable at this time because of the high cost of transmission associated with the use of a television channel on an exclusive basis. The cost per channel hour given in Table 1 is an average transmission cost that would have to be paid by an individual subscriber desiring his own motion video service. The price during prime time would be greater than this. In addition, there would be costs associated with a video tape or video cassette player at the head-end and the cost of the tape or cassette. If these costs were acceptable, remote controlled video jukeboxes providing on-demand, motion video with slow motion, stop action, and instant replay under the viewer's control could be made available. A more probable development is that video cassettes in the home will provide the motion video capability, with requested "movies" perhaps being recorded onto home cassettes from the cable during nonpeak hours. Alternatively, motion video could be made available on a shared basis by means of cable; groups of 10 to 100 subscribers sharing a channel might be adequate to reduce the cost to an acceptable level.

There are a variety of means for interconnecting local cable television systems into a national information network. Conventional, terrestrial microwave links provided by American Telephone and Telegraph (AT & T) are now used to interconnect broadcast television stations. Communication satellite systems appear to provide the most economical long-term approach. Hughes Aircraft has proposed to the FCC that it be permitted to construct a domestic communication satellite system for the purpose of interconnecting cable systems. Special-purpose common carriers, such as Datran, might also play a significant role in the interconnection of cable systems.[14]

AN INFORMATION UTILITY

The information utility that we propose be established might be visualized as a communication network providing access to a large number of retrieval systems in which nearly all information, entertainment, news, library archives, and educational programs are available at any time to any person wanting them.[15] Many of these services, such as retailing in the home, entertainment, and various specialized business services would be provided by private enterprise. Other services would depend on public support.

The social goal of such an information utility could be to provide all persons with equal opportunity of access to all available public information about society, government, opportunities, products, entertainment, knowledge, and educational services. From the subscriber's perspective such a system would look like a combination of a television set, telephone, and typewriter. It would function as a combined library, newspaper, mail-order catalog, post office, classroom, and theater.

The configuration of the information utility is likely to be that of a number of overlaid computer-communication networks, some competing with one another to provide similar functions, others providing different functions. These separate networks could share many of the same physical facilities, such as subscriber terminals, communication lines, and a switching computer. Each different network or service would probably have its own separate computer, central data file, and computer software.

Although competition might develop between the telephone system and the cable system for some of the services, the different physical characteristics of the two networks would probably lead to different and complementary services. The cable network would, like the telephone system, develop a local monopoly in each geographic area because it would be too costly to lay competing cables. To guarantee both freedom of speech and freedom of access on such a communication system, regulatory means would have to be found to guarantee nondiscriminatory access to both the sending and receiving ends of the information utility. Present FCC regulations for cable television are moving in that direction.[4]

ECONOMIC POTENTIAL

We have shown that the capital cost per subscriber for a system of this type, apart from the cost of the television set, is likely to be around $500 to $700. Of interest as a basis of comparison is the fact that the U.S. telephone system has a total capital investment of about $50 billion, which is an investment per telephone of $500 or an investment per household or business office of $700. Eventually, cable television will probably reach residents of every small town in the United States, but perhaps not every isolated farm house. On this assumption the total capital investment might be of the same order of magnitude as that for the telephone plant, or about $50 billion. This capital investment for hardware will be accompanied by an annual expenditure for programming and personnel that may be substantially greater than the equivalent annual cost of hardware. In the telephone system, annual operating costs are about $130 per telephone which is about equal to the equivalent annual cost of the hardware for the system. Both hardware and software segments of the information industry are thus likely to grow and to create new jobs during the coming decades.

Electricity, transportation, and communication facilities provide a basic economic structure that permits and stimulates further economic development. In the early stages of industrial development, production and distribution of goods dominated economic development. Now, production and distribution of information has taken on increasing economic importance. Although some people consider any services other than entertainment that might be provided by cable television as speculative, most knowledgeable observers expect strong growth to take place in additional services developed for or made more economical by large capacity, two-way communication. That such growth will take place may depend on there being guaranteed, non-discriminatory access to the information utility. This will provide incentives for large numbers of entrepreneurs to invest in the development of the programs and services that will be necessary if all potential customers are to be reached. The development of such an information utility in the next decades may provide an infrastructure for economic growth somewhat analogous to that provided by the development of railroads more than a century ago.

An economic analysis of the sources of economic growth in the United States attributes 23 percent of the growth from 1929 to 1957 to increases in the level of education and 20 percent to advances in knowledge. When this figure is translated into economic growth per person employed, 42 percent (the largest single factor) of the economic growth is attributed to improvements in education and 36 percent to advances in knowledge.[1] This indicates that if the United States adopts a policy of continued economic growth while reducing the rate of population growth, we should plan more productive investment in education. The information utility may permit the needed increases in productivity of educational services that could, in turn, spur general increases in economic productivity. The total costs of such a technology-intensive system will be higher, but the economies of scale in reaching many more students without extra building costs or labor costs should permit an increase in productivity.

When a majority of the working force was engaged in agriculture and industry, concentrated investments in the acquisition and distribution of new knowledge and technology related to these activities paid handsome dividends. By providing agricultural experiment stations and extension services, and by setting up land-grant colleges and investing in science and education generally, the federal government played a major role in the growth of the U.S. economy over the past century. Now that the productivity gains in agriculture and industry have significantly reduced the percentage of the labor force engaged in such pursuits, the next place to look for major productivity gains is in the knowledge "industries" themselves.

By making quality education readily available to those not now able to take full advantage of opportunities in present educational institutions (including culturally deprived minorities, those beyond school age, and some women), additional economic and social gains should be possible. Such facilities for education could reduce the unemployment rates of people undereducated for the kinds of jobs available in a technologically advanced society. The present, temporary underemployment of highly trained scientists and engineers could also be alleviated if the information utility that we propose were to be established, because of the research and development that would be required to make the system effective.

Communication technology without the development of educational content and human services would not be sufficient to accomplish the ambitious goals we are proposing.

SOCIAL POTENTIAL

The low cost, large capacity, and local nature of cable television relative to over-the-air broadcasting could lead to a greater amount of local programming and greater variety of program content that would satisfy many minority interests not now served by television. Regulations permitting pay-by-program television on cable would stimulate even greater diversity because some viewers will be willing to pay more than the approximately 1 cent per viewer hour paid by advertisers for "free" television.

As access to information becomes easier and the cost of this accessibility is decreased by improvements in communication technology, it might also become harder for the subscriber to maintain privacy. In the absence of legal barriers, the general trend would be to more openness (less privacy) as information costs come down. However, if there are legal guarantees of non-discriminatory access to both the sending and receiving ends of the cable system, the resulting openness should make it more difficult for any single viewpoint to dominate the media.

While an impersonal communication source cannot be sensitive to the individual receiver's emotional state, it can present the same content consistently and fairly to everyone because it is also blind to the age, sex, color, religion, or hair style of the receiver. The impersonal information system is likely to be valued as being more responsive to social needs because it makes information available to larger numbers of people.

If access to these information services is not universally available throughout the society, then those already "information-rich" may reap the benefits while the "information-poor" get relatively poorer. A widening of this "information gap" may lead to increased social tensions. On the other hand, policies stimulating universal availability may permit those presently economically or culturally deprived to gain information that could help them narrow the gap in economic and political power between themselves and the rest of society.

The present location, distribution, and congestion of many urban areas can be attributed to earlier stages of transportation and communication technology. The development of an information utility could reduce the need for transportation. The information utility could also lead to greater physical decentralization of business and other facilities, while maintaining the same or greater administrative centralization of control. Improved communication services may thus provide a key component for the solution of other urban problems. The National Academy of Engineering committee on telecommunications has recently suggested the importance of this possibility as a means of encouraging portions of our population to move into uncongested regions of the country.[16] This overall trend may be important also in slowing down the rates of energy consumption by providing access to information by means requiring less energy and creating less pollution.

POLITICAL POTENTIAL

To some extent, information is power. More widespread access to a greater variety of information will lead to an increasingly enlightened electorate and consequently to their greater participation in the political process. It will thus become more difficult for political power to be concentrated in a small group of people. A greater variety of information services may be the most effective way to bring power to all the people in a nondisruptive way.

Political candidates for other than national or statewide office often can not afford television coverage in their districts because it requires paying for coverage in a wide region, most of which lies outside their district. By means of cable television, local candidates would be able to reach only the voters in their district (or precinct) without having to pay the large costs of present television campaigning. The services provided by the information utility could permit voters to retrieve information about the candidates and their records in detail not possible with present media. Thus there would be various ways of increasing the subscribers' opportunities for political participation.

EDUCATIONAL POTENTIAL

In a recent article in *Science,* Pake discussed the crisis in higher education in the United States and pointed to the productivity problem as a key issue.[17] He cited costs per unit of instruction that increased by a factor of 4 during the decade of the 1960's in many universities. He said a major challenge to educational institutions is to find a way to use technology to increase the teaching productivity of the individual teachers. The same comments can be applied equally well to education at all levels. The difficulty is that given the financial crisis in most of our educational institutions, the research and development funds needed to make possible productivity gains must come from outside sources, presumably the federal government.

Changed conditions in society are placing the three following demands on educational institutions: equality of access to educational opportunity, lifelong learning, and diversity of curriculum content.

1) Demands for open enrollment in institutions of higher education are increasing, but the limitations of classroom and laboratory space and the costs of teaching personnel may make it difficult for many institutions to

respond to those demands. In the Open University in the United Kingdom, television is being used to provide higher education to those not served by the traditional universities. This concept could be extended here to include all levels of education. Thus any person would be able to attempt any course he wanted to without requiring classroom space or teacher time. If success were rewarded without failures being recorded or there being other potential penalties for the student, many inhibitions about learning might be avoided and people might find their own levels of ability without others telling them what they can and cannot do. Regardless of economic efficiency, political and moral judgments will eventually require the provision of educational systems providing equal opportunity of access to education.

2) Formal education learned early in life can seldom last a lifetime. The need for periodic (or continuous) retraining is particularly great in occupations with a large scientific or technical component (for example, medicine, engineering) and is well recognized. It seems unlikely that the concept of industry sabbaticals would be quickly implemented as a response to this need. In any case, much learning is often required between sabbaticals. Night school classes may provide a partial answer for some, but busy people or people with irregular schedules are often unable to make the kind of commitment required. An information utility that made education available on demand in homes and offices would provide a more flexible solution.

Lifelong learning in the home could start with appropriate preschool instruction. Supplementary or extracurricular instruction could be made available for school children as well as adults.

3) The trend in mass media and in education itself is toward more variety. This cultural pluralism is already evident in the variety of special-interest magazines available and in the decrease in the number of mass-circulation magazines now published. The diversity of curricula now available to students lags behind the variety of occupations and interests available in society. Because it is already evident that no fixed curriculum will meet the present requirements for relevance and variety, the logical culmination of the situation is the provision of completely individualized instructional programs—a state we are unlikely to attain without significant technological help.

If we project the labor costs and the building costs of meeting these three educational needs by traditional means, the projections become absurd. No matter how rich a society we become the percentage of resources needed would be too high to permit other essential activities.

FEDERAL PLANNING AND COORDINATION

The forces of the market will cause the information utility to take shape in some form without any governmental initiative. However, we believe that a more effective and widely useful system would come into being if there were a federal program to coordinate the planning and development of the system.

For example, if the market for new entertainment services turns out to be the first to develop, the hardware that is first installed may not be adequate for the provision of education and information services that develop later.

If there is adequate planning, it should be possible to design a system that can readily be adapted to the provision of new education and information services when they become available. Without adequate planning and a minimum level of standardization it may be unnecessarily costly to add new services to an existing system.

A similar favorable effect in the area of software and programming could be brought about by federal planning and coordination. Some minimum level of standardization or format would be helpful. A catalog of materials available and a mechanism for national distribution of such materials could facilitate the development of services on the information utility.

The need for federal planning and coordination is partly a result of the fact that the development of the information utility requires the cooperation of a number of otherwise separate industries. Hardware systems will be provided by the computer industry, the telephone industry, and the cable television industry; and components will be supplied to all of these by the electronics industry. The aerospace industry and the National Aeronautics and Space Administration are also involved in communication satellite subsystems. The provision of information content for the utility involves another set of industries including the entertainment industry, the education industry, and new information service industries. The establishment of minimum technical and administrative interface standards under federal supervision will greatly facilitate the interaction of these industries. Similarly, the establishment of nondiscriminatory rules of access to the utility for providers of entertainment, education, and information services will encourage the development of new services by providing assurance to these service industries that their products will have access to potential markets.

The total federal investment needed for planning and coordination of the utility is likely to be much less than 10 percent of the total investment in the utility. Yet this part of the total may be critical to the development of the utility in a form best suited to the provision of many of the most socially significant services.

PILOT PROJECTS

A very significant part of the planning process is the gathering of information by means of experiments or pilot projects. In the case of the information utility many experiments are likely to be performed by the private sector to gather information needed in order to plan private sector services. Similarly, federal investment in pilot projects is needed in the very near future, in order to plan public sector services and to coordinate the interface between public and private sector services.

The National Academy of Engineering committee on telecommunications recommends several pilot projects for demonstrating various portions of the information utility.[16] The next step would be to plan in more specific detail a number of demonstration projects in specific communities, some of which might be interconnected by an experimental satellite service.

A start has been provided by the recent Mitre Corporation study of cable television for Washington, D.C., and the Rand Corporation study of metropolitan Dayton.[18] These studies are focused on the economic viability of cable systems rather than on public service demonstration projects, however. Since the major difficulties in demonstration projects are more likely to be social and political than technical, it would be a mistake to plan only one or two such projects. Any single project could fail because of local political or management problems quite extraneous to the national potential being tested. Pilot demonstration systems should be undertaken in perhaps a dozen different locations spanning the major geographic regions of the country, and ranging from inner city to rural locations, from new towns to established communities, and from profit to nonprofit (or municipal) systems of ownership. Although most of the communities used for these projects would be expected to use cable television for the local distribution of information, at least one pilot project should be based on broadband telephone technology (for example, Picturephone). There should be some experimentation with direct access to satellites for remote rural locations as well as with the use of satellites for system interconnection. The technology is available; no breakthroughs are needed. What is required is a systematic mission-oriented research, development, and demonstration program to bring together the hardware components, to develop necessary software and programming, and to study how best they can be made to work in different social, political, and economic settings.

In each of the communities used for pilot projects funds will be needed for upgrading existing or proposed cable television or telephone systems in order to provide sufficient broadband channel capacity and permit two-way communication. Other costs will be incurred in the development and distribution of special user-terminal hardware, such as frame-grabbers and keyboards. The largest portion of the budget will be required for developing the most effective techniques for programming and delivering information over the new utility; these costs will be significantly greater than the cost of developing programs for a known technology, such as one-way television. The cost of developing new computer systems can also be expected to be substantial. Additional funds will be required for social science studies of the utilization and social effects of the information utility.

Several federal agencies may be interested in the development of experimental telecommunications systems in the pilot projects, including the departments of Housing and Urban Development, Transportation, Commerce, the National Aeronautics and Space Administration, and the Department of Health, Education, and Welfare (HEW). Because the information utility's most significant potential lies in the educational services that it can provide, it may be desirable to establish a new organization in HEW to oversee the educational uses to which the utility is put. The proposed National Institutes of Education (patterned after the National Institutes of Health) might be used for this purpose. Because of the interest of many federal departments, a coordinating role would have to be played by some central agency such as the Office of Science and Technology or the Office of Telecommunications Policy.

If a start were made immediately on detailed technical, financial, legislative, and management plans, it might be possible to have new authorizing legislation and appropriations for the fiscal year starting 1 July 1973. Phase 1 (1973-76) could include system development, policy planning, development of a research support program, and actual demonstrations and field tests. Both urban cable systems and low-population density satellite systems could be included in the phase 1 pilot programs. Phase 2 (1976-1985) would permit the national implementation of an information utility, making use of the most successful results of the phase 1 pilot programs. Legislation designed to encourage the development of this national telecommunication system may be needed during phase 2 to stimulate local and state development, as was the case for rural electrification and the interstate highway system.

CONCLUSION

The information utility that we have described is a system designed to provide better quality education and information to everyone in the United States, with unit costs of service substantially less than the costs of present systems. In order to accomplish these positive social goals a detailed plan for federal action and participation is needed. Since most of the funds for this utility will come from the private sector, the principle needs for federal action are in the areas of coordination, policy analysis and assessment, and the funding of pilot projects and demonstrations designed to stimulate the development of new public-sector education and information services.

REFERENCES

1. E. F. Denison, *Sources of Economic Growth in the United States and the Alternatives Before Us* (New York: Committee for Economic Development, 1962).

2. *Television Factbook* no. 41, (Washington, D.C.: Television Digest, 1971-72).

3. *On the Cable: The Television of Abundance.* Report of the Sloan Commission on Cable Communications, (New York: McGraw-Hill, 1971).

4. Federal Communications Commission, *Cable Television Report* (2 February 1972); *Federal Register,* vol. 37, no. 30, part 2 (12 February 1972).

5. The capital cost of a cable system per subscriber depends strongly on the density of homes. For typical urban locations with medium to high density, 50,000 homes or apartments can be served by 100 miles (1 mile = 1.6 km) of trunk cable. If we take $15,000 per mile as the cost of the underground trunk line cables, allowing $45 per subscriber for the line from the trunk cable to the house (house-drops), and $50,000 for head-end buildings, antennas, and related costs, a 10,000-subscriber system with 50 percent market penetration would cost $110 per subscriber. These cost estimates are for typical underground systems and are based

on information provided by the National Cable Television Association as reported by Comanor and Mitchell.[6] It should be noted that although $15,000 per mile for underground trunk cables is the present national average cost, $50,000 or more per mile is typical of some metropolitan areas. If $50,000 is used in place of $15,000 in the above cost estimate, the resulting capital cost per subscriber increased from $110 to $250. To convert capital cost to monthly cost, we can assume a system life of 10 years, an interest rate of 8 percent per year, and maintenance cost of 10 percent per year, obtaining a monthly cost of 1/48 of capital cost. The monthly cost that goes with the capital cost figure of $110 is then $2.29 per month per subscriber. If we assume 80 hours per month of usage by each terminal, the average cost per terminal hour is $0.03. If we assume 400 hours per month of transmission on each channel and 24 channels, the average cost per channel hour is $2.38.[7]

6. W. Comanor and B. Mitchell, *Bell J. Econ. Manage. Sci.*, vol. 2 (1971) p. 154.

7. D. A. Dunn, *Eascon '71 Record* (Proceedings of the IEEE Electronics and Aerospace Systems Convention, October 1971), p. 157.

8. S. Edelman, *Electron. Eng.*, vol. 30 (1971), p. 41; R. Jurgen, *IEEE (Inst. Elec. Electron. Eng.)*, vol. 8 (1971), p. 39; W. S. Baer, "Interactive television: Prospects for two-way service on cable," (Rand Corporation Report R-888-MF, November 1971).

9. R. T. Callais and E. W. Durfee, "The subscriber response system," Proceedings of the 20th Annual National Cable Television Association Convention, (1971), pp. 28-48.

10. P. Baran, in *Planning Community Information Utilities*, H. Sackman and B. Boehm, eds., (Montvale, N.J.: American Federation of Informational Processing Societies, in press).

11. J. Volk, "The Reston, Virginia test of the Mitre Corporation's interactive television system," (Mitre Corporation Report, MTP-352, May 1971).

12. D. Alpert and D. L. Bitzer, *Science* no. 167 (1970), p. 1582.

13. M. Gerald Walker, *Electronics* no. 45 (10), (1972), p. 91.

14. Federal Communications Commission Docket 18920, Entry of Specialized Carriers.

15. E. B. Parker, in *Handbook of Communication*, I. deS. Pool, W. Schramm, N. Maccoby, E. B. Parker, eds., (Chicago: Rand McNally, in press); see also B. Bagdikian, *The Information Machines* (New York: Harper, 1971).

16. *Communication Technology for Urban Improvement* (Washington, D.C.: Committee on Telecommunications, National Academy of Engineering, 1971).

17. G. Pake, *Science* no. 172 (1971), p. 908.

18. W. F. Mason, "Urban cable systems," (Mitre Corporation Report M71-64, November 1971); L. L. Johnson et al., "Cable communications in the Dayton Miami Valley: Basic Report," (Rand Corporation Report R-943 KF/FF, January 1972).

NOTE

Supported by NSF grant GR 86. We thank Dr. P. Sherrill for assistance in the preparation of this article.

Education's New Majority

by Fred Hechinger

A recurring media cliché is the "human interest" story about the grand-mother graduating from college, preferably as a member of her grand-child's class. The implication is that there is something cute about the accomplishment—the reverse of the precocious youngster who has bested his elders in a television quiz.

The absurdity of such attitudes has struck me with particular force ever since I started to teach an adult undergraduate seminar in the Adult Col-legiate Experience program (ACE), which City University of New York offers under the auspices of Queens College. My students' ages range from the mid-20s to the upper 60s. Their backgrounds vary just as widely, for the group includes nurses, teachers, businessmen and businesswomen, govern-ment employees, truck drivers, police officers, and just ordinary family people. The students' common trait is their extraordinary motivation. Even though most of them lead busy non-academic lives, their attendance record has been nearly perfect; their default rate on the delivery of term papers has been a straight zero.

These adult students personify the much-debated trend toward contin-uing education or, to put it more aptly, lifelong learning. Although a small sample, they are sufficiently real to render redundant those interminable academic discussions as to whether continuing education ought to be taken seriously as a legitimate part of higher education.

The reason why those discussions persist is mainly that the education establishment has always found it more convenient to think of school and college in those tidy terms of the pedagogical lockstep: children entering school at a universally fixed age, leaving high school 12 years later in unison, and graduating from college after another "normal" four years. True, graduate students, having at last attained the courage of their inde-pendence, have been more prone to challenge the administrative schedule (as have undergraduates in increasing numbers since the rebellious Sixties), usually to the dismay of deans who still tend to make part-time study appear a social disgrace and an academic weakness. (Until recently, such attitudes had the effect of freezing great numbers of women, who wanted to raise families, out of the inner sanctum of graduate studies.)

Even the GI Bill of Rights was initially viewed by most university admin-istrators as a threat to scholarly standards, simply because the veterans were already on the wrong side of that magic divide—college age. Within the last two years, however, academic attitudes have begun to change. Continuing education, long viewed with disdain by many university regulars, has sud-denly been discovered as the wave of the future. Some of the continuing education specialists at such pioneering institutions as New York University and the New School for Social Research, and a handful of others who have spent a lifetime teaching adults may be slightly amused by the novelty label that is being attached to their field, but they are not likely to object to the experience of suddenly being "discovered."

The movement is clearly worldwide. In recent weeks the education ministers of 21 European countries, meeting in Stockholm, have endorsed an extensive program for international cooperation to promote "lifelong learning opportunities." In the United States, the most obvious reason for the sharp turn to adults as tomorrow's students is the prospect of declining college enrollments. The sagging birthrate has already led to a shrinking elementary school clientele, an average of 600,000 fewer first-graders each year since 1973. Within the next five years, the number of young Americans between the ages of 18 and 21 will reach an all-time high of about 17 million, but 10 years later, that group will have shrunk to about 13.5 million. At a time of inflated costs and troubled budgets, no growth and actual decline constitute a serious threat. Under such circumstances the prospect of a new category of students, not counted in previous projections, makes a college president's heart beat faster.

Even without such demographic changes, continuing education would undoubtedly assume new importance in the last quarter of the century. Growing demands are certain to be made on education as the knowledge and the expertise required for success in the modern labor market shift and expand. Highly educated older professionals are in danger of becoming obsolete, their success and earning power threatened by younger professionals.

In addition, increasing numbers of middle-aged and old people, faced with early retirement and boredom, will seek new interests and skills to prevent stagnation. More and more women, in particular, will turn from homemaking to careers, entering entirely new ones or retooling for those they have temporarily abandoned in order to raise children.

These predictable changes in the pattern of American life will challenge some assumptions about institutionalized education. "To the American mind," says Cyril O. Houle, professor of education at the University of Chicago and one of the leaders in the continuing education movement, "education is understood only in terms of the ladder, and the college and university provide its upper rungs. More than that, in tradition though not in fact, the ladder is climbed almost entirely by young people."

Professor Houle sees adult and part-time students as "a new majority." This concept clashes with the traditional view of graduation and "commencement," the end of schooling and the beginning of life. It is at odds with the old image of a student body that Ernest Boyer, chancellor of the State University of New York, has described as the Youth Ghetto. Dr. Boyer and others who are advocating a more open-ended view of education insist that learning should always have been considered a lifelong enterprise and that the part-time students ought to be the rule rather than the exception.

Old-fashioned administrators look down on "subway circuit" students and characterize as a dropout anyone who does not graduate within the pedantically fixed number of years. Yet the process of phasing in and out of organized learning could actually place a higher value on the contribution to be made by the academy. Under economic pressure, the purists' "better never than late" view of education, and particularly of higher education, is giving way. Within the past year even Princeton and Berkeley have succumbed to the growing practice of letting students enroll in less than "the full program."

Stephen Graubard, in his introduction to a two-volume assessment of higher education in *Daedalus*, the journal of the American Academy of Arts and Sciences (fall 1974 and spring 1975), called for "a wholly new concept of studentship." He termed it "extraordinary that so few institutions have made any substantial commitment to the education of adults." "Higher educational institutions," Dr. Graubard continued, "cannot wait for the demand to manifest itself and then respond by offering specific courses. . . . They ought, rather, to engage in systematic studies of what adults in a society like ours need to know or would profit from knowing, and seek to make these things available to ever-larger groups during the day, at night, on weekends, in the summer, and at many convenient sites. . . . When many colleges and universities enroll men and women of all ages, they will have the large public constituency they currently lack."

The most obvious appeal of continuing education is clearly to be found in such professions as medicine, law, teaching, the sciences, and engineering, of which even the best-trained practitioners find that new developments make their past schooling inadequate. Such pioneers as Abbott Kaplan, during his years at the University of California, Los Angeles, created extension courses for doctors and lawyers that enjoyed a statewide following long before the present movement began. Similarly, the Department of Postgraduate Medicine of the Albany, N.Y., Medical College of Union University has been running a Two-Way Radio Conference since 1955, permitting family physicians to "keep up" with recent medical findings by way of professional seminars with leading medical authorities. In the past two decades these teaching conferences, conveniently scheduled around the lunch hour, have totaled more than 160,000 hours of medical education, conducted by a contributing faculty from nearly 50 medical schools. Similar programs have since been established in Ohio, Utah, Wisconsin, Maryland, and California.

Medicine is an obvious example of the need for continuing education. Each year the profession is inundated with an estimated 2 million pages of new literature and about 170,000 abstracts. Changes in the legal profession are no less formidable and rapid. Entirely new categories vie with changes in existing law—public-interest law, new tax laws, Internal Revenue Service regulations, consumer-protection statutes, the no-fault approach to growing numbers of areas, anti-discrimination provisions, environmental-protection legislation, to cite but a few—and have affected the field.

Earlier this year the Minnesota Supreme Court ordered the state's lawyers either to go back periodically to formal studies or to get out of the practice of law. Several other states are moving toward a system of periodic relicensing, based on a required number of courses completed under a system of continuing education. In California, public accountants must complete 80 hours of continuing study in any two-year period in order to retain their licenses.

During the recent session of the American Assembly on "Law and a Changing Society" at the Stanford University Law School, Howell Heflin, the chief justice of Alabama, made a successful plea for the recommendation that judges be required to undergo special training, both before they ascend to the bench and periodically thereafter. The implication was clearly that judges who lack special training or have allowed their knowledge of a rapidly changing body of law to get rusty constitute a threat to the administration of justice.

As professional people move up on the ladder of their careers, they frequently enter into largely unfamiliar spheres of action and decision making. A good teacher may not be prepared to function successfully as a principal. The instances of able physicians turning into incompetent administrators are legion. But the expectations for continuing education transcend the essentially utilitarian goals of those who find it necessary to shore up their professional standing and earning power by returning to the classroom. Thousands of men and women sense that their formal education stopped short of their intellectual capacities, others want to fill in gaps or strike out in new directions, and many want to explore interests unrelated to their daily work and lives. Occasionally, the dramatic examples are cited—Dwight Eisenhower turning to painting late in an active and successful life or, only a few months ago, former British Prime Minister Edward Heath joining a group of professional jazz musicians. In fact, these examples merely dramatize the more ordinary drive of countless adults to seek personal satisfaction in new intellectual exploration.

At its best, the continuing education movement runs counter to the obsession with degrees and credentials that often dominates and debases traditional undergraduate and professional studies. In the Thirties, Robert Maynard Hutchins, at the time of his efforts to reform collegiate education, once quipped that the true process of learning could best be aided if every American baby were given a bachelor's degree at birth. Because more and more of those who enroll in continuing education courses already have their Bachelor's and even their "terminal" graduate and professional degrees, they can afford to approach their studies with all the unconcern over credentials intended for the Hutchins babies.

No account of the movement, however, would be complete without a warning concerning its inherent dangers. For instance, continuing education mandated by the state or by establishment associations could easily deteriorate in precisely the manner in which so much of the existing increments-oriented teacher education has turned sterile and time wasting. Particularly at a time when colleges and universities seek to add to their revenues, the temptation will be powerful to spawn required make-work (and make-pay) courses and to emphasize the number of credits completed rather than relevancy, quality, and excitement.

Adult education, moreover, has always been vulnerable to hangers-on and dilettantes. Some years ago, in a parody of the pretentious nothingness of some of these courses, Woody Allen included in a fictitious but not entirely implausible-sounding catalog this offering: "Yeats and Hygiene, a Comparative Study: the poetry of William Butler Yeats is analyzed against a background of proper dental care."

In addition, continuing or, as it is increasingly referred to in Europe, "recurring" education is subject to misuse by educational elitists as a subtle device to keep the masses out of the regular university enrollment. Some indications reveal that conservative university administrators, particularly in France and Sweden, where the recurrent movement is gathering momentum, have embraced their liberal colleagues' appeals to persuade the public that they need not forfeit their chances of going to college if they postpone actual entry into higher education—not because they share the liberals' hopes of an ever-expanding higher educational constituency, but rather because they hope that those who are told to come later may not come at all. Thus, we run the risk that a new dichotomy may unwittingly be created between the children of the traditionally university-trained families, who would remain the social and educational elite, and the more amorphous clientele of recurring education.

Finally, we face the imminent danger that the colleges will view and treat the adult students as mere office temporaries—welcome to fill vacancies and shore up sagging gate receipts, but nevertheless expected to adjust to the academic status quo. Such attitudes could defeat the very purpose of continuing education and squander the mature students' extraordinary potential for giving a new dimension to old institutions. Ultimately, such a policy could so alienate adult students that they might leave existing colleges and universities in favor of specially created adult institutions.

None of this need happen provided that the academic leadership is alert to the opportunities inherent in the dramatic new demand. Milton Stern, dean of University Extension at Berkeley, sees the continuing education movement as an "invisible university" of enormous promise but warns: "These people are not automatically ours to educate. We do not get them to enter merely by opening the doors. Adult students who pay for their courses —or whose companies pay—will look carefully at what we have to offer."

Thus, the challenge is to take a new look at the campus constituencies. What the universities are asked to do is to think of their graduates as continuing, active members of their community, not just as alumni who have been processed and packaged and are henceforth expected merely to pay off their debt of eternal gratitude for services already rendered.

Some academic leaders have recognized this need to shift gears. For example, John Kemeny, soon after assuming the presidency of Dartmouth College, moved toward the establishment of intensive recurring alumni education. This year at Stanford some of the university's leading professors of economics, history, and sociology staffed a 10-day summer alumni college dealing with "The Reshaping of the American Dream."

But such efforts are clearly only a beginning. The future of many colleges and universities may well depend on their capacity to grasp the needs of this great unknown constituency and to respond to them. This will require a flexibility few of the existing institutions have exhibited in the recent past. Fortunately, American higher education has managed at crucial junctions to respond to changing realities, the most dramatic example of which is the Land Grant colleges' original response to the manpower needs of the agricultural and industrial revolutions.

In many instances degree programs for adults have to consider the granting of credits for proven practical experience. Academic departments must show a greater readiness to let students work independently both on and off campus. The creation of Empire State College, as part of the State University of New York, is a useful example. There mature students may complete much of their requirements by working at home, by following academic outlines individually designed for them, and by pursuing their studies with the aid of supervising tutors at conveniently located centers throughout the state.

Ultimately, the huge network of this country's 3,000 colleges and universities ought to be able to create indigenous replicas of the relatively small New York experiment and perhaps even of the giant, centrally administered television- and computer-assisted British Open University, which has made higher education accessible to tens of thousands without regard for their precious formal educational attainments.

Progress has been made. The University of Michigan, for instance, runs more than 30 separate continuing education programs as part of a wide variety of existing departments, schools, and research institutes, including one large continuing education center for physicians and another for engineers.

Stanford University operates an Instructional Television Network, which last year transmitted over 200 classroom courses to more than 4,000 off-campus students. Broadcasting from 7 A.M. to 7 P.M. on weekdays, the network delivers regular instruction directly to employee-students at their jobs throughout the San Francisco Bay area, under contracts with industry. Last year at the Santa Rosa plant of an electronics firm, engineers who enrolled in the videotaped courses, with the help of a local tutor, completed their academic work with higher grades than did on-campus undergraduates, who had been carefully screened at this highly selective university. Eventually, Stanford spokesmen say, the network could readily go national or even international via satellite. Indeed, five of the engineering courses are currently being offered in Japan by videotape.

But on the whole, traditional institutions have been slow to realize the potential of continuing education and to make the necessary readjustments to offer and reap the benefits of a movement of rapidly accelerating momentum. In addition to welcoming mature and even old people to their regular classes, American campuses will be called upon to extend their influence into former students' homes, lives, and careers. Colleges may have to help employers, labor unions, civic organizations, medical and bar associations, and other agencies to create new academic patterns for lifelong learning; they ought to be able to tape and package courses for home study; they should, in other words, overcome their own static view of themselves as enclaves reserved largely for post-adolescent resident students—to be visited for brief and rigidly defined periods of time.

What is clear is that the American "consumer" pedagogy will demand continuing education in ever-greater volume and in more readily accessible form. It therefore follows that unless the existing institutions are willing and able to deliver the goods, they may well be by-passed.

At a time when the universities are increasingly despondent over the prospect of a shrinking pool of applicants, the elitist opponents of such unconventional, quasi-populist expansion of the universities' role are almost certain to be out-voted by the economic pragmatists who, in the end, have carried the day at every previous critical turn in American academic history. In a declining youth market, adults of all ages can make higher education once again a growth industry.

The Underlying Assumptions of Advocacy Planning: Pluralism and Reform

by Donald F. Mazziotti

THE PLURALISM ASSUMPTION

Following the introduction of the concept of advocacy planning to the planning profession by Linda and Paul Davidoff, Lisa Peattie, and Marshall Kaplan, a persistent series of assumptions concerning community power structure have been asserted and, with some notable dissenting views (Funnye, 1970; Hartman, 1971; Kravitz, 1970; Piven, 1970)[1] accepted by the vast majority of planners practicing advocacy planning. The assumption which is central to the concept of advocacy planning, as presently practiced, is that of pluralism:

> The prospect for future planning is that of a practice which openly invites political and social values to be examined and debated. Acceptance of this position means rejection of prescriptions for planning which would have the planner act solely as a technician.
>
> Determinations of what serves the public interest, in a society containing many diverse interest groups, are almost always of a highly contentious nature. In performing its role of prescribing courses of action leading to future desired states, the planning profession must engage itself thoroughly and openly in the contention surrounding political determination.[2]
>
> Advocate planners take the view that plan is the embodiment of particular group interests, and therefore they see it as important that any group which has interests at stake in the planning process should have those interests articulated. In effect, they reject both the notion of a single 'best' solution and the notion of a general welfare which such a solution might serve. Planning in this view becomes pluralistic and partisan—in a word, overtly political.[3]

Although the nature of the "pluralism" described is never carefully examined by the initiators of the advocate planning concept, the arenas within which advocate projects are to operate, i.e., the political parties, ad hoc protest groups, and chambers of commerce[4] suggest a rather protracted analysis of the "overtly political" processes with which the advocate planner must deal. Given the political context described by the adherents of this pluralistic model, it seems reasonable to classify the Davidoffs' pluralism as only the broadest kind of generalization. A synthesis of data concerning our urban condition would result in a three-dimensional model of America's social structure, revealing a complex, dispersed network of competing interest groups at every scale. Below the social strata one would find an even more complex aggregation of natural and social resources which are, at once, the subject of competing claims and the measure of society's potential for exploitation and development. Thus, it is this array of conflicting public and private interest groups—a surface characteristic of virtually all modern, industrialized societies[5]—to which the term "pluralism" is ascribed.

Used in this very broad way, the overt political strategies which are consistent with this kind of pluralism amount to little more than the process of advocacy restated by Paul Davidoff in 1971:

> In trying to reshape the nature of America's urban communities, there is one area, one set of institutions, practices, within America, that allows you to contribute greatly to the work that you seek to do as a professional planner. This is work with political parties that are shaping policy for this urban community.[6]

To suggest that advocacy planning responds to the condition of pluralism by participation in the traditional political process leaves unanswered the more fundamental question of whether the reality of pluralism is but a smokescreen called democracy. It can be argued that the Davidoff definition of pluralism is the standard by which advocate planners plan, wherein the suboptimal planning which characterizes both public and private groups becomes the operational criteria for social change.

If, on the other hand, by pluralism we mean that the opportunities and resources necessary for the exercise of power are *inclusively* rather than exclusively distributed and that neither the enjoyment of dominance nor the suffering of deprivation is the constant condition of any one group[7] then the issue of whether we exist within a pluralistic society is neither patently apparent nor easily resolved. The analysis proposed here is that, in point of fact, political pluralism is a well-constructed social myth which provides the rationale for instituting social programs designed to placate the politically and economically disenfranchised. The purpose and scope of this inquiry is to critically analyze the pluralist assumptions of advocacy, the constraints these assumptions impose, and to raise issues which will stimulate a discussion of alternative modes of advocacy given the existing political economy.

ASSUMPTIONS CONCERNING POLITICAL PLURALISM

From a purely technical perspective, the antithesis of pluralism is "monism" which means that the state, or some institutional surrogate, is the supreme sovereign power, to which all its constituent parts are legally or ethically bound. As traditionally expressed, pluralism is a political philosophy which assumes the validity of a representative democracy as the decisionmaking vehicle and argues that private interest groups of all kinds should enjoy an active, legitimatized, and influential role in the formulation of public policy. This political philosophy specifically rejects the Hegelian nation-state as well as anarchism:

> The common life of society is lived by individuals in unions, institutions of all kinds. The religious, the scientific, the economic life of the community develop

through these. Each has its own development. There is in them a sphere of initiative, spontaneity, and liberty. That sphere cannot be occupied by the state with its instruments of compulsion.[8]

In essence, political pluralism conceptualizes the process of decisionmaking as a system of social relationships whereby the expression of power among and between competing group interests ultimately shapes the direction and structure of the social system. Legal scholars,[9] sociologists,[10] social critics,[11] political scientists,[12] and economists[13] have embraced the pluralist interpretation of the American social system since at least the beginning of this century. This widespread acceptance of the theory, despite radical structural and institutional changes in the social fabric of the United States, makes it possible to note the basic assumptions of pluralism and critically examine its mythological character.

A first assumption of pluralism is that the existence of diverse interest groups provides the broadest representation of private interests within the state. John R. Commons' economic pluralism provides the rationale for this assumption when discussing the free enterprise market mechanisms which in his view, could not operate with fairness unless the existence of economic pressure groups were a reality:

> To get back to first principles of representative government (historically as well as logically), each of these diverse interests should be permitted to assemble itself and elect a spokesman. The negroes would then elect Booker T. Washington; the bankers would elect Lyman J. Gage and J. Pierpont Morgan; . . . the trade unions would elect Samuel Gompers and P. M. Arthur; the clergy would elect Archbishop Comigan and Dr. Parkhurst; the universities would elect Seth Low and President Eliot.[14]

The structural and institutional disparities for the pluralists are solved only when the control of vested interests over governmental bodies are wrested from them by the bargaining power of plural pressure groups; conflict among plural groups results in social progress and reform in an otherwise irrational market system. What Commons and others overlook is the fact that the collision of group interests may and frequently does result in policies which are at variance with the asserted and unasserted claims of a broader, unorganized public, usually composed of individuals in their role as consumers.[15] The pluralism assumption fails to account for the inherent inequality of bargaining power as between groups; in this sense, the first assumption of pluralism ignores the realities of disequilibrium in the relative distribution of power among interest groups, the inequitable nature of access routes into the political structure, and the unorganized majority of citizens who are unrepresented by a particular group or set of pressure groups. Using the group interest representatives listed by Commons, it becomes apparent that while J. Pierpont Morgan and President Eliot may have represented differing interest groups, both were from the same economic elite or class and both wielded effective power over the system which had little or nothing to do with their relationships with the railroads or universities, per se. This same class-power condition exists in present-day society. Thus, the mere representation or advocacy of a group's interests in no way significantly disturbs the existing pattern of status and power distribution in society.

A second critical assumption of political pluralism is that spirited completion and participation between organized *groups*—and not individuals—occur over time within the existing social structure. As has been discussed by Mancur Olson and others, effective group influence can occur only where the group *organization* is given access and the opportunity to participate in the decisionmaking process.[16] Because the reality of organizational behavior is one which places the definition of group interests in the hands of a few, it cannot be logically argued that the representative organization exhibits the interests of the group while enjoying an existence which is apart from its members. The group advocates, who may be synonomous with group leaders, operate under an assumption that the group will act in a way which in fact advances group interests without examining individual group member interests. An impressive body of empirical data exists which makes the second assumption of pluralism little more than a contentious, illogical distortion of social reality;[17] interest groups tend to develop goals and objectives which become increasingly at variance with the interests of the members of that group. Advocates or leaders of the organization's goals and objectives increasingly depart from representation of the individual interests of group members. Although this development can be explained in a number of ways, Olson argues that it is primarily a function of group size and the behavior which is associated with size:

> One obstacle, it would seem, to any argument that large and small groups operate according to fundamentally different principles, is the fact, emphasized earlier, that any group or organization, large or small, works for some collective benefit that by its very nature will benefit all of the members of the group in question. Though all of the members of the group therefore have a common interest in obtaining this collective benefit, they have no common interest in paying the cost of providing that collective good. Each would prefer that the others pay the entire cost, and ordinarily would get any benefit provided whether he had borne part of the cost or not.[18]

The tendency of individual members to take this anticollectivistic attitude, however, depends upon the size of the group and the opportunities for members to become intimately familiar with the goals of the group and the decisionmaking process. The larger the group, the further it will fall short of providing an optimal amount of a collective good; like the American trade unions, the organizational interests become primary to the interests of the worker and the individual worker shows less interest in the organization, ultimately becoming manipulated by the organization's decisions.

A third assumption concerning pluralism has recently emerged as a modification of the first two and a shifting of the pluralist theory to accommodate changed social conditions. Because voluntary associations and interest groups have become oligarchically governed bureaus,[19] pluralists have accepted a redefinition of the concept of pluralism to mean a condition which exists only if no single elite dominates decisionmaking in every substantive area; thus, competition among elite interest groups becomes the criteria by which we are asked to judge the condition of pluralism. The pluralists fail to examine or explain how this redefinition affects the central notion of individual representation through interest groups or how a theory centering on the operation and influence of elite pressure groups can pretend to remain consistent with notions of representative democracy—both of which were essential components of the pluralistic argument.

It would appear reasonable, given the inconsistencies of the pluralist position, to assert a set of preconditions for the existence of pluralism which can be evaluated. Robert Presthus has suggested five conditions upon which pluralism must rise or fall (demurring on the logical inconsistencies and accepting—for purposes of analysis—the redefinition of pluralism):

1. That competing centers and bases of power and influence exist within a political community;
2. The opportunity for individual and organizational access into the political system;
3. That individuals actively participate in organizations of many kinds;
4. That elections are a viable instrument of mass participation in political decisions, including those on specific issues; and
5. That a consensus exists on what may be called the 'democratic creed.'[20]

The extent to which these five prerequisites of pluralism exist in American society gives a fair evaluation of the concept as the basis upon which advocates of social change may rely upon it in formulating strategies or mechanisms to accomplish change. That so-called competing centers and bases of power and influence exist within a political community is a social reality in America. The pluralist criteria discussed before, however, requires that the competition must be among a number of groups and that the bases of power associated with groups are variable (e.g., economic power conflicting with technical power, communications power, etc.). This competition is critical to the validity of pluralism and the corollary concept of countervailing power, i.e., the assertion that there exist social stabilizers wherein the movement toward dominance by one power base will inspire or mobilize another power base which will bring the social system into a relative balance.

A test of this first condition for pluralism can be constructed around the resource allocation system—the corporate economy. The central fact about the American economy is that it is a highly concentrated, nonatomistic system of centralized industrial firms. In virtually every important manufacturing industry, a handful of firms produce a major share of output, employ a significant portion of the work force, and make the decisive investment-production decisions.[21] The concentration of the American economic system is vividly illustrated by examining Census Bureau statistics:

(a) second look at the very biggest giants offers a strong hint that more and more of manufacturing is being drawn into fewer and fewer hands. Between 1947 and 1958, the top 50 firms enlarged their share of the industrial pie from 17 percent to 23 percent; the biggest 200 from 30 to 38 percent. In other words, the 200 greatest corporations increased their slice of a much bigger pie by more than one quarter.

In the eleven years from 1950 through 1961, the 500 biggest industrial firms picked up 3,404 other companies, an average of seven apiece. The top 200 acquired 1,943 or an average of nearly ten each.[22]

Because the "new" pluralism finds the growth of competing elite groups consistent with the pluralist faith, the mere concentration of economic wealth is a tolerable, even a healthy, social condition. If concentration of economic power does not interfere with other power bases, the pluralist notion remains tenable; the fact is, however, that other power bases are not left intact. Hegemony of corporate capitalism over the economy, despite decades of progressive taxation, unionization, Social Security, Medicare, and antitrust legislation, has not resulted in a significant redistribution of income or power to other groups. The social power of capital is as great as it was at the time of the trust-monopolists; expanded social welfare benefits and government programs have served to rationalize the system, not change it.[23]

The condition of economic concentration does not end with the trend toward corporate merger. Beyond this trend lies the existence of "finance capitalists" which represent an even more centralized, concentrated power group—a fact ignored or unknown to the political pluralism theorists. During the period of competitive capitalism, industrial corporations in the United States became increasingly dependent upon a small group of banks that were alone capable of financing capital growth or rescuing failing enterprises. Financial control of industry or "finance capitalism" characterized the end of the era of competitive capitalism in the United States at the close of the nineteenth century.

Most political economists, including leftist theorists, believed that the finance capitalism which continued through the first quarter of the twentieth century would disappear as the split between the banks or finance capitalists and the corporate managers widened. Such a belief was based upon the reasonable assumption that the speculation interests of the finance capitalists and the growth and development interests of the corporate managers would result in the end of finance capitalism. A recent assessment of this condition reveals that, in fact, the condition of finance capitalism continues to exist and is growing:

> As the corporation grows, owners must delegate power to the managers and carry out public financing. In the case of stock offerings, their ownership is diluted; in the case of long-term financing, both owner and management are subjected to conditions demanded by finance capital. Either type of public financing makes outside directors *mandatory*, with a resulting formalization of the board. The trend toward outsider, i.e., finance capital, domination appears in corporations with sales between $50 million and $500 million. At this level of enterprise the issue of control is most sharply fought. Generally speaking, however, managers are not the principal figures in the struggle, although they are frequently the spokesmen for the competing stockholder and financial interests. As the corporation reaches sales of a billion dollars or more, the domination of the corporation by outsiders is generally complete.[24]

Studies based upon evidence of the Patman Committee, reports of the United States Internal Revenue Service, and the Securities and Exchange Commission indicate that the sheer size of finance capitalists' assets has grown to 46.3 percent of all assets held by U.S. financial institutions. Between 1950 and 1955, there were 376 consecutive bank mergers without a single disapproval by the United States Comptroller; between 1953 and 1962, there were 1,669 mergers and absorptions, the largest of which occurred at the very top of the commercial banking empire. As a result of this series of mergers, the top five New York City banks by 1962 held 15 percent of all deposits in New York City. This is more than double the concentration ratio of 1922, the height of unrestrained financial power.

The significant point, in terms of this analysis, is that the condition of finance capitalism goes beyond even the vision of huge corporate giants, controlling different parts of the economy. The fact is that major U.S. financial institutions control the five hundred largest corporations in America through a series of interlocking devices which place the control of aircraft, mining, paper production, electronics, automobiles, resources exploitation, and so forth, in the hands of a very few financial institutions.

Even if the dominance of wealth and production is overlooked, however, the pluralists neglect to face what two scholars have called the power of "nondecisions."[25] This means that there exists an institutionalized bias in a society dominated by concentrations of economic and political power which makes the theory of pluralism nothing more than an euphemism for corporate capitalism. When the pluralists ignore the implications of corporate dominance and a nationwide institutional bias which favors such blatant singularity, they perform the questionable service of perpetuating a myth which prompts individuals to view society as one based on diffused power, where every person may have a significant impact on the decisionmaking process.

In a system dominated by interlocking corporate giants, individual and organizational access into the political system (a second, essential condition of pluralism) is conditioned by the extent to which such access will not disturb existing centers of power. A crucial point to note, which links the concentration of economic and political power to the exercise of power by individuals and organizations, is the fact that the social demands made by a group outside of the prevailing structure are predetermined by the capitalistic structure. For the urban and regional planner, this linkage should be immediately apparent: the private automobile becomes a social necessity, urban space is organized in terms of private transportation; public transportation becomes a secondary infrastructural consideration, land-use decisions are made in conformance with industrial demands and development markets, the social costs generated by industry, i.e., use of air, light, space, water, land, animals, etc., are absorbed by consumers, and the beat goes on. The de facto dictatorship of concentrated interests displaces less organized groups. As suggested by Gorz,[26] "it passes through a certain number of intermediate steps, it asserts itself essentially through the priorities it controls, by the subordination and conditioning of the range of human need according to the inert exigencies of capital."

In an environment where capital equals political power, the opportunity for meaningful impact by the competing interest groups envisioned by the pluralists becomes a pathetic tribute to the conditions of access, participation, and democracy in the American decisionmaking process. The pluralist fails to recognize that the economic power base extends to affect control and access over a political power base; the myth of pluralism may mask the institutional bias of a corporate-controlled state, but an analysis of the political process negates the validity of the pluralist view:

Politics is not an arena in which free and independent organizations truly connect the lower and middle levels of society with the top levels of decision. Such organizations are not an effective and major part of American life today. As more people are drawn into the political arena, their associations become mass in scale, and the power of the individual becomes dependent upon them: to the extent that they are effective, they have become larger, and to that extent they have become less accessible to the influence of the individual.[27]

The third criterion or condition of pluralism, i.e., that individuals actively participate in and make their will felt through organizations of many kinds, is subject to the same analysis which has been set out above and is inextricably related to the fourth condition of pluralism—that elections are a viable instrument of mass participation in political decisions. The new pluralist theory produces a political theory which is at variance with classical liberal democratic thought; the dangerous populist notions of the classical model are eliminated to accommodate the elitist character of modern corporate statism, the passive nature of the electorate is especially vulnerable to modern pluralism, and mass politics are encouraged to transmit a feeling of participation while operating in accordance with power centers which are unrelated to individual or small group interests within society.[28] As discussed at length by Michael Parenti, widespread and effective mass participation in the decisionmaking process, at any level, is atypical of our contemporary "pluralist" society. As discussed by Parenti,[29] "politicians are inclined to respond positively not to group *needs* but to group *demands*," and in "political life as in economic life, *needs* do not become *marketable demands* until they are backed by 'buying power' . . . for only then is it in the 'producer's' interest to respond." Parenti's exhaustive analysis of community power in Newark confirms this view:

> Furthermore, in places like Newark, the one institution theoretically designed to mobilize and respond to the demands of the unorganized lower strata, the local political party, fails to do so. One of the hallowed teachings of American political science is that the political party is the citizen's means of exercising collective power; the stronger the party system the abler will it effect the polyarchic will. But the party organization in Newark is less a vehicle for democratic dialogue and polyarchic power and more a pressure group with a rather narrowly defined interest in the pursuit of office, favor and patronage.

Political elections in this context do not provide a meaningful method of generalized mass influence over political leaders. The electoral instrument appears less accessible as a means of influence than as a means of expressing issue-oriented disturbances. The most potent mechanism in the pluralist theory is a facade for the reality of corporate concentration, elitist decisionmaking, formed and around that concentration, institutional bias, nondecision, and the patent lack of competing power bases.

The fifth condition of pluralism, that a consensus exists on what may be called the "democratic creed," requires that the value system of the society support the normative propositions underlying the social system, and that voting, organizational membership, and other political activity[30] are made operational by a system of decisionmaking that conforms to principles of representative democracy. The crucial, analytical distinction to note regarding this condition of pluralism is that it must be *operational*—not a social myth.

The growing feelings of political alienation—notwithstanding the myth-making and supporting effects of the mass media, market conditioning, and the psychology of mass politics—have been empirically recorded and studied. These studies have shown that large numbers of people, while subscribing to democratic principles, feel that they are not part of the political process, that their role makes no difference.[31] Feelings of alienation grow out of the perception that political decisions are made by a group of political insiders who are not responsive to the average citizens which, as has been discussed, are valid perceptions of the operational characteristics of the political economy. Applying the pluralist theory in the context of social reality produces an inherent challenge to democratic theory; it becomes a system of proportional representation at best and an elitist state at worst. Joseph A. Schumpeter described the nature of such a system, calling itself one thing and operating as another: "it merely means that the reins of government should (are) be handed to those who command more support than do any of the competing individuals or teams."[32]

The central assumption made by leading writers and practitioners of advocacy planning has been the uncritical acceptance of a social myth called "pluralism." Because the assumption is incorrect, the strategies associated with advocacy planning are developed in a way which responds to a myth and not a social reality. If acceptance of the pluralist theory merely meant recognition that the forces of influence and power in the public decisionmaking process go through cycles of influence, changing from one group to another, one might argue that advocacy planning is a relatively new and realistic method of accomplishing social change. The fact is, however, that pluralism is *not* an operational feature of American society, even if all of the modifications of the new pluralists are considered. Basing strategies on a faulty assumption about the decisionmaking process renders those techniques ineffective, illusory, and, in many cases, counterproductive in light of the gross inequity which is an inherent part of corporate capitalism in the urban-industrial state.

A radical interpretation of the political economy takes the basic position that structural change and reform within an inherently defective and corrupt system is not possible. The pluralist theorists fail to recognize the fact that social, cultural, and regional underdevelopment on the one hand and rapid development of "affluent" consumer goods and services industries on the other are simply two sides of the same reality. If collective needs of people are not being satisfied in social and public services, education, urban and rural development, and the entire spectrum of conditions which have been identified as "social problems," while at the same time the oligopolies, monopolies, and conglomerates which produce articles for individual consumption enjoy a spectacular prosperity and control over the political economy, the reason is not that the collective needs are public in nature and the individual consumptive needs are private in nature. On the contrary, the reason for the scandalous disparities between social need and social satisfaction of those needs is explained by the phenomenon of contemporary corporate capitalism—supported and advanced by the state—which has secured the position of the driving role in economic development and political control of present-day society.

THE ADVOCATE ANALOGY: A LIBERAL METAPHOR

Since the inception of the concept of advocacy planning in 1965, the *modus operandi* of this new planning technique was based upon an analogy drawn between the role and function of the legal advocate and the role and function of the advocate planner.[33] The planner-advocate would plead for his or her client's point of view: furthermore, the planner would provide more than information, analysis, and simulations—specific substantive solutions would be argued. Davidoff's analogy between lawyer and planner was stated specifically in his classic article, "Advocacy and Pluralism in Planning":

> Thus, the advocate's plan might have some characteristics of a legal brief. It would be a document presenting the facts and reasons for supporting one set of proposals, and facts and reasons indicating the inferiority of counterproposals.[34]

While the analogy was constructed around the adversary dimension of the legal advocate, and makes no pretense that both lawyer and planner would or should possess the same technical skills, the generalized analog even raises some crucial issues concerning the appropriateness of the comparison.[35]

The argument made here with respect to the analogy between the advocate lawyer and planner is that the uncritical acceptance of such a comparison assumes that the adoption of the legal-advocate model will somehow establish an effective urban democracy, one in which citizens may be able to play an active role in the process of deciding public policy. The analogy is an extension of the pluralist faith that given the opportunity to be heard, the demands of competing groups will go through an adversary process through which the best decisions concerning planned community change will result.

There is substantial danger in using analogy carelessly, i.e., using only logical rationalizations and never resorting to testing or making a discovered induction without proving the degrees of similarity. In this case, the danger of drawing an analogy between the legal-advocate and the planner-advocate has materialized into another unrealistic guidepost. A fair test of the analogy is to examine the nature of legal advocacy and whether that model, in fact, maximizes citizen participation or access into the realm of decisionmaking, results in the best or most justified decision, or arrives at a truth which is the synthesis of groups competing equally before public tribunals (given the opportunity to be heard).

As the socioeconomic organization of American society is based upon property rights and the balancing of public and private relations, so the law serves the most powerful property interests; as argued in the section dealing with the myth of pluralism, the masses of people and interest groups who have no direct connection to the bases of power are governed by rules intended to maintain and fortify existing power relationships.[36] To the assertion that the adversary process establishes equality before the law, a radical critique of such a sweeping statement can be placed with a well-constructed and documented syllogism: law serves power, the law is made by those holding power, it perpetuates those in power, it decides what the tolerable limits of justice are—law is made by the power elite to protect and enshrine its own interests.

The good liberal, particularly the good liberal lawyer will respond to the radical critique by pointing to the host of legal decisions which have expanded the civil rights of men and women, the extensive social welfare system which has been constructed to help, not control, the economically disadvantaged. They may well allude to, as do the pluralist-advocate planners, the "guarantees of fair notice and hearings, production of supporting evidence, cross examination, reasoned decision(s)."[37]

The ostensible goal of the advocate planner is, through the use of advocacy, to meet the "just demand for political and social equality on the part of the Negro and the impoverished"[38] to provide social change which will benefit "those who are, through lack of education and of technical sophistication, particularly ill-prepared to deal with the presentation of issues in a technical framework"[39] and "defend or prosecute the interests of his clients."[40] The critical issue is whether the superimposition of the legal-advocate model upon the planner will work to achieve these goals. Clearly, recent court decisions, based upon an expanded theory of equal protection, used very broad egalitarian rhetoric in the criminal law area, encouraging attorneys for the poor to apply this same argument to other social problems, e.g., inequality in education and the unequal provision of state and municipal services.[41] Again, the problem of myth versus reality rolls into operation; the general public, including naive planners, assume that headline cases mark "high impact" social decisions which serve to ameliorate the position of the poor and disenfranchised. The analysis of the impact of a visible social decision, however, falls short of examining anything but the outcome, without asking whether the process of decisionmaking has been materially affected.

A critical view of the process would reveal that legal advocacy, like planning, has severe institutional restraints imposed upon it. A cursory examination of the criminal courts in America would reveal that enforcement and conviction is almost always directed at the working person, the poor, and the political activist. A corporate official who conspires to fix prices, utilize deceptive advertising, and proffer limited guarantees on products sold at inflated prices, rarely suffers the demise of the poor, the working, or the activist. The poor are arrested more often, convicted more frequently, sentenced more harshly, rehabilitated less successfully than the rest of society. Just as economic inequality within the United States has remained virtually constant throughout this century, inequality before the law, despite rigorous substantive and procedural safeguards, has remained relatively unchanged.

CONCLUSION

That persons occupying positions of control over capital are among the key wielders of local influence and control has long been one of the most commonplace assumptions of American sociologists and, more recently, planners. While it is clear that to ignore particularly local configurations of economic and political power in developing strategies for advocacy planning efforts would be inappropriate, this analysis has attempted to suggest that there are clear and growing indicators of power concentrations which are apart from the local community. Furthermore, the development of capital concentration within a growing corporate structure imposes rather substantial external controls over local decisionmaking. There is increasing evidence which suggests that local planning decisions are becoming the function of private market decisions and that this characteristic is an inherent component of the way corporate capitalism has developed in the United States.

This analysis does not suggest that elitism and concentration of power is an inherent element of capitalism—anymore than to suggest, for example, that a socialized economy would be inherently free of such control. What is specifically suggested is that the evolution of capitalism in the United States has developed into a system with inherent defects which can be modified only by changes in the nature of that system per se. The analysis raises significant implications for both planning education and planning practice.

From a conceptual and theoretical standpoint, the great majority of commentators on advocacy planning either explicitly or implicitly make inaccurate, misleading, and incongruent assumptions regarding the political economy within which advocacy must be made operational. Acceptance of the assumptions discussed here requires an endorsement of the political myth of pluralism, a posture which must ultimately embrace the status quo or the liberal-reformist approach to solving complex social problems, and the adoption of a set of tactical strategies which emulate existing professions so as to preserve centers of power and frustrate the notion of participatory democracy.

Given this radical critique of the theoretical foundations of the Davidoff-Peattie-Kaplan model of advocacy planning, the classroom disaffection with planning strategies which embrace a pluralist framework, and the spread of advocacy-like positions in the planning job market, it would appear that the profession of urban and regional planning is faced with a series of criticisms which deserve something more than casual discussion. The bulk of planning literature concerned with advocacy fails to suggest new strategies to confront persistent social problems, continues to assume the necessity for gradualist or reform-oriented solutions, and implies that the prime criteria for effectiveness must be the existing institutional setting.

The final and fundamental point to be made in this brief discussion is to suggest the infirmities of existing advocacy planning theory and to stimulate renewed debate and contention over alternative strategies of advocacy planning—especially with respect to the so-called "radical" techniques of advocacy which have received scant attention in the literature.

REFERENCES

1. C. Funnye, "The Advocate Planner as Urban Hustler," *Social Policy* 1:35–37 (July–August 1970); C. Hartman, "Community Planning and the Advocate in The City," *Planning Comment* 7:16–22 (Winter 1971); A. S. Kravitz, "Mandarinism: Planning as Handmaiden to Conservative Politics," in T. L. Beryle and G. T. Lathrop, eds., *Planning and Politics* (New York: The Odyssey Press, 1970), pp. 240–267; and F. F. Piven, "Whom Does the Advocate Planner Serve?," *Social Policy* 1:34–41 (May–June 1970).

2. P. Davidoff, "Advocacy and Pluralism in Planning," *Journal of the American Institite of Planners* 31:331–332 (November 1965).

3. I. R. Peattie, "Reflections on Advocacy Planning," *Journal of the American Institute of Planners* 34, no. 2 (March 1968) p. 81.

4. Davidoff, "Advocacy and Pluralism in Planning."

5. A. Etzioni, *Modern Organizations* (Englewood Cliffs, N.J.: Prentice-Hall, 1964).

6. P. Davidoff, "Community Planning and the Advocate in the Suburbs," *Planning Comment* 7:2–13 (Winter 1971).

7. M. Parenti, "Power and Pluralism: A View from the Bottom," unpublished revision of a paper sponsored by the Caucus for a New Political Science. (Washington, D.C.: Annual Convention of the American Political Science Association, 1968).

8. A. D. Lindsay, *The Modern Democratic State* (London: Oxford Univ. Press, 1943), p. 245.

9. O. von Gierke, *Natural Law and the Theory of Society: 1500–1800,* trans. by Ernest Baker. (Cambridge, Eng.: Cambridge Univ. Press, 1950).

10. E. Durkheim, *The Division of Labor in Society,* trans. by George Simpson. (Glencoe: Free Press, 1947).

11. J. W. Dewey, *The Public and Its Problems* (Denver: Allan Swallow Publishers, 1954).

12. F. Hunter, *Community Power Structure* (Chapel Hill: Univ. of North Carolina Press, 1953).

13. J. R. Commons, *Institutional Economics* (Madison: Univ. of Wisconsin Press, 1959).

14. J. R. Commons, *Representative Democracy* (New York: Bureau of Economic Research, n.d.).

15. R. Presthus, *Men at the Top: A Study in Community Power* (Oxford, Eng.: Oxford Univ. Press, 1964).

16. M. Olson, Jr., *The Logic of Collective Action* (New York: Schocken, 1968).

17. J. M. Burns and J. W. Peltson, *Government by the People* (Englewood Cliffs, N.J.: Prentice-Hall, 1960); V. O. Key, *Politics, Parties, and Pressure Groups* (New York: Crowell, 1958); D. D. McKean, *Party and Pressure*

Politics (Boston: Houghton Mifflin, 1949); and B. C. Roberts, *Trade Union Government in Great Britain* (Cambridge, Mass.: Harvard Univ. Press, 1956).

18. Olson, *The Logic of Collective Action*, p. 21.

19. H. Kariel, *The Decline of American Pluralism* (Stanford: Stanford Univ. Press, 1961).

20. R. Presthus, "Community Power Structure: Theoretical Framework," in F. M. Cox et al., *Strategies of Community Organization* (Itasca, Ill.: F. E. Peacock, 1970), pp. 109–110.

21. B. D. Nossiter, "Corporate Power in the Economy," in T. Christoffel, et al., *Up Against the American Myth* (New York: Holt, Rinehart and Winston, 1970), pp. 19–32.

22. *Ibid.*, p. 10.

23. E. Greer, "The Public Interest University," in Christoffel, *Up Against the American Myth*, pp. 338–343.

24. R. Fitch and M. Oppenheimer, "Who Rules the Corporations," *Socialist Revolution* 1:85–86 (September/October 1970).

25. P. Bachrach and M. Baratz, "Two Faces of Power," *American Political Science Review* 56:947–952 (December 1962).

26. A. Gorz, "Private Profit versus Public Need," in Christoffel, *Up Against the American Myth*, pp. 32–47.

27. C. W. Mills, "The Structure of Power in American Society," in I. L. Horowitz, ed., *Power, Politics and People: The Collected Essays of C. Wright Mills* (New York: Oxford Univ. Press, 1963), p. 28.

28. R. Blackburn, "Defending the Myths: The Ideology of Bourgeois Social Science," in Christoffel, *Up Against the American Myth*, pp. 154–69.

29. Parenti, "Power and Pluralism: . . . ," p. 16.

30. Presthus, "Community Power Structure: . . . ," pp. 103–111.

31. M. Levin, "Political Alienation," in E. and M. Josephson, eds., *Man Alone: Alienation in Modern Society* (New York: Dell Publishing Co., 1962), pp. 227–239.

32. J. A. Schumpeter, *Capitalism, Socialism and Democracy* (New York: Harper and Row, 1950), p. 273.

33. Piven, "Whom Does the Advocate Planner Serve?," pp. 34–41.

34. Davidoff, "Advocacy and Pluralism in Planning," p. 333.

35. Roger Starr, "Advocates and Adversaries," *Planning 1968* (Chicago: American Society of Planning Officials), pp. 33–38. This article records the author's distaste for advocacy planning, viewing advocacy efforts as frustrating urban renewal efforts. Starr also, for the wrong reasons, challenges the notion of equating the role of an urban planner to that of the "noble profession of law."

36. R. Lefcourt, *Law Against the People* (New York: Random House, 1971).

37. Davidoff, "Advocacy and Pluralism in Planning," p. 332.

38. *Ibid.*, p. 331.

39. Peattie, "Reflections on Advocacy Planning," p. 81.

40. M. Kaplan, "Advocacy and the Urban Poor," *Journal of the American Institute of Planners* 35:96–101 (March 1969).

41. G. Goodpaster, "The Integration of Equal Protection, Due Process Standard and the Indigent's Right of Free Access to the Courts," *Iowa Law Review* 56:223–266 (1970).

On High and Popular Culture

by Raymond Williams

What is the relationship between high culture and popular culture? This question, which is common in contemporary discussions of the humanities, is sometimes real but as often rhetorical. Two positions usually follow from the rhetorical question. First, it is said that high culture—"the best that has been thought and written in the world"—is in danger, or is indeed already "lost," because of widespread popular education, popular communications systems, and what is often called "mass society." Secondly, that high culture —"the tradition"—is, in the main, the product of past stages of society, that it is ineradicably associated with ruling classes and with elites, and that it is accordingly being replaced in modern democratic conditions by a popular culture. The debate between these two positions has practical results in social policy both in the allocation of resources and in the political shaping of cultural institutions. Yet the two common positions and the debate between them are intolerably confused by failures of definitions, and the social policies that follow from them largely ignore the realities of contemporary society.

In its earliest senses, in several major languages, the term "culture" always referred to the culture *of* something: originally the culture of natural products and then, by metaphorical extension, the culture of mental or spiritual faculties. In either case it was a process defined by the object of cultivation. In the late 18th and early 19th centuries it was given a very different additional meaning. This begins in the universal histories, which offered a largely secular and developmental account of the growth of human civilization. To avoid identification of this process with any particular modern state (and hence to avoid the crude distinction between civilization and barbarism) but even more to emphasize the self-acting (secular) and growing (developmental) factors of human history, the term "culture," which already expressed human process, was distinguished from and often preferred to the alternative term "civilization." In the work of Herder and others a further decisive development occurred. We had to speak, Herder insisted, of "cultures" rather than "culture." At a certain level the process might be universal, but its reality was in a range and series of specific cultures: the whole ways of life of particular groups. This is the origin of the ordinary modern use of "culture" in anthropology.

But the older sense of culture as a process survived. In the course of the 19th century it acquired a specific association with the practices on which mental and spiritual cultivation were thought to depend: intellectual work and the arts. "Culture" is now often a shorthand not only for these practices but for their products. It implies at once the general process of human development and the specific organizations of such development in different societies. It implies also both the whole way of life of a people and the

practices and products of intellectual work and the arts. These two implications become sources of difficulty in our notions of "high culture" and
"popular culture."

What does "high culture" mean? Its most plausible use is to describe the
great body of cultural skills and the great works which embody and represent them. There would be argument about which skills to include or
exclude, but in common usage the skills of organized thought, writing,
music, the visual arts and architecture would certainly be included.

We then also recognize that high culture has no specific social structure.
It is, by definition, a body of work from many different societies and many
different periods of history. Indeed, only in abstraction can it be seen as a
"body" of work at all. No individual and no single society receives or uses this
whole body of work. Rather, particular societies, for historical reasons,
receive selections of this body of work, which they perceive as their effective
cultural traditions. There is great unevenness in this process of selection, as
is quickly evident when, for example, Asian and European scholars compared their notions of "tradition" or of "classics." Moreover no society makes
available to all its members anything like the whole of even its selected area of
the tradition. In the processes of international conquest and domination, as
most evident in imperialism and in neo-colonialism, there is not only unevenness of distribution but a deliberate process of imposition of alien forms
of selection.

"High culture," then, has no real social structure, but at best a professional structure or series of professional structures in which people inherit
and practice a selection of skills and maintain and disseminate a selection of
works. Such professional structures have important common interests, from
an international perspective, in such activities as the study of alternative
traditions, visiting, exchange-teaching, translation and so on. They also have
important common interests, in national perspectives, in maintaining and
extending the skills and works that they value.

Nevertheless all these professional structures exist within social structures. As members of particular institutions, and as members of particular
societies in definite relationships with other societies, their work cannot be
abstracted from their real social existence. "High culture" in any particular
society is not only a selection from universal high culture, but a selection that
relates, explicitly or implicitly, to wider elements of the society. Thus high
culture, the work of more than one's own class, society, period or even
epoch, is commonly incorporated into a particular contemporary social
structure—a social class or such institutions as universities or churches—that
owes its real contemporary existence to factors other than high culture, and
that indeed often confuses its temporary, local or self-interested features
with the received and selected high culture that it offers to justify or to ratify
them. Similarly, between nations, an invading or dominant society projects
—by imposition or by suppression of a native culture—a version of "high
culture" that cannot in practice be abstracted from its direct political and
economic interests.

Thus whether within or between societies, respect for "high culture" in
its purest and most abstract sense must find a critical rather than a justifying
form of expression and action. Within societies it is necessary to become

conscious of the selective character of the "high culture" or "cultural tradition" that is currently active, and to explore the relations between the selection and contemporary social structures (including such directly relevant social formations as universities). Between societies, when in any good faith the selective character of particular versions of high culture will quickly become obvious, we must explore the connections between these variations and the real historical and contemporary political and economic relationships, and, above all, to avoid the error of supposing that a selective version made by some temporarily dominant society is "universal" whereas the selective version of some temporarily dominated society is merely "local" or "traditional." The interaction between particular local selections and what can be conceived theoretically as a universal high culture must, for cultural as well as other reasons, take place in conditions of equality and mutual respect. This, of course, does not mean that what is sought is some bland consensus; there is much necessary opposition and conflict between variant cultural traditions, as well as honest recognition of alternatives.

At this point the meaning of "popular culture" becomes critical. First, there can be no simple contrast between "high culture" (universal) and "popular culture" (local). This is because every available version of high culture is always, in the senses described, local and selective, and because, in the process of being made available in a real society, it includes (whether these are noticed or not) elements of the popular culture, in the widest sense, of its own society. Universities, which transmit and sometimes practice selections of universal high culture, are in their internal organization, which has been shaped by the selection and in their relations with the rest of the society, parts of the popular culture of their own time, with discoverable resemblances to the values, criteria and methods of organization of other institutions in the social structure that are not concerned with high culture at all. The culture of a people, in the sense of its whole way of life, inevitably shapes and colors our explicitly "cultural" institutions.

Secondly, there can be no simple contrast between the "high culture" of a social class or occupational group and the "popular culture" of the rest of the people. There are evident and important differences of degree of access and use, but these are contingent social and historical relationships. In certain societies, of the past and still in some cases of the present, there are distinguishable cultural situations: for example, court and peasant cultures, aristocratic and folk cultures, metropolitan-imperial and native-colonial cultures. Often the separated cultures will have evident differences of degree of access to a more universal high culture, but none of them can be identified with high culture as such, and increasingly, as societies develop, there is influential interaction between previously separated spheres. In industrial societies, and especially in societies with developed and developing systems of general education and communications, we are beyond the stage of influential interaction between distinguishable cultures and into a more complex process that needs to be seen from the beginning as a whole.

This brings us to the most crucial distinction between different senses of "popular" culture. There is a kind of culture that has been developed *by* a people or by the majority of a people to express their own meanings and values, over a range from customs to works. There is also a different kind of culture that has been developed *for* a people by an internal or external social group, and embedded in them by a range of processes from repressive imposition to commercial saturation. The distinctions between these two kinds are not simple; influential interaction constantly occurs. The choice of process, in the popularization of an alien culture, depends on variable historical and social conditions but usually includes close attention to the culture that is already popular. The sources of cultural activity have nevertheless to be precisely identified, in every case. In some cases this is easy, as in internationally exported religions or political ideologies or television programs. In other cases, when in particular social conditions certain kinds of adaptive, imitative or incorporated activity begin among those who were previously only the objects of external popularization, identification may be very difficult. No simple presumption of values can in any case be made. But unless the process is made conscious, by critical examination and discussion, the state of any particular popular culture will not be understood.

Comparative and historical definitions of high culture lead us toward situations in which, by recognizing the existence of many centers of meaning and value, and by further recognizing the dynamic processes of selection, formation and interaction we can envisage precise kinds of study and work. By contrast abstract and pseudo-universal definitions of high culture and popular culture, restricting meaning and value to a single tradition and contemplating the meanings and values of the majority of people and peoples as intrinsically inferior, lead us to evade true cultural values and contemporary reality.

In the area that we consider as belonging to high culture we can properly think of some universally valuable (although very general) skills and of a considerable number of generally important and interesting works. While we treat these specifically, and follow their action through history and across frontiers, we learn deep and extending respect for their kinds of achievement, but we do not learn, except in the case of some of the most abstract skills, anything like a set of available values.

Thus, to take one major example, the *Antigone* of Sophocles has been a major work in most periods of European culture. In its dramatization of a conflict between duty to a brother and duty to a state, it raises permanent social and ethical questions. But the play gives no available answer to these. When Antigone, having chosen her duty to her brother, adds that she would not have done this for a husband, she so shocked one Victorian scholar that he "proved" the passage spurious. But the distinction is valid within the relevant kinship system, and this has to be included, with all its other definitions and problems—some of which we must now necessarily reject, or reject other whole areas of our real cultural tradition—before any available value can be abstracted.

Our contacts with some of the greatest philosophical and artistic work will often lead to questioning, rejection or a sense of ineluctable strangeness and otherness, and this is as much a part of the true process of high culture as the more commonly cited experience of learning, enlargement and enrichment. Given the highly variable and extraordinary character of the more enduring elements of high culture, this is not only not surprising; it is a condition of recognizing the true conditions and qualities of this remarkable human enterprise. All traditions can become less selective and culture-bound than they now are, and every genuine effort in this direction is important. But there can be no short-cuts. The meanings and values of all particular peoples and cultures have to be respected, with no prior selection of universal values, if the next necessary stage, of contact, interaction and the dynamic processes of agreement and disagreement, intellectual conflict as well as consensus are to be reasonably conducted under conditions of equality.

Meanwhile within societies and between societies, there is very important work to be done in the recovery, and where possible and relevant the reanimation of suppressed, neglected and disregarded cultures: the meanings and values, in some cases the works, of dominated peoples and classes, and of minorities that have suffered discrimination. This is one crucial kind of popular culture program.

But it is insufficient, and could decline into mere antiquarianism and folklorism if the real present is not connected to the recovered past. To do this we have not only to study contemporary cultural change (in spite of the persistent reflex of humanistic scholars toward the past). We have also to study contemporary cultural media (in spite of the persistent prejudice of humanistic scholars against what are thought of as vulgar subcultural manifestations). We shall not now understand any popular culture unless we study, for example, the press, the cinema, broadcasting and sport. Indeed the movement toward versions of universalism is much more evident in these spheres than in those of traditional philosophy and arts. Yet it is becoming universal only in the sense that it is widely exported from a few powerful centers, within radically unequal terms of exchange. What has been called, for broadcasting, the "global village" will be neither founded nor governed by all its putative inhabitants. Rather in hitherto unimaginable terms, the use of powerful new media will enable a few to speak to and apparently for the many, and, unless powerful safeguards are constructed, to drive out of competition the more varied and authentic voices that are the true discourse of any society and of humanity.

In culture as in other matters, human resilience and creativity are still our major resource. High culture has no social structure, but the professional structures that have direct responsibility for it, in artistic, intellectual and scholarly work, have much to do of a new as well as a traditional kind: the maintenance and extension but also the critical review and intercultural examination of their own received high cultures; the understanding and critical review of received and changing popular cultures; and, in work that now necessarily takes them beyond their own frontiers, whether of country or of discipline, the understanding and critical review, leading to such action as is necessary, of the new forms and new media that reflect now our most active and vital cultural processes.

V

LIBRARIES
IN POST-INDUSTRIAL
SOCIETY

The Information Function: A Theoretical Basis for the Development of Information Networks and Centers

by Major R. Owens

INTRODUCTION

It is generally recognized that there is a great need for the development of adequate information services; however, the continued generation of a vast body of information has overwhelmed the library profession and fostered a paralysis which has prevented the examination of a set of practical points of departure.

A set of simple definitions accompanied by the exploration of certain elements and characteristics of information may begin to throw light on the road ahead. Of equal importance is the introduction of new theories and principles related to the flow of information in our computerized, democratic and capitalistic society. In its 1972–73 Annual Report, the National Commission on Libraries and Information Science summarizes the importance of the information function:

> The informational role is not new to libraries, but its importance is heightened because society demands that the individual and the corporate group be knowledgeable on a broader front than previously was expected. As society changes, better information—supplied more quickly—is needed in order to cope with events and trends. Information is of paramount importance to world economy and individual well-being. Information, a prime product of government and of private industry, has become the basis for improved functioning of industry, agriculture, trade and services.
>
> One goal of information is to produce consistently a better yield at a lower cost. In industry the requirement for information may be a need for market forecasts or tariff data or the machinability characteristics of an alloy. Improved productivity as a result of current and valid information is the goal. At all levels of experience and activity the pressing requirement for trustworthy information is a critical and universal feature of our times.[1]

To avoid encouraging an impending schism between those who want to provide information only to the *information literates,* defined by Paul G. Zurkowski, President of the Information Industry Association, as "people trained in the application of information resources to their work," and those who want to provide information for the general public, this discussion will focus on a comprehensive approach which insists that the only adequate system is a system which recognizes every citizen as a potential "information literate" and therefore seeks to serve the total populace. All people must be encouraged to apply information resources to their home, civic and community life as well as to their work.

DEFINITION AND ELEMENTS OF INFORMATION

After citing the fact that information scientists are reluctant to try to define *information*, Faibisoff and Ely, in a commissioned paper, "Information and Information Needs," offered their own operational definition: *"Information is a symbol or a set of symbols which has the potential for meaning."*[2] In this same paper it was noted that a study of thirty-nine definitions of information science included only eight definitions of information and that none of these eight definitions had any common element. One should not minimize the difficulty of defining the word or concept of information; however, fear of being vanquished in linguistic jostling should also not paralyze us and prevent the offering of a definition more workable than the one stated above.

Information is a record of phenomena observed or decisions made. The record may merely be the impression on the mind of an individual or it may be an elaborate array of data stored in a computer. A tree in a forest burning as a result of being hit by lightning is a phenomenon which becomes information only when a human being sights it or a planted instrument records the occurrence. A decision made by a president or a king at breakfast is information even before it is announced. Information is not synonymous with fact or truth. Information may reduce uncertainty or it may promote confusion.

That decisions made by individuals may be classified as information is an assumption which should be examined more closely. We readily accept the notion that information can always be communicated; however, a contention that almost everything that is communicated is information will be challenged. An eccentric on a street corner proclaiming the end of the world is communicating a decision he has made; most listeners label it as misinformation or incorrect information and ignore him. The same eccentric in a crowded theater yelling "fire" is taken seriously and most of the audience will act first to evacuate the building and then later check the accuracy of the information. The example is a bit extreme; however, it is not unrelated to what happens when bureaucrats and public officials proclaim food shortages or oil shortages. Although common sense instructs us to trust the official pronouncements and accept without question the massive amounts of supporting data they are able to manipulate, we often find that months and years later, after the hysteria dissipates, a closer and more thorough examination indicates the self-evident true information was an elaborate fabrication. In time the voices of the doubters and dissenters who questioned the official positions become accepted as the generators of the "correct" information.

Despite the fact that it makes the task of managing information more difficult, the point here is that all viewpoints from all sources are part of the ongoing information output and premature judgments with respect to what should be excluded because it is incorrect, inaccurate or unreliable should not be made by librarians or other information managers. Our focus should instead be on the achievement of a better understanding of certain key elements of information: *public significance, value* and *level.*

All information is potentially significant and a comprehensive, all-inclusive system which gives equal attention to all of the information being generated represents the ideal; however, for practical working purposes we must recognize that we are light years away from such an ideal. Very real limitations on our resources and capacity for managing information make it necessary to be selective and act in terms of such concepts as *public significance.* Some considerations determining public significance are:

1. The number and categories of people affected by the phenomena or decisions;
2; The degree to which citizens are affected; Is it a matter of life and death, necessity or convenience?
3. The duration of the problem;
4. The immediacy of the impact and the possibility of escalation;
5. The capacity to act possessed by the generator of information.

We must learn how to identify items more rapidly which have *public significance* and after such information items are identified we must understand that the only truly adequate information system is the system which is designed to provide access to everything that is recorded concerning that item. Every problem or subject has its own information milieu or environment—statistics, data, pronouncements, laws, rules, etc.—and the goal must be to expose as much of that environment to scrutiny as possible.

Closely related to the concept of *public significance* we should consider the notion of *value.* The value of information is not absolute but relative. Value is determined primarily by the nature of and the situation of the consumer of information. Information that has *public significance* will of necessity be of great *value* to large numbers of consumers; however, all information that has *value* for individuals is not publicly significant. For the one individual on a bus tour who is allergic to the pollen from apple blossoms, the fact that the road ahead passes through an apple orchard is information of great value while it seems trivial and irrelevant to all others. The announcement that the President of the United States has decided merely to consider the possibility of imposing a tax on gasoline would be information with *public significance* for millions of people. For the commuter considering the possibility of joining a car pool; for the owner of a small trucking firm; for the business man considering the purchase of stocks in an oil refinery; for all of these the information also has value. The consequences of the decisions they make or postpone may be quantitatively or qualitatively measured.

Understanding the concept of value is of primary importance in satisfying group and individual information needs. As it becomes more specific and focuses more on specific concerns, information acquires value. Formats for the delivery of information should be determined primarily by the nature of the perceived value of the information to the consumer. Will the information be of value in making a household management decision, in launching a campaign to change public policy or in formulating a major business or industry decision? Food prices are a matter having great public significance; however, the local housewives are not interested in information on Department of Agriculture policies; they merely want to know where to find information which shows which food product prices are rising and declining from day to day. Members of the local school board want statistics, forecasts and projections which support their effort to gain greater federal subsidies for the school lunch program. The local food wholesalers association wants copies of confidential newsletters which discuss internal developments within the food industry and the government agencies that influence food pricing policies. Purpose and manner of utilization are important determinants of value.

For information to meet a need and acquire increased value it must be provided in the appropriate format or at the proper *level.* Information exists on a continuum from the simple to the complex; from the current output to that which has been sifted, edited, time-tested and scientifically proven. The fact sheet, press release, pamphlet, position paper, magazine article, government regulation, scholarly treatise, book, television documentary, slide show, film, etc., are all physical manifestations of this continuum. The needs of target populations serviced by libraries and information centers are likely to be more homogeneous with respect to the levels of information needed than with respect to the subject or category of information needed. Training and specialization in the processes of transforming and translating information into needed levels and formats may be as important as training with respect to subject content.

THE FLOW OF INFORMATION

Awareness of these three elements of information—public significance, value, level—enhances a new approach to the discussion of flow of information. How does information of public significance presently move in our society? Are there any clearly discernible streams from generators to consumers? Who are the information generators?

There is a macro-flow and a micro-flow of information from generator to consumer. Some major information generators—originators, creators, discoverers, commanders—are international bodies, scientific and technological groups, business and corporate leaders, professional associations and government at every level—national, state, local. Among these generators, government is unequaled with respect to frequency and quantity of output.

MACRO-FLOW

To illustrate the concept of macro-flow of information, government provides the best model. We shall describe macro-flow as the movement of information from a high point of recognized public significance downward in a spreading pattern where for an ever increasing number of consumers it provides value. For most governmental information there is a pyramidal movement. At the top of the pyramid are the laws made by the legislative branch; the executive orders or policy statements of the executive branch; the decisions and opinions of the judicial branch. The pattern is nearly the same for national, state and local governments.

At the first level down on the pyramid are the rules and regulations developed to interpret the law. In the federal structure, the cabinet secretaries and their administering departments are the generators, the issuing bodies for such interpretations which inevitably grow and multiply, assuming a volume far greater than that of the original law. For a law which covers less than a hundred pages, hundreds of volumes full of rules and regulations accumulate as time passes. On the federal pyramid further down one must add the state policies and regulations which result from the exercise of certain options allowed by the federal law. Still further down near the base of the pyramid are the local government regulations which are concerned chiefly with the administration and implementation of the law or program created by the law. Agencies of local government may add still another set of important conditions and regulations.

At the base of this pyramid the agencies of local government are the prime implementers of the law or the chief deliverers of the service provided for in the law. In order to gain maximum benefits from the law which rests at the top of the pyramid, consumers must know how to obtain information that is present at the base within the local agencies; however, if purposefully or by accident the agency does not provide the information, then knowledge of how to scale the pyramid becomes vital. But an adequate information system should relieve the consumer of this necessity and also avoid placing the burden for providing all of the information on the local agencies at the base of the pyramid. Usually it is at the base of the pyramid that the information acquires the greatest value for the consumer. For example: an unemployed worker seeking a job provided by the federal Comprehensive Employment and Training Act wants to know what jobs are available in his city or neighborhood. Information concerning job titles, job descriptions and rate of pay will not be available at any level except the local agency level. Federal and state agencies may explain many features of the law but they will have no specific information about jobs.

To lubricate the operation of government and its programs it is desirable to have consumers who are already informed to some degree when they approach the local deliverers of service. An adequate information system must be based on consciously developed dissemination or exposure strategies. Although it cannot direct an unemployed person to a specific job, the federal government can maximize the amount of information it provides concerning the rights of the unemployed, eligibility requirements and priorities for assigning workers as stated in the law and regulations related to CETA. Because it is a national program covering millions of potential users, whether the information is provided by television, radio, newspaper or pamphlet, the cost per person per unit of information provided would be far lower than any per person cost for a local agency.

MICRO-FLOW

To understand the micro-flow of information, an examination of how information moves from small scientific and cultural groups to the mainstream is necessary. Prior to the launching of the Russian Sputnik, no science was considered by the general public to be more esoteric and ivory tower than the science of astronomy. Groups working in this area received no support or acclaim from government decision-makers. The same Secretary of Defense who had harsh words for research which sought to determine why grass is green and potatoes are brown would have used worse language in denying a proposal for funding of a project to determine the temperature on the planet Mars. But small groups interested in astronomy labored to continue gathering information which had value within their limited circle. The launching of the national space race moved this information which had value only for a small number into the mainstream where overnight it became information of great public significance. In the same fashion a war in Korea or Viet Nam catapults collections of material on Asian culture into the mainstream of publicly significant information.

It is highly probable that any body of information systematically collected will at some time prove to be useful to more than the immediate circle of compilers. It is in the best interest of society to avoid information vacuums. Governments should encourage groups who nurture specialized collections and seek to link them to larger networks. Information on American Indians, blacks, the deaf, Mexican-Americans, older people, migrant workers, rural people, prisoners, etc., is information which possesses enough value for the particular group involved to justify support for its cumulation. It must be remembered that material of public significance means little until it acquires value for a particular user. Information which begins with value should therefore never be assumed to be trivial. One must also remember that certain groups or users of specialized information are large enough to be considered "publics" by themselves. The definition of public significance is a flexible one and does not involve any percentage of the population cutoff point.

INFORMATION FOR DECISION-MAKING

The information of greatest value is information that aids decision-making. An examination of the role of information in decision-making will enable us to better understand the concept of information of value. The presence of information creates options, sets the stage for meaningful decision-making. Before decisions are finalized, the alternatives should be examined. Information is the raw material from which options and alternatives emerge.

It must be remembered that most decision-making takes place without benefit of research assistance and therefore the information made available must be as compact and clear as possible in order for the alternatives to be visible. The National Commission on Libraries and Information Science is on target when its report highlights the need for "filtering and packaging" information.

Participants pointed out that some groups have optimized their lives in such a way that the search and gathering of information useful to them has been relegated a very low priority and thus they obtain and use very little recent and germane information. It could be inferred that information services should take this into account and provide a filtering apparatus to give them only the information most essential to their life tasks. Filtering and packaging, however, are very expensive and the Commission representatives were concerned about the element of cost in regard to meeting users' needs.[3]

The conclusion that the desirable "filtering and packaging" would prove too costly is a questionable one. Systems, appropriately designed, for "filtering and packaging" may produce a better costs-benefits ratio than the present information gathering practices. One necessary part of such systems should be the establishment of a set of special categories as information priorities for the target population being served. Priorities will vary as the clientele served varies with respect to education, economic level, ethnicity, and other basic characteristics. Interesting outlines have been developed by the Appalachian Adult Education Center[4] and by the students and staff of the Columbia University Community Media Librarian Program. The latter group developed the following eleven information priorities for inner-city residents:

1. General Know-How and Community Action
2. Community News, Studies, History
3. Job Training, Employment and Career Development
4. Education: Formal and Non-Formal
5. Social Services and Income Maintenance
6. Health and Environment Protection
7. Civil and Criminal Legal System
8. Housing and Community Development
9. Economic Development
10. Consumer Education and Protection
11. Transportation

From the great mass of publicly significant information, guided by this listing, items may be extracted and packaged at a level which meets the need and provides information of value to inner-city residents. Pinpointing the need by subject or contents category, however, is not the only basic concern in providing information for decision-making. Again the commission report is on target.

The user requires content only when the content can be assimilated and when it arrives during the period of need. Contents in an ideal format and delivered on a timely basis to one group of users in an emergency situation may be invaluable while the same information in the same format may be of no use to others in a different situation. . . .[5]

Timeliness is the second basic concern in the provision of information for decision-making. It is possible to establish a set of types of decisions and to determine at what point in the problem solving process is the information input most valuable. A young widow should not be first informed of her social security benefits at the hospital which has just admitted one of her children for malnourishment. The federal employment office in Alaska should not be the only place with detailed job information related to the oil pipeline project. Workers should be able to obtain reasonably reliable information in their own states and home communities before they make the trip to Alaska. Citizens must be able to obtain information about legislation at the point when it is drafted and submitted and not after it has been passed. The regulations of the federal cabinet level departments should receive wider circulation in draft form before they are finalized.

In providing information for decision-making, prepackaging and the anticipation of the most timely points of delivery are important; however, selective, individualized, personalized service is also necessary. To provide the specific information which best helps to make a decision, one must be responsive to the person or group making the decision. The need is for the development of collections for maximum group use. Details are important and therefore to be adequate such collections must specialize. Where needs have been identified properly there should be no fear of making the necessary investment for specialization. A special library is not of necessity a research library. Networks of special libraries may serve the general public better than the traditional branch approach. We are again in agreement with the commission report.

> One of the operational modes postulated for the future was an 'information environment' in which the content of information would not change appreciably, but the format would change in response to the social and educational preparation of the individual user.
>
> The participants also foresaw the development of a community information network in which affiliations among different institutions that provide access to recorded knowledge in any form would provide the user with an interlaced system of collections, formats and access points that would readily adapt to changing needs. So-called 'hotline' information services that are always available to give specific information or counsel may be the prototype of such community information networks.[6]

PROPOSED INFORMATION NETWORKS

That information system which is based on an understanding of the way in which information flows and is designed to facilitate the extraction of the raw material needed; and has the capacity to refine the raw data by packaging it at a level and in a format which converts information of public significance into information that has value for a particular individual or group consumer; such a system represents the ideal which we must strive to build.

In different language and from a different point of view Faibisoff and Ely reach a similar conclusion:

> In order to create effective information systems, a number of studies indicate that the following needs must be met:
>
> 1. The need for more prompt dissemination of information. Several user studies have determined that the greatest information problem today is the time lag between the production and dissemination of information.

2. The need for quality filtering of information. All information should be screened for accuracy, relevancy, and quality before it enters an information system. This would lessen the effects of the information explosion.

3. The need for the right amount of information at the right time.

4. The need for receiving information in the desired form, usually oral or written, and in understandable language.

5. The need for active, selective switching of information. The ideal would be to receive the right information without having to ask for it.

6. The need to browse. Perusal of peripheral documents allows scientists to fulfill, through serendipity, needs that they have not yet formulated.

7. The need to get information easily and inexpensively.

8. The need for awareness of current literature, and the need to know of work in progress.

9. The need to know about and how to use available information systems.

10. The need for syntheses of the literature, state-of-the-art reviews, and introductory surveys of subjects.

11. The need to expedite interpersonal communication. If informal communication is considered a kind of information system, many of its characteristics are included in the above list. As a part of this system, each scientist reads documents, stores bits relevant to himself and others, and disseminates these relevant bits rather than transferring the whole document. He also translates the information into terms that his colleagues understand. He saves information and selectively disperses it to those he knows want it. Unpublished and unpublishable information is also transmitted through interpersonal communication (Menzel, 1968).

One scientist said that "he had never found that anyone failed to get the information he wanted, provided he knew the right person to ask!" The informal communication system is convenient and easy to use. However, it is only as reliable as the people involved. It is not systematic, cannot possibly be complete in itself, and must be combined with formal systems.[7]

In more concrete terms the National Commission on Libraries and Information Science in its 1972–73 Annual Report sets forth six major points that will assume increasing importance as a national effort to develop adequate information services is mounted.

1. A top-level agency in the Federal Government should be designated or created to develop, guide and lead the nation's effort to coordinate its library and information services.

2. A policy establishing certain encyclopedic and specialized library and information collections and national resources must be developed and implemented.

3. Bibliographic services that cover wide segments of the printed or non-printed literature and that serve extensive groups of users with the means to identify and obtain it must be designated and supported as national information utilities.

4. National telecommunication linkage of information service facilities including computers must be extended and subsidized to provide nationwide access to national resource library collections and to national information utility services from any inhabited location that has telephone service.

5. Improved efforts must be made to select, train and retrain information system managers to deal with the complicated problems in this area of endeavor.

6. Existing state and regional library and information programs can become the building blocks of a national program. The partnership of Federal-state-local services must be developed to make the best use of resources, reduce duplication and accomplish at each level the tasks best suited to that level. State programs that mirror the Federal program in organization and operation can contribute greatly to a unified attack on this important problem.[8]

The kind of information system implied in these six points is compatible with the macro- and micro-flow of information described above. A top level federal agency would guarantee the proper management of the all important federal information flow. Indexes of presidential executive orders and press conferences may be created. The vital regulations developed and issued by the cabinet level departments may receive wider dissemination before they are finalized. The laws in process and under immediate consideration by Congress may become more widely publicized and local groups concerned with public policy may gain more immediate access to the information which allows them to exert meaningful influence on their representatives. The proposal that state programs be designed to mirror the federal program in organization and operation would probably guarantee that the information output from governors, state legislatures and departments will be better managed.

The call for specialized library and information collections is a recognition of the importance of the micro-flow phenomenon in establishing a comprehensive information system. Certain specialized collections may be established at the initiative of the government; however, a large proportion of specialized information flows from certain "natural" sources which evolve out of felt information needs or result from certain geographic, historical and ethnic circumstances and these cannot be "established." What exists already or what lies within the potential of a special group to create must be subsidized by government. Contracts which establish a legal relationship between specialized information units and federal, state and local information systems must be explored as one method of providing financial support while avoiding any compromise of organizational independence and autonomy. A government grant to the Fortune Society, an organization which advocates prison reform and assists ex-inmates in rehabilitation efforts, to improve their information center and related information dissemination activities is not a contradiction. The information managed with great dedication by this group may be channeled into the mainstream information flow.

INFORMATION IN TELECOMMUNICATIONS

The commission's statement on telecommunication is significant only if it is the seed for a much larger effort to utilize all forms of telecommunication. The authority of the federal government to mandate the direction of all broadcasting over the air waves should not be neglected in any master plan for an information system. If information is vital for a smoothly functioning modern democratic society, then the mass media of radio and television must reflect the government's commitment to the provision of information. A loose charitable arrangement presently governs the quantity and quality of information programmed by the networks and stations. At some place in the top-level federal agency which coordinates information service there should be a unit which determines those information items having maximum public significance at a given time and directs the mass media to select from a list of possibilities and use their own ingenuity to provide appealing prime-time programs. In addition to prime-time, a certain percentage of each hour of broadcasting should be required to focus on publicly significant information. By leaving the exact format for presentation to the discretion of the networks and stations, competition would not be inhibited. On the contrary, information which is generally thought to be dull would present a challenge to the mass media entrepreneurs. The month of August 1975, for example, might mandate prime-time documentaries on a combination of the following topics:

- Energy Supply Forecast for the Fall and Winter
- Grain Sales and Their Possible Impact on Food Prices
- The New Health Act Passed by Congress Over the President's Veto
- A Discussion of All Legislation Vetoed By The President
- The Amount and Meaning of the 1975 Federal Deficit
- New York City's Fiscal Emergency And Its Implication For Other Cities
- Review and Status Report On the Comprehensive Employment and Training Act

At the regional, state and local level, similar lists could be developed. Periodically the bills before state and local legislatures should be given wide exposure. The implications of executive orders promulgated by governors and mayors and their numerous administrative departments should be periodically examined under the mass media searchlight. In addition to mass media, the minicommunications media of cable television, sixteen millimeter films, slides and audio cassettes are also available to take up the telecommunication effort at the local and neighborhood levels where mass media is no longer feasible.

In point five the commission calls for improved efforts to select, train and retrain information system managers. For a national information system such trained managers are the *sine qua non,* the vital element without which the system does not exist. The know-how of the information specialist or librarian is necessary to bind all the other pieces of the structure together. Massive buildings and the most modern equipment may be highly desirable; but in truth, a library exists wherever there is a trained librarian and people seeking information. The kingpins of the system are librarians who are highly trained generalists who have the ability to interpret and analyze consumer needs and the ability to scan the entire information spectrum to search out appropriate information that meets the identified needs.

INFORMATION SERVICE AT THE LOCAL PUBLIC LIBRARY

As the final point of delivery, the public library remains the most important unit in the structure for the provision of information services. It may be beneficial to view the local library or information center as a switchboard site, the librarian as a switchboard operator and the information consumer as a caller trying to obtain the best possible connection within the environment of a particular information item. Arrayed on the switchboard before the librarian are lines, switches and plugs representing choices which must be made in the effort to provide information of value. Some lines carry the macro-flow of information from large primary (government, business, science) information generators; some lines are connected to specialized (civil rights, drugs, Chicanos) interest groups from all parts of the country; still other lines carry the micro-flow from immediate local generators of information (tenants, taxpayers, ethnic organizations). The consumer is seeking information to meet an immediate need, information useful for decision-making, information of value. It must be remembered that the connection will have no value unless it is also on a level that facilitates effective communication. The consumer must be connected with a response that is digestible and understandable in order for the need to be satisfied.

Level, value, public significance are three concepts which must be understood if the librarian as switchboard operator is to function effectively. The switchboard becomes comprehensible when these elements of information are understood. Such awareness will greatly assist in the task of imposing order on the great continuous outpouring of information. Of crucial importance is the avoidance of the problem of being overwhelmed. The notion that there is "so much" available on a subject that only the consumer himself has the time needed to search for the answers is self-defeating and challenges the public library's reason for being. No layman can "cope" where librarians fear to tread. Making connections (with the switchboard) to produce information of value is a primary library function which must be practiced widely and with perseverance in order for the library profession to move continuously closer to the goal of the provision of adequate information services.

A new philosophy and sense of mission must guide the library's management. Consideration must be given to the fact that the public library must serve as a terminal point for information flowing downward from national and state generators and for information flowing across from specialized interests. At the local level the library must serve as the information management component within an overall local service delivery system. Librarians must also provide options for decision-making. Of final but vital importance is the library's capacity to "know" the group and individual consumers within the community. In the discussion above we have illustrated how information flows downward to local outlets. In most instances each national, state, science, business or other MACRO-flow generating source has a local counterpart or designated outlet. Federal social service information will end its flow in the local department of social services. Government employment information will be deposited first at the local public employment agency.

The local chamber of commerce will be the primary recipient of information from the national chamber of commerce. In addition to aggressively assuming the role of receiver for information which has no regular local receiver the library must be concerned with the optimum utilization of the information which accumulates in all of the other local receivers. Because it is best equipped to manage—acquire, classify, compile, arrange, retrieve, disseminate—information, the public is best served when other agencies assign this function to the library and actively cooperate and support its implementation. The information "tasks" of each component within the system are better performed by the designated information management component. A more expanded description of this process is provided in "The Public Library and Advocacy: Information for Survival."[9]

The provision of information of value, information for decision-making, is the end for which information management serves as the means. We have explained the concept of information for decision-making above; however, it would be useful to elaborate further on one aspect: Timeliness, or having the information available at the point where it facilitates an understanding of the number of options and the nature of the options before the decision is made. In some instances it is a matter of making information available in order to alert the appropriate citizens that it is necessary to make a decision. A family seeking a larger apartment should be able to obtain information regarding government rent subsidies, low-interest loans for cooperatives, recent large rent increases in certain housing complexes and other similar matters related to the housing market. On the other hand, when a state or city government begins to consider assigning a large portion of its federal rent subsidies to one housing development or one locality, the public should know in advance and thus be given the opportunity to make a decision in opposition to the proposed action.

Timeliness is made possible by an awareness of how to retrieve publicly significant information quickly and by a heightened sense of what the target consumer population needs. The librarian should be so attuned to and should "know" the consumers being serviced so well that a large proportion of the information requests may be anticipated. One system for the identification of needs is explained in detail by Owens and Braverman in eight basic steps.[10] Such categorization forecasting and predicting makes it possible to select material from the information grid in advance and to process and remold it for the level most appropriate for the local consumer. Creative forecasting also makes it possible to make optimum use of the other components of the local service delivery system.

> Following the identification of needs, systems must be developed which most effectively and efficiently meet those needs. Like the patient entering a hospital each client is a unique case; nevertheless, just as standardized procedures, predesigned equipment and established formulas increase the possibility of the patient's successful recovery, in similar fashion an adequate information delivery facility must be prepared. The facility must be developed to the point where routine and recurring problems are taken care of swiftly and almost automatically. The system should leave the professional librarian free to do the necessary improvisation and creative problem-solving for clients with complex information problems.[11]

> Before the inventory of information can be set in order and utilized, the problem must be pushed into the most suitable holding pen. For any information priority or category the related body of general information is the starting point for the solution to a specific problem. For example: A problem related to food stamps may be handled more rapidly if it is already known that food stamp programs are usually administered not through health departments but through local social services agencies. Familiarity with the general structure and functions of the social service agency and its basic literature will lubricate the process of assisting with the food stamp problem.[12]

The goal is to place as much useful information at the disposal of the consumer as rapidly as possible. Studies indicate that a large proportion of the people who approach the public library for information do not receive responses which may be called reasonably relevant, complete and practical. The continuing rejection by the masses of the public library may be due to this failure of consumers to obtain information that is thorough and timely enough to give high value and the satisfaction which triggers the chain reaction of word-of-mouth referrals that would produce a steady flow of new consumers.

A simple innovation that would cost nothing but would greatly enhance the provision of satisfactory service is increased citizen participation through library advisory committees. Since the value received by the public will determine future support for information and referral activities, it is imperative that the closest liaison be maintained with the citizens in order to guarantee ongoing relevant service. Such advisory committees, when properly utilized would not be interesting appendages but a vital element of the ongoing needs identification process.

> The process is a circular one. When citizens are involved in the process of identifying needs and planning information services, the probability that those needs will be effectively satisfied is increased. Positive experiences with libraries increase public support and with greater public support, more resources are made available to continue expanding and improving library services. Conversely, services which isolate themselves from the clientele served are likely to become less and less relevant and eventually will experience the most devastating act of hostility, the refusal to recognize the library as an institution worthy of action or reaction. . . .[13]

Value is highly subjective and relative; value requires movement from the general to the specific; to provide value, information must undergo a humanizing process. Of all the persons employed within the various units of the ideal information service structure, it is the local public librarian who will most frequently look into the eyes of the human beings who are helped in some concrete way by the information made available through the efforts of the entire system. It is the public librarian who will pass the vital feedback up through the structure. Upon the librarian and the public library effort an adequate information system will fall or stand and be further expanded and developed.

SUMMARY

Our complex society demands that all individuals and groups be knowledgeable on a broader front than previously was expected. All citizens are potentially "information literates" and must be encouraged to apply information resources to their home, civic and community life, as well as to their work. Information is a record of phenomena observed or decisions made. The record may merely be the impression on the mind of an individual or it may be an elaborate array of data stored in a computer. Awareness of three elements or characteristics of information—public significance, value, level —enhances our ability to understand and design adequate information delivery systems. Among the major generators of information of public significance, goverment is unequaled with respect to frequency and quantity of output. Information flows downward from major generators or from small specialized groups. The information of greatest value is information that aids decision-making by providing the raw material from which options and alternatives emerge.

As the final point of delivery the local library or information center may be viewed as a switchboard site, the librarian as a switchboard operator and the information consumer as a caller trying to obtain the best possible connection within the environment of a particular information item. In order for the connection to have value the consumer must receive a response on a level that facilitates communication, a response that is digestible and understandable. In addition to serving as the terminal point for information flowing downward and across, the public library must serve as the information management component within an overall local service delivery system. The goal is to place as much useful information at the disposal of the consumer as rapidly as possible. To achieve this goal, a system which begins with a national agency and moves through the state level to the local library must be developed. A theoretical understanding of a structure that never has existed but might be created may end the paralysis within the library profession and open the way to the step-by-step development of adequate information networks and centers.

REFERENCES

1. National Commission on Libraries and Information Science, *Annual Report to the President and the Congress, 1972–1973* (Washington, D.C.: Govt. Print. Office, 31 January 1974), p. 2.

2. Sylvia G. Faibisoff and Donald P. Ely, "Information and Information Needs," Commissioned Paper under the Commissioned Paper Project, (Teachers College, Columbia Univ., Division of Library Programs, U.S. Office of Education, 1974), p. 6.

3. National Commission, p. 27.

4. Beverly Rawles, *Materials Selection for Disadvantaged Adults* (Morehead, Ky.: Appalachian Adult Education Center, Morehead State Univ., July 1974).

5. National Commission, p. 27.

6. Ibid., p. 28.

7. Faibisoff and Ely, pp. 26–8.

8. National Commission, pp. 3–4.

9. Major R. Owens and Miriam Braverman, "The Public Library and Advocacy: Information for Survival," Commissioned Paper under the Commissioned Paper Project, (Teachers College, Columbia University, Division of Library Programs, U.S. Office of Education, 1974), p. 38.

10. Ibid., pp. 42–8.

11. Ibid., p. 50.

12. Ibid., p. 51.

13. Ibid., pp. 72–3.

The Need for Cooperation Among Libraries in the United States

by Roderick G. Swartz

The title of this article is deceptive. It assumes that traditional library cooperation is valid. About a decade ago, one state library had as its slogan "cooperation is the key." Similar terms such as library cooperation, regional library, library system, and networking—all of which imply cooperative action—have become sacred in the profession. From time to time, someone needs to ask: Cooperation—the key to what and for whom?

In addition, the title does not indicate whose needs are fulfilled by traditional library cooperation, i.e., shared resources and shared jurisdiction. There is no doubt that it has been of benefit to those citizens who now have some type of regional library, or to researchers who receive library materials on interlibrary loan. There is no doubt that it has been beneficial in providing jobs for hundreds of library employees. But how valid is library cooperation based on an analysis of contemporary user needs for library and information services?

The title also implies that cooperation among libraries is the only valid and important type of cooperation. There is certain historical justification that interlibrary cooperation has been very beneficial; yet, how important is it today in relation to all other types of cooperative ventures with the various agencies and groups to which a library now has access?

It is the purpose of this article to take a critical look at the validity of library cooperation based on the recent increase of user need and demand studies and to determine whether cooperation really has been and will continue to be the key to meeting those needs and demands, based on the information and library needs of users and potential users.

Shared library resources and jurisdictions have prospered in the United States based on the assumption that *more* is good, and that a well-coordinated and well-financed *more* is even better. Regional public library development grew out of projections made by Carleton Joeckel in 1935 that the answer to the poor distribution of library resources in the United States was a series of regional libraries which would provide nationwide library service, including service to rural and suburban areas.[1] Joeckel argued that by forming regional units of communities and counties too poor to provide library service, adequate levels of library service would span the country. Aided by federal legislation such as the Library Services Act of 1956, regional libraries did begin to provide a pattern of library service to the country.

Cooperation among college and university libraries was based on the assumption that the problems of too much growth within any one library could be offset by well-coordinated and cooperatively financed efforts. Spurred by threatening projections, college and university librarians began to develop joint acquisition programs such as the Farmington Plan, cooperative storage centers such as the Center for Research Libraries in Chicago, and the development of a nationwide system of interlibrary loans.

Networking continues to stress the better coordination of existing resources in all types of libraries. Bibliographic networks are allowing for the decrease in repetitious processing of library materials, while telecommunication networks are connecting a variety of library materials in all types of libraries, and administrative networks are working toward better coordination of library and information services. The National Commission on Libraries and Information Science, in developing its program for a national network, calls for this coordination factor to protect and sustain the United States' national resources of information.

These trends show that library cooperation has become an economically feasible way to improve traditional library service, a pattern which emphasizes the importance of improved access to a growing number of library materials. Regional library service is better than no library service, access to several university libraries via interlibrary loan is better than the availability of just one university collection, and the coordinated access of library materials in the United States through a national network would be even more advantageous. The argument has been that the more library materials available locally, or at a reasonable distance, the better the library service will be. If the financing of this service is shared by several jurisdictions, the service will be better and the costs more equally distributed.

From the point of view of library management, cooperation is certainly reasonable. But how does it rank in view of recent studies in user information need and demand?

USER STUDIES OF THE INFORMATION RICH AND THEIR IMPLICATIONS

User studies traditionally have been examinations of how libraries were used and by whom. They have been analyses of circulation statistics, of the use of particular library areas such as the reference department, or of the socio-economic backgrounds of library patrons. Tobin points out that this type of user study grew in popularity after World War II and was used as a management tool to "improve [the] existing condition." However, over the years little attention was given to the potential user or to citizen information demands or needs.[2]

This review looks at users and potential users of information rather than only at those who currently use libraries. In viewing their demands and needs, groups of information users should be distinguished. Edwin Parker uses the terms *information rich* and *information poor*.[3] The former includes leaders from scholarly governmental and business communities who have an overabundance of information, who use libraries and other formal information sources, and who are familiar with techniques for securing information. The information poor are those who have little acquaintance with traditional information sources such as libraries, and whose information needs in many cases would not be met by these sources. For purposes of this discussion, Parker's distinction will suffice.

Next, one should distinguish between an information demand, or articulated information need, placed on the formal information community, and an information need which the individual has not articulated, perhaps even to himself. Demands on formal information sources have been a growing concern for a number of years, while the study of information needs is still in its infancy—there is little standardization at this point and the methodology is still in a formative stage of development. The major tool of measurement is the written questionnaire combined with an interview. From time to time there is serious doubt as to whether it is possible to discover information needs by querying an individual or group of individuals.[4]

Information demand research meanwhile has evolved into two separate strands: one which focuses on the literature patterns of use, and one which concentrates on the individual and his information gathering habits.

The study of literature use emphasizes the frequency and the depth to which particular segments of the library collection are utilized. The Fussler and Simon book on *Patterns in the Use of Books in Large Research Libraries,* which examines use patterns of various collections at the University of Chicago, is an example of this type of study.[5] The field of bibliometrics, in which fields of literature are analyzed for frequency and duration of use, has added much to the knowledge of user demands on library collections.

The other trend in user demand studies has been toward the investigation of information gathering techniques, i.e., the way scientists and other professional people search for information, what service they use, and how they evaluate and rank the various sources they use. Patterns and networks of the information flow are the central concerns of this research.

In examining the literature of user demand by the information rich, one notices two factors. First, there seems to be little relation between the groups concerned with information demand and need studies, and the groups involved with the development and design of library and information services.[6] In other words, library administrators and information technologists seem to draw little from the research in information need and demand. One notable example which has been documented is the development of the Educational Resources Information Center (ERIC); no user studies of demand and need, user behavior, or user requirements were included in the development of the ERIC system. As a result, Paisley found that after five years of operation the system was still not being brought to the attention of the educational practitioner.[7]

The second startling factor is that much of the work in information demand and need is being done abroad. There is, of course, the work being done at the Institute for Communication Research at Stanford University, the Massachusetts Institute of Technology, Johns Hopkins University, and the studies of the American Psychological Association. However, much progress is being made abroad. England is a prime example; in preparing the background work for cooperative plans such as the National Lending Library, numerous studies were made of user demands for information and on library collections.

There are several major themes which run through the information studies of the information rich. Perhaps the most recurring is the choice by scientists, researchers and other professional people of an informal information network over, or in equal importance to, any formal network of libraries and information centers. Watson's discussion of the informal communication of scientists in his book, *The Double Helix,* has been corroborated by numerous user studies. Studies of astronomers, anthropologists and agricultural experts show that informal discussion among colleagues is a major source of information.[8]

The use of informal discussion has led to a series of studies on information flow in professions, associations and organizations. It has allowed investigators to project the concept of an invisible college where scholars of a particular discipline are interconnected in an informal network akin to the organizational grapevine.[9]

In formal information channels, the right amount of information is more important than access to a quantity of information. For example, studies among physicians and physicists show that use is limited to a restricted number of primary journals in the field. One writer claims that in reader studies based on journals in the field of physics, even these basic journals are not well read. Another author claims that the "quick fix" was more often the norm than an exhaustive use of available collections.[10]

In fact, the question of accessibility—both in terms of time and geography—proved to be a more important factor than the quality of the source. One study asked individuals in a research sample to rank sources of information for several hypothetical problems. In each case, the sources of a personal library, a knowledgeable person close by, or the telephone were given priority over the services of a more distant library.

When such individuals are drawn into a formal information channel such as a library, numerous studies have shown that they are not sophisticated in their use of the tools of library and information science. Studies of citations from abstracting and indexing tools, for example, show a small number of references drawn from these sources.

One researcher speculated that the twin features of accessibility and the right amount of information were the reasons many researchers went to informal sources. There the individual gets "the right information in the right amount and within the time required."[11]

Finally, librarians are not seen as active participants in the procurement of information. They are seen as housekeepers, organizers, or managers perhaps, but not people who aid in the complexity of securing information and data.[12]

USER STUDIES OF THE INFORMATION POOR AND THEIR IMPLICATIONS

User studies of the information poor are even more limited than are studies of the information rich. Tobin, studying the 477 user studies of all types listed in *Library Literature* for 1960-73, could find only five studies of nonusers and three studies of the disadvantaged. She hypothesized that there may have been more, but the results in terms of library use were minimal and not disclosed.[13]

Studies of the information demands of this group have shown that the logical, formal, information source—the public library—contributes little toward fulfilling their needs. A study conducted by the System Development Corporation (SDC) called for a "new outlook" by the public library if it is to be responsive to the information needs and demands of the disadvantaged.[14] An earlier study of the information needs of the information poor by Mary Lee Bundy showed the public library in a position of nonimportance.[15] A study of adult information needs in Indiana indicated that even for business, industry, agriculture and labor, the public library had little relevance.[16]

Data on information needs of the information poor are even more restricted. The most recent efforts appear to have been conducted by the SDC and the National Commission on Libraries and Information Science (NCLIS). SDC, in a study of Library Services and Construction Act projects to special target groups, looked at the information needs of the various groups of the information poor. The study focused on users and nonusers of federally financed library projects, finding a high interest in audiovisual formats. This was especially true of nonusers of the projects. Subject interests favored were employment information, health care, ethnic materials, and hobbies.[17] Similar trends were noted by the NCLIS in evaluating total information needs and relating this evaluation to planning for nationwide library cooperation and networking. After an early study by Patrick and Cooper indicated that the previous user studies did not provide enough data for national information planning,[18] the NCLIS made various attempts to identify user needs as a basis for national planning. An NCLIS study conducted by Bourne and others for the Institute of Library Research, University of California, Berkeley, identified nineteen subgroups whose information needs would vary from the norm. Among the nineteen groups with special information needs, the following information poor groups were identified: the economically and socially disadvantaged, ethnic minorities, the mentally and physically handicapped, the geographically remote, the aged, and the institutionalized.[19]

Another NCLIS study, written and researched by Edwin Parker of the Stanford University Institute for Communication Research, projected the impact of socio-economic change on information needs.[20] Again, emphasis was placed on information needs of the information poor, with a special stress on life information, and on information in an audiovisual format.

A third, less scientific attempt to evaluate potential user needs was a series of regional hearings scheduled in various parts of the country. Invitations to testify were sent not only to library and information specialists, but also to users and potential users of library service. The major impact of these hearings was on the growing awareness by the NCLIS of a greater variety of information needs being expressed by a wider potential clientele.[21] The commission found itself face to face with representatives of the information poor and heard them describe their information needs. While many of these needs were only partially or incompletely explained, the commission did begin to gain a broader understanding of the information needs of the information poor.

Still another effort to analyze user needs was the NCLIS's conference on user needs, held in Denver in May 1973. Building on the work of the Institute of Library Research, the commission invited sixteen specialists in user information needs to present papers on the information requirements of a particular subgroup. Each participant found that the description of information needs was a difficult task, even when one is extremely knowledgeable of the subgroup and its information interests.

In all sixteen subgroups, two factors which remained consistent were the importance of time and the usability of format. Unless information arrived on a prescribed time schedule and was in a format which could be used, the information itself was useless.

Nine of the papers looked at information needs of social and demographic subgroups which varied from the norm, the norm being defined as a "white male, middle class, healthy 'normal' adult, aged 21-65 years." These groups included women, homemakers, parents, children, young adults, the aged, the geographically remote, the economically and socially deprived, the institutionalized, the mentally and physically handicapped, and Mexican-Americans. The major information needs of these groups were for life information, including survival, general life maintenance, and self-enrichment and growth.[22]

While the commission made these efforts to comprehend user needs, it is evident that there is still a great deal of basic research to be done on user information needs. It is encouraging, however, that the commission's study is one of the first times that library/information system planning and research on user needs are being conducted by the same group.

As many writers have pointed out, research in user information needs and demands is a fairly new field. More is known about information demands than about information needs. Work has concentrated on the information rich, with special attention to the requirements of scientists and technologists. As late as 1970 Brittain could identify only eighteen useful studies on the users of social science material.[23] Even less is known about the information needs of the information poor. While it is premature to draw too many conclusions from this total body of work, it is perhaps possible to make several observations about user information needs and demands, and library cooperation. There seem to be definite implications at the local, regional and national levels.

Despite limited knowledge of information needs, it is obvious that well-coordinated and well-financed library cooperation is not enough. More and better traditional library service is not the complete answer, which may suggest an entire new approach to the local delivery of information, especially to the information poor.

In his book entitled *Management*, Peter Drucker takes public service institutions to task for simply asking for more money to do the same old things. It is "effectiveness, not efficiency which the service institution lacks . . . they tend not to do the right things. . . . All service institutions are threatened by tendencies to cling to yesterday rather than slough it off."[24]

From the viewpoint of the information poor, and to a certain extent that of the information rich, it is necessary to reevaluate information and library services to determine which are important, and to ascertain the types and extents of information needs.

The first step in this process of moving from efficiency to efficient effectiveness is a better understanding of the potential user and his or her information needs. The use of marketing research techniques has proved helpful in some developments. This does not imply the creation of false needs, but rather a true analysis of a segment of the potential clientele, an assessment of their information needs, and then development or alteration of services to meet these needs. The needs of potential patrons are studied to project the types and varieties of demands they could place on an institution. One marketing expert examined the marketing approaches for an information system such as ERIC and found that marketing techniques could be applied,[25] and a public library in Manchester, England, has experimented with market research training for its staff.[26] The work done at Hamline University in Minnesota in studying the information needs of the campus, and then using the data to make the library responsive to these needs, is another illustration.[27]

This marketing approach emphasizes a different type of library cooperation, a closer user-professional working relationship. It implies a closer working relationship with all potential users in the community and community involvement in the planning of new and revitalized programs and services. It requires the library administration to work with the leadership and staff members of other groups serving the same community. In the SDC study of special target groups, people from other agencies ranked community involvement important to the success of the projects studied, whereas community involvement was not a significant point cited by the librarians questioned.[28]

User studies imply that the user-professional relationship needs to be strengthened within the walls of the library. The librarian needs to be more adept at isolating an information demand when it is articulated. Studies by Crowley and Childers show that the librarian is deficient in responding to even elementary information demands.[29] Merely to call on the vast resources of library cooperation and interlibrary loan is not enough. The importance of the professional's role in interpreting the demand and delivering the right amount of information is reflected in user studies. Studies show that the information rich are satisfied with less information than was supposed and that the information poor often require smaller amounts of information than most libraries will supply. This would indicate that it is crucial for a professional directly serving the public to identify correctly an information demand and then to produce the right amount of information to appropriately satisfy that demand.

Improved information demand analysis implies a greater concern with the interview process. The professional needs to know not only the literature and the channels for securing it, but also how to query the client to be sure the correct demand has been ascertained. It also indicates a greater responsibility for the librarian as an information transfer facilitator. Special librarians have long espoused this role in meeting the information demands of their companies, but librarians from other types of libraries have been slower to accept this responsibility. If even the information rich are partial to informal and personal channels of information, and are unskilled in the use of library and information science tools, the growing importance of the trained librarian or information transfer specialist is obvious.

At the same time, there is a strong need for the library to explain its function to the user. Studies show that even if the user can overcome the difficulty of translating a generalized need into an information need and then into an information demand, it is very unlikely that the library is credited with satisfying that demand. This requires a total public relations program by the library (which starts with marketing or needs assessment), the development of new or revamped programs, and then the explanation to the public of the function and availability of these programs. This goes beyond elementary publicity to the very image that the library has in its community, whether it is town, campus, or school building.

User studies indicate that this need for closer user-professional co-operation is balanced by a need for closer cooperation with technological improvements. Users are making information demands which can no longer be filled by traditional formats or traditional sources. The growing importance of audiovisual formats for the information poor has been stressed by several authors. The valve of technology—especially telecommunications and computers—in aiding the receipt of information at the right time is becoming increasingly important to users of all types. Participants at the NCLIS Denver conference on user needs stressed that information not received in time was not useful information.[30] The ability to relay data about information, as well as information itself, via faster processes will be of growing importance to the information user.

At the regional and national levels, the improvement of the traditional form of library cooperation, i.e., the coordination and interchange of library materials, is rivaled by the importance of new and different types of library cooperation. Illustrative is the need for a coordinated program for continuing education, which updates and revitalizes the librarian's view of user needs, service patterns, and library cooperation. Better coordination of newer formats—such as audiovisual materials, microforms, and computerized data bases—is needed. The applicability of the technologies of computers and telecommunications to user information requirements demands better understanding.

One effort, hopefully cooperative, is the developing study of user needs and the demands for information. Work with the information poor lags far behind the work conducted with the information rich. Even more important, there must be closer cooperation between researchers in information needs and administrators who are designing and providing library and information services. The developers of new or revitalized library and information services and products should be aware of and benefit from research in user needs studies. Finally, there is the effort to increase the effectiveness of traditional library cooperation by the infusion of technology and the planning of standardized networks.

From the user's viewpoint, the four important cooperative trends appear to be: (1) the effort to increase the effectiveness of traditional library cooperation by the infusion of technology and the development of a system of networks; (2) the development of other regional and national cooperative endeavors, such as the coordination of continuing education for library and information personnel; (3) a growing cooperation between the user of information services and the professional librarian or information specialist in order to reassess the way in which information is dispensed at the local level; and (4) the initial, although limited, cooperation between researchers on user information needs and demands, and the developers and administrators of library and information services. Just what the highest priority should be among these four trends depends to some extent on the group of users with which one is identified. For example, developments in the first trend have been criticized as being of more benefit to the information rich than to the information poor. The National Commission on Libraries and Information Science, although sharply criticized for it, has provided leadership for the first and second trends. However, clear leadership patterns are not as obvious for the third and fourth trends.

Traditional library cooperation, improved by technology, may still be a key to the fulfilling of user information needs and demands. Nevertheless, to ensure improved service to all user groups, it is essential that all aspects of these cooperative trends be utilized.

REFERENCES

1. Carleton Joeckel, *Government of the American Public Library* (Chicago: Univ. of Chicago Press, 1939).

2. Jayne C. Tobin, "A Study of Library 'Use Studies,' " *Information Storage and Retrieval* 10:102 (March/April 1974). See also Marcia Bates, *User Studies: A Review for Librarians and Information Specialists,* ERIC Document 047738 (March 1971).

3. Edwin B. Parker, "Information and Society," *Library and Information Service Needs of the Nation; Proceedings of a Conference on the Needs of Occupational, Ethnic, and Other Groups in the United States* (Washington, D.C.: Govt. Print. Off., 1974), pp. 9–50.

4. J. M. Brittain, *Information and its Users: A Review with Special Reference to the Social Sciences* (Bath, Eng.: Bath Univ. Press, 1970), p. 147.

5. Herman H. Fussler and Julian L. Simon, *Patterns in the Use of Books in Large Research Libraries* (Chicago: Univ. of Chicago Press, 1969).

6. Nan Lin and William D. Garvey, "Information Needs and Uses," in Carlos A. Cuadra, ed., *Annual Review of Information Science and Technology* 7:30 (Washington, D.C.: American Society for Information Science, 1972). See also Brittain, *Information and its Users,* p. 147.

7. William Paisley, "Improving a Field-based 'Eric-like' Information System," *Journal of the American Society for Information Science* 22:403 (November/December 1971).

8. J. Watson, *The Double Helix: A Personal Account of the Discovery of the Structure of DNA* (New York: Atheneum, 1968). See also D. N. Wood,

"User Studies: A Review of the Literature from 1966 to 1970," *Aslib Proceedings* 23:11–23 (January 1971).

9. Derek J. De Solla Price, *Little Science, Big Science* (New York: Columbia Univ. Press, 1963).

10. Wood, "User Studies." See also Ching-chih Chen, "How do Scientists Meet Their Information Needs?" *Special Libraries* 65:272–80 (July 1974); and Margaret Slater, "Meeting the Users' Needs Within the Library," in Jack Burkett, ed., *Trends in Special Librarianship* (London: Clive Bingley, 1969), pp. 99–136.

11. Wood, "User Studies," p. 14. See also Brittain, *Information and Its Users*, p. 157.

12. Chen, "How do Scientists Meet Their Information Needs?"

13. Tobin, "A Study of Library 'Use Studies,' " pp. 105, 107.

14. Jean Wellisch et al., *The Public Library and Federal Policy* (Westport, Conn.: Greenwood Press, 1974). Summarized in Donald V. Black, "Library Needs of the Disadvantaged," *Library and Information Service Needs* . . ., pp. 281–314.

15. Mary Lee Bundy, *Metropolitan Public Library Users: A Report of A Survey of Adult Library Use in the Maryland Baltimore-Washington Metropolitan Area* (College Park: Univ. of Maryland School of Library and Information Services, 1968).

16. Charles Bonser and Jack Wentworth, *A Study of Adult Information Needs in Indiana* (Bloomington, Indiana: Indiana Univ. Graduate School of Library Science, 1970).

17. Donald V. Black, et al., *Evaluation of LSCA Services to Special Target Groups: Final Report* (Santa Monica: System Development Corp., 1973). Summarized in Black, "Library Needs of the Disadvantaged."

18. Ruth J. Patrick and Michael D. Cooper, *Information Needs of the Nation: A Preliminary Analysis* (Berkeley, Calif.: Univ. of California School of Librarianship, 1972).

19. Charles P. Bourne et al., *Preliminary Investigation of Present and Potential Library and Information Service Needs* (Berkeley: Univ. of California Institute of Library Research, 1973).

20. Parker, "Information and Society," pp. 9–50.

21. National Commission on Libraries and Information Science, *Annual Report to the President and the Congress, 1972–73, 1974* (Washington, D.C.: Govt. Print. Off., January 31, 1974).

22. *Library and Information Service Needs* . . ., pp. 253–54.

23. Brittain, *Information and Its Users*, p. 146.

24. Peter F. Drucker, *Management: Tasks, Responsibilities, Practices* (New York: Harper, 1974), pp. 138, 146.

25. Philip G. Kuehl, "Marketing Perspectives for 'Eric-like' Information Systems," *Journal of the American Society for Information Science* 23:356–64 (November/December 1972).

26. D. A. Yorke and D. I. Colley, "Meet the Public: Public Libraries and Marketing Research," *Library Association Record* 75:203–04 (October 1973).

27. Herbert F. Johnson and Jack B. King, "Information Systems Management in the Small Liberal Arts College," *College and Research Libraries* 30:483–90 (November 1969).

28. Black, "Library Needs . . .," pp. 301–302.

29. Terence Crowley, and Thomas Childers, *Information Service in Public Libraries: Two Studies* (Metuchen, N.J.: Scarecrow, 1971).

30. *Library and Information Service Needs . . .*, pp. 254–56.

Proposals for a Dynamic Library

by Gerald Salton

INTRODUCTION

The paper which follows contains a blueprint for a new mechanized library environment which emphasizes methods for automatic document and query analysis, automatic document classification, rapid searches of the collections in response to incoming queries, interactive modifications of query and document identifications designed to keep the collections current with changes in user interests and needs, and, finally, automatic procedures for accommodating document growth and for retiring less useful materials to auxiliary storage.

The current library scene is dominated by two main approaches to the library crisis: on the one hand, one implements small-scale changes in some of the technical processing—a new circulation control system here, a different serials acquisitions system there—and at the same time one continues to clamor for larger budgets and more space, buildings, and people to service the library. Because a piecemeal mechanization is almost never cost effective this approach does little to affect the library problem. On the other hand, one speaks about library networks, cooperative procedures, and long distance transmission of library materials from one "node" of a network to another; but the reality of collection sharing and joint library acquisitions is different from the theory, and the ultimate library in which all users are tied to mechanized library networks by console terminal devices is not likely to alter current library practices for a long time to come.

One reason why the progress made in library processing is so excruciatingly slow—the current library procedures were all well known in the last century and no fundamental changes have taken place in our lifetime—is that we appear to be locked into a given methodology and framework which turns out to be much less useful than generally assumed. Everyone uses a hierarchical library classification system consisting of nonoverlapping classes in which each library item is placed into a unique class. The storage and retrieval operations, if implemented, are invariably based on key word indexing, Boolean query formulations, so-called "inverted" files, and a search strategy which aims at retrieving all and only those items indexed by the given keyword combination. Procedures exist for adding items to existing collections, but the reverse process of removing older or less used materials is one about which little is known.

The dynamic library, introduced in this paper, is based on a new type of "clustered" file organization in which the classes can be adjusted to fit the characteristics of the user population. Items that appear important are promoted into active regions of the collection; other less important items are pushed to the periphery from where they can eventually be "retired" if it becomes necessary to make room for new items. The document and query processing is "dynamic" in the sense that the user population affects all processes; each library center then operates in an environment tailored to its user population, and mistakes, if made, need not be final.

Whether the proposals made in this paper will lead to actual implementation in operational situations remains to be seen. Some small-scale, experimental evidence obtained in a laboratory environment is included to show that the proposed methodology may well be worth considering as a substitute for alternative proposals that have been tried in the past without success.

Background

It is no longer controversial to affirm that all over the world there exists a library crisis and that some changes are in order if the traditional library services are to be maintained in the future. Following a recent study of large university libraries, Mason put the situation in the following terms:[1]

> "the great university libraries are largely in a state of quiet crisis, ill-housed, ill-served, and ill-fed . . .; within ten years, the full impact of overloading and undersupporting the research libraries will become painfully apparent. . . ."

The difficulties stem from a combination of factors: the increase in the amount of material to be processed and stored; the greater demands for service from a growing user population; the larger costs for goods and services; and the availability of new types of materials which cannot be treated by conventional methods. The obvious results are a breakdown of the established operations, an intellectual crisis among the people responsible for library management, and a deepening space and budget problem.

The latter, in particular, has led many observers to conjecture that the continually increasing requirements of the modern library and the growing budgetary needs cannot long be met by expanding the traditional library functions: "one cannot expect that an ever-increasing fraction of the available resources be allocated to some one function [the library], regardless of its importance."[2] Rather, it is argued, the need arises for new organizational structures and new procedures which may better cope with the existing problems than conventional approaches.

In the remainder of this study, the current thinking concerning the library problem is briefly reviewed, and proposals are made for the implementation of a new environment for the future library.

Current Approaches to the Modern Library

Three main approaches to the library problem are apparent at the present time. The most obvious—although not necessarily the most painless —way of proceeding consists in retaining the current operations conceptually intact, while attempting to mechanize some of the procedures using data processing or computing equipment.

A second approach is based on the creation of compacts and cooperative arrangements whereby several libraries decide to share resources or experiences to accomplish some common task; alternatively, a central agency may perform a given operation jointly for a number of different libraries. In either case, the hope is that the resources to be invested by individual participants become smaller, and the expenditure and upheaval inherent in the library processing turns out to be more bearable.

A final trend to be mentioned consists in postulating certain more drastic alterations of the present methodologies involving the creation of large library networks, the implementation of mechanized records for all library holdings, and the replacement of normal hard copy storage and standard circulation procedures by a (long distance) transmission of the corresponding stored records, and the reproduction of the information as required by the various user populations.

THE MECHANIZATION OF STANDARD LIBRARY PROCESSES

Most large libraries have introduced mechanized procedures to a greater or lesser extent. In decreasing order of popularity, the following operations are principally affected:[3]

i)   the treatment of business operations, such as budget and accounting work, as well as the handling of book funds, bindery records, gifts, and related matters;

ii) the processing of document acquisitions, including the ordering and control of serial and monograph items, and the handling of the accounts payable following the receipt of new documents;

iii) the control of circulation records, including load procedures, check out and check in of material, automatic dissemination and transmission methods, and so on;

iv) the generation and maintenance of lists and records of many types, including the library catalog, acquisition lists, index and subject listings, shelf lists, technical abstract bulletins, dictionaries of various types, and so on;

v)   the handling of reference and search work, often called "information retrieval" in the literature, including bibliographic (catalog) searches, demand searches by subject or content specification, and recurrent searches of the type used with selective dissemination systems where users are automatically notified, on a continuing basis, of interesting materials;

vi) the content processing, including the indexing, cataloging, abstracting and classification of documents and journals.

In the majority of libraries the mechanization efforts are restricted to business-type operations such as accounting and the production of printed lists of various kinds. Several hundred organizations have also mechanized their acquisition procedures and circulation records. Comparatively few use automatic search and retrieval operations—one major impediment being the creation of the voluminous mechanized files required for this purpose; finally, only very few are venturing into the areas involving the mechanization of intellectual tasks such as cataloging or classification.

For the most part, the mechanized housekeeping procedures are carried out *off-line* in a *batch processing* mode; that is, any file changes that occur are accumulated (batched), and all records that require updating are simultaneously treated in a single sweep through the file. A complete new acquisitions file may then be created once per week, or a new circulation file once a day.

The main disadvantage of the batch processing environment is the lack of *real time* control. That is, the exact status of a given record may not always be ascertainable, since changes are not incorporated into the files as they occur. To obtain a continually updated set of records, the operations must be carried out *on-line* by using computer terminals to initiate individual transactions whenever they take place. An on-line implementation may in time lead to a complete mechanization of all library operations, using a multi-terminal computer system in which the same bibliographic record, in various stages of completeness, serves all library functions.[4]

A number of on-line library acquisitions systems are now in operation,[5] as well as several on-line book circulation systems. Some of the latter may include provisions for queuing unfilled requests, followed by the automatic generation of notices to those customers whose requests had previously been held in abeyance.[6] Systems have also been implemented in which the user himself performs the necessary console operations for the charging and discharging of library items,[7] and in some cases, items may be charged out over the telephone.[8]

While the cataloging itself is normally carried out by trained experts, on-line methods, including, for example, the console display of bibliographic information and of vocabulary control data, may be used as an aid to the cataloger.[9] Furthermore, considerable thought has been devoted to the creation of mechanized procedures capable of using cataloging data from several different sources, such as locally generated data, and data originating at the Library of Congress.[10]

In summary, a considerable degree of sophistication has been achieved over the years in some areas of library mechanization and, while a great deal remains to be accomplished, most people concerned with library procedures feel that progress is being made in the right direction.

CENTRALIZATION AND COOPERATIVE EFFORTS

The second notable trend in the library field is a tendency to consider seriously the advantages of joint efforts and cooperative ventures in the mechanization area. Many observers, in fact, believe that a mechanization of library procedures should not be carried out separately by individual libraries, but that the investment is easier to justify in a somewhat different environment:[11]

"one concludes that the problems met in attempting to serve a large, growing, diverse community are not to be solved locally with more buildings and more employees, and that if a solution is to be achieved, it must be done either by altering the problem or by going beyond the local level . . ."

"Going beyond the local level" in this context implies the institution of centralized or cooperative ventures.

In principle, collaborative procedures are usable for all library procedures. In practice, the ends of cooperation are normally assumed to consist in the achievement of individual library goals rather than in the furtherance of a strong cooperative able to respond as a unit to its environment. As a result, most collaborative schemes are restricted in scope, and applied to simple, specific tasks such as card catalog production or accounting or printing of common catalogs and statistical data.[12]

A possible alternative to the introduction of collaborative arrangements is the delegation of certain tasks to a centralized agency. This is often easier to carry out because such a transfer of responsibility does not raise the usual fears concerning loss of autonomy or freedom of action on the part of any individual library. By far the best known and most influential activity of this type is the utilization by a variety of libraries and information centers of the tape distribution services that now make available bibliographic information prerecorded on magnetic tape. In the library field, the principal services of this type make use of the MARC (Machine Readable Cataloging) records originating at the Library of Congress.[13]

The MARC system makes available on tape in a standard format cataloging data for English language materials processed at the Library of Congress. Such data can be used by the recipients "passively" if the need for the particular citations has already been established within the library before the MARC records are received, or "actively" if the MARC record itself triggers an initial ordering or acquisitions operation. In either case, procedures must be available for searching MARC tapes by comparing the incoming information with individual current production needs, and for merging matched MARC records with internally generated data to produce a combined file for all items currently in process.

Centralized cataloging information can, of course, be used for a variety of purposes, including ordering, receiving, book accounting, cataloging, binding, labelling, and so on, and considerable savings may be produced, assuming that the tape formats are acceptable and that the service is timely and somewhat comprehensive. The same argument is put forward by a number of service bureaus that offer processing facilities to individual libraries, thereby eliminating, at least in theory, obvious overlapping.

A final approach toward cooperative endeavors in the library consists in the creation of *library networks,* where each component is connected to the others, and information can be exchanged by the several participants. The aim here is to institute common, or at least compatible, procedures, while at the same time making available to individual component members the resources of the whole network.

A number of such networks are now in existence, generally connecting organizations with common subject interests (Bio-medical Information Network, Medline-Medlars On-Line), or with close regional contacts (Ohio College Library Center, New England Library Network, and so on). For the moment, the network organizations are mostly concerned with the institution of common housekeeping operations, and their influence over the total library scene is still somewhat limited. However, as communication costs go down, and the use of on-line processing becomes more prevalent, one can expect that the importance of the network concept will grow. Eventually, a meaningful pooling of network resources may be undertaken by eliminating some duplicate holdings, combining subscriptions to some specialized journals, and instituting common storage facilities for certain portions of the collections.[14]

Such a development would dramatically change the library cost picture, but its realization requires a new understanding of the role of individual libraries, and some change in organization and attitude on the part of library managements.

THE LIBRARY OF THE FUTURE

A final development, illustrative of the thinking of some of the more influential observers on the library scene, is the conceptual design of the "library of the future."[15] In its most provocative form, such proposals postulate the complete elimination of books as we now know them:[16]

> ". . . any concept of the library which begins with books on shelves is sure to encounter trouble . . . we should be prepared to reject the schema of the physical library—the arrangement of shelves, card indexes, check-out desks, reading rooms, and so forth . . ."

Instead a centralized repository is suggested based on a combination of computer storage, microreduction, and remote transmission of information, from which information could be extracted by a suitable interactive search process. In each case, a variety of linguistic, processing, and display tools would be used to establish appropriate connections between the customers and the corresponding relevant information items:[17]

> "we are assuming that the average man of that year (2000 AD) may make a capital investment in an 'intermedium' or 'console'—his intellectual Ford or Cadillac—comparable to the investment now made in an automobile . . . the computer would be used as an interface in applying various sequences of procedures to named texts, graphs, and tables; observing the results; and intervening whenever a change or extension of plan is required."

Clearly, such a design is most appealing in that it eliminates the enormous duplication caused by the storage of multiple copies of the same material in many different places; it keeps the stored information continuously available for all comers because texts do not "circulate" in the normal sense of the word; it avoids delays in obtaining the desired information items and prevents losses; and, finally, it may improve not only the efficiency but also the effectiveness of the search. As Kemeny points out:[18]

> "I look forward with delight to being able to find in ten minutes everything relevant that has been written in a subject."

While no one has seriously proposed that a prototype of such an "ultimate" system be constructed at the present time, attempts have been made to implement more modest mechanized information transfer systems based on the simultaneous storage of full document texts as well as document surrogates and accessing information.[19] Such systems might be used to manipulate large data bases on-line, and to provide experience with a variety of information handling procedures, including the maintenance of stored library catalogs, the accessing of full document texts, the integration of different types of data bases, the utilization of text editing, reviewing, indexing and abstracting methods, the use of the on-line technology for the publication of new items, and the development of techniques for querying the data base.

Even this more modest on-line environment has not so far been realized for a variety of technical, financial, legal, and political reasons. Some of the impediments which must be overcome before progress can be made in building the "new" library are examined in more detail in the next section.

CRITIQUE OF THE CURRENT APPROACH

The Ultimate Library

Consider first the most advanced types of proposals which would eliminate books and libraries as we now know them, and replace these by man-computer interfaces for the dissemination of knowledge. While such systems may eventually come into being, it is unlikely that they will be seriously considered at the present time. The fact is that bound volumes of printed materials are likely to be in demand for some time, and the argument that books should be eliminated because they happen to be convenient for use only by human beings but not by machines appears insufficiently compelling.

Even if one were to grant that the users of information products might eventually get used to computer-produced copies of the stored information, the "procognitive" systems have little chance of realization in the foreseeable future: on the one hand, the usual manual content analysis operations would not be adequate to analyze and classify a vast store of diverse knowledge; on the other hand, the free and unrestricted kind of user-system interaction that is proposed to analyze and classify information, to find one's way in the information store, and to supply the necessary instructions for further processing cannot be utilized in any practical situation. Specifically, it is not possible to perform "a combined syntactic-semantic analysis of a text that reduces every sentence to a (linguistic) canonical form, or to a set of expressions in a (logical) predicate calculus;"[20] nor do we have capabilities that would easily mix question-answering and reference-retrieval routines;[21] nor is it reasonable to assume that machine translation facilities could be used when needed;[22] nor can we implement in a meaningful way even simple systems to simulate the operations of a computerized handbook.[23]

In other words, it appears that the reality of the library crisis will not be affected for some time to come by proposals which are still several levels removed from current capabilities. For this reason, attention will be restricted to systems more directly applicable to the libraries as we know them.

Prototype Centralized Networks

A theoretically easy way of introducing some degree of standardization into library processing, and of testing the effectiveness of collaborative library arrangements consists in creating a prototype library network. Unfortunately, the actual realization of such projects is more difficult than expected, and a great many questions are immediately raised by any proposal aiming at network construction.

There are first problems of scale and of strategy. Should one aim immediately at the implementation of a national policy, such as a national depository or the mechanization of a national union catalog, or should a start be made in a circumscribed subject area and geographical location. Should one implement only housekeeping operations that are well understood, or should the prototype network be used to experiment with new features—for example, a fact retrieval experiment, or an experiment to disseminate manuscripts prior to publication. Definite plans are difficult to generate in this area since no experiences are available upon which the necessary decisions might be based.

The next question relates to costs and cost-benefits. At a time when library budgets are subjected to critical examination everywhere, cost studies are conducted with considerable seriousness. Unfortunately, while reliable current costs may sometimes be ascertainable, a quantification of benefit remains elusive.[24] In particular, the quantitative contribution of information to the productivity or effectiveness of the user population is unknown and generally not determinable. This hampers the performance of cost-benefit analyses, and makes it difficult to adduce convincing arguments in favor of a mechanization of automatic information services.

The third question to be raised about the construction of prototype information networks covers legal and sociological problems, and more particularly the issues relating to copyright[25] and privacy.[26] The difficulty concerning the copyright is simply that the unlimited storage, reproduction, and transmission of copyrighted information tends to destroy the rights of copyright ownership and impairs the "fair use" concept under which copyrighted information can now be used for certain purposes. For this reason, the organizations that now depend on the copyright protection—including particularly the publishing industry—claim that the copyright restrictions should apply on input, that is, at the time the information is first entered into a computer network, rather than at the time of utilization when controls are more difficult to institute. Additionally, there is some concern among copyright owners that the "integrity" of a piece of information is difficult to preserve in the age of the computer utility, since the stored information can be manipulated in various ways—for example, by generating concordances, indexes, abstracts, translations, abridgements, and so on—again without controls over the utilization of these derivatives.

The privacy issue is equally tricky. While there is a realization that much information stored in mechanized data banks may be beneficial to the user population, there is also increasing concern about potential abuses. In particular, it may be desirable that information about private individuals or business enterprises be ethically or legally restricted to persons with a right to know. Unfortunately, privacy decisions which appropriately restrict or grant access are difficult to postulate and to enforce since insight can often be gained by cross-correlating or manipulating seemingly disparate and innocuous stored information items. Furthermore, even if the stored information were secured against unauthorized access, the accuracy of the stored information might not be guaranteed, so that harm might result even from authorized access and disclosure.

In summary, a variety of legal and ethical problems must be resolved before sophisticated information networks will prove acceptable for general use.

A last question pertaining to the implementation of information networks relates to the availability of adequate technologies. While the picture is still somewhat mixed in this area, improvements[27] are expected soon where they are needed.

Large-scale computing equipment is already available, and the performance of the small computers that might be needed to connect individual user stations to a central computer is improving relative to the large ones. The internal core or disc storage capacity at acceptable cost and with practical access times is also already on hand for many purposes and drastic improvements are foreseen in this area for the future.[28] At the moment, the less expensive microform technology is still mandatory as a primary medium for large-scale text and image storage.

The key problems relating to the computing and storage technologies remain lack of standardization and compatibility between various lines of equipment and, specifically, the problems arising in the interplay between photographic microform and computer technologies.

The input-output operations are less well understood. In particular, there still exists no easy process for converting hard copy text or images into machine-readable form. On the input side, optical character recognition equipment of sufficient sophistication and flexibility to process the needed variety of type fonts and character faces is still not available, and neither are output printers that can supply the character variations normally found on standard library cards. The long-term hope for the solution of the data entry problem rests on the continued evolution of the printing industry, and in particular on the use of computer-controlled typesetting routines able to generate data tapes that can later be read into a computer for storage and retrieval purposes. Alternatively, the available tape distribution services which currently supply bibliographic information on tape might be expanded to include also the distribution of document abstracts or text excerpts. In the meantime, much of the source data information must still be elaborately processed by keypunching techniques.

The terminal equipment necessary to carry out the normal user-computer interaction forms another problem area. A large variety of different consoles is currently used, ranging from simple keyboard devices and touch-tone telephones to elaborate graphics and audio terminals. However, users complain that the more sophisticated consoles are difficult to use and too expensive to acquire for many standard applications.

The data communications area presents what is likely to be the most serious challenge of all in the equipment area. Everyone agrees about the technological feasibility of transporting large volumes of data over long distances by electrical means. The problem is an economic one in that channels of sufficient transmission capacity and speed are out of reach for normal library applications, whereas narrow-band transmission techniques —for example, by facsimile methodology—are very slow.

In several hardware areas, including notably high capacity storage, input-output, and transmission equipment, a concurrent performance improvement and cost reduction will be required before information networks can be implemented comfortably. And overall, one must conclude that too many loose ends remain to be tied up before centralized networks may be expected to offer the kind of services now provided by the conventional environment.

In the immediate future, an improvement in the library situation must then come from a reevaluation of the standard library practices and procedures. This question is examined in the next subsection.

Library Software Assumptions

The strategies currently used for library mechanization appear to be based on a number of assumptions that are widely believed and accepted. The first of these states that *the clerical (housekeeping) operations constitute the most promising area for the institution of mechanized operations in the library*. Cost is believed to be the main obstacle to the implementation of mechanized housekeeping; as Locke says:[29] "We will bring in computers the minute they can do the same job for less money, or a better job at a price we can afford." The implication is that sooner or later the cost picture is bound to improve, and that the negative experiences that have accumulated in this respect in many places are a temporary phenomenon.

Unfortunately, an examination of library housekeeping operations from a data processing viewpoint reveals a considerable number of problem areas:

a) the library files to be processed are large, including sometimes many millions of items;
b) the file maintenance and updating operations required on a day-to-day basis are extensive;
c) a great variety of inputs are used and several dozen different output products are normally generated;
d) real time control of the library collection is considered desirable in the sense that the whereabouts of each item should be ascertainable at any time.

Obviously, such a set of requirements is certain to impose great strains on the computing facilities because no application involving large files subject to a great deal of updating is easy or cheap to mechanize; and the real time control by itself requires for implementation a large complement of expensive, fast-access files. In these circumstances, it is not surprising that the application of computers in the library has not proven to be cost-effective for the most part. Nor is it likely that the plea of many librarians for cheaper and more rational computational processes will be heeded because costs are not coming down by orders of the magnitude that is apparently needed to produce a viable mechanized process.

Thus, contrary to popular assumption, the library problem does not appear to be solvable by a superficial mechanization, one operation at a time, carried out separately in each individual library. Instead a change in administrative practice is needed first, and a good deal of justification exists for waiting with the introduction of computers until common standardized procedures can be introduced cooperatively into many different environments. When each item will be cataloged once only, instead of hundreds of times, and a given mechanized card catalog will prove acceptable for use by many organizations, instead of only by a single one, the existing cost projections may no longer apply and mechanized library housekeeping operations will have a much better chance of proving cost-effective than under present operational conditions.[30]

The second assumption relating to the introduction of computers in the library field states that *computers are not suitable for carrying out the content analysis operations required for document indexing and cataloging.* The arguments brought forward are based largely on sentiment rather than facts. Specifically, one demonstrates (correctly) that a complete semantic analysis of document texts cannot be carried out reliably by automatic means, and one concludes (falsely) that the resulting automatic indexing products are necessarily inferior to manual ones produced by trained catalogers or subject experts. In the process one forgets that manual indexing and cataloging products are also unreliable and that perfect performance, either manual or automatic, is not attainable in the library field. As Swanson points out: "though machines may never enjoy more than a partial success in library indexing, . . . people are even less promising."[31]

The available evidence, collected over the last ten to fifteen years, indicates that practically useful indexing products are obtainable fully automatically with comparatively little effort.[32] In the most recent comparison between a conventional, intellectual indexing process performed under controlled conditions by trained subject experts (MEDLARS) and an automatic term extraction process using document abstracts as the principal machine input (SMART), it was found that a deficiency in performance of 30 to 40 percent in recall and precision[33] produced by a raw, automatic term extraction process can be turned into an advantage of 15 to 30 percent in recall and precision over the conventional, manual process by using a variety of mechanized processing features for language normalization such as dictionaries generated fully automatically and partly automatic thesauruses, ranked document output in decreasing query-document similarity order, and interactive searching based on feedback information supplied by the user.[34]

In any case, the mechanization of content analysis and indexing operations should not automatically be excluded from the design of the future library.

The third assumption in the library mechanization area is that *a combination of standard library classification methods and inverted indexes of subject indicators and keywords are adequate for storage, searching, and retrieval.* Concerning first the standard library classifications, every available test result indicates that classificatory indexing languages—that is, languages in which hierarchical relations can be specified between terms—are unrewarding in a retrieval environment. In this connection, Keen says that "the theory is sound enough, but no way has been found to realize the benefits of classificatory languages in practice."[35] The evaluation results seem to indicate that the use of the hierarchical linkages for indexing purposes leads to an over-specification of document content, and that it is easier to supply any missing controls at the search stage in the form of a thesaurus or other language normalizing tools, or through interactive search methods, than to have them built into the indexing language.

Misgivings have also been voiced about the existing library classification systems in their role as links between catalog and the classified arrays of volumes, and as an aid in promoting browsing at the shelves. The main complaints relate to the static quality of most classification systems, the difficulties of updating and maintaining the schedules, and the need to classify a given item uniquely into the tree structure provided for that purpose.

While it is, of course, necessary to choose a sensible shelving arrangement—for example, by placing items dealing with a common subject area in adjacent positions in the library stacks—and to keep this reasonably fixed, there is no need to tie the shelving order to a hierarchically classified catalog. Instead, a flexible cataloging method can be used in which the classes are easily adjusted and items may be simultaneously entered into several overlapping classes. Moreover, the same class identifiers should be used for query formulation and for search and retrieval, as well as for the normal classification purposes.

It should be noted in this connection that the inverted file organization method, now considered standard for search and retrieval purposes, exhibits flaws somewhat similar to those inherent in the conventional library classification methods. An inverted file search is normally conducted by consulting an inverted directory which supplies for each index term acceptable to the system a list of references, or accession numbers, for all documents identified by the given term. The accession lists corresponding to the various query terms are then merged to reflect the correct query formulation, and the document citations for all items exhibiting the appropriate combination of terms are retrieved from a citation file. As usual for keyword retrieval systems, the retrieval process separates the collection into two parts, containing respectively the retrieved items—those identified by the appropriate term combination—and the rest which are not so identified. No ranking or order of preference is normally provided within either set, and each retrieved item is inherently considered to be as important as any other. Thus to obtain a desired level of performance in terms of recall and precision, it is necessary to find just the right kind of query formulation. For if the formulation is too broad, the retrieved set is likely to be very large, thereby imposing a great burden on the user and producing low precision even when the recall is fairly high; on the other hand, a narrow formulation is likely to restrict severely the level of recall which may be attained.

The main virtue of an inverted file search is the search speed, since it is normally necessary only to examine those file portions corresponding to index terms actually used in the query statement.

The disadvantages, however, of the standard Boolean searches used with inverted files are serious and varied and a reexamination of the normal search and retrieval methodology may well be needed:

a) an inverted file organization makes it difficult to vary the search depth so as to retrieve a greater or lesser amount of material, depending on user requirements; specifically, to obtain adequate performance variations, a user must be intimately familiar with the properties of the vocabulary and the effects to be obtained by adding and/or subtracting terms from the query statements, or by changing the Boolean formulation;

b) it is awkward to carry out "partial matches" between queries and documents so as to retrieve items that exhibit varying degrees of closeness with the Boolean search statement; while the construction of a set of nested subsearches can ideally produce the desired performance, the required multiple query formulations are difficult to generate for the average user;

c) the set of output documents cannot be presented to the user in ranked order, for example, in decreasing order of query-document similarity; instead a partial ranking must be simulated by using weighted query terms, and by listing the output in decreasing order of the matching term weights;

d) the indexing information attached to queries and documents cannot easily be changed in an inverted file organization, because the set of keywords belonging to any one item is scattered throughout the file and, in general, as many file accesses are needed to collect the full term set belonging to a given item as there are index terms attached to each document (to reach a decision even for selected term changes, the full term vectors are normally needed, as will be seen);

e) the index term vocabulary is difficult to change since the introduction of new terms or the deletion of old ones requires wholesale changes in file organization; for this reason, inverted file organizations invariably lead to quasi-static indexing systems.

The output of Table 1 exhibits partial results obtained in the previously referred to comparison between the conventional Boolean search environment used at MEDLARS, and the automatic SMART system.[36] It is seen that the "partial match" policy used by SMART (which utilizes a correlation coefficient ranging from 0 to 1 to reflect query-document similarity), followed by a ranking of the documents in strictly decreasing order of the similarity coefficient, improves the SMART output by about twenty percent in recall and precision.

This assessment is confirmed by Lancaster's evaluation studies of currently existing retrieval services, all of which operate with the conventional inverted file organization: "the use of Boolean algebra for querying computer-based retrieval systems may have been a mistake . . . arising through the similarity of early computer-based systems to systems employing edge-notched cards or the optical coincidence principle. . . . There was no possi-

TABLE 1
SMART-MEDLARS COMPARISON SHOWING
IMPORTANCE OF DOCUMENT RANKING
(450 documents, 29 queries, adapted from Salton)

	Analysis Method	Recall	Precision
MEDLARS	(controlled terms assigned by trained indexers)	0.3117	0.6110
SMART	(word stems extracted from abstracts; simulation of Boolean search)	0.1814 (−42%)	0.4141 (−32%)
SMART	(word stems using ranking feature, and displaying documents in decreasing query-document order)	0.2622 (−16%)	0.4901 (−19%)
SMART	(thesaurus consisting of groups of related terms, and using ranking feature)	0.3232 (+ 4%)	0.6106 (0%)

bility for partial match and the retrieval of lists of references ranked according to degree of match with the search strategy. Computer-based systems, on the other hand have no reason to be so restricted. . . ."[37]

Indeed they haven't, and the conclusion is that the standard storage organizations and retrieval strategies currently used in library and information centers for both classification and search and retrieval might usefully be replaced by more flexible methodologies affording the same search speeds without the accompanying disadvantages.

A last assumption currently popular in the library environment relates to the role of the library user in influencing systems and procedures. Specifically, it is taken for granted that *the library is user responsive in its service aspects* (for example, by acquiring items of interest to the user population, and by improving circulation and related services), *but users do not influence internal processes such as classification and indexing methods, storage organizations, or collection control methods.* That is, although the library lives in a dynamic environment characterized by a constant interaction with a changing user population, the feedback information which could potentially be secured from the users concerning various aspects of the collection processing is wholly ignored, and the users are insulated from the library environment, which moves with a momentum of its own, regardless of what happens around it.

The picture that emerges from the current assumptions regarding library software is one based on unproven assertions, and on habits stemming back to the days of punched-card technologies: that the clerical operations are the ones that can easily be mechanized; that intellectual operations must be carried out by humans; that current library file organizations have proven themselves; and, finally, that there is no place for user control over the internal library processing.

A new dynamic library environment is outlined in the next section in which clerical procedures are carried out cooperatively, while the intellectual search and retrieval and collection control operations are influenced by the user population. It is believed that the proposed system can alleviate the current library crisis without requiring an abandonment of books and journals, and without leading to dream situations that cannot be implemented under current conditions.

THE DYNAMIC LIBRARY

Basic Principles

The library processing should ideally be based on three main principles:

a) a "total" library system in which one basic input serves to initiate a chain of successive processing steps—the basic inputs undergoing successive modifications as a result of the various steps in the processing chain;[38]

b) the widest possible use of cooperative and shared operations, including collaborative or centralized acquisitions policies, shared cataloging, and standardized library housekeeping operations[39] and;

c) an adaptive environment in which the user population influences the main intellectual processes such as the indexing vocabulary and practices, the storage organization, the search and retrieval operations, and, finally, the collection control necessitated by document growth and retirement.[40]

Specifically, the mechanization of the basic input and housekeeping operations cannot be justified if performed separately in each individual organization. It should therefore be undertaken cooperatively and/or centrally, using the greatest possible degree of procedure standardization and work sharing. Ideally, the work might be performed on-line using real time procedures; however, the type of centralized off-line processing now inherent in the MARC tape distribution service is also most encouraging. It is already the case that fewer and fewer organizations now claim convincingly that their requirements are so specialized, and their user population so unusual, that a standardized process will not fit. One may hope that the developments in the direction of greater standardization and cooperation in the housekeeping area will continue to be pushed rapidly, because they constitute the best hope for an eventual improvement in the cost-benefit picture.

On the other hand, while the clerical input operations should be standardized, the collection management itself can certainly be handled by each library in accordance with its own environment. Not everyone must necessarily maintain the same file arrangement, nor must the same indexing vocabulary be used everywhere regardless of the orientation of the user population; and certainly, when the time comes to retire the less-used materials to an auxiliary store, each organization should use its own experience to decide what portion of the collection can best be demoted.

The dynamic system outlined in the next few paragraphs makes it possible for each library to be directly responsive to its user population, and overcomes the common failures which now arise from the use of static indexing and classification systems, the need to learn specialized, controlled indexing languages, and the lack of user-system interaction during information search and retrieval.

The main idea is to maintain the library cataloging system in a continuous state of flux. Documents are first tentatively indexed—hopefully automatically—by assigning to each item a set of weighted terms representing document content. These *term vectors* are then used automatically to classify the items into affinity groups, in such a way that items with similar vectors wind up in the same classes. During the processing, both query and document vectors are subjected to small changes—for example, by increasing or decreasing the weights of certain terms, or by adding a new term, or subtracting an old one. As the individual term vectors change, so will the document classification. In the end, a file is obtained in which "interesting" items wind up in the center of the file, whereas unwanted items wind up on the periphery.

The file organization and the main processing steps are described in the remainder of this study.[41]

Clustered File Organization

A *direct* file organization in which documents are not stored in subject order but in some random document order—for example, in chronological order of the acquisition dates would obviously not be suitable for library processing since subject or author searches would then require a complete match of every document with a search request, thereby producing excessively long search times. An *inverted* file, on the other hand, organized in order by permissible keywords leads to a static indexing system and inadequate search strategies. A *clustered file* organization is therefore recommended in which documents carrying somewhat similar content descriptions are automatically grouped into *clusters*.[42] Each cluster is identified by a representative cluster profile, or *centroid*, somewhat akin to the center of gravity of a set of mass points. A cluster centroid is simply a weighted set of terms, derived from the document vectors included in the corresponding cluster.

A clustered file is then similar in concept to a normal classified library file, except that the classes and the assignment of documents to classes are automatically generated, and that some overlap may exist between classes, that is, certain documents may be included in more than one class. A search in such a clustered file is carried out in several steps: each query is first compared with the index file of centroid vectors; for those centroids which exhibit a sufficiently high similarity with the query, the individual document vectors in the corresponding clusters are examined next, and the document citations are ranked for output purposes in decreasing query-document order, as previously explained.

It is clear that the "depth" of the search, as measured by the number of query-document comparisions, can be controlled in a clustered file, since it is possible to search only the "best" cluster—the one exhibiting the highest query-centroid similarity—or the top two clusters, or the top ten, as may be required. Moreover, since all document vectors and citations belonging to a given cluster are stored adjacently in the same storage area—for example, on the same track or cylinder of a given disc assembly—only one access operation is needed for each document cluster, as opposed to one access for each document citation in an inverted file.[43]

A detailed comparison of inverted and clustered file organizations comes to the conclusion that the clustered file is more economical of storage, leads to faster retrieval operations, and permits more flexible, feedback-type searches.[44] The one disadvantage of the clustered organization, namely the requirement to generate the clusters in the first place, is not as serious as might appear, because fairly inexpensive clustering methods are known which require of the order of n log n vector comparisons to cluster n document vectors (as opposed to n² comparisons for the conventional methods that are based on a comparison of each document vector with all others).[45]

Since the feedback searches and file reorganization methods are considered essential in future library processing systems, a clustered file organization is assumed in the remainder of this study.

Automatic Analysis with Dynamic Vocabulary

An automatic generation of document or query vectors must necessarily rely on the analysis of query and document texts. Normally, a term extraction process is used as a basis for all subsequent processing.[46] The following principal steps may be involved in a typical automatic word stem analysis and retrieval process:

a) the individual words included in document abstracts and in query texts are isolated;
b) certain words, such as function words listed in a negative dictionary, are removed from the document and query word lists;
c) one of two types of suffix cut-off procedures is used to reduce the word lists to word stem lists: the suffix "s" or the *word form* method removes only final "s" endings, and the regular *word stem* process cuts off all normal suffixes to produce word stems;
d) weights are assigned to the word stems based on the frequency of occurrence of the stems in the document abstracts or query formulations;
e) the resulting weighted word stem vectors representing documents and queries respectively are compared, and a correlation coefficient is computed for each query-document pair reflecting the similarity between the corresponding vectors;
f) document citations are presented to the user in decreasing order of the correlation coefficients.

It was seen in Table 1 that the retrieval effectiveness produced by such a system comes to within ten or fifteen percent of a conventional manual indexing system, assuming that the cluster search process and output ranking systems are properly used.

In order to obtain output that is completely comparable in effectiveness to systems using intellectual indexing, it is necessary to introduce some word control in the form of dictionaries or control lists. Two of the more useful tools in this connection are, first, the *word discrimination list* which identifies any term determined to be a common identifier, or nondiscriminator and, second, the *thesaurus* which specifies a grouping of thesaurus entries into affinity groups to provide synonym recognition.[47]

FIGURE 1
TYPICAL TERM-DOCUMENT MATRIX

	Term 1	Term 2		Term k
Doc. 1	$t_1^1, \; w_1^1;$	$t_2^1, \; w_2^1;$	. . . . ;	$t_k^1, \; w_k^1$
Doc. 2	$t_1^2, \; w_1^2;$	$t_2^2, \; w_2^2;$	. . . . ;	$t_k^2, \; w_k^2$
Doc. n	$t_1^n, \; w_1^n;$	$t_2^n, \; w_2^n;$	. . . . ;	$t_k^n, \; w_k^n$

t_j^i = term j in document i

w_j^i = weight of term j in document i

Both dictionaries can be constructed fully automatically by using the standard word stem vectors, representing the documents of a collection. A typical set of sample vectors is shown in matrix form in Figure 1. Using the matrix representation of Figure 1, it is possible to compute a similarity coefficient between any pair of documents by comparing the corresponding rows of the matrix. This process is, in fact, used as a basis for the document clustering process previously mentioned.

The same process is also used to generate the automatic term discrimination list. Specifically, a *nondiscriminator* is defined as a term which increases the interdocument similarity (that is, which increases the average similarity coefficient between pairs of rows in the matrix) when the corresponding term is incorporated in the normal document vectors; the contrary is true for discriminators, which reduce the interdocument similarity when used for indexing purposes. By computing for each term a document space density function or, equivalently, some measure of average document-pair similarity, it is easy to obtain *term discrimination values* that can be used as criteria for judging the goodness of each term for purposes of content representation.[48]

To construct an automatic thesaurus it is necessary to group those terms judged to be valuable as content indicators into affinity classes. Clearly, the same clustering methods that generate document classes from the document-pair similarity coefficients can construct term classes by using term-pair similarities. Instead of comparing the rows of the matrix of Figure 1 to judge the similarity among documents, one uses pairs of columns of the matrix to obtain the term similarities leading to the thesaurus classes.

In the dynamic retrieval environment to be described later, information obtained from the user population during the processing will eventually be reflected in changes in certain document vectors. As the rows of the matrix of Figure 1 are changed, so will the columns be altered. Thus, a change in document indexing leads to a similar change in the thesaurus organization.

A number of experiments were recently conducted to evaluate the operations of such a *dynamic thesaurus* and to determine how the thesaurus classes would change with time.[49] In particular, regular feedback searches to be described later were conducted using about 120 original user queries. The feedback operations were then used to modify the document-term matrix, and this in turn was utilized to produce new thesaurus classes. Thirty new user queries, not previously utilized in the feedback operations, were then processed both with the original and the final thesauruses, and a performance improvement of about four or five percent in recall and precision resulted for the new updated thesaurus.[50]

No fundamental difficulty appears to exist about the utilization of changes in vocabulary usage and in user interest to effect automatic alterations in the corresponding vocabulary control tools.

Feedback Searches in a Dynamic Library

The main idea behind the dynamic library file is the utilization of customer experience in improving service and updating the file organization. A principle contribution to such a dynamic system is the incorporation of user inputs in an effort to improve the formulation of search requests submitted by the user population. The preferred method of query alteration used with the SMART system is known as *relevance feedback,* because the queries are automatically updated based on relevance information furnished by the user about previously retrieved documents.[51] Specifically, the relevance feedback process assumes that an initial search is first performed for each query entering the system. A small amount of output, consisting of some of the highest scoring documents, is then presented to the user and the user is asked to identify some of these documents as being either relevant to his information need (R), or nonrelevant (S). These relevance judgments are then returned to the system and used automatically to adjust the search request in such a way that the query terms present in the relevant documents are promoted (by increasing their weight), whereas terms occurring in the nonrelevant documents are simultaneously demoted.

The R previously identified relevant documents and the S nonrelevant ones then serve to construct a new query formulation q' which may be expected to be more similar to the relevant, and less similar to the nonrelevant documents, than the original query q. If the terms from the relevant items are added to the search request, whereas terms from the nonrelevant are subtracted, the query updating which implements the relevance feedback operation can be represented by equation (1)

$$q' = q + \alpha \sum_{i \in R} r_i - \beta \sum_{j \in S} s_j \qquad (1)$$

where r_i is the ith document included in the relevant set R, s_j is the jth document included in the nonrelevant set S, and α and β are constants.

An evaluation of the relevance feedback process indicates that of the various interactive retrieval methods, relevance feedback produces the best results, while at the same time placing the least burden on the user.[52] When the relevance feedback process is applied to the medical collection previously used for the SMART-MEDLARS comparison of Table 1, the output of Table 2 is produced. It may be seen that after two feedback searches the SMART output is at least ten percent better than MEDLARS for the word stem analysis process, and twenty to thirty percent better when the thesaurus is used for analysis purposes. (No feedback procedures were used with MEDLARS; however, sophisticated relevance feedback methods are in any case not implementable either with the off-line MEDLARS system using sequential files, or with the on-line Medline service based on inverted files, since the full document indexing information is not easily obtainable for these file organizations.)

TABLE 2
SMART—MEDLARS COMPARISON USING FEEDBACK FEATURE
(450 documents, 29 queries; from Murray)

Analysis Method	Recall	Precision
MEDLARS (controlled terms)	0.3117	0.6110
SMART word stem		
0—initial search	0.2622 (−16%)	0.4901 (−19%)
1—iteration feedback	0.3235 (+ 4%)	0.6385 (+ 5%)
2—iteration feedback	0.3433 (+10%)	0.6892 (+13%)
SMART thesaurus		
0—initial search	0.3232 (+ 4%)	0.6106 (0%)
1—iteration feedback	0.3915 (+25%)	0.7427 (+18%)
2—iteration feedback	0.4029 (+29%)	0.7438 (+22%)

The previously described query alteration process is based on information obtained from the user population in the course of the normal retrieval process. No good reason exists, however, for not utilizing customer intelligence to help improve the document vectors themselves by promoting, so to speak, document representations about which the user has reported favorably, while similarly demoting the others.

Specifically, when a number of document citations retrieved in response to a given query are labelled by the user as "relevant," it is possible to render them more easily retrievable in the future by making each of them somewhat more similar to the query used to retrieve them. Similarly, retrieved documents labelled as nonrelevant are rendered less easily retrievable by being shifted away from the query. Hopefully, following a large number of such interactions, documents which are wanted by the users can be moved slowly into the active portion of the document space—that part in which a large number of user queries are concentrated, while items which are rejected are moved to the periphery from where, eventually, they may be discarded.

Brauen[53] had implemented and tested a document space modification process using the following strategy:

a) the document vector for an item identified as *relevant* during the feedback process is altered by adding query terms or incrementing the weights of terms jointly present in the document and query vectors; on the other hand, document terms absent from the query are decreased in importance by being assigned a lower weight;

b) similarly, for documents identified as *nonrelevant,* the document terms jointly included in the document and query vectors are reduced in weight, while document terms absent from the query are increased in weight.

In both cases, the assumption is that the query vectors represent active subject areas. Thus documents moved closer to the active queries are "promoted" by being placed closer to the centers of interest. The reverse is true for documents removed from the main query areas.

The procedure was tested by first using a set of 125 user queries to modify the given document space. A new set of 30 queries was then processed against the original document collection (prior to document vector modification), and also against the final, modified space, following the processing of the earlier 125 queries. The evaluation output shows that the 30 new users profited from the earlier user interaction, since the retrieval results with the new, modified space are improved by 3 percent in normalized recall, and 8 percent in normalized precision[54] over the results obtained with the orginal space.[55]

In a practical library environment the document space modification process may be considered to be a permanent feature of the file system: if the user population is fairly homogeneous, an equilibrium condition will be attained rapidly with most relevant items clustering around the corresponding query areas. As user interests shift, or new subjects become popular, the document organization will slowly change to take care of the new conditions.

If the user population is not sufficiently homogeneous, or if users submit "unusual" relevance judgments with which subsequent customers may disagree, no permanent damage should result from the document space modification, although a certain amount of "thrashing" will occur in that some items moved out to the periphery will come back in, and vice versa.

Obviously, when a large number of document vectors change as a function of incoming user queries, the corresponding document class (centroid) vectors will in time become ineffective as a representation of the altered documents. Several possible strategies can be used to update document centroids, including the addition of new and deletion of old terms from the centroids, or weight alterations in the existing terms. Eventually, as the number and magnitude of the document space alterations increases, it will become necessary to allow for a shifting of documents from cluster to cluster. Such a reclustering operation is envisaged in the next section.

Library Growth and Retirement[56]

The document vector modifications discussed up to now are performed in response to the normal query processing, the intention being to keep the collection updated with changes in user interests. There are, however, even more important reasons for insisting on a dynamic catalog environment, and these have to do with *collection growth and retirement*. For the most part, library and information center personnel are aware of the severity of the problems created by normal collection growth, and by the lack of viable retirement policies for journal issues and monographs. Unfortunately, the state-of-the-art is such that the inevitable response of library administrations faced with accelerating document growth rates is an insistence on additional buildings, funds, and personnel.

In the document environment stipulated in the present study, it is possible to institute document retirement policies based on actual experiences with the local user populations. Furthermore, new documents introduced into existing collections can be accommodated within the framework of the existing operations. Both the collection growth and retirement operations affect, initially, only the library files by keeping the catalog current, and removing to a secondary file obsolete items that clutter up the catalog and impede the search operations. Subsequently, the addition and/or deletion of catalog items may improve also the physical arrangement of the library shelves.

Consider first the question of *collection growth*. In the clustered environment, the principal question to be resolved concerns the manner of updating the clusters when new documents are introduced. The illustration of Figure 2 shows the two typical clusters on the left side of the figure. If new documents are simply added to the cluster identified by the closest centroid vectors, a situation similar to that illustrated in the center of Figure 2 results after some time. Eventually, it becomes necessary to generate completely new centroid vectors if an accurate representation of the collection is wanted. The results of the required reclustering operation are shown for the sample document space on the right-hand side of Figure 2.

In principle, it is desirable to reorganize the file as often as possible. In practice, the work involved in reclustering a sizeable file is considerable and alternative methods must be used whenever possible. Murray[57] finds that the normalized recall and precision figures decrease by about 4 percent for a 50 percent updating range (that is, when about 50 percent of the document vectors in the collection are modified once or are newly introduced), and that the loss increases to 8 percent for a 75 percent updating rate. Murray concludes that "enough decay in the file organization occurs with 25 to 50 percent updating to warrant a complete reclustering operation; the break even point is probably on the low side of this range."[58]

FIGURE 2
CLUSTER UPDATING WITH PROFILE ALTERATION
(new document addition)

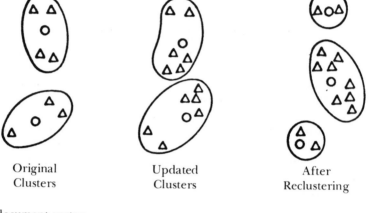

Original	Updated	After
Clusters	Clusters	Reclustering

△ document vector

○ cluster profile

Between reclustering operations the collection can be updated by suitable changes in the centroid vectors as new documents are introduced into the clusters. Three modes of centroid alteration appear possible:

a) new document vectors are associated with the best existing cluster (the cluster for which the centroid-document similarity is highest), but all centroid vectors remain unchanged;

b) new document vectors are associated with the existing clusters, and the centroids are changed by updating only existing centroid terms, that is, the weights of existing centroid terms may be altered, but no new terms added, thereby insuring a constant centroid dimension;

c) new documents are associated with the existing clusters, and the centroids are changed by updating the existing terms and introducing new terms taken from the documents added to the clusters.

To determine which of the centroid updating methods operates most satisfactorily, an experiment was performed by Kerchner[59] in which a collection of 700 documents in aerodynamics was augmented by a new set of 700 additional documents in the same subject area, thus accounting for a total updating rate of 50 percent for the complete collection. For each added document all 3 centroid updating methods were utilized, that is, no updating, updating of existing profile terms only, and updating of existing as well as addition of new terms. Furthermore, the organization of the collection was also regenerated by a complete reclustering procedure.

The output of Table 3 represents the average performance of fifty queries using each of the four document organizations. As expected for a fifty percent updating rate, the completely reclustered collection provides the best performance, and the unaltered profiles are least effective. Of the two centroid alteration methods, the one keeping a constant profile length is somewhat preferable, particularly for high recall values; it is, of course, also the preferred method from the viewpoint of storage space utilization.

TABLE 3
DOCUMENT PROFILE UPDATING FOLLOWING ADDITION OF NEW ITEMS
(1400 documents, 50 queries; adapted from Kerchner)

Precision / Recall	Original Space	Centroid Mod. 1 (updating of existing terms)	Centroid Mod. 2 (updating and addition of new terms)	Reclustered Space (addition of 700 documents)
0.1	0.3981	0.4234 (+ 6%)	0.4296 (+ 8%)	0.4313 (+ 8%)
0.3	0.2190	0.2432 (+11%)	0.2460 (+12%)	0.2631 (+20%)
0.5	0.1390	0.1547 (+11%)	0.1526 (+10%)	0.1408 (+ 1%)
0.7	0.0422	0.0458 (+ 9%)	0.0444 (+ 5%)	0.0717 (+70%)
0.9	0.0282	0.0287 (+ 2%)	0.0285 (+ 1%)	0.0388 (+38%)

One other collection growth policy deserves investigation, and that involves the maintenance of user *query-clusters*, in addition to the normal document clusters. Under this policy, incoming queries are clustered in a manner similar to the documents, each query cluster thus representing a composite user profile. New documents entering into the collection can then be matched against the existing query profiles (rather than the document profiles) before being assigned to the appropriate document clusters. Such a strategy remains to be fully investigated.[60]

Possibly the most important current problem in library management—one which has been attacked with remarkably little success—is the question of *document retirement*. By retirement is meant not a complete loss of an item, but merely its removal from the central file system—the one searched every time—to an auxiliary storage area which may be accessed only in special circumstances.

The classical approach to collection retirement consists in introducing concepts such as the *half-life* of a collection, that is, the time required for obsolescence of one-half of the currently published literature,[61] or the *utility* of a document in terms of the number of references that it can be expected to attract in its context during the remainder of its existence.[62] In each case, a short half-life, or a low utility factor, implies rapid obsolescence and, therefore potential retirement of an item. In order to translate concepts such as these into an active retirement policy, measurements must be made to be translated into an obsolescence threshold, and these measurements often cover one or more of the following forms: a count of the number of citations to a given item in the literature which post-date the item in question (e.g., the number of bibliographic references in later journal papers); the usage of a given item as measured by the number of times it is removed from the library shelf, or the length of the borrowing period when the item circulates; or the age of the item, that is, the number of years since it was first published. In each case, a low citation count, a small rate of usage, and high age lead to a high obsolescence figure.

Unfortunately, the approach based on measurements is difficult to implement, for practical purposes, because accurate values of these parameters (except for the age factor) are basically unobtainable. First of all, each measure depends on a specific library or user environment and the calculated values cannot be translated into other environments. Second, it is not clear what periods of observation and sample sizes are required in order to obtain reliable measurements.[63] Finally, for the technical literature, at least, it is important to distinguish the general scientific usage of a document from its historical usage (for survey and other retrospective purposes). Obviously, the rates of obsolescence are different for the two cases. In summary, a retirement policy based on measures which cannot accurately be determined is not likely to be successful.

A policy is therefore proposed which directly uses the dynamic document environment. Specifically, a generalized document vector modification policy is suggested based on the following three factors:

a) the closeness of a given document to the set of query centroids, measured by the size of the similarity coefficients between query centroids and the documents;
b) the rank of a given document in the list of retrieved items, whenever it is retrieved in response to a given user query;
c) the user response whenever a given document is retrieved, that is, the judgment which the user renders concerning its potential utility to his information needs.[64]

The idea is that documents located close to the centers of user interest (close to existing query sets), or retrieved with a low rank in response to a query (say in the top 50 documents), or known to be relevant to the users' needs, should be promoted by being shifted closer to the respective queries where user interest is concentrated; at the same time, documents which are far removed from the query sets, or which are retrieved with very high rank (in the bottom 50 for example), or which are known to be nonrelevant to the users' needs, are demoted by being shifted away from the current query positions. If such a policy is implemented correctly, it is clear that items which are never wanted, or which are always near the bottom of the retrieved list, will be shifted toward the periphery, away from the active part of the file, and will eventually become irretrievable. Simultaneously, documents which are promoted will become more easily retrievable in the future if new queries, similar to the currently active ones, should be received.

A number of problems will be met in such a dynamic retirement environment. First, it is important to pick adjustment parameters for the term weights that are large enough to make themselves felt eventually, but not so

FIGURE 3
SIMPLIFIED DOCUMENT RETIREMENT STRATEGY

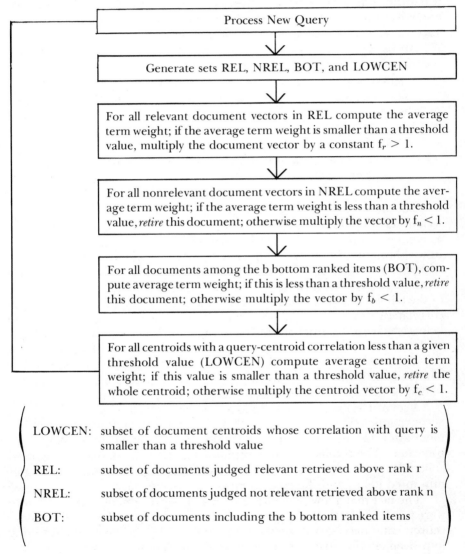

LOWCEN: subset of document centroids whose correlation with query is smaller than a threshold value

REL: subset of documents judged relevant retrieved above rank r

NREL: subset of documents judged not relevant retrieved above rank n

BOT: subset of documents including the b bottom ranked items high as to cause violent perturbations in the document space. In particular, it is likely that different adjustment rates must be used for items about which something specific is known; for example, in the form of a user relevance judgment, and for those which merely happen to be retrieved with high or low document ranks. This leads to the fast and slow increment functions which have been used successfully to update user profiles in certain information dissemination systems.[65] Second, when documents are demoted, that is, when the shift is away from a given item (rather than toward a specified area), it is necessary to take special precautions to prevent the "disappearance" of a vector, that is, the reduction of all term weights to zero.[66]

An experiment was recently performed in which the candidates for retirement were chosen from among the following sets:[67]

a) documents that are retrievable—that is, that exhibit a sufficiently high query-document correlation—but that are repeatedly judged to be nonrelevant;

b) documents that are not retrievable because the query-document correlation is too low;

c) document *clusters* that are never expanded, the corresponding documents never being matched against any query because the query-centroid correlations are too low.

The retirement policy actually implemented consisted of an up-weighting of relevant document vectors retrieved above a given rank r, up to a maximum value of the average term weight beyond which no further upweighting would occur; a downweighting of nonrelevant documents retrieved above rank n, down to a minimum value of the average document term weight, below which the document would be retired; a downweighting of the b bottom documents in the list ranked according to query-document correlation, down to a minimum value of the average document-term weight below which the document would be retired; and finally, a downweighting of all document *centroids* with a query-centroid correlation less than a threshold value, down to a minimum value of the average centroid term weight below which the centroid (and all included documents) would be retired. A simplified flowchart of the retirement policy is shown in Figure 3.

A set of 155 queries was used together with 424 clustered documents in aerodynamics. The particular strategy chosen for the test led to the retirement after 155 user responses of 24 documents—about 6 percent of the collection. The recall-precision output of Figure 4 shows that the reduced collection gives somewhat better results because of the downweighting of unwanted items, and the retirement of the useless ones.

The fact that a few percentage points of improvement in performance were produced by the retirement strategy is of course irrelevant. Document retirement is necessary in a library environment regardless of any resulting improvements in retrieval effectiveness. In fact, a reduction of collection size is desirable even when a loss in performance is produced, provided only that the loss can be kept within bounds. The results of Figure 4 shows the viability of the experimental automatic retirement policy which is being proposed.

More extensive experimentation is needed in the areas of document growth and retirement. The rate of retirement can be altered by parameter

FIGURE 4
RECALL-PRECISION COMPARISON OF ORIGINAL
COLLECTION (424 DOCUMENTS) AND MODIFIED ITEMS
FOLLOWING RETIREMENT (400 DOCUMENTS)

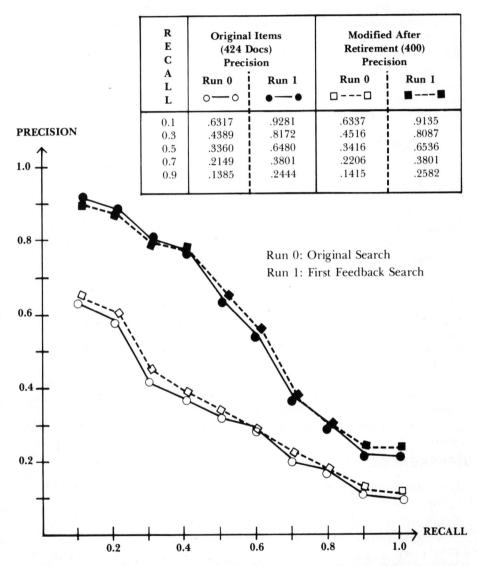

R E C A L L	Original Items (424 Docs) Precision		Modified After Retirement (400) Precision	
	Run 0 ○——○	Run 1 ●——●	Run 0 □---□	Run 1 ■---■
0.1	.6317	.9281	.6337	.9135
0.3	.4389	.8172	.4516	.8087
0.5	.3360	.6480	.3416	.6536
0.7	.2149	.3801	.2206	.3801
0.9	.1385	.2444	.1415	.2582

Run 0: Original Search
Run 1: First Feedback Search

variations, and the updating method of document and centroid vectors can be modified—for example, by shifting close to, or away from, the queries instead of multiplying the term weights by a constant parameter.

Still, a retirement policy appears feasible which is self-correcting in the sense that user input forms the basis for decisions concerning document promotions or demotions. As user opinions change, items that are suddenly needed but have been pushed out of the way can be rescued, or contrariwise, items found near the top can eventually be discarded. Moreover, the policy is implemented without computing or maintaining statistical data concerning age or utility of each document, so that the entire storage space gained through retirement can be utilitzed to accommodate collection growth. Finally, the retirement strategy produces gains in retrieval performance.

Eventually, appropriate cost studies will have to be made for the dynamic environment. Any dynamic file process will obviously require some apparatus (such as document vector modifications) not needed for static file management. On the other hand, the costs presently inherent in the maintenance of ever-growing files are large and the trained personnel, storage space, and new buildings are becoming scarcer. A self-monitoring, dynamic environment such as the one proposed may then be easier to justify than would appear, both economically and technically.

CONCLUSIONS

It may be time to discard the old assumptions and priorities in the library mechanization area. The static environment in which an item is cataloged for eternity and the user population contributes little to the efficiency of the procedures is not conducive to effective library management. Neither are the one-shot operations in which every organization goes off on its own, each one in a somewhat different direction. No amount of additional land, buildings, space, people, or money will solve the library problem, but a combination of new ideas and the rejection of old prejudices may.

In the present study, a new dynamic library file environment is proposed. It emphasizes procedures oriented toward the customer population, and generates for each organization a catalog organization optimized for its own user group. It does not require new technologies not now available, nor is it based on a replacement of the current information carriers (books and journals) by alternative, unproven products.

The dynamic environment should appeal to library users because services will be far more effective; it should also help librarians overcome the current operational crisis conditions and reduce the growing budget problems. It may constitute the best hope for a viable library system for the future.

REFERENCES

1. E. Mason, "Along the Academic Way," *Library Journal* (15 May 1971), pp. 1671–76.

2. *Libraries and Information Technology–A National System Challenge* (Washington: National Academy of Sciences, 1972).

3. B. E. Markuson, "An Overview of Library Systems and Automation," *Datamation* (February 1970); R. H. Parker, "Library Automation," in *Annual Review of Information Science and Technology,* vol 5, C. Cuadra, ed., *Encyclopedia Britannica* (Chicago, 1970); G. Salton, "On the Development of Libraries and Information Centers," *Library Journal* (15 October 1970), pp. 3433–3442; and R. A. Wall, "Computer Applications in Libraries," *Int. Journal of Math. Educ. in Science and Technology* 2:51–74 (1971).

4. R. W. Alexander and R. W. Harvey, "An Overview of the Experimental

Library Management System (ELMS)," Laboratory Report 16:197 (Los Gatos, Calif.: IBM-ASDD Division, May 1970).

5. T. Burgess and L. Ames, *Lola–Library On-Line Acquisitions Subsystem* (Pullman, Wash.: Wash. State Univ. Library, July 1968); and F. G. Spigai, and T. Mahan, "On-line Acquisitions by Lolita," *Journal of Library Automation* 3:4 (December 1970), pp. 276-294.

6. R. A. Kennedy, "Bell Laboratories Library Real-Time Loan System (Bellrel)," *Journal of Library Automation* 4:2 (June 1968), pp. 128-146.

7. J. S. Aagaard, "An Interactive Computer-based Circulation System: Design and Development," *Journal of Library Automation* 5:1 (March 1972), pp. 3-11.

8. G. D. Guthrie, "An On-Line Remote Catalog Access and Circulation Control System," Proc. ASIS National Meeting, Washington (1971), pp. 305-309.

9. J. L. Bennett, "On Line Access to Information: NSF as an Aid to the Indexer/Cataloger," *American Documentation* 20:3 (July 1969), pp. 213-220.

10. F. G. Kilgour, "Concept of an On-Line Computerized Library Catalog," *Journal of Library Automation* 3:1 (March 1970), pp. 1-11; C. T. Payne, and R. S. McGee, "The University of Chicago Bibliographic Data Processing System," Reports PB 195836 and PB 204205, Univ. of Chicago (October 1970 and April 1971); and A. H. Epstein, and A. B. Veaner, "A User's View of Ballots," Stanford University (June 1972).

11. *Libraries and Information Technology* . . . .

12. P. J. Fasana and A. Veaner, eds., *Collaborative Library Systems Development* (MIT Press, 1971); D. C. Weber and F. C. Lyndon, "Survey of Interlibrary Cooperation," in *Interlibrary Communications and Information Networks*, J. Becker, ed., (Chicago: American Library Association, 1971), pp. 69-81; and A. E. Jeffreys, "Centralized Services for University Libraries," in *Interface*, C. K. Balinforth and N. S. M. Cox, eds., (Oriel Press, 1971), pp. 115-125.

13. Kilgour, "Concept of an On-Line Computerized Library Catalog"; Payne and McGee, "The Univ. of Chicago Bibliographic Data Processing System"; Epstein and Veaner, "A User's View of Ballots"; R. McGee, and R. C. Miller, "MARC Utilization in the Univ. of Chicago Library Bibliographic Data Processing System," Eighth Annual Clinic on Library Applications of Data Processing, (Univ. of Illinois, April 1970); R. Bregzis, "The Univ. of Toronto MARC Pilot Project," in *Organization and Handling of Bibliographic Records by Computer*, N. S. M. Cox and M. W. Grose, eds., (Newcastle: Oriel Press Ltd., 1968); and F. G. Kilgour, "Computerized Cooperation," presented at the Annual Meeting of the Association of Research Libraries, Columbus (May 1972).

14. F. B. Ludington, "Hampshire Interlibrary Center," *ALA Bulletin* 46:10-11 (January 1952); and H. J. Harrar, "Cooperative Storage Warehouses," (Doctoral Dissertation, Rutgers University, June 1962).

15. J. G. Kemeny, "A Library for 2000 A.D.," in *Management and the Com-*

puter of the Future, M. Greengerger, ed., (MIT Press and John Wiley and Sons, 1962), pp. 134-179; J. C. R. Licklider, *Libraries of the Future* (MIT Press, 1965); and C. F. J. Overhage, "Project Intrex Planning Conference, Summary of Report," Woods Hole, (August 1965).

16. Licklider, *Libraries of the Future.*

17. *Ibid.*

18. Kemeny, "A Library for 2000 A.D."

19. Overhage, "Project Intrex Planning Conference. . . ."

20. Licklider, *Libraries of the Future.*

21. *Ibid.*

22. Kemeny, "A Library for 2000 A.D."

23. Overhage. "Project Intrex Planning Conference. . . ."

24. F. W. Lancaster, "The Cost Effectiveness Analysis of Information Retrieval and Dissemination Systems," *JASIS* (January/February 1971), pp. 22-27; and F. W. Lancaster, *Information Retrieval Systems–Characteristics, Testing and Evaluation* (Wiley, 1968), chap. 13.

25. S. Allen, S. Green, J. Friedman, B. E. Harrington, and L. R. Johnson, "Information Storage and Retrieval by Computer—An Emerging Problem for the Law of Copyright," in *Reader in Library Services and the Computer,* L. Kaplan, ed., (Microcard Editions, 1971), pp. 149-168; 1967 ABA Copyright Symposium, "Computers and Copyright: The New Technology and Revision of the Old Law," *Bulletin of the Copyright Society of America* 15:1 (October 1967); and R. P. Bigelow, "The Computer as a Copyright Infringer," *Law and Computer Technology* 1:7 (May 1968), pp. 2-5.

26. R. W. Conway, W. L. Maxwell, and H. L. Morgan, "On the Implementation of Security Measures in Information Systems," *Communications of the ACM* 15:4 (April 1972), pp. 211-220; R. M. Graham, "Protection in an Information Processing Utility," *Communications of the ACM* 11:5 (May 1968); L. J. Hoffman, "Computers and Privacy—A Survey," *Computing Surveys* 1:2 (June 1969), pp. 85-103; D. N. Michael, "Speculations on the Relation of the Computer to Individual Freedom and the Right to Privacy," *George Washington Law Review* 33:270-286 (1964); and A. Westin, *Privacy and Freedom* (New York: Atheneum, 1967).

27. *Libraries and Information Technology* . . . .

28. *Ibid.*

29. W. N. Locke, "Computer Costs for Large Libraries," *Datamation* (February 1970).

30. This statement is likely to prove correct, even though the local processing costs in each library are liable to be higher for a mechanized card catalog than for a conventional manual one.

31. D. R. Swanson, "Searching Natural Language Text by Computer," *Science* 132:1099-1104 (October 1960).

32. Swanson, "Searching Natural Language Text by Computer"; C. W. Cleverdon and E. M. Keen, "Factors Determining the Performance of Indexing Systems," Aslib-Cranfield Research Project Reports, vol. 1 and 2 (Cranfield, Eng., 1966); G. Salton and M. E. Lesk, "Computer Evaluation of Indexing and Text Processing," *Journal of the Association for Computing Machinery* 15:1 (January 1968), pp. 8-36; G. Salton, "Automatic Text Analysis," *Science* 168:335-343 (17 April 1970); and G. Salton, "A New Comparison Between Conventional Indexing (MEDLARS) and Text Processing (SMART), *Journal of the ASIS* 23:2 (March/April 1972), pp. 75-84.

33. *Recall* is the proportion of relevant material actually retrieved, while *precision* is the proportion of retrieved material actually relevant. Ideally, everything relevant is retrieved while at the same time everything extraneous is rejected, producing recall and precision values equal to one.

34. Salton, "A New Comparison between. . . ."

35. E. M. Keen, "Prospects for Classification Suggested by Evaluation Tests Carried Out 1957–70," in *Classification in the 1970's*, A. Maltby, ed., (Linnet Books and Clive Bingley, 1972), pp. 193-210.

36. Salton, "A New Comparison between . . . ."

37. F. W. Lancaster, "Evaluation of On-Line Searching in MEDLARS (AIM-TWX) by Biomedical Practitioners," Report no. 101, Univ. of Illinois Graduate School of Library Science, (February 1972). The utilization of Boolean algebra for the formulation of query statements, and the requirement to retrieve *all and only those* items containing the precise combination of requested keywords are intimately connected to the optical coincidence (peek-a-boo) search principle devised for inverted file organizations. In principle, a partially matching document exhibiting some imperfect degree of connectedness with a Boolean search query might be retrieved even from an inverted file, but this requires a much more complete search of the file than currently practiced, thereby giving up the main advantage of the inverted organization—its fast search characteristics. Lancaster's criticism should not then be directed so much at the Boolean algebra used for the query statements, which is incidental, as at the philosophy of retrieving all and only those items requested, and at the (inverted) file organization capable of supplying this output efficiently.

38. R. M. Hayes, "The Concept of an On-Line, Total Library System," Library Technology Reports, American Library Association, May 1965.

39. Fasana and Veaner, *Collaborative Library Systems Development;* Weber and Lyndon, "Survey of Interlibrary Cooperation"; Jeffreys, "Centralized Services for University Librarians"; McGee and Miller, "MARC Utilization . . . "; Bregzis, "The Univ. of Toronto MARC Pilot Project"; Kilgour, "Computerized Cooperation"; Ludington, "Hampshire Inter-Library Center"; and Harrar, "Cooperative Storage Warehouses."

40. G. Salton, "Dynamic Document Processing," *Communications of the ACM* 15:7 (July 1972).

41. It should be understood that the dynamic operations described in the remainder of this study are applicable to the organization and processing of the mechanized catalog files, and to the software aids used in obtaining access to the stored items. The physical arrangement of books on shelves need not be affected, except of course for the addition of new items, and the removal to remote storage of items designated for retirement.

42. G. Salton, *The SMART System–Experiments in Automatic Document Processing* (Englewood Cliffs, N.J.: Prentice Hall, 1971), chaps. 10-13; and D. M. Murray, "Document Retrieval Based on Clustered Files," (Doctoral Dissertation, Cornell Univ., Scientific Report no. ISR-20, Dept. of Computer Science, June 1972). Murray has undertaken a detailed comparison of the main classes of file organization, including sequential, chained, calculated access, inverted, and clustered files. Sequential and chained files do not provide sufficiently fast access for on line operations, while calculated access methods are difficult to implement successfully for large files. Inverted and clustered files are therefore of most immediate interest in a retrieval environment.

43. The access is needed in an inverted file for a complete list of documents indexed by the same term, followed by one access per document citation for those items for which the full bibliographic information is needed.

44. Murray, "Document Retrieval Based On Clustered Files."

45. Salton, *The SMART System* . . . ; and D. B. Johnson and J. M. Lafuente, "A Controlled Single-Pass Classification Logarithm with Application to Multi-level Clustering," Scientific Report No. ISR-18, sec. XII, Dept. of Computer Science, Cornell Univ., (October 1970).

46. Cleverdon and Keen, "Factors Determining the Performance of Indexing Systems"; Salton and Lesk, "Computer Evaluation of Indexing and Text Processing"; Salton, "Automatic Text Analysis"; and Salton, "A New Comparison between. . . ."

47. Salton, "A New Comparison between. . . ."

48. *Ibid.;* K. Bonwit and J. Aste Tonsman, "Negative Dictionaries," Scientific Report no. ISR-18, sec. VI, Cornell Univ., Dept. of Computer Science, (October 1970); and G. Salton, "Experiments in Automatic Thesaurus Construction for Information Retrieval," Proc. IFIP Congress-71 (Amsterdam: North Holland Publishing Co., 1972).

49. K. Hamilton and J. Leslie, "Thesaurus Class Modification Based on User Feedback," Scientific Report no. ISR-21, Dept. of Computer Science, Cornell Univ., (1972); and A. Wong, R. Peck, and A. van der Meulen, "An Adaptive Dictionary in a Feedback Environment," Scientific Report no. ISR-21, Dept. of Computer Science, Cornell Univ., (1972).

50. Hamilton and Leslie, "Thesaurus Class Modification. . . ."

51. Salton, *The SMART System* . . .; and G. Salton, *Automatic Information Organization and Retrieval* (New York: McGraw-Hill, 1968).

52. G. Salton, "The Performance of Interactive Information Retrieval," *Information Processing Letters* 1:35-41 (1971).

53. T. L. Brauen, "Document Vector Modification," in *The SMART Retrieval System–Experiments in Automatic Document Processing,* G. Salton, ed., (Englewood Cliffs, N.J.: Prentice Hall, 1971), chap. 24, pp. 456-484.

54. Normalized recall and precision are global measures derived from the standard recall and precision parameters, (Salton, *Automatic Information Organization and Retrieval*).

55. Brauen, "Document Vector Modification."

56. Some of the experiments examined in this section are described in more detail in reference (Salton, "Dynamic Document Processing").

57. Murray, "Document Retrieval Based on Clustered Files."

58. *Ibid.*

59. M. D. Kerchner, "Dynamic Document Processing in Clustered Collections," (Doctoral Dissertation, Scientific Report no. ISR-19, Dept. of Computer Science, Cornell Univ., October 1971).

60. V. R. Lesser, "A Modified Two-Level Search Logarithm Using Request Clustering," Scientific Report no. ISR-11, sec. VII, Dept. of Computer Science, Cornell University, (June 1966); and S. Worona, "Query Clustering in a Large Document Space," in *The SMART Retrieval System– Experiments in Automatic Document Processing,* G. Salton, ed., (Englewood Cliffs, N.J.: Prentice Hall), chap. 13, pp. 298-310.

61. R. E. Burton and R. W. Kebler, "The Half-life of Some Scientific and Technical Literatures," *American Documentation* 11:18-22 (1960); A. Sandison, "The Use of Older Literature and Its Obsolescence," *Journal of Documentation* 27:3 (September 1971), pp. 167-183; and R. S. Grant, "Predicting the Need for Multiple Copies of Books," *Journal of Library Automation* 4:2 (June 1971).

62. B. C. Brookes, "Obsolescence of Special Library Periodicals: Sampling Errors and Utility Contours," *Journal of the ASIS* (September/October 1970), pp. 320-329; and B. C. Brookes, "The Growth, Utility and Obsolescence of Scientific Periodical Literature," *Journal of Documentation* 26:4 (December 1970), pp. 283-294.

63. A. K. Jain, "Sampling In-Library Book Use," *Journal of the ASIS* 2:3 (May/June 1972), pp. 150-155.

64. Such a policy judges not only document obsolescence but also document quality, because negative user responses may imply that the documents are useless rather than obsolete.

65. C. R. Sage, R. R. Anderson, and D. R. Fitzwater, "Adaptive Information Dissemination," *American Documentation* 16:3 (July 1965), pp. 185-200.

66. J. Kelly, "Negative Response Relevance Feedback," in *The SMART Retrieval System–Experiments in Automatic Document Processing,* G. Salton, ed., chap. 20, pp. 403-411.

67. K. C. Tai and C. S. Yang, "Document Retirement in Automatic Retrieval Systems," Scientific Report no. ISR-21, Dept. of Computer Science, Cornell Univ., (1972).

Libraries in the Information Marketplace

by Kas Kalba

Public libraries have traditionally defined their mission as distinct from the commercial marketplace. They have strived to fulfill information needs that for one reason or another could not be met by the private sector. In practice, this has meant providing free access to a greater collection of print materials than would otherwise be available to most citizens. More recently, libraries have sought to expand their service offerings in new directions, including audiovisual programming, specialized collections, information and referral services, and the online retrieval of citations and abstracts.

But in the process of seeking new ways to remain viable, public (and often other) libraries have paid insufficient attention to developments in the information marketplace. These developments, as the following analysis will attempt to show, have in many instances rendered traditional library services obsolescent. And they once again raise the question of what role libraries should assume in relation to the private sector. Should libraries imitate marketplace innovations? Should they take the lead in certain areas? Or should they recognize that in a society and economy increasingly preoccupied with information activities, their own function is bound to decline?

To take a first step in answering these questions, one must walk a thousand miles (to invert a Chinese proverb). Specifically, it is important to understand the burgeoning array of information services that have come into being over the past two or three decades—their statistical parameters, their produce and service characteristics, and their relationship to societal and consumer requirements. This will be the purpose of the following analysis of library functions in the information marketplace.

THE INFORMATION MARKETPLACE

Let me begin the analysis by reviewing a few recent statistics on how much individuals, businesses, and government agencies spend on information services in the United States. For example, in 1973, 3.5 billion dollars was spent on broadcast television, another half a billion on cable TV, and 1.5 billion dollars on radio. 8.3 billion dollars was spent on newspapers, 4.1 billion dollars on books, and 3.7 billion dollars on periodicals.

But these expenditures are only the tip of the iceberg—the most manifest forms of information consumption in our society. A whopping 25.5 billion dollars was spent on telephone services, 8.3 billion dollars on postal services, and over 3.7 billion dollars in computer software. Over 50 billion dollars was spent on marketing and advertising and almost 90 billion dollars on schools and educational institutions.

In fact, if one adds up the revenues of all of the information industries, including motion pictures, telegraph, business consulting, research and development, federal information services, and others, the total figure for 1973 is over 300 billion dollars, and this climbs even further, to over 500 billion dollars, if one adds on banking, insurance, and legal activities, the bulk of which are, after all, highly specialized information services of one kind or another. These 300 and 500 billion dollar figures can be compared to a GNP for 1973 of 1,294.9 billion dollars.[1]

Given the added fact that the information industries have grown more than twice as fast as GNP during recent years, we are led to conclude that our economy is rapidly moving from a manufacturing base to an information base. In fact, the emergence of a broad information sector is emphasized even more, if we look at labor statistics. One recent study projects that by 1980 some 55 percent of the labor force will be working in the information industries.[2]

What does the emergence of this information sector mean for us as a society? And what does it mean for libraries?

At the societal scale, it is clear that the mining, processing, distribution, warehousing and retailing of information resources is becoming as important to our social and economic livelihood as the production of goods, oil included. Conversely, the consumption of information by individuals and organizations may soon surpass the consumption of products or raw materials as a national pastime. In short, the generation and application of information has become a complex and elaborate socioeconomic process, far removed from the time when information was conveyed primarily within the family circle or village square, with the occasional intervention of a scribe or oral historian.

The emergence of the professions; our immersion in radio and television; the growth of bureaucracy and the computer industry; our credit card-filled wallets; the rising costs of postage and the paper shortage; our dependence for retail information on newspaper ads and the yellow pages; the space-shrinking impact of satellite communications; and our increasing acceptance of higher and continuing education, are all manifestations of the information marketplace that is being created.

What are the societal implications of these developments? This is hard to predict. The information experts are themselves in disagreement. For example, Japan's Yoneji Masuda predicts that advanced industrial societies are on the verge of a utopian age, where voluntary information-based communities will constitute the core of a new global social system. By contrast, others such as France's Jean Voge, argue that we may be reaching a point of economic and social stalemate, since productivity in advanced economies can only decline as the manufacturing sector itself declines.

LIBRARIES UNDER COMPETITION

In other words, the jury is still out on how the growth of information services will affect our overall economy and society. But the impact of this growth on libraries is easier to detect. All one needs to do is compare the status of libraries in earlier times with their current state.

At one point, libraries constituted the only available multi-purpose information marketplace. Then, along with education, they became one of several major information sectors, coexisting peacefully, on the one hand, with the *consumer-information sector,* as represented by newspapers, television, telephone and entertainment services, and, on the other, with the *corporate information sector* of computer software, marketing, management consulting and financial services. It was at this stage that libraries began to define their function as distinct from commercial information services.

But now, and probably increasingly so in the future, libraries find themselves in a statistical quandry; for as the numbers indicate, libraries represent, in revenue terms, less than one percent of today's information marketplace. (I am comparing here the 3.5 billion dollars of expenditures for libraries every year to the 300+ or 500+ billion dollars for the information sector as a whole.) If they continue to consider themselves distinct from commercial services, they must accept a declining role in the information marketplace. Or, if they wish to remain in the mainstream of information delivery, they must recognize that they are now competing for revenues not only with school libraries, newspapers, consultants, and universities, but also information brokers, government data banks, information and referral services, newsletters and special-interest magazines, online information retrieval systems, suppliers of films and audiotapes, computer and microfiche storage systems, telephone hotlines, all-news radio stations, professional and technical conferences and, perhaps most painfully, with the Xerox® machine and Sesame Street.

I would only add that ironically the very factors that preserved the institutional credibility of libraries in the past may now be acting to undermine library survival. Libraries have traditionally served as one-stop information supermarkets. They served the needs of diverse users in diverse subject areas. More importantly, they were proficient in a variety of information functions: information procurement, indexing, storage, retrieval, and circulation, to mention only the most obvious ones. However, as the need for information services in our society has become more pervasive, immediate, and complex, newcomers to the information marketplace have challenged the library's traditional role.

One such challenge arose because the library, despite its multi-purpose character, placed two specific constraints on its clientele, namely, functional literacy and physical proximity, restrictions which radio and television have avoided.

Another challenge has come from the growing need for, and application of, scientific, technical and business information. Without budgetary windfalls, it has simply become impossible for the average public library and often even the research library, to acquire and process the growing volume of scientific knowledge. The assembly-line procurement, indexing and shelving of books and magazines, which was perfectly adequate in early days, has become much too slow to satisfy the information needs of most specialized users. Today's specialized user first finds out about research results at a professional association meeting or even earlier, if he or she is on the author's mailing list for preliminary drafts or progress reports. By contrast, formal publication may follow the professional conference by six months to two years, with the library then taking another one or two years to order the publication and make it available to its users. By the time the specialized user obtains research results from the library (i.e., three or four years late), they have, more likely than not, been outdated by subsequent studies, given the rapid turnover of scientific knowledge.

The result of this knowledge explosion has been the rise of more specialized libraries in universities, within industrial R & D Labs, and at special government centers—all of which operate outside of the traditional public library structure; along with the proliferation of professional and scientific meetings, specialized newsletters, and special-purpose information banks, including online information retrieval services.

Finally, the library has been challenged by new specialized information services aimed at the general public. While, in theory, the general public should be able to obtain relevant occupational, political, consumer, and leisure-related information from the library, the growing need for specialized information in everyday life, whether in dealing with medical problems, learning a new sport, or coping with government codes and regulations, has spawned a variety of new information services from specialized consumer magazines to telephone-based hotlines. What these sources offer the consumer is greater convenience, specificity, timeliness and/or choice of information than provided by most libraries.

In sum, the library, to the extent that it is to be judged in marketplace terms, has not fared well; it has not maintained its market share. Paradoxically, as the very marketplace it was organized to serve—the information marketplace—expanded in size and complexity, it has been outpaced by a host of new information suppliers and services. This conclusion, in turn, raises questions concerning the future of libraries in America, particularly those that are continuing to provide a diversity of services to a diverse clientele. But before addressing these future prospects, it may be useful to examine in more specific terms several competitors to the library.

The examples I will focus on are three relatively new sources of information: special interest magazines, online retrieval services, and the so-called "information brokers." In my opinion, each presents some useful lessons for the library that is searching for survival amidst frozen budgets, apathetic customers, and the intense competition of the information marketplace.

SPECIAL-INTEREST MAGAZINES

By definition, special interest magazines are those that appeal to a narrower segment of the magazine public than general interest magazines. But, in practice, the distinction between special and general interest publications is harder to make. The problem is that some "special interests" may be pursued by virtually the entire population. Is *TV Guide* a special interest magazine? Can *Money* Magazine claim the special interest label? For promotional purposes, *Money* does. Some of its promotional materials refer to it as "the special interest magazine that's of special interest to everyone." *Time*, when its circulation was under 20,000, was probably also considered a special interest magazine.

The point is that labelling a publication "special interest" is largely subjective. One would have to ask a variety of people whether they consider a magazine to be specialized before making a reasonable judgment. This, in fact, is what was recently accomplished in a study of some 45 magazines. The results that were compiled in this way showed that what readers perceive is a spectrum of magazines running from the most general to the most specialized; specifically, from *Reader's Digest* and *Newsweek* and *Good Housekeeping* and *The New Yorker* or *Modern Romance* to *Business Week* and *Rolling Stone* and *Psychology Today* and, finally, to *Gourmet, High Fidelity, Wilderness Camping* and *Railroad Magazine*.[3]

More generally, we should note that most special interest magazines divide the public by sex (such as *Ms, Viva, Gentlemen's Quarterly*), age (e.g., *Cricket, Silver Foxes*), occupation (*MBA, Firehouse*), life style (e.g., *Career Woman, Cruising World, Suburban Singles*), or by ethnicity, locality, or hobbies and leisure pursuits. (For example, over 20 magazines now cover citizens band radio.) Beyond this there are the subspecialties and subsubspecialties, for instance *The Texas Fisherman, Texas Bass Fisherman, Second House Guide, Arabian Horse News* (and its competitor *Arabian Horse World*), and *International Flying Farmer*.

This explosion of special interest magazines is a very recent phenomenon. In earlier days, and by this I mean as late as the 1960's, libraries, along with book stores, were privileged sources of special interest information, at least insofar as the average consumer was concerned. Then came the paperback book and special interest magazines. As consumers gained time, affluence and education to pursue special interests, whether gourmet cooking, tennis, or hi-fi systems, magazine publishers recognized that they could support the pursuit of these special interests by direct mail, and advertisers, seeking more focused demographic or psychographic markets, agreed to help them out.

A recent study of thirteen special interest magazines, from *Hot Rod* to *National Review*, shows that their average circulation rates per issue rose 88.4 percent between 1963 and 1973 and that the percentage of sales handled through subscriptions (rather than newsstands) rose from 48.8 percent to 73.3 percent during the same period.[4] By comparison, a parallel sample of general interest magazines, including *Family Circle, TV Guide, Playboy*, and *Newsweek*, exhibited only 55.3 percent growth during the same ten years and continued to rely on the newsstand or supermarket counter as their principal distribution channel. It should be added that the mass magazine sample did not include *Look* or *Life*, whose termination during this period contributed to a minimal 15 percent in growth in circulation for the general circulation magazine market as a whole.[5]

What do these trends imply about the growth of specialized information services? First, they indicate that a new market does exist and that it is a consumer (and not only institutional) market. Second, with the exception of regional publications such as *Boston Magazine,* or *Texas Monthly,* or *New West,* that the market is best organized at the national level. Most special interest magazines with circulations from 30,000 to 300,000 could not aggregate enough subscribers on a regional or local level to be viable. Third, that the principal and often unstated selling point of special interest magazines is the convenience they provide the consumer compared to other sources of specialized information. They deliver directly to the home; they provide regular updating of information; and they offer the consumer readability as well as choice of relevant information, given the different types of information (e.g., feature stories, how-to articles, special columns, ads, and book reviews) that most special interest magazines cover.

From a financial viewpoint, the viability of special interest magazines is based on their ability to aggregate isolated *afficionados* of a particular subject or activity into a national market, often with considerable subsidization by advertisers. But from a service perspective, the key characteristic of special interest magazines is *convenience.* This, in effect, is the key difference between the marketplace of magazine publishing and that of libraries. The one offers convenience at a cost, the other access (to a far greater volume of information) at no nominal cost whatsoever. It would seem that libraries should have nothing to worry about. Yet in assessing the trade-offs between going to a library several times a year to read special-interest publications (including the travel time, parking time, gasoline cost, adherence to library schedules, and time lost for actually engaging in the activity that is to be read about) and paying, on the average, about eight dollars a year for the subscription, most consumers choose the latter opportunity. Convenience makes the difference.

ONLINE RETRIEVAL SYSTEMS

Convenience does not necessarily make the difference in my second example of a new information marketplace. The online retrieval services that exist today are essentially in the accessing business rather than the convenience business. What they offer is rapid access to citations and abstracts from a particular data base. To the extent that they reduce or eliminate the need for searching through card catalogs, journal citations, and bibliographies, they do provide convenience. But their main service is to help institutional users identify relevant information sources in the face of the scientific and technical information explosion.

The majority of existing online retrieval services provide citation searches in specialized fields such as engineering, chemistry, psychology, medicine, and law. However, the services vary in their degree of comprehensiveness, which simply depends on how the data base that they access has been assembled. In some cases, several data bases may need to be searched and this can involve the use of several retrieval services, each employing a separate protocol, each storing information in a different manner and each charging a separate fee.

In addition, once all the potentially relevant citations have been assembled—and "all" can mean several hundred—the user is still left with the problem of deciding which ones are the most important for his or her purposes and how to track down the source documents. This is no easy task, although the increasing online availability of abstracts, as well as citations, is at least reducing the sorting problem.

Finally, from the viewpoint of the suppliers of online information retrieval services, the absence of clearcut copyright rules for computer-based intellectual property often limits, or at best complicates and confuses, the collection of relevant data inputs.

A copyright law is intended to protect the rights of the author of an original manuscript at the point where it is copied. But, as my partner in Kalba Bowen Associates, Anne Branscomb, has often asked, who is the author in the case of scientific content that is available online? Is it the scientist, the government or private sponsor of his or her research, the system designer, the author of the abstract, the service provider, the computer programmer, the user, or who? What is the *original,* when updating of computer-based content can occur frequently, and what is a copy, when only a small portion of the "original" can be accessed? And what is fair use?[6]

In short, convenience has not, to date, proven to be the mainstay of online retrieval services, neither for the supplier nor the user. *If* the user knows exactly what information is being sought; *if* he knows what online data base to find it in; *if* he knows how to translate the information request into the language and protocol of the retrieval system; *if* the information is not bound by copyright restrictions and has been stored in the data base being accessed; and *if* the user knows where to find what the outpouring of citations and abstracts will indicate are potentially important, then the online service can be a convenience. But these are a lot of *ifs.*

In that case, why are online retrieval services proliferating so rapidly? What are they offering that libraries do not? In my judgment, they represent, primarily, a response to the increasingly perishable nature of scientific and technical information. As the effective lifespan of this information is shortened due to the volume of scientific and technical information that is being produced, libraries—even large research libraries—can no longer acquire and process specialized information rapidly enough for it to be of value to the user once it becomes available through this traditional channel. The fact that much of the sought-after information is a journal article or a report released through a non-traditional publishing channel (e.g., the mimeograph machine of a research laboratory in Tucson, Arizona) made the library acquisition and indexing problem so much more severe. Consequently, for the user who can put up with the various inconveniences, online retrieval services do facilitate access to relevant information before it joins the data burial ground of our knowledge-obsessed society.

INFORMATION BROKERS

This brings me to my third and final example of the new information marketplace that libraries are faced with: the information broker. The concept of an information broker was first introduced in France in the 1940's by S'il Vous Plait, a firm that provided businesses with quick responses to telephone inquiries on a monthly subscription basis. (However, I am told by Carroll Bowen that the Budapest Telephone Newspaper, a similar service, operated in Hungary as early as 1923.) Curiously, it has taken several decades for the formal idea of an information broker to catch hold in the United States. But now, most major metropolitan areas have at least one commercial information broker, operating under such names as Find/SVP (the French firm's domestic licensee), Information Resources, Information Unlimited, and Packaged Facts.

What do information brokers do? The answer is a multitude of things. They finger through reference books to provide quick answers to quick questions. They compile statistics, mailing lists, and abstracts. They research specific topics from the state of the plastics industry in Denmark to the distribution of clothing retail outlets in Denver. They provide current awareness services. They access multiple citation indices and online retrieval systems to assemble comprehensive, yet customized, bibliographies. They retrieve source documents. They help clients organize their own information files. And, in some cases, they also provide consulting, market research, and/or translation services.

But the key service they provide is rapid, customized, one-stop information brokerage. As Andrew P. Garvin, the chairman of Find/SVP has put it: "We refer to ourselves as a one-stop, information-on-demand service. We're one-stop because whether our clients need a quick fact, specific data, or in-depth research, they can go to just one source . . . . We're information-on-demand because . . . (when) our clients have any kind of information need, all they have to do is call us, state their question, and we immediately go to work on the assignment."[7] This sounds almost like a library.

Of course, the information broker business is not really as simple as that. The client's information need first has to be understood, a process that often involves several contacts, not to mention negotiation. Second, the brokerage firm has to have the requisite talents and resources to fulfill the request. And third, to do an effective job in answering a given question, it has to cope with the queuing up of requests—if it is a successful firm—which is very much what a busy library reference desk contends with.

Nonetheless, information brokerage firms are at least surviving, if not prospering. They do so because they reduce the library queuing problem; because they provide customized responses at several levels of detail; because they are one-stop for the kinds of information that one might ordinarily have to consult a directory, a market research firm, and a scientific data base for; and because they provide, in some cases, a less expensive way of retrieving specialized information than setting up an in-house information unit. In fact, in many respects, they survive by doing what libraries have traditionally claimed they could do; although, in practice, the differences between information brokers and libraries may be more instructive than the similarities.

The most obvious difference is that information brokers cater primarily to business clients, who pay directly for the services involved, rather than to the general public, which pays through taxes. Beyond this, information broker firms are less likely to stockpile information: books, periodicals, files, etc., unless they know they will utilize this information and can't access it easily somewhere else. This also makes it possible to organize and re-organize stored information along problem- or market-centered categories rather than on the basis of an unchanging Dewey Decimal System or other architectonic classification scheme, and, much more than libraries, they depend on rapid access to external information sources. For example, Find/SVP supplements its core staff capabilities with part-time researchers; outside consultants; a dozen outgoing WATS lines for contacting trade groups, research centers, government agencies, and other sources of expertise; and access to 30 computerized data bases and some 200 libraries (the latter, still apparently being a good free source of information).[8]

Finally, two other distinctions are pertinent. One is that information brokers promote their services extensively, whether by means of direct mail, radio and magazine advertising, conference exhibits, directory listings, or word-of-mouth. The second is that their employment policies are more entrepreneurial. They seek individuals who are curious, imaginative, and self-starters, and not necessarily only those with formal library training. Marketing or writing skills, for example, are often valued as highly as indexing.

While I cannot document the fact, I suspect that if a budgetary comparison were made between libraries and information broker firms, the latter would have proportionately higher marketing expenses, but lower administrative overhead than the former. Correspondingly, the brokerage firm's expense for computer time and telephone would be higher than the library's, while its costs associated with acquiring information materials for in-house storage would be lower.

In summary, information brokers are doing what some have argued libraries should be doing, and they are surviving by providing their services to relatively prosperous clients on a fee-for-service basis.

LIBRARY RESPONSES TO COMPETITION

Having reviewed several recent developments in the information marketplace, let me now attempt to draw some generalizations concerning the present and future course of public libraries. Let me begin by returning to the original goals of the public library, whose mission, traditionally, was to increase access to information in a society that had not yet accepted formal information as a basic ingredient of social, economic, and cultural life.

This was in the nineteenth century. Now, a hundred or more years later, the everyday dependence on information has infiltrated our social fabric. At the same time, the fulfillment of this social dependence on information has far outpaced our library resources and capabilities. The general public's regular diet of news and current affairs information, consumer information, career and employment information, government services information, or legal information, is not being served by libraries, but instead by television, radio, newspapers, magazines, commercially-distributed books, and by specialized or professional information sources. By contrast, today's public libraries are serving segments of the public primarily in the areas of general fiction and non-fiction, history, general reference materials, and education-related books.[9] In many respects, the public library has become a residual distribution system for those individuals who cannot afford book club memberships or discount book store prices, and a supportive service for local schools, and even this latter role is being reduced as schools invest more heavily in library resources. The only unique marketplace the public library seems to retain is as a source of materials about local history, a market that, because of its geographical confines, the special interest magazine has not sought to penetrate—and a market that is a stark caricature of the public need that libraries were initially constituted to serve.

In a recent study of the *Information Needs of Urban Residents,* it was found that, "only three percent of respondents overall used a library to obtain information on their most important problems."[10] Clearly, this kind of demoralizing statistic is not news to the administrators and staff of public libraries. The message that libraries are trying to play a catch-up game rather than acting as a vanguard in the information society hits home almost every time libraries ask for budget increases, launch membership drives, or compete for employees with the private sector. Nor, on the other hand, have public libraries remained dormant in the face of user apathy and market competition. Selectively, at least they have attempted to institute new programs, from bookmobiles to reference answering services; to take on expanded functions such as outreach and information and referral; to accept new technology, including video cassettes and the use of local cable television; and even to reduce their self-reliance through networking with other libraries by mail, teletype or online access to information retrieval systems.

Take, for example, the attempt to introduce online retrieval services into four public branch libraries in California, the so-called *Dialib* program. This program attracted not only a considerable amount of press attention (and often press hyperbole, since the media still gets carried away with anything involving computers), but also a fair amount of usage. During its first year over 1,000 searches were performed, primarily for technical, professional, and college students (the latter presumably doing research for term papers). Most of these users (62 percent), I should add, were not previous users of the libraries involved.[11]

But there is a catch, or at least there may be. This online service was made available at no charge during its first year. In the second year users were to pay one-half of the search costs, and usage is bound to drop off. In the meantime, the librarians involved in the program are trying to cope with the additional work created by this new service, both in helping users utilize the system and in retrieving source documents once citations are made available. Moreover, the costs of a typical search are hard to determine. Connect time and offline citation printing is running about 15-25 dollars per search, depending on the data base that is accessed, but this does not include online staff assistance or offline preparation time. A more complete cost per search estimate could run in the 100 dollar range, which could mount higher still if less technical users were attracted to the service.[12] (This should be compared to about $1.00 per transaction for most conventional public library services.)

Another innovative thrust of public libraries in recent years has been in the area of television. Since broadcast television has already been preempted by *Kojak, Sesame Street,* and the *Today* show, the focus has been on alternatives to the over-the-air system, principally cable television and video cassettes. As of about two years ago, over a hundred public libraries were involved in video and cable TV projects.[13] Four other libraries have provided viewing facilities for video cassettes distributed by the public television library, a branch of the public broadcasting service. This "Watchabook" program may, in fact, represent a preview of things to come, as video players become available on a mass basis over the next five to ten years, and rental libraries are created to serve this new video programming market.[14]

A third direction that some libraries are taking, particularly those in large cities, is the development of information and referral services. The chief purpose of these services is to improve the urban citizen's ability to deal with the bureaucratic maze of government services, laws, codes, and eligibility requirements that have proliferated over the past 30 years to the point where interpersonal communications are no longer capable of informing the citizen of how to access them. Operationally, these "I&R" services are similar to the information broker activities described earlier, in that they rely heavily on telephone contacts, directories and reference files, which, in some cases, are computerized, and on the maintenance by libraries of external contacts with various service delivery agencies.[15] But again, their introduction by public libraries reflects the search for new directions and competition with the private sector that libraries are undergoing.

FUTURE LIBRARIES AND "INFOBUSINESS"

In reviewing the preceding analysis, the most pressing question that emerges is whether a viable role in the information marketplace is, in fact, conceivable for public libraries. Or is obsolescence predetermined, mitigated though it may be by the willingness of public decision-makers to continue subsidizing libraries to a minimal extent—in that way leaving them in a kind of twilight zone, neither dead nor alive? To begin answering this question realistically, one has to first recognize that in many ways the public library today is like the small "Ma and Pa" farm, trying to make a living side by side with agribusiness, only that "infobusiness" is already several times the size of agribusiness.

The new directions that libraries are taking, some of which have been described above, will not necessarily insure their viability. The basic problem is that public libraries are still trying to serve a general public with a very broad array of subject matter. This places an operational burden on public libraries, simply in terms of the acquisition, indexing, and storage of materials, which limits their ability to compete with other information services in terms of the convenience, timeliness, or selectivity that information consumers have come to expect. And it relegates the librarian to the role of an information generalist in a time when specialization is the name of the game.

The key lesson to be learned from the recent evolution of the information marketplace is that viable information services specialize in the content they cover or the audience they seek (*or* both), and that to attempt to cover a broad array of content for a broad public is simply no longer in the cards. Special-interest magazines specialize in content while still appealing to a broad audience. Information brokers cover a wide array of subjects but only attempt to serve a relatively narrow institutional clientele. Online retrieval services are generally very specialized in the content they cover (e.g., medicine, or engineering, or chemistry) *and* serve only a professional or institutional market. Libraries, by contrast, are still trying to be broad-based in terms of both content and user population.

Given this perspective, the attempts by libraries to expand their services into new areas, such as information and referral, video programming, or online retrieval, may ultimately prove as frustrating as more traditional strategies such as branch libraries, school-related collections, or membership drives. In the short run, as long as federal subsidies are supporting these innovative programs, they may well represent an opportunity for ad hoc institutional survival. But once the subsidies are removed, either the service will have to be downgraded or users will be asked to reimburse the cost of the service.

The problem is that no matter which alternative the library pursues at this point, its viability is not likely to be ensured. If it abandons or downgrades a new service, it is pushed back to square one with a declining user base. If it charges for the service, it places itself into competition with the private sector—with "infobusiness," which, because of greater specialization and without a geographically-circumscribed market, will win in the price or convenience war that will inevitably take place.

In fact, the private sector may be grateful to the library for doing some R&D and advance promotion of new services, prior to its entry into the consumer-oriented video cassette or online retrieval or telephone referral marketplace.

But again, this will not help the public library. Its last resort will be to return to the federal or state or municipal decision-maker in order to plead for funds to continue subsidizing the new service. Unfortunately, others will be there pleading also. The state university or local science museum may also want to set up online information retrieval services for the general public. The local school system or arts council may also want to program a cable TV channel or initiate a video cassette program. And the health and welfare council or municipal consumer affairs office may also want to launch an information and referral service. And, unfortunately, there is no preordained reason why the public library will be able to convince the budget allocators why it can provide any of these services more effectively than some of its competitors in the public sector, not to mention the private one.

In short, the complexity and competitiveness of today's information marketplace does not leave much room for an institution that tries to serve most of the people with most of the information.

But, I do not want to conclude this analysis with the impression that there is no exit from the situation the public library finds itself in (or, at least, from the situation as I have described it). There are, in my view, three possible exits, but pursuing any of them will require giving up or changing one of the three key ingredients of the public library system that exists today. These ingredients are:

1. The value of universality of service;
2. The physical resources of the library, namely, its central and branch facilities and book collections; and
3. The orientation and training of its professional staff.

The first exit I have in mind is the one already opted for by many commercial and academic libraries; it is specialization. A public library could play a viable role in programming a cable television channel or circulating video materials, just as it could by being a truly specialized children's library, or historical library, or legal library, or best sellers library, or consumers library, or what have you. But in order to be viable, it would have to concentrate all of its resources and imagination on a more specialized service concept or a narrower subject spectrum or a more limited public than existing public libraries. In the process, the value of universal service would have to be abandoned.

Exit number two is for the public library to become a full-fledged information and referral agency, with the emphasis on referral. Given the complexity of today's information marketplace, the role of a one-stop information traffic director does have an innate appeal, and while specialized information services exist for everthing from suicide prevention to where to buy antiques, no single source facilitates access to the array of currently-available information sources.

In this sense, the library as an "information broker's broker" could be a very valuable institution for an increasingly information-dependent society.

But to move in this direction effectively libraries will have to warehouse their book collections and move to streetcorner retail outlets or telephone banks in office complexes. Their operational focus will have to shift to updating a limited number of directories that are pertinent to the most frequent inquiries, rather than to acquiring, indexing, and storing large volumes of books and periodicals; and to maintaining contacts with numerous external organizations, from special purpose libraries and information services to service delivery agencies in order to be able to refer clients to the most relevant and responsive source.

Finally, the third exit, and undoubtedly the most challenging one, is for libraries not only to refer their clients to appropriate information sources, but to help them cope with their new identities as members of an information society and as producers, consumers, and intermediaries in the information marketplace. The role of libraries, in this context, would be to promote, instruct, and facilitate information literacy in our society—not only visual literacy, or computer literacy, but all-information literacy: CB radio literacy, newsletter literacy, graphic arts literacy, bureaucratic literacy, online retrieval literacy, legal literacy, consumer information literacy, and pocket calculator literacy.

How to establish such an information literacy program will be in itself a major agenda-setting task. The first step could well be to stop indexing individual materials, whether books or magazines or video cassettes, and to start indexing information experiences, problems, and outlets that residents of the information society regularly cope with. The second, a more long-range endeavor, could be to re-orient and re-train library staffs so that they become information facilitators rather than information compilers.

The promise of this third exit is that it would allow the library to continue to serve a universal public, since we are all informationally handicapped in the face of the overabundant and overloaded produce that "infobusiness" provides us each and every day. And it would take advantage of the physical facilities of the library, since video or computer or graphic arts workshops do require physical as well as pedagogical spaces to thrive in. Finally, it would allow the library to do what our educational system has not been able to, caught as it is in the fear of curriculum change and the possible displacement of human labor by media technologies. Most importantly, it would create new libraries for a new age, which is already upon us.

REFERENCES

1. The above statistics are taken from Harvard Program on Information Technologies and Public Policy, *Annual Report 1974–75,* vol. 1. (Cambridge, Mass.), p. 3.

2. Edwin B. Parker and Marc Porat, *Social Implications of Computer/Telecommunications Systems,* report no. 16, Program in Information Technology and Telecommunications, Stanford University (February 1975).

3. Benjamin M. Compaine, *Consumer Magazines at the Crossroads* (White Plains, N.Y.: Knowledge Industry Publications, Inc., 1974), pp. 30–32.

4. *Ibid.,* pp. 52–54.

5. *Ibid.,* p. 59 (based on Audit Bureau of Circulation figures for 100 leading general and farm magazines).

6. See Anne W. Branscomb, "The Future of Computerized Information Systems: The Legal, Political, and Regulatory Environment," paper presented at the EDUCOM Fall Conference, November 10–12, 1976.

7. "The Information Brokers: Who, What, Why, How," *Bulletin of the American Society for Information Science* 2:7, p. 11, (February 1976).

8. *Ibid.,* pp. 15–16.

9. See, for example, Colorado State Library, *A Survey of the Attitudes, Opinions and Behavior of Citizens of Colorado with Regard to Library Service,* General Statewide Summary, vol. 1, (November 1973), p. 54.

10. Edward S. Warner, et al., *Information Needs of Urban Residents,* Office of Education, U.S. Dept. of Health, Education, and Welfare, (December 1973), p. 137.

11. Alice E. Ahlgren, "Providing On-line Search Services Through the Public Library," Paper presented at the annual meeting of the American Society for Information Service, (October 26–30, 1975).

12. For a discussion of the difficulties in extending online retrieval services to the general public, see Andrew E. Wessel, *The Social Use of Information: Ownership and Access* (New York: Wiley, 1976), especially pp. 66 ff.

13. Based on information compiled by Brigitte L. Kenney and Susan Bunting at Drexel University's Graduate School of Library Science.

14. For a description of the"Watchabook" experiments, see Public Television Library, "Have you Watched a Book Today: An Experimental Project of the PTL," final report (undated).

15. See also Cleve Hopkins, *Community Information and Services Centers: Concepts for Activation,* Office of Telecommunications, U.S. Dept. of Commerce, (July 1976).

Bibliography

PART I: THE NATURE OF POST-INDUSTRIAL SOCIETY

Bell, Daniel. *The Coming of Post-Industrial Society: A Venture in Social Forecasting.* New York: Basic, 1973.

Bellini, James. "The Economics of Decline: A Neglected Scenario," *Futures* 8 (Feb. 1976).

Boulding, K. *Meaning of the Twentieth Century: The Great Transition.* New York: Harper and Row, 1964.

Bouvier, L. F. "U.S. Population in 2000," *Population Bulletin* 30, no. 5:2–33 (1975).

Cole, H. S. D.; Freeman, Christopher; Jahoda, Marie; and Pavitt, K. L. R. *Models of Doom: A Critique of the Limits to Growth.* New York: Universe, 1973.

Davisson, William I. "Technology and Social Change," *Review of Politics* 34:172–184 (October 1972).

Ginsberg, Eli. "The Pluralistic Economy of the U.S.," *Scientific American* 235:25–29 (December 1976).

Heilbroner, Robert L. *An Inquiry Into the Human Prospect.* New York: Norton, 1974.

Hill, Richard Child. "The Coming of Post Industrial Society," *The Insurgent Sociologist* 4,3: 37–51 (Spring 1974).

Janowitz, M., and Olsen, M. E. "Coming of Post-Industrial Society: A Venture in Social Forecasting; Review Symposium," *American Journal of Sociology* 80:230–41 (July 1974).

Jungk, Robert, and Gultung, Johan, eds. *Mankind 2000.* Oslo: Oslo University Press, 1969.

Lamberton, D. M., ed. "Information Revolution," (symposium), *American Academy of Political and Social Science Annals* 412:1–162 (March 1974).

Levitt, Theodore. "Management and Post-Industrial Society," *Public Interest* 44:69–103 (Summer 1976).

Masuda, Y. "The Plan for Information Society—A National Goal Toward the Year 2000." Final report, Japan Computer Usage Development Institute, Computerization Committee, Tokyo, Japan, May 1972.

Meadows, Donella; Meadows, Dennis; Rangers, Jorgen; and Behrens, William W. III. *The Limits to Growth.* Washington: Potomac Associates Books, 1972.

Mesarovic, Mihajlo, and Pestel, Eduard. *Mankind at the Turning Point: The Second Report to the Club of Rome.* New York: E. P. Dutton, 1974.

Miller, S. Michael. "Notes on Neo-Capitalism," *Theory and Society* 2:1–35 (Spring 1975).

Piel, Gerard. *The Acceleration of History.* New York: Knopf, 1972.

Piven, Frances Fox, and Cloward, Richard. *The Politics of Turmoil.* New York: Pantheon, 1974.

"Special Issue of Smithsonian as America's Third Century Begins." *Smithsonian* 7:26–40 (July 1976).

Stavrianos, L. S. "Promise of the Coming Dark Age; Western Civilization," *Nation* 221:204–208 (13 September 1975).

Teichert, Pedro C. M. "Scarcity and the Uncertain Future of Industrial Societies," *Rivista Internazionale di Scienze Economiche e Commerciali* 23:358–372 (1 April 1976).

Wolfgang, M. E., ed. "Future Society: Aspects of America in the Year 2000," (symposium), *Annals of the American Academy* 408:1–102 (July 1973).

Young, J. P. "Prophet of Post-Industrialism versus Politics of Nostalgia," *Polity* 8, no. 2:269–85 (1975).

PART II: PROFESSIONALS IN POST-INDUSTRIAL SOCIETY

Aaron, Shirley Louise. "The Making of a Differentiated Staffing Model 1973," *School Media Quarterly* 2:1:36–40, 57–59 (Fall 1973).

Astin, M. S.; Suniewick, N.; and Dweck, S. *Women: A Bibliography on Their Education and Careers.* Washington, D.C.: Human Service Press, 1971.

"Beyond Awareness: Women in Libraries Organize for Change," *School Library Journal* 23:5:31–36 (January 1977).

Biblarz, Dora. "Professional Associations and Unions: Future Impacts of Today's Decisions," *College and Research Libraries* 36:121–28 (March 1975).

Blake, Judith. "Changing Status of Women in Developed Countries," *Scientific American* 231:136–47 (Spring 1974).

Blasingame, Ralph, and Lynch, Mary. "Design for Diversity," *PLA Newsletter* 13:5–22 (June 1974).

Blumberg, Paul. "The New Academic Proletariat," *Nation* 223:102–104 (14 August 1976).

Braverman, Harry. "Labor and Monopoly Capital; the Degredation of Work in the Twentieth Century," *Monthly Review* 26:1–134 (July 1974).

——. *Labor and Monopoly Capital; the Degredation of Work in the Twentieth Century.* New York: Monthly Review, 1975.

Bundy, Mary Lee, and Wasserman, Paul. "Professionalism Reconsidered," *College and Research Libraries* 29:3–26 (January 1968).

Chaplan, Margaret A., ed. "Employee Organizations and Collective Bargaining in Libraries," *Library Trends* 25:419–557 (October 1976).

Corbett, Edmund V. "Staffing of Large Municipal Libraries in England and the United States," *Journal of Librarianship* 3:81–100 (April 1971).

DeWeese, L. C. "Status Concerns and Library Professionalism," *College and Research Libraries* 33:31–38 (January 1972).

Dicesare, Constance B. "Changes in the Occupational Structure of U.S. Jobs," *Monthly Labor Review* 98:24–34 (March 1975).

Edwards, Ralph. "Management of Libraries and the Professional Functions of Librarians," *Library Quarterly* 45:150–160 (April 1975).

Epstein, Cynthia Fuchs. *Women's Place: Options and Limits in Professional Careers.* Berkeley: Univ. of California Pr., 1970.

Etzioni, Amitai, ed. *The Semi-Professions and Their Organization.* New York: Free Press, 1969.

Flanagan, Leo N. "Professionalism Dismissed?," *College and Research Libraries* 34:204–14 (May 1973).

——. "The Unionization of Library Support Staffs," *Wilson Library Bulletin* 48:491–99 (February 1974).

Freidson, Eliot. *The Profession of Medicine.* New York: Dodd, 1970.

Goffman, Erving. *The Presentation of Self in Everyday Life.* New York: Doubleday, 1959.

Guttsman, W. L. "Subject Specialization in Academic Libraries. Some Preliminary Observations on Role Conflict and Organizational Stress," *Journal of Librarianship* 5:1, 1–8, 27 (January 1973).

Haga, W. J.; Graen, G.; and Dansereau, F. "Professionalism and role making in a service organization," *American Sociological Review* 39: 122–33 (1974).

Halmos, Paul, ed. "Professionalisation and Social Change," *Sociological Review Monograph*, no. 20. Keele, England: University of Keele, 1973.

Hanks, Gardner, and Schmidt, C. James. "An Alternative Model of a Profession for Librarians," *College and Research Libraries* 36:175–187 (May 1975).

Haug, Marie R. "The Erosion of Professional Authority: A Cross-Cultural Inquiry in the Case of the Physicians," *MMFQ/Health and Society* :83–106 (Winter 1976).

Henderson, Lenneal J., Jr. "Public Technology and the Metropolitan Ghetto," *Black Scholar* 5:9–18 (March 1974).

Keller, S. "Future Role of Women; with Questions and Answers," *Annals of the American Academy* 408:1–12 (July 1973).

Luck, Carolyn. "Staff Training for the Information Center," *Drexel Library Quarterly* 12:69–80 (January-April 1975).

Lynch, Beverly. "The Role of Middle Managers in Libraries," *Advances in Librarianship* 6:255–277 (1976).

Maslow, Abraham H. *Motivation and Personality*. New York: Harper, 1970.

Merton, Robert K. "Role of the Intellectual in Public Bureaucracy," *Social Theory and Social Structure*. Glencoe, Ill.: Free Press, 1957.

Myers, Margaret, and Scarborough, Mayra, ed. *Women in Librarianship: Melvil's Rib Symposium*. New Brunswick, N.J.: Rutgers Univ. Pr., 1975.

"Papers on Women and Work: An Issue in honor of Caroline Rose," *Social Problems* 22:467–547 (April 1975).

Patterson, Susanne. "Job Satisfaction of Librarians: A Comparison between Men and Women," *College and Research Libraries* 36:45–51 (January 1975).

Presthus, R. *Technological Change and Occupational Responses: A Study of Librarians*. Washington, D.C.: U.S. Office of Education, Bureau of Research, 1970.

Ritzer, G. "Professionalization, Bureaucratization, and Rationalization: the Views of Max Weber," *Social Forces* 53:627–34 (June 1975).

Rosen, B. "Dual-career Marital Adjustment: Potential Effects of Discriminatory Managerial Attitudes," *Journal of Marriage and Family* 37:565–72 (August 1975).

Saltman, Ray. "Educating Public Administrators for Managing Science and Technology," *Public Administration Review* 34:394–96 (July 1974).

Schiller, Anita R. "Women in Librarianship," *Advances in Librarianship* 5:103–147 (1974).

Simonds, Michael J. "Work Attitudes and Union Membership," *College and Research Libraries* 36:136–142 (March 1975).

Theodore, Athena. *The Professional Women*. Cambridge, Mass.: Schenkman, 1971.

Vaughn, William J., and Dunn, J. D. "A Study of Job Satisfaction in Six University Libraries," *College and Research Libraries* 35:3, 163–77 (May 1974).

Vollmer, Howard M., and Mills, Donald L., eds. *Professionalization*. Englewood Cliffs, N.J.: Prentice-Hall, 1966.

Warner, Alice S. "The Library Volunteer," *Library Journal* 97:1241–45 (1 April 1972).

Wasserman, Harry. "The Professional Social Worker in a Bureaucracy," *Social Work* 16:89–95 (January 1971).

Weatherford, John. "Librarians in Faculty Unions," *Library Journal* 99:2443–2446 (1 October 1974).

Weibel, K. "Toward a Feminist Profession: Impact on Librarians," *Library Journal* 101:263–7 (1 January 1976).

Wetherby, P. "Librarianship: Opportunity for Women," *Sixteen Reports on the Status of Women in the Professions.* Pittsburgh: KNOW, 1970.

Wilensky, Harold L. "The Professionalization of Everyone?," *American Journal of Sociology* 70:137–158 (September 1964).

"Women and the Future," (a symposium), *Futures* 7:362–435 (October 1975).

PART III: ORGANIZATIONS IN POST-INDUSTRIAL SOCIETY

Argyris, Chris. *Integrating the Individual and the Organization.* New York: Wiley, 1965.

——. "Personality and Organizational Theory Revisited," *Administrative Science Quarterly* 18:747–767 (June 1973).

Arrow, Kenneth J. "Control in Large Organizations," *Management Science* 10:397–408 (September 1964).

Atkins, Neil P. "Leadership and Support for School Media Programs," *School Media Quarterly* 2:1, 15–18 (Fall 1973).

Axford, William H., ed. "Effective Resource Allocation in Library Management," *Library Trends* 23:549–664 (April 1975).

Bolton, Earl C. "Response of University Library Management to Changing Modes of University Governance and Control," *College and Research Libraries* 33:4, 305–311 (July 1972).

Bommer, Michael R. W. *The Development of a Management System for Effective Decision Making and Planning in a University Library.* Philadelphia: Univ. of Pennsylvania, Wharton School of Finance and Commerce, 1972.

Bonjean, C. M., and Grimes, M. D. "Bureaucracy and Alienation: A Dimensional Approach," *Social Forces* 48:365–373 (March 1970).

Booz, Allen and Hamilton, Inc. *Organization and Staffing of the Libraries of Columbia University: A Case Study.* Westport, Conn.: Redgrave Information Resources Corp., 1973.

Buckland, M. K. "The Management of Libraries and Information Centers," *Annual Review of Information Science and Technology* 9:335–379 (1974).

Castagna, Edwin. "Public Librarian and the City Manager," *Public Management* 43:32–35 (February 1961).

Chamot, Dennis. "The Effect of Collective Bargaining on the Employee-Management Relationship," *Library Trends* 25:489–496 (October 1976).

Chaplan, Margaret, ed. "Employee Organizations and Collective Bargaining in Libraries," *Library Trends* 25:419–557 (October 1976).

Drucker, Peter. *Management.* New York: Harper, 1974.

Evans, Edward G. *Management Techniques for Librarians.* New York: Academic Press, 1976.

Flener, J. G. "New Approaches to Personnel Management: Personalizing Management," *Journal of Academic Librarianship* 1:17–20 (March 1975).

Frantz, John C. "The Role of the Federal Government," *Library Trends* 23:239–251 (October 1974).

Friedman, Nathalie, and Rogers, Theresa. *Administration Decentralization and the Public.* New York: Bureau of Applied Social Research, Columbia Univ., December 1974.

Gardner, N. "Non-hierarchical Organization of the Future: Theory vs. Reality," *Public Administration Review* 36:591–598 (September 1976).

Granger, C. H. "The Hierarchy of Objectives," *Harvard Business Review* 42:63–74 (May–June 1964).

Hall, Richard H. "Professionalism and Bureaucratization," *American Sociological Review* 33:92–104 (February 1968).

Hill, L. B. "Institutionalization, the Ombudsman, and Bureaucracy," *American Political Science Review* 68:1075–85 (Spring 1974).

Holley, E. G. "Organization and Administration of Urban University Libraries," *College and Research Libraries* 33:175–89 (May 1972).

Jun, Jong S., ed. "A Symposium: Management by Objectives in the Public Sector," *Public Administration Review* 36:1–45 (January–February 1976).

Kaplan, Louis. "The Literature of Participation: From Optimism to Realism," *College and Research Libraries* 36:473–479 (November 1975).

Lynch, Beverly P. "The Academic Library and Its Environment," *College and Research Libraries* 35:126–132 (March 1974).

Maccoby, Michael. *The Gamesman.* New York: Simon and Schuster, 1977.

MacKenzie, Alexander Graham. "Systems Analysis as a Decision Making Tool for the Library Manager," *Library Trends* 21:4, 493–504 (April 1973).

McAnally, Arthur M., and Downs, Robert B. "The Changing Role of Directors of University Libraries," *College and Research Libraries* 34:2, 103–125 (March 1973).

Michalko, James. "Management by Objectives and the Academic Library: A Critical Overview," *Library Quarterly* 45:235–252 (July 1975).

Michner, Roger E. "Unions and Libraries," *Southeastern Librarian* 23:15–25 (Winter 1974).

Morrissey, E., and Gillespie, D. F. "Technology and the Conflict of Professionals in Bureaucratic Organizations," *Sociological Quarterly* 16:319–332 (Summer 1975).

Pritchard, Alan. *The Library as an Industrial Firm: An Approach to Library Management.* London: City of London Polytechnic, Library and Learning Resources Service, March 1973.

Rose, Richard. "Implementation and Evaporation: The Record of MBO," *Public Administration Review* 37:64–71 (January–February 1977).

Rosengren, W. R., and Lefton, M., eds. *Organizations and Clients.* Columbus, Ohio: Charles E. Merrill, 1970.

Schlachter, Gail. "Quasi-Unions and Organizational Hegemony with the Library Field," *Library Quarterly* 43:185–198 (July 1973).

Shapiro, Lillian L. "Bureaucracy and the School Library," *Library Journal* 98:1346–1351 (15 April 1973).

Sheriff, Peter E. "Unrepresentative Bureaucracy," *Sociology* 8:447–62 (Spring 1974).

Thomas, Pauline A., and Ward, Valerie A. *An Analysis of Managerial Activities in Libraries.* London: Aslib, 1974.

Trezza, Alphonse F., and Halcli, Albert. "The Role of Local and State Governments," *Library Trends* 23:229–238 (October 1974).

Yin, Robert, and Yates, Douglas. *Street Level Governments: Assessing Decentralization and Urban Services.* Santa Monica, Calif.: Rand Corporation, October 1974.

PART IV: SERVICES IN POST-INDUSTRIAL SOCIETY

Anderla, J. Georges. *Information in 1985: A Forecasting Study of Information Needs and Resources.* Paris: Organization for Economic Cooperation and Development, 1973.

Blanc, Robert P. *Review of Computer Networking Technology.* Washington, D.C.: National Bureau of Standards, 1974.

Brady, Edward L., and Branscomb, Lewis M. "Information for a Changing Society," *Science* 175:4025, 961–66 (3 March 1972).

Buckelew, D. P., and Penniman, W. D. "The Outlook for Interactive Television," *Datamation* 20:8, 54–58 (August 1974).

Budington, William S., ed. "Library Service in Metropolitan Areas," *Library Trends* 23:179–317 (October 1974).

Childers, Thomas, and Post, Joyce A. *The Information-Poor in America.* Metuchen, N.J.: Scarecrow, 1975.

Clunies-Ross, E. "Educational Technology in Adult and Community Education," *Community Development Journal* 9:206–11 (October 1974).

Coté, Lawrence G. "Data Bases and Libraries," *EDUCOM* 9:4 (Winter 1974).

Curley, Arthur. "Social Responsibility and Libraries," *Advances in Librarianship* 5:77–101 (1974).

Donahue, Joseph C., and Kochen, Manfred. *Information for the Community.* Chicago: ALA, 1976.

Drolet, L. L. "Metropolitan Library Service via the Cable in the United States of America: A Thing of the Future," *UNESCO Bulletin for Libraries* 29:75–9 (March 1975).

Edelson, Burton I. "Global Satellite Communications," *Scientific American* 236:58–73 (February 1977).

Gee, Sherman. "The Role of Technology Transfer in Innovation," *Research Management* 17:6, 31–36 (November 1974).

Hale, C. E. "Continuing Education: An Educational/Library Interface," *Focus* 28:9–124 (Winter 1974).

Haug, Marie R., and Susman, M. B. "Professional Autonomy and the Revolt of the Client," *Social Problems* 17:153–161 (Fall 1969).

Illich, Ivan. *Deschooling Society.* New York: Harper, 1971.

"Information Brokers: Who, What, Why, How," *Bulletin of the American Society for Information Science* 2:11–20 (February 1976).

Josey, E. J. *New Dimensions for Academic Library Service.* Metuchen, N.J.: Scarecrow, 1975.

Kutner, N. G. "Poor vs. the Non-Poor: An Ethnic and Metropolitan–Nonmetropolitan Comparison," *Sociological Quarterly* 16:250–63 (Spring 1975).

Myrdal, Gunnar. "Case against Romantic Ethnicity," *Center Magazine* 7:26–30 (July 1974).

National Academy of Sciences. Committee on Scientific and Technical Communication (SATCOM). *Scientific and Technical Communication; A Pressing National Problem and Recommendations for its Solution.* Washington, D.C.: National Academy of Sciences, 1969.

Nilles, Jack M. *The Telecommunications–Transportation Trade off: Options for Tomorrow.* New York: Wiley Interscience, 1976.

Novak, Michael. "New Ethnicity," *Center Magazine* 7:18–25 (July 1974).

Oettinger, Anthony G., and Zapol, Nikki. "Will Information Technologies Help Learning?," *American Society of Political and Social Science Annals* 412:116–26 (March 1974).

Orr, Richard H. "Measuring the Goodness of Library Services: A General Framework for Considering Quantitative Measures," *Journal of Documentation* 29:3, 315–332 (September 1973).

Rees, M. B., and Paisely, W. J. "Social and Psychological Predictors of Adult Information Seeking and Media Use," *Adult Education Journal* 19:11–29 (1968).

Reif, F. "Educational Challenges for the University," *Science* 184:537–542 (3 May 1974).

Robinson, D. Z. "Will the University Decline as a Center for Scientific Research?," *Daedalus* 102:101–10 (Spring 1973).

Ryan, William. *Blaming the Victim*. rev. ed. New York: Vintage, 1976.

Shaw, M. E. "Education is Not a Place: Connecting Learning and Living," *Public Administration Review* 33:516–22 (November 1973).

Sjoberg, G.; Brymer, R. A.; and Farris, B. "Bureaucracy and the Lower Class," *Sociology and Social Research* 50:325–337 (April 1966).

Strange, John. "The Impact of Citizen Participation on Public Administration," *Public Administration Review* 32:457–470 (September 1972).

Turn, Rein. *Computers in the 1980's*. New York: Columbia Univ. Pr., 1974.

Urban Resource Systems. *A National Network for the Acquisition, Organization, Processing and Dissemination of Materials by and about Blacks*. Haslett, Mich.: Urban Resource Systems, January 1974.

West, Celeste, and Katz, Elizabeth. *Revolting Librarians*. San Francisco: Booklegger Press, 1972.

Withington, Frederic G. "Five Generations of Computers," *Harvard Business Review* 52:99–108 (July–August 1975).

Yin, R. K.; Kenney, B. L.; and Possner, K. B. *Neighborhood Communications Centers: Planning Information and Referral Services in the Urban Library*. Santa Monica: Rand Corp., 1974.

PART V: LIBRARIES IN POST-INDUSTRIAL SOCIETY

Atkinson, Hugh C. "Extension of New Services and the Role of Technology," *Library Trends* 23:305–317 (October 1974).

Benge, R. C. *Libraries and Cultural Change*. London: Archon Books, 1970.

Bone, Larry E., ed. "Community Analysis and Libraries," *Library Trends* 24:429–643 (January 1976).

Braverman, Miriam, ed. "Information and Referral Services in the Public Library," *Drexel Library Quarterly* 12:1–179 (January–April 1976).

"Cooperation: A Library Journal Mini-Symposium," *Library Journal* 97:10, 1767–1775 (15 May 1972).

DeGennaro, Richard. "Research Libraries Face the Future," *Library Journal* 101:917–22 (15 May 1975).

Eastlick, J. T., ed. *The Changing Environment of Libraries*. Chicago: ALA, 1971.

Fussler, Herman H. *Research Libraries and Technology: A Report to the Sloan Foundation*. Chicago: Univ. of Chicago Pr., 1973.

Grove, Pearce S., ed. "Library Cooperation," *Library Trends* 24:157–423 (October 1975).

Jussim, Estelle. "Confronting our Media Biases," *School Libraries* 21:12–17 (Summer 1972).

Karatygina, T. F. "Central Specialized Scientific and Technical Libraries Serving Different Branches of the Soviet Economy," *UNESCO Bulletin for Libraries* 27:2, 92–97 (March–April 1973).

Kenny, Brigitte. "The Future of Cable Communications in Libraries," *Journal of Library Automation* 9:4, 299–317 (December 1976).

Kochen, Manfred. "WISE: A World Information Synthesis and Encyclopedia," *Journal of Documentation* 28:4, 322–42 (December 1972).

"Libraries in America's Future," *Library Journal* 101:1–292 (1 January 1976).

Rawles, Beverly A. *Planning the Expansion of Library Services to Disadvantaged Adults.* Morehead, Ky.: Morehead State Univ., Appalachian Adult Education Center, 1974.

Robbins, Jane B. *Citizen Participation and Public Library Policy.* Metuchen, N.J.: Scarecrow, 1975.

Schmidt, James C. "Resource Allocation in University Libraries in the 1970's and Beyond," *Library Trends* 23:643–648 (April 1975).

Schuman, Patricia Glass, ed. *Social Responsibilities and Libraries.* New York: Bowker, 1976.

Soules, Gordon. *What People Want in a Library; the Kind of Information Every Library Needs to Provide the Best Possible Service to its Community.* Vancouver: Gordon Soules Economic and Marketing Research, 1975.

U.S. National Commission on Library and Information Science. *Towards a National Program for Library and Information Services: Goals for Action.* Washington, D.C.: Govt. Print. Off., 1975.

Weizenbaum, Joseph. *Computer Power and Human Reason.* San Francisco: Freeman, 1975.

Index

Compiled by Eric Johnson